Miikka E. Anttila
Luther's Theology of Music

Theologische Bibliothek Töpelmann

Herausgegeben von
Bruce McCormack, Friederike Nüssel
und Christoph Schwöbel

Band 161

Miikka E. Anttila

Luther's Theology of Music

Spiritual Beauty and Pleasure

DE GRUYTER

ISBN 978-3-11-055215-7
e-ISBN 978-3-11-031027-6
ISSN 0563-4288

Library of Congress Cataloging-in-Publication Data
A CIP catalog record for this book has been applied for at the Library of Congress.

Bibliografische Information der Deutschen Nationalbibliothek
Die Deutsche Nationalbibliothek verzeichnet diese Publikation in der Deutschen
Nationalbibliografie; detaillierte bibliografische Daten sind im Internet
über http://dnb.dnb.de abrufbar.

www.degruyter.com

Contents

1 Introduction

1.1. Theology of music

For many, the spiritual dimension of life manifests itself through music. While the power of religious institutions, symbols, and practices is in decline, music keeps offering comfort to the stressed and creating at least an illusion of sense in a senseless world. To some extent, the same applies to the arts in general. Deprived of religious beliefs, people today encounter what remains of the sacred in works of art. The modern idea of an artist is suggestive of a visionary, a prophet, or a priest more than it is of an artisan. However, that has not always been the case. Historians of art and aesthetics date the origin of the quasi-religious understanding of art to some time in the eighteenth century. According to musicologist Carl Dahlhaus the romantic view of music employed words such as "devotion" and "contemplation" to describe it even as religious sentimentality became more aesthetic around the year 1800.[1] Herbert Marcuse's *The Aesthetic Dimension* gives a closer examination of art's important spiritual dimension:

> Art breaks open a dimension inaccessible to other experience, a dimension in which human beings, nature, and things no longer stand under the law of the established reality principle. Subjects and objects encounter the appearance of that autonomy which is denied them in their society. The encounter with the truth of art happens in the estranging language and images which make perceptible, visible, and audible that which is no longer, or not yet, perceived, said, and heard in everyday life.[2]

As a form of art, music has the advantage of being easily accessible, facilitated by electronic portable devices. In that regard it surpasses not only sculpture and literature, but even television. In terms of omnipresence, it is the supreme art. Given its ubiquity and the spiritual dimension assigned to it, studies in theology of music that address this spiritual dimension are long overdue. The issue is related to other philosophical problems peculiar to music. For example: How does music represent anything? The idea of "absolute music" denies the possibility of understanding music in terms of an extra-musical meaning. In other words,

---

1 Dahlhaus 1983, 12–13. The theologian Nicholas Wolterstorff (2004, 337) for his part, comments on the development in the last two centuries as follows: "According to the modern grand narrative of art ... art in the eighteenth century finally freed itself from service to religion. What strikes anyone who follows out the various tellings of the narrative, however, is how often this liberated art is described in religious terms, and how often religious hopes and expectations are lodged in it."
2 Marcuse 1979, 72.

music is understood entirely within itself. Although this view does not have wide support, it is a viable option and, as such, it illustrates the difficulties we face when talking about music.[3] One of the basic philosophical problems with music is that we experience it as deeply meaningful, yet it is impossible to tell what this meaning is. Another approach to meaning in music is to claim that music does not convey ideas but emotions. Not only does this view introduce a vexed philosophical discussion on emotions, it also raises the question whether emotions perceived in music are due to the composer, musician, listener, or to the music itself. If we decide that emotions reside in the music itself, how can one say that a non-personal entity, such as a piece of music, is joyous or angry?[4] Is it possible to conclude that the reason we sense the sacred in music is its inexplicability? Music's historical openness to Christian theology suggests that it contains more than that. According to one of the foremost theologians of music of our day, Jeremy Begbie, "music can serve to enrich and advance theology, extending our wisdom about God, God's relation to us, and to the world at large."[5] That music can "enrich and advance" theology means that it can make us rethink our relation to time and space. Both dimensions are experienced in music differently than in physics, and this holds true for theology, too.[6] Music as a language of emotion also has a theological bearing. To

---

3 Scruton (1999, 125–139) gives three musical examples: Arthur Honegger's Pacific 231 imitates the sound of a steam locomotive. If imitation of this kind is tantamount to representation, it would be a defect of music that it can represent only the sounds of things – those that it also reproduces. On the contrary, a typical example of program music like Debussy's *La Mer* can be understood perfectly as music without knowing its representational claims. Extramusical thoughts occur in appreciation of music, but they have an "ostensive" character, as though music were making a gesture towards something it cannot define. There is a peculiar "reference without predication that touches the heart but numbs the tongue." Scruton says that it is one thing for a piece to be inspired by a subject, another to imitate the subject, another to evoke or suggest a subject, another to express an experience of the subject, and yet another to represent the subject. A noteworthy phenomenon is the leitmotif in Wagner operas. It has complex ways of expressing underconscious action. Yet Wagner's music can be understood perfectly as music without the dramatic context. The mystery in music is that we know that it is meaningful, yet this meaning cannot be understood as a language without crossing the barrier between sound (i.e. physical sound-phenomenon) and tone (i.e. a sound that exists within a musical 'field of force').
4 Kivy 1989 presents a theory of emotions in music, in which he distinguishes between "to express" and "to be expressive of" something. Music is expressive of emotions in that it resembles and is analogous to human expressive behavior. Although Kivy's position has gained support, the issue is far from settled.
5 Begbie 2000, 3.
6 Begbie (2005, 728–729) gives the example of musical triad as an illustration of the Holy Trinity. "It may be that a large part of our chronic tendency to treat the Trinity as essentially

"understand" means both in music and in theology more than being able to analyze the salient features of a particular piece of music or a theological doctrine. Upon closer examination, music reveals many features that bring it close to theology.

1.2. Music and Luther studies[7]

Martin Luther (1483–1546) thought that theology and music held many features in common. Any profound account on the theology of music cannot bypass him, given his position on the history of theology in general and the fact that he spoke about music on several occasions. Yet, it is hard to say whether or not Luther's theology of music is a profoundly discussed topic. As early as in 1924 Hermann Abert wrote that there is hardly any musically gifted pastor who had not touched upon the topic of "Luther and music" in an essay or a paper.[8] On the other hand, as late as 1994 Christoph Krummacher wrote that it is a futile endeavor to search for special studies focusing on Luther's view on music in recent literature (e.g. in the bibliography of *Luther-Jahrbuch*).[9] The truth is that there are a vast number of seminary papers and short articles about Luther and music but few analytical accounts on the subject. Some of the most noteworthy studies are briefly summarized.

The first academic dissertation on Luther and music in the 20th century was Karl Honemeyer's *Luthers Musikanschauung* (1941). Accessible only as a manuscript in the library of Münster University – not to mention the unfortunate wartime conditions of its emergence, this remarkable study has remained in obscurity. In many respects the study is outdated, but still it contains many interesting details. As the subtitle alludes (*Studien zur Frage ihrer geschichtlichen Grundlagen*), Honemeyer contextualizes Luther's thought in its historical background. One of Honemeyer's most fascinating findings is the school book of an unknown boy in Chemnitz (1506–1508) that contains a *laus musica*, a musical poem ex-

---

problematic, an intellectual and fundamentally mathematical conundrum, has been fuelled by an excessive reliance on visual conceptions of space, according to which 'three in one' will always be deeply problematic. The disarming simplicity of a three-note chord facilitates conceptions of Father, Son, and Spirit 'in' and 'through' each other (perichoresis) far more naturally."

7 See also the detailed overviews on the previous research by Krummacher 1994, 11–14, 26–33 and Block 2002, 15–24.

8 Abert 1924, 103.

9 Krummacher 1994, 12.

hibiting a close reminiscence of some Luther's texts. Honemeyer discusses the view of music in scholastic theology, monastic education and humanism. He makes an interesting move with a tentative statement that the musical theology of German mysticism could have influenced Luther.[10]

Christoph Wetzel wrote another unprinted German dissertation in 1954. Wetzel's study has three parts: the historical background, music in Luther's biography, and a more systematic account on the purpose of music. For Luther's conception of the purpose of music, Wetzel sees it as a helpful device to make people more receptive to the Word of God.[11] There are two basic convictions in his dissertation that Wetzel subsequently developed: that music is a part of the temporal realm (*weltliches Regiment*) and that its office in the Church is to praise God.[12]

Oskar Söhngen's *Theologie der Musik* (1967) is a classic in the field. As a general introduction to the theology of music, it is not actually a Luther-study. Luther is, nonetheless, the most quoted theologian in the book. Luther's views provide for Söhngen the only adequate basis for Protestant theology of music.[13] Söhngen's discourse runs from the New Testament through the Reformation,

---

10 Honemeyer 1941, 75–79. In Honemeyer's opinion the German mystics have perhaps taught Luther about the connection between singing with one's heart (corde) and one's mouth (ore). Johann Tauler sees three ways to praise God, of which the highest is complete silence. "Wenn solche Gedanken von Luther bei Tauler gefunden wurden, so mochten sie ihn wohl in den frühen Kampfjahren um 1520 bei seinem Urteil über die veräusserlichte Kirchenmusik, bei welcher der von religiösen Glut erfüllte Mönch die innere Kraft des Glaubens vermisste, mitbestimmen. In der späteren Zeit verstummen solche Äusserungen, und nichts wäre verkehrter, als in ihnen den massgeblichen Zug in Luthers grundsätzlicher Haltung gegenüber der Musik zu sehen." (79) Later, Wetzel (1954, viii) sees Honemeyer's idea of the possible influence of German mysticism in Luther's theology of music as poorly substantiated.

11 Wetzel 1954, 185: "Der Musik kommt hier also keine weitere Aufgabe zu als auf die Menschen einen natürlich-sinnlichen Reiz auszuüben und gewisse in der Natur des Menschen liegende Hemmnisse beiseite zu räumen: so z.B. die Trägheit des Herzens und Willens sich aufzumachen, um dem Wort zu begegnen. Und dann erfüllt die Musik ihren Zweck darin, dass sie es durch ihre ‚Süssigkeit' menschlich angenehmer macht sich täglich unter das Wort zu stellen. So ist die Musik geradezu cooperator Evangelii, weil sie domina et gubernatrix affectuum humanorum ist."

12 Wetzel 1961.

13 Söhngen 1967, 260: "[S]o dürfte deutlich geworden sein, dass für den Versuch einer Theologie der Musik auf evangelischem Boden nur bei Martin Luther Anknüpfungsmöglichkeiten gegeben sind. Das schliesst nicht aus, das sich auch von den anderen Reformatoren, Huldreich Zwingli und Johannes Calvin, manches Wichtige für die Erkenntnis des Phänomens der Musik und für die Beantwortung der Fragen nach der Möglichkeit und den Voraussetzungen ihrer gottesdienstlichen Verwendung lernen lässt. Aber zu einer theologischen Bewertung der Musik, geschweige denn zu einem Topos de musica im System der evangelischen Dogmatik kann man von ihren Positionen aus nicht vorstossen."

highlighting the discussion on manifestations of music.[14] Although Söhngen explicates at the beginning of the study that the problem of church music is but a special case within the larger question of music's theological import, a large section of the work is dedicated to church music.[15] At the end of the book, Söhngen provides a tentative Trinitarian account of music.[16] Söhngen's study is a major source for many articles on Luther and music, and one of the enduring merits of the book is that it also contains a separate chapter on the musical thought of young Luther.[17] Winfried Kurzschenkel's encyclopedic account on the theology of music from a Catholic standpoint, *Die theologische Bestimmung der Musik* (1971), is in many respects indebted to Söhngen. Kurzschenkel considers Luther to be the foremost theologian of music since Augustine. Moreover, Kurzschenkel acknowledges the ecumenical potential of Luther's ideas arguing that they need not be confined to particularly Protestant points of view.[18]

Wetzel continued to develop his ideas in his study *Die Träger des liturgischen Amtes im evangelischen Gottesdienst* (1961).[19] Here he tries to find a proper place for music in the Lutheran doctrine of worship. Wetzel's precise standpoint is the office of the Church, in which he distinguishes between the preaching office (*das Predigtamt*) and the praising office (*das Lobamt*), the latter being the office of church music. Wetzel's objective is to guard Lutheran primacy of the Word in re-

---

14 Söhngen 1967, 11–112: "Die Stellung des Neuen Testaments und der Reformatoren zur Musik"; 113–166: "Erscheinungsweisen und Bedeutungsgestalten der Musik." The account on the history of theology is often lacking in the studies on Luther and music. Although Söhngen later comments on the views of Augustine, Boethius etc. the historical part itself switches from the NT to the Reformation.

15 Söhngen 1967, 167–225: "Theologische Voraussetzungen der Kirchenmusik." Cf. Vorwort.

16 Söhngen 1967, 261–340: "Versuch einer trinitarischen Begründung der Musik."

17 Söhngen 1967, 100–112.

18 Kurzschenkel 1971, 153–154:"Zugegeben, die einseitige Hervorhebung von im Laufe der Zeit entstellten, abgesunkenen oder verdunkelten Wahrheiten bot Luther dazu fruchtbare Anregungen, und es ist sein bleibendes Verdienst, in seiner geschichtlichen Stunde die theologische Sicht der Musik vertieft und das Musizieren als eine treibende Kraft im christlichen Leben entdeckt zu haben. Jedoch scheint es nicht so zu sein, die gewonnenen Einsichten unablöslich evangelisch-lutherisches Sondergut wären oder bleiben müssten ... Obwohl nun manche Gesichtspunkte lutherischer Musikauffassung eng mit spezifisch reformatorischen Lehren verknüpft erscheinen ... so scheint doch der wesentliche Gehalt von Luthers Musiktheologie nicht angetastet zu werden, wenn wir darauf verzichten müssen, in unsere Darstellung die betreffenden Gebiete lutherischer Theologie mit einzubeziehen."

19 The essay is a part of *Leiturgia. Handbuch des evangelischen Gottesdienstes*. Bd 4, which also contains the first version of Söhngen's opus.

lationship to music, thus he states that the purpose of music is not to proclaim the Gospel, but to praise God.[20]

Christoph Krummacher took a critical stance toward the previous studies in his work *Musik als praxis pietatis* (1994).[21] Krummacher was anxious to show that when Luther is speaking about music, he means music *as* music, not just as related to the spoken word. He criticizes Söhngen by noting that although Söhngen expressly wants to safeguard the theological significance of music, he speaks exclusively about *vocal* music.[22] Against Wetzel, Krummacher points out that the distinction between proclamation and praise does not work. If a musician should abstain from proclaiming the Gospel, should the preacher abstain from praising God?[23] Krummacher's own emphasis on the significance of music in Luther's thinking is the *freedom to make music*. As a consequence, Krummacher argues, music in the Church is not based on the doctrine of the two realms (as in Wetzel) or on it being instituted in the New Testament (as Söhngen sees), but on the Christian freedom to sing.[24]

The most systematic account thus far on the topic is Johannes Block's *Verstehen durch Musik: Das gesungene Wort in der Theologie* (2002). The specific angle from which Block approaches Luther's theology of music is the hermeneutics of Gerhard Ebeling. Ebeling's hermeneutical method means that the reader tries not only to understand the text, but also becomes understood by the text.[25] Ac-

---

20 Wetzel 1961, 316: "Es ist nicht sachgemäss, wenn innerhalb der lutherischen Theologie vom Verkündigungsauftrag der liturgischen Musik geredet wird. Viel angemessener findet der Sachverhalt in dem Begriff ‚Lobamt' seinen Ausdruck. Überall, wo betont vom Verkündigungscharakter der Kirchenmusik geredet wird, ist man in der Gefahr, Luthers Anschauung zu verkennen und Chor- und Orgelempore zur zweiten Kanzel zu befördern."

21 This book is not actually a study on Luther, but written for self-understanding of the Lutheran church music (zum Selbstverständnis evangelischer Kirchenmusik) in the context of the German discussion of renewal of church music (die kirchenmusikalische Erneuerungsbewegung). Many German studies are related to this renewal movement in Germany after the First World War. A good introduction to the history and theology of this movement is Krieg 1990.

22 Krummacher 1994, 26.

23 Krummacher 1994, 30. Actually the question is posed to Matthias Silesius Viertel, who presents a modified version of Wetzel's position (Viertel 1985).

24 Krummacher 1994, 51–52:" Kirchenmusik ist nicht da, weil sie von Gott gefördert wäre, sondern weil der Glaube an Artikulationsmöglichkeiten verlöre, wenn er sich nicht auch der Musik bediente."

25 Block refers several times to the following passage by Ebeling (1971, 3): "Was Verstehen im tiefsten Sinne bedeutet, nämlich dass es nicht nur zu einem Begreifen des Textes, sondern auch zu einem Ergriffenwerden kommt, dass das comprehendere von der Schrift ausgeht und nicht vom Ausleger, dass das Verstehen etwas Passives ist und alle Aktivität beim Text liegt, dass der Text zum Subjekt und der Verstehende zum Objekt wird, zum Gefangenen des Textes, das wird

cordingly, Block emphasizes the existential nature of music according to Luther. From this perspective, understanding music occurs only when one is understood *through* music – touched and moved by it.[26] The larger context to which Block's study is associated is the self-understanding of practical theology. He aims to define what he calls *hermeneutical hymnology*, in which singing a text requires something more than analyzing and explaining it. The singer is personally involved in the song, leading to an existentialist redefinition of practical theology.[27]

Hubert Guicharrousse's *Les Musiques de Luther* (1995) is probably the most exhaustive study on the subject. This interdisciplinary book takes into account the musical environment in the beginning of sixteenth century, the theological background and musical agenda of the Wittenberg Reformation, Luther's Bible translation and its musical implications, and nearly all discussions in Luther's works regarding music, musical instruments, or singing.

Joyce L. Irwin's *Neither Voice nor Heart Alone* (1993) tells the story of the later development of Lutheran theology of music, up to Johann Sebastian Bach. Irwin attests that Luther's positive attitude to music was cherished in Lutheran Orthodoxy and Pietism. As a matter of fact, future generations went to the extreme. In contrast to Calvinism, it was even maintained that music is not an *adiaphora*, but an obligation in the Church.[28] Criticizing Lutheran scholars broadly and Söhngen in particular, Irwin states that it is not plausible Luther assigned a kerygmatic function to music. That view is based on insufficient sources and selective reading of Luther. That music can proclaim the Gospel is, according to Irwin, a thought first uttered by Johann Mattheson, an eighteenth century composer and music theorist.[29] Robin A. Leaver did not share Irwin's opinion, claiming

---

wohl an kaum einem anderen christlichen Exegeten so eindrücklich wie an Luther. Denn: Scripture virtus est hec, quod non mutatur in eum, qui eam studet, sed transmutat suum amatorem in sese ac suas virtutes … Quia non tu me mutabis in te … sed tu mutaberis in me."

26 Block 2002, 45. There is an interesting resemblance – though no dependence – between Block's standpoint and the way Begbie (2000, 4) speaks about the "theology about music" and the "theology through music."

27 Block 2002, 178 – 189. Block employs in this regard words "theologisieren", that means the traditional, objective way of practising theology, and "theologieren" by which he refers to personal, existential encounter with the issue in text.

28 Irwin 1993, 11 – 22.

29 Irwin 1993, 147: "In spite of all that has been said about music as the viva vox evangelii in Lutheranism, there is indeed no evidence that anyone prior to Mattheson dared to suggest that music could serve as well as the sermon for proclaiming the Gospel. Söhngen's evidence that Luther regarded music as a means of proclaiming the word rests on two brief passages from Table Talk which are hardly explicit on this topic and on the Smalcald Articles which specify the various means by which the Gospel is made available: preaching, baptism, the sacrament of the altar, the power of the keys and 'mutuum colloquium et consolatio fratrum'. Only by connecting

that although not all points of Söhngen are defensible, his basic conviction is plausible: that music is important to Luther throughout his literary output.[30] Leaver himself has collected and edited some of his numerous articles[31] on Luther for the book *Luther's Liturgical Music* (2007) which contains not only discussions on the theological significance of music, but chapters on Luther as a musician, Luther's liturgical reforms, and analyses of his hymns. Of special value is Leaver's critical edition and translation of one of the most important sources, Luther's preface to the *Symphoniae iucundae* (1538).[32]

In addition to these major studies, two shorter articles deserve mention, as they have been somewhat influential in the Anglo-Saxon world. The first of these is an article by Brian L. Horne entitled "A Civitas of Sound" (1985). Instead of dissecting the word-music relationship, Horne establishes Luther's theology of music on the order of creation. Horne claims that for Luther, the creation of the world is the revelation of a divine order, which is in the mind of the creator. Music and theology are therefore the two sole survivors from the disaster of the Fall. Since music also represents the divine order, it is "a sure indication of the stability of God in a shifting and unstable world."[33] Horne is mindful of Luther being terrified of disorder, noting the Reformer turned to the most formal of all arts, "the most remote from the untidiness of life; that which is least susceptible to false interpretation; that which ... does not 'mean', but only 'is.'"[34] Another American author, the musicologist Paul Helmer, also defines Luther's theology of music in cosmological terms. Grounded in the medieval theory of music and well-versed in the numerical symbolism in fifteenth century polyphony, Helmer posits that music was for Luther, first and foremost *numerus sonans*, a sounding number. Luther's ideas on music thus fell in the continuum of the mathematical discipline of music in medieval universities.[35]

---

this phrase with the words of Col 3, 16 and Eph 5, 18 is it possible to understand music as included in this mode of proclamation. A recent article by Matthias Viertel points out that Söhngen's translation of Col 3, 16 connects Word and singing in a way that Luther's does not. Placing more importance on the critical comments by Luther which Söhngen attributes to an earlier phase of Luther's development, Viertel calls into question the view of Söhngen and others that Luther assigned music a kerygmatic function."

30 Leaver 1994, 682–683.
31 Above all, Leaver 1995; 2001a; 2004; 2006.
32 Leaver 2007, 313–324.
33 Horne 1985.
34 Horne 1985,28.
35 Helmer 2010.

In addition to the monographs and articles mentioned here, Luther's view on music has been mentioned in numerous other articles,[36] dictionary entries,[37] and accounts on church music history.[38] Moreover, hymnologists and other practical theologians refer to Luther's theology of music recurrently.[39] Nonetheless, one group of scholars is conspicuously absent – systematic theologians, the experts in Luther's theology. Although this topic has not been a cause for major academic dispute, there is one problem that has puzzled scholars and deserves to be discussed separately.

1.3. The relationship between music and the Word of God in previous scholarship

The relationship between word (or the Word) and music is perhaps the most discussed detail in the subject regarding Luther's theology of music. This has been the concern of German studies in particular. In his study entitled *Musik als Problem lutherischer Gottesdienstgestaltung* (1947), Alfred Dedo Müller coined the expression *Naturform des Evangeliums*, the idea that music would be a natural form of the Gospel.[40] He himself did not advocate this view, but nevertheless launched the discussion on how the indisputable high esteem that Luther assigns to music is interpreted in light of the principle of *sola scriptura*. The question was: If music is a part of proclamation of the Gospel, how is it related to the Word? Is it an indirect and secondary form of proclaiming the Word, comparative to images and Church architecture, as Peter Brunner describes in his authoritative account on theology of Christian worship?[41] As a result, several models for

---

36 The most important articles are: Grew (1938), Buszin (1946), Spelman (1951), Wetzel (1955), Blankenburg (1957), Hoelty-Nickel (1960), Schneider (1997), Mannermaa (1991), and Anttila (2010).

37 Blankenburg (1960, 1961b), Joncas (2002), Leaver (2001b), Stalmann (2004), and Schilling (2005).

38 Blume (1975, 5 – 14)

39 Considering hymnological studies, very useful are those of Markus Jenny (1983) and Patrice Veit (1986). Jenny is also the editor of the second ##fourth??## volume of *Archiv zur Weimarer Ausgabe* (AWA), which contains Luther's hymns. For practical studies especially in Nordic countries, see e.g. Thestrup Pedersen (1983), Sariola (1986), Krokfors (1993) and Tobin (1996, 49 – 73). Some Luther biographers comment on the role of music in the Reformer's life, see Brecht (1987, 244 – 247) and Bainton (2002, 340 – 344). Stolt (2000, 127 – 146) discusses music at length from a rhetorical point of view.

40 Dedo Müller 1947, 10.

41 Brunner 1954, 204 – 207.

the word-music relationship emerged. For Söhngen the secret of music was its *Wort-förmigkeit*, while Christhard Mahrenholz conceived of it as *wortverhaftet, wortgebunden, wortfragend und wortdarbietend*.[42] That music is "Word-formed" implies that there is a close connection between music and word. Music therefore somehow naturally belongs to the Word of God (*von Hause aus dem Worte Gottes zugeordnet*)[43]. In other words, there is an inherent ability to preach the Gospel within music itself, which according to Söhngen becomes apparent in the way Luther accepted the Gregorian chants. The argument is that Luther preserved the old tunes and only composed new words. This reflects the conviction that the proper words merely gave expression to the Gospel already present in the music.[44] *Wortförmigkeit* also posits aesthetic criteria for music in the church. Söhngen criticizes Friedrich Blume, who says that church music is not a separate genre of music.[45] Söhngen observes that this is a one-sided statement, noting that not all music is suitable for the purpose of the church. Only music that has a peculiar "cultic" character is capable of fulfilling the mission of church music.[46] Söhngen notices that there is a difference between Luther and Calvin in understanding the "spiritual" in music. For Calvin it is mostly a question of *understanding*, whereas Luther sees the issue in more existential terms. Spirituality means that the whole personhood is involved in singing, and that music can benefit Word owing to its *Wortförmigkeit*.[47]

Walter Blankenburg interprets the existential encounter that occurs in music in the following celebrated formula:

---

42 Söhngen 1967, 84; Mahrenholz 1937, 14.

43 Söhngen 1967, 259.

44 Söhngen 1967, 109: "Darum kann er sich auch an die Unterlegung reiner, schriftgemässer Texte wagen, in der Gewissheit, damit erst richtig zum Ausdruck zu bringen, was die Musik schon von sich aus aussagt und eigentlich meint … Weil die Musik von Hause aus ‚wortförmig' ist, darum muss Luther auf Schriftgemässheit ihrer Texte drängen, weil sich nur so der Einklang von Wort und Weise herstellen lässt."

45 Blume 1974, 3. This is also the view promoted by Wetzel in his dissertation (1954, 205) "Es gibt im strengen Sinne weder geistliche noch weltliche Musik, sondern nur die Musik als Geschöpf und Gabe Gottes, die den Menschen zu rechten Gebrauch oder widernatürlichen Missbrauch ausgesetzt ist."

46 Söhngen 1967, 196: "Nicht jede Musik lässt sich durch Verbindung mit dem ‚Wort' zur Kirchenmusik adeln. Nur eine Tonsprache, die ‚kultische' Grundhaltung besitzt, vermag die Funktion und den Auftrag gottesdienstlicher Musik zu erfüllen."

47 Söhngen 1967, 108: "Es geht nicht mehr um das begriffliche Verständnis des Textes (wie bei Calvin), sondern um die existentielle Begegnung mit dem ‚Wort'; und diese Zielsetzung wird nicht etwa tangiert, sondern nur noch unterstrichen, wenn Luther bemerken kann, dass die Musik bei solchem Geschehen mithelfen kann – eben weil die ‚Wortförmigkeit' der Musik Grundlage der Musikanschauung des reifen Luther ist."

```
WORD  –  REASON   –  THEOLOGY
              and
VOICE  –  EMOTION  –  MUSIC⁴⁸
```

Singing and reading a text have a different effect. This is a reworking of the traditional teaching: *qui cantat, bis orat*; who sings, prays twice. Reading speaks solely to the intellect, but singing takes the emotional side of a person into an encounter with the Word. Johannes Block emphasizes the hermeneutical potential of music, arguing that singing enables one to transcend the subject-object relationship that prevents a personal, participatory understanding.[49] To portray the benefits of music, Block uses antithetic pairs such as *Verstehen/Ergehen* and *Auslegen/Ausgelegtwerden*. To sing the word is not just to understand it, but experience it. To sing a psalm is not to explain it, but to become explained by it.[50] The theology of music is deeply emotional. Jean-Denis Kraege sees Luther's theology of music as a bulwark against the over-intellectualization of Protestant Christianity.[51] Many scholars, even those not related to Luther-and-music studies, have noted that for Luther the Word is primarily a vocal and auditory thing, a *leibliches Wort*.[52] Bernd Wannenwetsch boldly states that *sola scriptura* is a misreading of Luther's theology altogether, arguing instead that the Word of God was for Luther a sound event (*Klangereignis*).[53]

---

[48] Blankenburg 1957, 21.

[49] Block 2002, 219: "Im Grundinteresse einer hermeneutisch fragenden Hymnologie steht jene Öffnung im Verstehen, die sich jenseits erklärender, also historischer, formanalytischer und liedexegetischer Gesichtspunkte aufschliesst. Solch ein existentiales Verstehen ist das Bezugsfeld der jüngeren hermeneutischen Theologie. Diese zielt darauf, jene Subjekt-Objekt-Relation zu überwinden, die ein teilnehmendes, lebenspersönliches Verstehen unmöglich macht. Unter dem Horizont der hermeneutischen Theologie findet das gesungene Wort als ein der Sache der Schrift angemessenes Verstehensmittel (Hermeneuticum) Beachtung."

[50] Block 2002, 86–87: "Das gesungene Wort wiederholt nicht blosse Inhalte (vivere literaliter), sondern beteiligt am actus des Wortes Gottes, das sich unter dem Einsatz der eigenen Existenz eröffnet (vivere spiritualiter). Hier erscheint der hermeneutische Rang der vox humana bzw. der vox musicae, die den Ausleger im Sinne eines vivere spiritualiter ausstreckt – daraufhin, dass das Wort Gottes im Hören steht, der Ausleger hingegen als illustrandus hört und empfängt."

[51] Kraege 1983, 450–453.

[52] Bayer 1992, 57–72; Beutel 1998, 104–123.

[53] Wannenwetsch 2004, 341: "An dieser Stelle zeigt sich wiederum, was hier nur angemerkt sei, warum Luthers Lehre von der Schrift in der Formel ‚sola scriptura' missverständlich repräsentiert ist. Wenngleich der dramatische raptus, der Affektsturz des Glaubens, vermittels der Schrift bewirkt wird, so ist das medium salutis eben hier dezidiert nicht die Schrift als Schrift, sondern die Schrift als Stimme, als Klangereignis, wie es etwa aus der gemeinschaftlichen Form des Psalmodierens entsteht. Wenngleich Luther die Schrift immer wieder als Autorität gegenüber bestimmten kirchlichen Traditions-Missbildungen ins Feld führen musste, so bleibt doch festzuhalten, dass er die Rezeption der Schrift selbst für keineswegs voraussetzungslos hielt, son-

Luther's unreservedly positive attitude toward music is problematic for theologians who try to take it seriously while maintaining a genuine Lutheran understanding of the Word. Seeing music as a gift of God with no explicit connection to the Word is suspect because it seems to promote some kind of *natural theology*. For that reason Mahrenholz, although saying that Luther considers instrumental music to be as effective as vocal music, hastens to add that without the Word music cannot lead to Christ.[54] In the same manner Blankenburg asserts that music cannot be revelatory and awaken faith by itself, although the sung word is the most effective form of the word.[55] According to Krummacher, these attempts to safeguard the primacy of the Word articulate a problem that the unity of creation and redemption dissolves. To say that something is *creatura*, as Luther argues concerning music, is already a statement of faith. In creation the Word of God is already present. Thus music as a gift of God does not necessarily need to be connected strictly outwardly to the word.[56]

---

dern als einen Vorgang gemeinsamen Hörens und Hörbarmachens der Schriftworte verstand, wie er ihm innerhalb der kirchlichen Tradition des Psalmodierens vertraut war: ‚Vox est anima verbi.'"

54 Mahrenholz 1937, 18: "Luther schreibt der Musik eine Wirkungsmöglichkeit im positiven Sinne auch ohne Bindung an Gottes Wort zu ... aber eins kann sie aus sich selbst nicht: zu Christus hinführen."

55 Blankenburg 1957, 24. On an earlier occasion Blankenburg holds to the kerygmatic ability of music. He does not consider music only as a medium of praise, but also that of proclamation. "Neben dem gesprochenen Wort der Verkündigung hat das gesungene eine legitime kerygmatische, ihm eigentümliche Aufgabe ... Wort und Antwort, Verkündigung und Lobopfer [sind] durch den ganzen Gottesdienst miteinander verwoben und unzertrennlich miteinander verknüpft. Das aber bedeutet, dass das gottesdienstliche Singen – nur von ihm haben wir gesprochen und nicht auch vom Spielen – unmittelbaren Anteil hat an dem, was den Gottesdienst begründet und trägt, nämlich an der Vermittlung des Evangeliums. Seine Zurücksetzung ist Verschmähung eines Gefässes der Verkündigung, das Gott zu seinem Sprachrohr erwählt hat [emphasis mine]." Blankenburg 1953, 16.

56 Krummacher 1994, 19–20. Tuomo Mannermaa (1991, 2) sees music as being distinct from, but concomitant with the Word of God: "According to the Lutheran view there is another 'good' [besides the Word] which should be able to control human hidden will. This good is music. As the written and spoken language is an instrument, in and through which God himself approaches man, so is music with its elements and structures another 'language' in which God approaches man. All music is a good gift of God, the purpose of which is to delight human heart. The meaning of music is to bring the hidden human inner will in connection with the 'good' and 'delightful' and thus control it. 'Frau Musica' turns human will at herself, overwhelms it with her wondrous splendor and ties the human heart to herself. Especially that kind of music, where the Word of God is connected to melody, is delighting the soul and the bowels, because in it it is possible to taste the Good itself and its sweetness. Like the word of God is 'cloud and darkness', so can music also be a kind of 'shining cloud' where God comes near as hidden, but real and

1.4. The aim, method and sources of the present study

The aim of the present study is to explain Luther's position on the theological significance of music, a question approached from the point of view of *pleasure*. This approach was selected because this topic has not been fully addressed in previous studies, while a very superficial reading of Luther's texts on music shows that one of the greatest advantages of music is its ability to produce pleasure, to delight the human heart. This is also an interesting standpoint in the history of theology, because the history of Christian thought has seldom been read in terms of the positive evaluation of pleasure. Therefore the background chapter offers an account of the delight of music in the history of Western philosophical and theological thought. Before proceeding, however, the terminology of pleasure needs to be detailed. The word "pleasure" (mainly *voluptas* in Latin) refers to a gratification of the senses. Pleasure is more related to the physical phenomena than "delight" (*delectatio*) which, although overlapping with pleasure, bears the connotations of an aesthetic perception. The third word, "joy" (*gaudium*), is a more dispositional term describing the inner attitude toward that which causes pleasure. This is adopted in the present study as a technical division and as a tool for the analysis. Luther does not use these words with precision, nor do the other theologians discussed.

The method adopted in this study is systematic analysis. Theology of music can be practiced in the different branches of theological studies; for example, exegetical studies of music can explain the musical expressions and instruments in the Old Testament and the way singing together was a part of the life of New Testament congregations. On the other hand, historical accounts of church music begin with early church hymns and the psalmody of desert fathers, chronicling the Gregorian chant of the early medieval times, the rich Renaissance polyphony, German Baroque organ music, and finally modern Church music with its jazz and pop influences. This study, however, belongs to the area of systematic theology, which means that Luther's statements about music are treated as theological statements. Systematic analysis as a method covers a number of methods used in textual analysis and is focused in the use and meaning of central concepts in the textual material, as well as in their mutual relatedness and in the structure of argumentation. Choosing this approach is justified by the conviction that music is not a theological *bagatelle*, but reflects something essential in Lu-

---

able to be sensed. The abyss calls upon the abyss to the endless depth. There is the bright darkness. In this bright darkness, the hidden inner will of man has come home." Translation mine.

ther's theology. It is related to central concepts such as "the Word of God," "faith," and "gift." Therefore questions are posed such as: If music is a gift of God, what does it mean to be a "gift"? If Luther says that music is the best gift of God, what is the feature in music that makes him say so? If music's ability to produce pleasure is the reason why it is the best gift of God, what does this mean for the theological appreciation of pleasure? Luther's high estimation of music was intact throughout his career. Therefore the study is presented in thematic order with less attention to the development in the Reformer's thinking. I am not claiming that there was no development concerning Luther's ideas of music. Certainly there was a significant shift of emphasis between young and old Luther (e. g. concerning the import of *canticum novum*). Nonetheless, I believe that Luther's theology of music can be viewed as a consistent whole without dissecting it into developmental stages.

Luther's theology of music did not, of course, emerge in a vacuum. He was a part of the rich Western history of music and theology. A historical survey on musical thought, with special attention to pleasure and emotions, begins the analysis of this study. This account is needed to give us the conceptual equipment and the context of philosophical and theological discussions that we must understand when we analyze Luther's ideas.

This is strictly a theological study, which means that no musical expertise is required either from the author or the reader. However, in the last part of this study an attempt is made to identify theological aesthetics of music. Given the theological significance of music, it is fitting to ask what kind of music offers the required pleasure that seems to be essential. In other words, are there some kinds of aesthetic standards according to which Luther judges music? A tentative sketch of Luther's conception of beauty is required to address these questions.

This study concentrates on the literary production of Martin Luther. I am well aware that this kind of restriction may well be seen as a defect, as many of the previous studies, those of Leaver and Guicharrousse in particular, benefit from encompassing the sixteenth-century musical tradition and environment, biographical details and Reformation policy with their theology of music. All this is important in order to understand the emergence of Lutheran church music, because the Lutheran theology of music is not all about defining music, but also about how it sounded and how ordinary people participated in it.[57] My focus on Luther, and particularly on the texts of Luther is partly due to a need to limit the scope of the present study. The sixteenth century was a time of musical

---

[57] Rebecca Wagner Oettinger's dissertation (1999) provides the basic study for how average 16th century Germans experienced the music of the Reformation.

reform and innovation. Many other Wittenberg reformers apart from Luther, such as Philip Melanchthon,[58] Andreas Karlstadt,[59] and Johannes Bugenhagen influenced music, not to mention Luther's closest musical collaborator Johann Walter[60] or the other branches of the Reformation: Thomas Müntzer,[61] Martin Bucer,[62] John Calvin,[63] or Huldreych Zwingli.[64] Music in the thought of Erasmus of Rotterdam[65] and the decrees of the Council of Trent carry some relevance as well.[66] Sixteenth century music theory was also fascinating. It was then that remarkable treatises by Johannes Cochlaeus (1514), Andreas Ornitoparchus (1517), Franchino Gaffurio (1518), and Heinrich Glarean (1547) were written, among others.[67] While for the purposes of this study the texts by Luther provide a sufficient basis for analysis, those texts need not, and must not, be isolated from their historical environment.

In keeping with the postulated theological significance of music, all the works of Luther serve as plausible sources for this study. It is obvious that one cannot consult them all, nor are all of them relevant to the subject. Those texts that are dedicated especially to music cover hardly more than a dozen pages in *Weimarer Ausgabe*.[68] In the following I will briefly present the most significant texts of Luther that are related to the topic.

The largest single text concerning music that Luther ever wrote is *Praefatio zu den Symphoniae iucundae* (1538). The occasion for the preface was the publishing of a motet collection by Georg Rhau. Rhau (1488–1548) was a Wittenberg printer, publisher, musician, and composer, who also edited motet collections that consisted of works by the best composers in his day, including Ludwig

---

58 Krummacher 1994, 41–49.

59 Sider 1974, 149–153.

60 Gurlitt 1933; Blankenburg 1991; Sander 1997.

61 Honemeyer 1974; Bräuer 1974.

62 Mayer 1993, 215–226.

63 Begbie 2003.

64 Jenny 1966; Söhngen 1979.

65 Miller 1966.

66 Fellerer 1953.

67 For the history of the theory of music in 16th century Germany see Niemöller 2003. All these treatises on music (with lots of ancient and medieval sources) are accessible at the database *Thesaurus musicarum latinarum* (http://www.chmtl.indiana.edu/tml/start.html).

68 *Weimarer Ausgabe* (WA) is the main edition of Luther's texts. In this study, H. U. Delius' *Studienausgabe* (StA) will be used, when available. *Archiv zur Weimarer Ausgabe* (AWA) is used in *Operationes in Psalmos* and Luther's hymns. The English translations are mostly taken from the American edition of *Luther's Works* (LW). As for the texts belonging to the Lutheran Confessions, I use the translation made by Timothy Wengert and Robert Kolb in *The Book of Concord* (BC).

Senfl, Heinrich Isaac, and Pierre de la Rue. *Symphoniae iucundae* contained fifty-two motets for each Sunday of the church year. In fact, it was the first volume of a twelve-part series of collections. Melanchthon and Bugenhagen wrote the prefaces to the subsequent volumes, which affirm that in Wittenberg, the connection between frontline theologians and musicians was extremely strong.[69] This important text has at least three extant versions: *Weimarer Ausgabe* includes both a Latin and a German version.[70] There has been some discussion as to which of these is Luther's original. According to one hypothesis, Luther himself penned the German version, with its characteristic Lutheran pleonasms, while the Latin version was thought to be a translation by Melanchthon that was written later. This theory was discredited by a scatological detail – again characteristic of Luther. The Latin text includes the word *merdipoeta*, "a shit-poet." The word is undoubtedly addressed to Simon Lemnius, who was active in Wittenberg in 1538, the year of the publication of *Symphoniae iucundae*.[71] It is difficult to determine why Melanchthon would later have replaced the German *"wüste, wilde Eselgeschrey des Chorals"* with an obscene reference to Lemnius. A more plausible theory is that Johann Walter, who published the German text together with his own *"Lob und Preis der himmlischen Kunst Musica"* in 1564, changed the text so that it is now addressed to Gregorian chants instead of to Lemnius, whom few remembered at that time. There exists also another German translation, published in 1575 by Wolfgang Figulus. This translation is somewhat shorter than the Latin version and remarkably shorter than the Walter translation. Walter Blankenburg was the first to suggest that the latter is not merely another translation, but the original draft by Luther, which he used as the basis for the 1538 preface.[72] *Praefatio zu den Symphoniae iucundae* is also known as *Encomion musices*, which is the name that will be used in the present study.

---

69 See Melanchthon's preface to the collection *Harmoniae selectae* in CR V, 918–920.

70 WA 50, 368–374.

71 Simon Lemnius (c.1514–1550) was a pupil of Melanchthon who in 1538 published libelous epigrams about Wittenberg personages, thus causing a local scandal. Brecht 1987, 95–97.

72 Blankenburg 1972. According to Blankenburg, there are several reasons to believe that the Figulus text is the original German version written by Luther. Figulus himself proclaims that it is "a German Preface of honorable father Martin Luther, not printed before," and there also are some text-critical remarks that make the point plausible: the Figulus text is not a learned study like the Latin text (which is addressed to students). The thoughts are presented in a less ordered way than in the Latin text. The greeting formula "alle Liebhaber der Musik" fits this text better than the Latin version or Walter's translation. The peculiarity of the text, the allusion to the song of nightingale, is well in line with Luther's poem Frau Musica, written in 1538, which likewise contains some strophes about nightingale. In addition, words characteristic of Luther occur in the Figulus text that are absent in Walter's translation, such as "grossen, unaussprechlichen,

Luther's theology of music cannot properly be treated without acknowledging his activity as a hymn poet and composer. Although his artistic endeavors are beyond the scope of this study, Luther's hymns– and hymnal prefaces in particular– provide a group of extremely important texts for the present study. Luther wrote his first hymnal preface for Johann Walter's *Geystliche Gesangk Buchleyn* (1524), which contained 24 of Luther's songs. In the short preface, Luther discusses the importance of singing spiritual songs and the educational usefulness of learning hymns, and expresses his wish to see all arts, particularly music, in the service of their Giver.[73] Luther's hymns became exceedingly popular across Europe, circulating more than any other writings produced by the Wittenberg Reformation. While some of the hymn publications were authorized by Luther, most of them were not. In the preface to J. Klug's *Gesangbuch* (1529), Luther touches on this copyright question. He declares that the names of the writers are now included in the original Wittenberg hymnbooks, and he makes a plea that no unauthorized versions of Wittenberg hymnbooks would appear.[74] In the year of the publication of *Encomion musices* – 1538 – another praise of music was published in a hymnal preface to *Vorrhede auff alle gute Gesangbücher*, which is better known by its subtitle, *Frau Musica*. In fact, it never was a hymnal preface, but was published to accompany the first edition of Johann Walter's aforementioned "*Lob und Preis der himmlischen Kunst Musica*." *Frau Musica* praises music in a similar way as the *Encomion*.[75]

The preface to J. Klug's *Begräbnislieder* (1542) is important for two reasons: first, in it Luther gives an account on his ideas on funeral music, and second, he explains his policy of using Gregorian tunes (that some other Reformers claimed should be abandoned as "popish"). The last of Luther's hymnal prefaces was written for Valentin Bapst's *Geistliche Lieder* (1545). In it Luther discusses a theme that dates back to his early Psalm lectures – the new song of the new covenant.[76]

A short draft from 1530 with the Greek title of Περι της μουσικης ("On Music") is an oft-quoted document.[77] Robin Leaver has suggested that it is a

---

unbegreiflichen und erforschlichen Weisheit gottes." Nevertheless, Blankenburg considers the Latin version as the best.

[73] WA 35, 474, 1– 475, 10. For the emergence of the first Lutheran hymnal, see Brecht 1986, 132– 138.

[74] WA 35, 475, 11– 476, 15. Note that here it is dated in 1528. It is, however, most likely written not earlier than in 1529, see the volume introduction WA 35, 303.

[75] WA 35, 482, 12– 484. There is an ambiguity in the dating: The text is dated 1524, although its first publication was 1538.

[76] WA 35,476, 16– 477, 36.

[77] WA 30 II, 696.

draft for a larger treatise on music that was never completed by Luther. The date of the draft suggests that Luther planned to work on it during his sojourn in Veste Coburg at the time of the Diet of Augsburg. The lines of the draft would have served as subtitles for separate chapters.[78] For the sake of convenience, I will refer to this text by its English title *On Music*. Its thoughts are often echoed in *Table Talk* (*Tischreden*), to which it lends certain credibility. The source-critical problem of the topic at hand is that many of the most celebrated and interesting quotes from Luther on music are derived from second-hand reports collected in the *Tischreden* volumes of the Weimar edition. Without *On Music*, which is a genuine Luther text, these quotations would have no significance whatsoever for an academic study, but in light of this text they may be consulted – albeit with extreme cautiousness. Also from the same period as *On Music* is a letter to the composer Ludwig Senfl that ranks among the most important sources on Luther and music.[79]

In addition to the writings already mentioned, Luther's psalm commentaries, such as *Dictata super Psalterium* (1513–1515) and *Operationes in Psalmos* (1519–1521) provide some material related to music. These are often comments on musical terms made in passing. Besides the psalm commentaries, there are some other texts that have often been quoted in discussions on the topic. *The Last Words of David* (1543) contains a passage on music, as do some of Luther's sermons. The role of music in Christian worship is discussed in Luther's liturgical writings *On the Public Order of Worship*, *Formula Missae*, and *The German Mass*. To support the claim that music belongs to the core of Luther's theology, one must also consult Luther's Catechisms and other major writings, because a thought of Luther related to music may occur where least expected.

The study begins with an account on the history of theology that discusses the evaluation of music's pleasure in antiquity and medieval times. Other important factors related to that discussion are the theory of affects and the notion of Christian aesthetics. The first main chapter examines Luther's understanding of music as a gift of God, and it includes the analysis of *Encomion musices*. The analysis continues in the next chapter, which presents music as the ruler of human affects. After these opening chapters, two topics that have appeared to be crucial in Luther's theology of music (joy and pleasure) receive a separate discussion from an analysis of Luther's most important works. The final chapter enters the field of theological aesthetics and discusses Luther's view of beauty and the particular virtues of music.

---

78 Leaver 2007, 85–97.
79 WA Br 5, 639.

2 Voluptates aurium: the pleasures of music in Antiquity and the Middle Ages

This chapter examines how Christian authors evaluated the pleasure of music beginning from the early church until the fifteenth century. That issue is related to two others: the role of emotions in faith and the appreciation of beauty (aesthetics). A section is devoted to each of these topics. Serving as a background chapter of a study on Luther's theology, the present account focuses on the theological tradition of the West, and as a consequence the rich musical theology of the Eastern Church has been omitted. Furthermore, no immediate historical or literary dependence is postulated here. Some scholars suggest that certain figures (notably Gerson and Tinctoris) may have had a direct impact on Luther's theology of music. In general, the authors and ideas presented in this chapter portray the spiritual tradition and musical heritage of which Luther was a part. This lengthy account also provides the history of the concepts that are important for the study, such as "pleasure," "affect," and "beauty."

2.1 Song of the heart: the appreciation of music in the early church[80]

"The words of institution" of church music are in Eph 5:19, where the Apostle admonishes Christians to be filled with the Spirit, "speaking to one another in psalms and hymns and spiritual songs, singing and making melody to the Lord with all your heart." Col 3:16 renders the same idea with the words "let the word of Christ dwell in you richly, teach and admonish one another in all wisdom, and sing psalms and hymns and spiritual songs with thankfulness in your hearts to God." These verses indicate that there was music in Christian gatherings from the church's beginning. One minor detail of some relevance to the theological treatment of music in the patristic era is an ambiguity concerning how "the heart" is involved in singing. The Greek text of Eph 5:19 may read τη καρδια or εν τη καρδια.[81] In the former case, the successful translation would be "with

---

80 The source quotations in this section are mainly derived from James W. McKinnon's *Music in Early Christian Literature*, which comprises patristic thought and references to music from Apostolic Fathers to Augustine. The texts in McKinnon collection are numbered, thus I use references as "McKinnon no.2"

81 In the Nestle-Aland edition (26th Ed.) of the New Testament, τη καρδια is in the corpus text and εν τη καρδια/εν ταις καρδιαις in the apparatus. From an exegetical point of view, neither of

(all) your heart," the latter being possible to read "in the heart." The Vulgate reading *in cordibus vestris* was less ambiguous and gave reason for some church fathers to think that the singing suggested here does not involve any kind of outer voice, although the context does not support that kind of interpretation. Jerome commented on Eph 5:19 by saying, "We ought to make melody and to praise the Lord more with our soul than with the voice."[82] The extreme conclusion that singing aloud should be prohibited in general was never made, thus nothing compared to the iconoclastic schism occurred with music.[83] As a consequence, theology of music remained a somewhat underdeveloped area of inquiry. Since there was no urgent need to defend the use of music in the church, ancient and medieval theologians speak about music only occasionally.

Jerome did not claim that one should abstain from using one's voice in singing but that emphasis should be on the words rather than on the sweetness of the singer's voice. "Thus let the servant of Christ sing, so that not the voice of the singer but the words that are read give pleasure."[84] The problem was accordingly not the voice, but the pleasure involved in it. Over-emphasizing the sweetness of the voice compromises the spiritual understanding of the words sung. Niceta of Remesiana expressly refuted the opinion – which he thought was more common in the east – that it is superfluous or even frivolous to produce sound with one's lips when singing a psalm. The words "singing in your hearts" were therefore to be understood so that one sings only with the attention of one's heart and moreover, one meditates the words that one sings.

> But I believe also that he frees our mouths, loosens our tongues and opens our lips, for it is impossible for men 'to speak' without these organs; and just as heat differs from cold so does silence differ from speech. And since he adds 'speaking in psalms and hymns and

---

these verses is understood as promoting "silent singing of the heart." Col 3:16 speaks about Christ dwelling "in you" (εν υμιν). It is not possible to understand this individually (as a matter of fact, "among you" would be a better translation). It continues with "teaching and admonishing one another." The aim of singing is to teach and admonish others. This social and communicative emphasis alone suffices to rule out the silent singing in the secrecy of the heart. The same applies to Eph 5:19. It is no use to translate λαλουντες εαυτοις as "speaking for yourself", as did Aquinas. Delling 1972, 499; Barth/Blanke 1994, 428; Barth 1974, 583.

82 PL 26, 528: "Et canere igitur et psallere, et laudare Dominum magis animo quam voce debemus."

83 Joncas 2002 mentions both Zwingli and Abbot Pambo as theologians who want to extirpate church music. As for Zwingli, both Jenny (1966) and Garside (1966) have attested that his view on music was more positive than was often viewed. As for the harsh denunciation of psalmody by Abbot Pambo, McKinnon (1987, 9) claims that the story is unauthentic.

84 PL 26, 528.

songs', he would not have mentioned 'songs' if he had wished those 'making melody' to be altogether silent, for no one can sing by being absolutely quiet.[85]

The scriptures did not cause trouble for the first Christians with regard to music.[86] The reason early church fathers harbored doubts about music was due to the prominence of music in the pagan cults. The suspicion was directed particularly toward musical instruments. Justin Martyr found pagan assemblies despicable because "there are excessive banquets and subtle flutes that provoke people to lustful movements."[87] Clement of Alexandria rebuked the Christians who, after attending the Christian service, "amused themselves with godless things," such as listening to music played with strings and *aulos*, and finally "defiling themselves with dancing, drunkenness and every sort of trash."[88] Tertullian disapproved not only of theatre, but also of music because they were closely related to the cults of Venus, Apollo, Minerva, and other pagan deities. "O Christian, you will detest those things whose authors you cannot but detest."[89] This kind of rigor was exceptional among the Latin church fathers. Novatian accompanied Tertullian by stating that even if music and theatre were not consecrated to idols, they would nevertheless be superfluous and hardly suitable for believers.[90] However, even Tertullian did not think that the Christians should not sing in their gatherings.[91]

---

85 De utilitate hymnorum 2 (McKinnon 1987, no. 303)

86 Although music is not a topic in itself in the New Testament, there are many places where singing is mentioned or implied. Jesus sang a hymn after the Last Supper (Matt 26:30, Mark 14:26), and Paul and Silas sang at night in the prison of Thyatira (Acts 16:25 – 26). The description of worship in the Corinthian church states that when coming together, each one has a psalm, teaching, tongue or interpretation (1 Cor 14:26 – 27) and praying as well as singing should happen both with the spirit and with the mind (1 Cor 14:14 – 15). There are a few passages, which are early Christian hymns (1 Tim 3:16, Eph 1:3 – 14, Phil 2:6 – 11), not to mention the many hymns contained in the book of Revelation.

87 Discourse to the Greeks IV (PG 6, 235)

88 Paedagogus III,11 (PG 8, 660)

89 Tertullian: De spectaculiis X, 8 (PL 1, 643)

90 Novatian: De spectaculiis VII, 1–3 (PL 4, 785 BC): "Haec etiamsi non essent simulacris dicata, adeunda tamen et spectanda non essent Christianis fidelibus; quoniam, etsi non haberent crimen, habent in se maximam et parum congruentem fidelibus vanitatem." (although PL attributes the text to Cyprian, McKinnon 1987, no. 92 sees more plausible to presume Novatian as its author)

91 As a matter of fact, Tertullian provides us with a unique report of musical improvisation in the liturgy of the first Christian centuries. Apologeticum XXX, 16 – 18:"... each is urged to come into the middle and sing to God, either from the sacred scriptures or from his own invention (de proprio ingenio)." McKinnon 1987, no. 74.

An essential part in the liturgies of the early church was "singing psalms and hymns and spiritual songs."[92] The three New Testament words for congregational song are psalms (ψαλμος), hymns (υμνος), and songs (ωδη), which have been interpreted in various ways. Two exemplary ways to differentiate them can be observed: Jerome makes the distinction within the Psalter, saying that a *hymn* declares the power and majesty of the Lord and usually contains the word *alleluia*. On the other hand, a *psalm* is directed to the ethical side of the human person, and a spiritual *song* is created to examine the harmony in the world and the order and concord of all creatures.[93] According to Gregory of Nyssa, the leading idea of a *psalm* is a musical accompaniment and that of a *hymn* is praise of God. Gregory considers ωδη to be the general word for a song, whether accompanied or unaccompanied, meant for praise or any other subject.[94] The role of psalmody in Christian spirituality was enhanced in what James W. McKinnon calls "the fourth-century psalmodic movement."[95] The new understanding of the virtue of music emerged under the austere conditions of the Egyptian desert. Indeed, the spirituality of the desert fathers influenced many of the most remarkable fourth-century theologians, notably Basil the Great, John Chrysostom, Ambrose, and Augustine. Psalm singing was also an essential part of desert monasticism, and the monks sang psalms many times a day. Actually the ideal was continuous psalmody: "The true monk must have prayer and psalmody in his heart without ceasing," states the *Apophthegmata Patrum*.[96] Simultaneously, metrical hymn poetry emerged, first in the East by Ephraem the Syrian, and then in the West by Hilary of Poitiers and eventually Ambrose of Milan. One interesting historical detail is that Ephraem used hymn tunes made by heretical Bardaisan and his son, Harmo-

---

92 Although Justin Martyr fails to mention singing in his early account on Christian service, the letter of Pliny to the Emperor Trajan (written c. 112) reports about Christians, who "were wont to assemble on a set day before dawn and to sing a hymn among themselves to the Christ, as to a god." (McKinnon 1987, no. 41)

93 PL 26, 527–528: "Quid autem intersit inter psalmum et hymnum et canticum, in Psalterio plenissime discimus. Nunc autem breviter hymnos esse dicendum, qui fortitudinem et majestatem praedicant Dei, et ejusdem semper, vel beneficia, vel facta mirantur. Quod omnes psalmi continent, quibus ALLELUIA, vel praepositum, vel subjectum est, psalmi autem proprie ad ethicum locum pertinent, ut per organum corporis, quid faciendum, et quid vitandum sit, noverimus. Qui vero de superioribus disputat, et concentum mundi omniumque creaturarum ordinem atque concordiam subtilis disputator ediserit, iste spirituale canticum canit. Vel certe (ut propter simpliciores manifestius quod volumus, eloquamur) psalmus ad corpus: canticum refertur ad mentem."

94 PG 44, 493.

95 McKinnon 1994.

96 McKinnon 1987, no. 124.

nios. He used the music of the heretics against the heresy itself. This incident witnesses both the belief in the power of music and the conviction that there is nothing wrong with music, even if it was used for wrong purposes.[97] In the later half of the fourth century one encounters several praises for psalmody written by prominent authors. These eulogies are impressive in their praise of *singing* psalms. Basil the Great (330 – 379) encapsulates the benefits of psalmody as follows:

> A psalm is tranquillity of soul and the arbitration of peace; it settles one's tumultuous and seething thoughts. It mollifies the soul's wrath and chastens its recalcitrance. A psalm creates friendships, unites the separated and reconciles those at enmity. Who can still consider one to be a foe with whom one utters the same prayer to God! Thus psalmody provides the greatest of all goods, charity, by devising in its common song a certain bond of unity, and by joining together the people into the concord of a single chorus.[98]

In the first place, there are the psychological virtues of music. John Chrysostom observed, "For nothing so arouses the soul, gives it wing, sets it free from the earth, releases it from the prison of the body, teaches it to love wisdom, and to condemn all the things of this life, as concordant melody and sacred song composed in rhythm."[99] According to Ambrose, a psalm softens anger, offers a release from anxiety, and alleviates sorrow.[100] Whereas Athanasius and to some extent Jerome taught that sacred songs should not be used for pleasure, Basil, Chrysostom and Ambrose discovered the benefit of psalmody precisely in being pleasing to the soul. Mindful of the possibility of licentiousness, Chrysostom states that God erected the barrier of psalms against impiety, so that the psalms would be a matter of both pleasure and profit. Furthermore, Niceta of Remesiana suggests that the word of God needs the pleasure of song to be fully effective: "For a psalm is sweet to the ear when sung, it penetrates the soul when it gives pleasure, it is easily remembered when sung often, and what the harshness of the Law cannot force from the minds of man it excludes by the suavity of song."[101] The delight of music is

---

97 Theodoret of Cyrus, Eccl.Hist IV 29, 1 – 3: "And since Harmonios, the son of Bardesanes, had composed some songs long ago, and by mixing the sweetness of melody with his impiety had beguiled his audience and led them to their destruction, Ephraem took the music for his song, mixed in his own piety, and thus presented his listeners with a remedy both exceedingly sweet and beneficial."(McKinnon 1987, no. 226) PG 82, 1189.
98 Hom. In Ps 1 (PG 29, 212). McKinnon 1987, no. 131.
99 PG 55, 156. McKinnon 1987, no. 164.
100 PL 14, 924D: "Ab iracundia mitigat, a sollicitudine abdicat, a moerore allevat." Also Evagrius Ponticus says "Psalmody lays the passions to rest and causes the stirrings of the body to be stilled."(McKinnon 1987, no. 115).
101 PL 68, 372AB: "Suaviter enim Psalmus auditur dum canitur, penetrat animum cum delectat; facile Psalmi memoria retinentur, si frequenter psallantur; et quod legis austeritas ab humanis

also of educational value. Ambrose pointed out that a child who refuses to learn other things takes pleasure in contemplating a psalm. In other words, it is a kind of play that advances learning more than stern discipline.[102] Other benefits of music concern social virtues. For instance, Basil thought that singing psalms together creates a bond of unity. Ambrose wrote: "A psalm joins those with differences, unites those at odds and reconciles those who have been offended, for who will not concede to him with whom one sings to God in one voice?"[103] The concord of the hearts was the equivalent for the Greek word *symphonia* for church fathers. Already Ignatius of Antioch had used the metaphor of strings of a cithara to depict the unity of the church, which sings to Jesus Christ with unity and concordant love.[104] "For this is a symphony", observes Ambrose in his Gospel commentary, "when there resound in the Church a united concord of differing ages and abilities as if of diverse strings."[105]

2.2 Evaluation of aural pleasures in Augustine

2.2.1 The temporal and eternal numbers of *De Musica*

The fourth-century psalmodic movement had, at least through Ambrose in Milan, an impact on the thought of Augustine, despite the fact that he never wrote a praise of psalmody. Instead, he wrote an important and authoritative account of music as a science among the *artes liberales*. *De Musica* is an early work of Augustine, consisting of six books, the last of them written after his baptism in 391. It is a treatise of numbers, movement, rhythm, and measure more than that of music (in the sense modern audiences understand the word). Initially Augustine aimed to dedicate a book to all the liberal sciences. However, the only accomplished works came to be *De Musica* and *De Dialectica*.[106] The vision behind

---

mentibus extorquere non poterat, hi per dulcedinem cantionis excludunt." (McKinnon 1987, no. 306).

102 PL 14, 925AB: "Hunc tenere gestit pueritia, hunc meditari gaudet infantia, quae alia declinat ediscere. Ludus quidam est iste doctrinae majoris profectus, quam cum seria traditur disciplina." (McKinnon 1987, no. 276).

103 PL 14, 925B.

104 Ign.Eph. 4:1–2.

105 PL 15, 1763 (McKinnon 1987, no. 284).

106 Retract. I, 6: "Per idem tempus quo Mediolani fui, Baptismum percepturus, etiam Disciplinarum libros conatus sum scribere, interrogans eos qui mecum erant, atque ab hujusmodi studiis non abhorrebant; per corporalia cupiens ad incorporalia quibusdam quasi passibus certis vel pervenire vel ducere. Sed earum solum de Grammatica librum absolvere potui, quem

these books was a prominently Neoplatonist one; through the study of sciences that belong to the physical world, one could arrive at the incorporeal reality of God (*per corporalia cupiens ad incorporalia quibusdam quasi passibus certis vel pervenire vel ducere*). *De Musica* was a highly influential textbook throughout the Middle Ages. All subsequent authors on musical theory – Cassiodore and Boethius as well as Isidor – relied upon Augustine in one way or another.

At the outset Augustine defines music as *scientia bene modulandi*.[107] This idea is difficult to translate concisely, but one alternative is to render it "the science of measuring well." Another equally acceptable interpretation is "the knowledge of proper movements." The verb *modulari* means to measure, and *modus* is not only "a measure", but also "a rule." To perceive a measure or a rule also presupposes movement. Therefore Augustine says that music can be also defined as *scientia bene movendi*, "the knowledge of moving well." If music is about moving, it easily suggests dancing. As with ancient Christianity in general, Augustine did not favor dance, therefore the word *bene* is important. Music does not mean any musical movement, but only good and proper ones. It is also important that music is *scientia*, not *ars*. For Augustine, the difference between them is the same as between *ratio* and *imitatio*. In short, it is far more valuable to understand (have a *ratio*) something than merely execute (*imitari*) it.[108] Augustine provides examples of artisanship or surgery, where the architect or doctor demonstrates less ability in practical matters than artisans or nurses, yet the mastery of these sciences is attributed to those who operate with science and meditation rather than by practice and imitation. In a similar manner, it is more valuable to have the knowledge (*scientia*) of music than to be able to sing or play (*ars*).[109] Music is therefore a mathematical discipline, dealing with numbers in their relationships and in their movements, and belongs to the *quadrivium* of the liberal arts with arithmetic, astronomy and geometry. At the end of the first book Augustine suggests the spiritual usefulness of this discipline: "Since music somehow issuing forth from the most secret sanctuaries leaves traces in our very senses or in things sensed by us, must

---

postea de armario nostro perdidi: et de Musica sex volumina; quantum attinet ad eam partem quae Rythmus vocatur. Sed eosdem sex libros jam baptizatus, jamque ex Italia regressus in Africam scripsi; inchoaveram quippe tantummodo istam apud Mediolanum disciplinam. De aliis vero quinque disciplinis illic similiter inchoatis; de Dialectica, de Rhetorica, de Geometria, de Arithmetica, de Philosophia, sola principia remanserunt, quae tamen etiam ipsa perdidimus: sed haberi ab aliquibus existimo." (PL 32, 591).

107 De Musica I, 2. The phrasing is not Augustine's invention. Scientia bene modulandi is the definition for music e.g. in Censorinus' De die natali X, 3 (c.238).

108 De Musica I, 4, 6.

109 De Musica I, 4, 9.

not we follow through these traces to reach without fail, if we can, those very places I have called sanctuaries."[110]

To Augustine, numbers are unquestionable, eternal, and real. Numbers also guarantee certainty, serving as a proof of immortality and God's existence. Numbers are the being of things and without them nothing exists. Furthermore, all beauty is based on numerical ratios and equality, and accordingly, knowledge of numbers is the core of all learning and understanding.[111] Like Plato, Augustine sees numbers as the mediating link between body and soul.[112] It also follows that being a science of numbers, music is a theologically relevant branch of knowledge. In the sixth book of *De Musica*, Augustine explains in terms of numbers what happens when we hear music. The relevant question that Augustine poses is whether the numbers are in the sound one hears, or whether numbers are formed in the ears as a sense perception. One can also consider them belonging to the act of one who utters with one's voice, or to memory, since one recognizes the sound.[113] Augustine answers this with a set of five classes of numbers. The first is generated by the beating of a physical body (*pulsu corporum*) and exists even when there is no one to perceive it, referred to as *numerus sonans* or "sounding number." Second, the numbers pertaining to ears are *numeros occursores*. It means numbers "occur" when they meet our ear. The task of these numbers is to receive the sounding numbers, thereby being completely dependent on them and opening to them the entrance of our soul. Hearing sounds also evokes in us the spontaneous movements of the third class of numbers, the *numeros progressores*. These are not necessarily connected to physical sounds, since a person can move to music without actually hearing it. The fourth class is the sound retained in the memory, even when neither heard nor thought of, and it is referred to as *numerus recordabilis*. Finally, there are *numeros iudiciales* according to which we evaluate the sounds. This evaluating number delights in the equality of a perceived number and is offended when it fails.[114]

Since *De Musica* is decidedly striving toward permanent and eternal numbers, the question remains as to which of these five classes of numbers are eter-

---

110 De Musica I, 23, 28 (PL 32, 1100): "Quamobrem cum procedens quodammodo de secretissimis penetralibus musica, in nostris etiam sensibus, vel his rebus quae a nobis sentiuntur, vestigia quaedam posuerit; nonne oportet eadem vestigia prius persequi, ut commodius ad ipsa si potuerimus, quae dixi penetralia, sine ullo errore ducamur?"

111 Thus summarizes Horn 1994, 389–390.

112 Cf. Timaeus 31b-c.

113 PL 32, 1163: "[I]n sono tantum qui auditur, an etiam in sensu audientis qui ad aures pertinet, an in actu etiam pronuntiantis, an quia notus versus est, in memoria quoque nostra hos numeros esse fatendum est?"

114 PL 32, 1165: "cum delectamur parilitate numerorum, vel cum in eis peccatur, offendimur."

nal. Except for *numeros iudiciales*, Augustine finds that the first four numbers do not endure. But the evaluating numbers belong permanently to the human nature that approves harmonies and rejects discords (*approbando numerosa, perturbata damnando*).[115] In short, the task of evaluating numbers is to be delighted (*delectari*) in recognizing orderly numbers. Delight appears as problematic; if *numeros judiciales* are the highest rank of numbers, delight is the highest thing to do. This necessitates a further class of numbers, with which the delight of *numeros judiciales* is judged. These numbers are pertaining to reason (*ratio*). These rational numbers are the true evaluating numbers, since they evaluate whether the delight of *numeros judiciales* is right.[116] As for delight, Augustine observes that "delight is a kind of weight in the soul. Therefore, delight rules the soul. 'For where your treasure is, there will your heart be also.' Where delight, there the treasure; where the heart, there happiness or misery."[117]

If delight is the weight of soul, it can only be governed by a greater weight. The carnal love of temporal things can be redirected only by some sweetness of eternal things.[118] In other words, numbers direct our delight toward its right source and force us to inquire about what it is that pleases us in perceivable objects. Augustine's answer is that we can only love beautiful things (*non possumus amare nisi pulchra*) and that beauty is established in *aequalitas* and *numerositas*. Moreover, God has created everything with numbers, so that even a sinner may be moved by numbers and set numbers into movement. These movements may be less beautiful, but they cannot be entirely without some of the beauty that resides in the numbers.[119] The aim of musical studies is that "with a restored delight in reason's numbers, our whole life is turned to God, giving numbers of health to

---

115 PL 32, 1172: "hi autem judiciales, utrum et in anima nescio, in ipsa certe hominis natura manent, judicaturi de oblatis, quanquam a certa brevitate usque ad certam longitudinem varientur, approbando in his numerosa, et perturbata damnando."

116 From De Musica VI, 9.24 on these former numeros iudiciales are called sensuales.

117 PL 32, 1179: "Delectatio quippe quasi pondus est animae. Delectatio ergo ordinat animam. Ubi enim erit thesaurus tuus, ibi erit et cor tuum (Matth. VI, 21): ubi delectatio, ibi thesaurus: ubi autem cor, ibi beatitudo aut miseria." I translate "ordinet" as "rules", unlike Taliaferro, who renders it as "orders."

118 PL 32, 1190: "Non enim amor temporalium rerum expugnaretur, nisi aliqua suavitate aeternarum."

119 PL 32, 1191: "Nos tantum meminerimus, quod ad susceptam praesentem disputationem maxime pertinet, id agi per providentiam Dei, per quam cuncta creavit et regit, ut etiam peccatrix et aerumnosa anima numeris agatur, et numeros agat usque ad infimam carnis corruptionem: qui certe numeri minus minusque pulchri esse possunt, penitus vero carere pulchritudine non possunt. Deus autem summe bonus, et summe justus, nulli invidet pulchritudini, quae sive damnatione animae, sive regressione, sive permansione fabricatur."

the body, not taking pleasure from it."[120] This reflects the Augustinean tenet that bodily sensations are the operations of the soul. The soul is therefore the very agent of the passions of the body. Should it be otherwise, it would jeopardize the soul being the ruling part of a human being.[121] Furthermore, the soul should not take pleasure from the sensations of the body, but strive toward eternal and spiritual numbers. The pleasures of music in *De Musica* are of an intellectual sort.

2.2.2 The scruples of *Confessions*

In the tenth book of his *Confessions*, Augustine discusses the sensual temptations he has experienced. Proceeding to the sense of hearing, he provides his most profound account of musical pleasure.[122] Augustine admits that he has been vulnerable to the delights of the ear (*voluptates aurium*), which is tantamount to the sweetness of music. Although Augustine thanks God for being liberated from the hold of the delights of the ear, he still finds it problematic when he finds contentment (*adquiesco*) in the sweet melodies by which the Word of God is sung (*cum suavi et artificiosa voce cantantur*). In sacred hymns the most important part are the words, and Augustine states that the sacred words give life to music (*sonis quia animant eloquia tua*). That notwithstanding, Augustine must admit that when holy words are sung, this elevates our mind to a flame of devotion more fervently. Moreover, he ascribes a hidden affinity (*occulta familiaritas*) between human affections and music. For example, let us examine more closely the following sentence:

> et omnes affectus spiritus nostri pro sui diversitate habere proprios modos in voce atque cantu, quorum nescio qua occulta familiaritate excitentur.

By saying this, Augustine refers first to the kinship between the musical modes and the movements of the soul. This is commonplace in Greek musical theory, as mentioned by Plato in *The Republic* and by Aristotle in *Politics*.[123] Given the common nature of the notion, one questions the word *nescio*, "I do not know." Although the theorists of Greek antiquity have explained the moods and their influences on the human mind, and although Augustine himself had striven to best

---

120 PL 32, 1181: "delectatione in rationis numeros restituta ad Deum tota vita nostra convertitur, dans corpori numeros sanitatis, non accipiens inde laetitiam."
121 De Mus. VI, 5, 10.
122 Conf. X, 33, 49–50.
123 Plato, Republic III, 398d-399c; Aristotle, Politics VIII, 7 (1341b, 19–1342b, 33).

understand the musical modulations and the *numerositas* of the soul in *De Musica*, the hidden affinity between the soul and music remains a mystery.

To be delighted by music is a gratification of the flesh (*delectatio carnis*), whereupon the sense presides over reason. This occurs in such a subtle manner in music that Augustine becomes aware of it only later. Struggling with the beauty of music leads Augustine to consider the advice offered by Athanasius to readers in Alexandria to read psalms with very slight inflections of voice, so that recitation resembled speaking more than singing.[124] However, Augustine is not comfortable with the idea that the effect of music is completely wicked. Augustine admits the power of music in his own soul as well as its pedagogical usefulness by recalling his own tears as a fresh convert to Christianity in Milan. To that incident, he ascribes music a spiritual power above words: "How much I wept at your hymns and canticles, deeply moved by the voices of your sweetly singing Church. Those voices flowed into my ears, and the truth was poured out in my heart, whence a feeling of piety surged up and my tears ran down."[125] Since then, Augustine seems to have reconsidered the pleasure involved. He admits that he is still "moved not by the song but by the things which are sung, when sung with a fluent voice and music that is most appropriate."[126] This statement reflects Augustine's vacillation between the dangers of sensuality and the

---

124 Conf X, 33, 50: "aliquando autem hanc ipsam fallaciam immoderatius cavens erro nimia severitate, sed valde interdum, ut melos omne cantilenarum suavium quibus daviticum psalterium frequentatur ab auribus meis removeri velim atque ipsius ecclesiae, tutiusque mihi videtur quod de Alexandrino episcopo Athanasio saepe mihi dictum commemini, qui tam modico flexu vocis faciebat sonare lectorem psalmi ut pronuntianti vicinior esset quam canenti." Athanasius has probably the most reserved attitude towards psalmody among the fourth-century theologians. In his Epistula ad Marcellinum Athanasius states that the psalms are not sung with a melody because it is pleasing the ear. Rather, the melody is a symbol of the spiritual harmony of the soul. "Hence to recite the psalms with melody is not done from a desire for pleasing sound, but it is a manifestation of harmony among the thoughts of the soul. And melodious reading is a sign of the well-ordered and tranquil condition of the mind." (McKinnon 1994, 518).

125 Conx IX, 6, 14: "quantum flevi in hymnis et canticis tuis, suave sonantis ecclesiae tuae vocibus commotus acriter! voces illae influebant auribus meis, et eliquabatur veritas in cor meum, et exaestuabat inde affectus pietatis, et currebant lacrimae, et bene mihi erat cum eis." Perl (1955, 506 – 507) is of the opinion that this passage has not been interpreted correctly. "Eliquabatur veritas in cor meum" has been taken in the sense of "creating a deep impression," although it quite unmistakably recalls the idea that music communicates a knowledge about God, indeed, the very knowing of God, and moreover, as becomes clear from the manner of expression, it mediates this knowledge more clearly and more directly than the words could by themselves.

126 Conf. X, 33, 50: "[E]t nunc ipsum cum moveor non cantu sed rebus quae cantantur, cum liquida voce et convenientissima modulatione cantantur."

undeniable benefits of music. In other words, through the pleasures of the ear a weaker mind may ascend to loving devotion. Still, taking pleasure in singing instead of the sense of the song remains reprehensible.[127]

2.2.3 The importance of delight

The overall suspicion toward sensuous pleasure is found throughout Augustine's works. Confronting Manichaeism, Augustine could not consider the palpable creation as altogether evil. In the early work *De Musica*, Augustine indicated that he could not detest the bodily existence because Christ had become flesh.[128] Yet Augustine is constantly vigilant that no creature comes between him and God because he acknowledges that nothing inferior to God can be the source of ultimate happiness. Augustine prayed in his *Soliloquia:* "I beg only for your mercy, that you convert me entirely to you, and let nothing stand in my way as I strive towards you."[129]

It is important to note that pleasure plays an essential role in striving toward God. In the last section of *On Christian Teaching*, Augustine discusses the use of rhetoric in the scriptures and in Christian teaching. Augustine defends the use of rhetoric by a Christian, asking whether it would be desirable that the defenders of the truth should be ignorant of the art of rhetoric while those who are trying to persuade men of that which is false use rhetoric to bring the hearer into a friendly or attentive frame of mind. In other words, while rhetoric can be used to promote both truth and falsehood, why should the defenders of truth withhold using it?[130] The duty of a Christian preacher is not solely the utterance of Christian doctrine but to speak convincingly and also address emotions. Augustine quotes Cicero, who states that the aim of the orator is "to teach, to delight, and to persuade." The delight in hearing speech is, of course, not sufficient alone. Besides, the truth itself may be enough to delight the hearer.[131] Neverthe-

---

127 Conf. X, 33, 50: "[i]ta fluctuo inter periculum voluptatis et experimentum salubritatis magisque adducor, non quidem inretractabilem sententiam proferens, cantandi consuetudinem approbare in ecclesia, ut per oblectamenta aurium infirmior animus in affectum pietatis adsurgat. tamen cum mihi accidit ut me amplius cantus quam res quae canitur moveat, poenaliter me peccare confiteor."

128 De Mus. VI, 4, 7.

129 Soliloquia I, 6.

130 Doct. Christ. IV, 3.

131 Doct. Christ IV, 28: it is not necessity to give pleasure; for when, in the course of an address, the truth is clearly pointed out (and this is the true function of teaching), it is not the fact, nor is it the intention, that the style of speech should make the truth pleasing, or that the style should

less, delight is inseparably involved in teaching generally and in Christian teaching particularly. It follows that the hearer must be moved as well as instructed. "To move" refers in this context not just to move emotionally, but also to move into action. Thus the Christian speaker ought to endeavor to both be clear and intelligible, and give pleasure and convince the hearer.[132]

Pleasure is a necessary means to move humans into action, and it is not possible to move human will without pleasure. This is not merely a rhetorical fact, but a deep question concerning salvation. In his treatise *De diversis quaestionibus ad Simplicianum*, Augustine deals with the question of justification through faith. St. Paul proclaims: "For the flesh lusts against the Spirit and the Spirit against the flesh; and these are contrary to one another, so that you do not do the things that you wish."[133] The question of free will is difficult. Paul admonishes us to live up to our calling in order to attain a heavenly reward. He is asking us to receive the gift of the Holy Spirit in order to do good out of love (*per dilectione bene operari possimus*). But who is able to tell one's will to want something that it does not want? The only source of human action is delight, since nothing else moves the will.[134] Nonetheless, to be chosen for salvation cannot be dependent on the human will. The problem is that the will does not move unless there is something that attracts it. Unfortunately, that which attracts the will is not under the will's authority. To summarize, the depth of delight is beyond human capacities and the processes that prepare the human heart to take delight in God are not under one's control. Thus Augustine may use the power of music as a proof for the lack of free will.[135]

---

of itself give pleasure; but the truth itself, when exhibited in its naked simplicity, gives pleasure, because it is the truth.

132 Doct. Christ. IV, 56.

133 Galatians 5:17.

134 PL 40, 127: "Quis habet in potestate tali viso attingi mentem suam, quo ejus voluntas moveatur ad fidem? Quis autem animo amplectitur aliquid quod eum non delectat? aut quis habet in potestate ut vel occurrat quod eum delectare possit, vel delectet cum occurrerit?" See also Brown 1967, 154–155.

135 PL 40, 128: "Restat ergo ut voluntates eligantur. Sed voluntas ipsa, nisi aliquid occurrerit quod delectet atque invitet animum, moveri nullo modo potest: hoc autem ut occurrat, non est in hominis potestate. Quid volebat Saulus, nisi invadere, trahere, vincire, necare Christianos?" Augustine mentions the power of music as an example of the lack of free will in *Contra Iulianum* V, 5, 23 (PL 44, 797–798), where he tells the story of Pythagoras calming the raging youths with the help of an *aulos* player.

2.3 The development of the concept of music from speculation to practice

2.3.1 The Mathematical concept of music: Boethius and his legacy

As a university discipline in the Middle Ages, music was part of the *quadrivium* of mathematical sciences. However, a slow development began toward a more practical understanding of music, which implied that music is more about sounds than numbers. This development also reflected the overall shift in the understanding of science. Since the rediscovery of the works of Aristotle, sense perception became increasingly important as a source of knowledge. In music, as in other sciences, the Pythagorean-Platonic abstract contemplation was superseded by the empirical methodology of Aristotle.[136] The result was that a different understanding of the virtues of music echoed a more practical view: the psychological effects of music – although always known and often appreciated before – gained theological prominence.

Anicius Manlius Severinus Boethius (c.480 – 525) was the author of *De institutione Musica*, which became even more influential in the Middle Ages as a university textbook for music than Augustine. Moreover, it served as a basis for further textbooks, extending to fourteenth-century *Musica speculativa secundum Boetium* by Johannes de Muris. The latter was still used in music education at Erfurt University where Luther studied. Boethius' great achievement was to transmit the Greek philosophy of music to the Middle Ages. Rather than Boethius' own contribution, *De institutione musica* is a compilation of Nicomachus' *Eisagoge musica* and Ptolemy's *Harmonica*, among others.[137] *De institutione musica* exemplifies the mathematical understanding of music, which incorporates the musical cosmology of Plato's *Timaeus*, in which the soul of the universe is joined together according to musical concord.[138]

---

136 This development is documented in Dyer 2007. For accounts of medieval musical thinking, see Seay 1965, Abert 1964. It is noteworthy that in the history of music, the word "medieval" often also comprises early Christian music.

137 See Calvin M. Bower's introduction to the English edition, "Fundamentals of Music", xix – xliv.

138 Timaeus 29d- 92c contains the creation myth of Plato. The universe is created according to the eternal image in God's mind, also called god, which is made in likeness of its Creator (παραπλησια). In the beginning God creates order in disorder. For making his creation as beautiful as possible, he endowed it with soul and reason. The emergence of the visible and tangible body of this god-model occurs through the harmonious proportions between earth, air, water, and fire. The body was made in the most perfect shape, a round sphere. The soul was put in the center of the body and diffused throughout it. In 35a-36d the creation of the god-pattern is

De Institutione Musica contains five books, of which only the first contains valuable remarks on the power of music. In the first pages, Boethius declares the peculiarity of music as compared to arithmetic, geometry and astronomy. Whereas all these disciplines share the task of searching for truth, music is associated not only with speculation, but with morality as well. Again, the moral dimension of music is based on its power over humans: "Nothing is more characteristic to human nature than to be soothed by pleasant modes or disturbed by their opposites." The argument here is that humans are naturally disposed to musical modes with a spontaneous affection (*naturaliter affectu quodam spontaneo modis musicis adjunguntur*).[139] Concerning the power of music, Boethius refers to the celebrated stories of Pythagoras, Terpander, and Arion. These examples are sufficient to demonstrate that the choice of musical modes is not a minor detail. Following Plato's argumentation in *The Republic*, Boethius concludes: "It is common knowledge that song has many times calmed rages, and that it has often worked great wonders on the affections of bodies or minds."[140] The power of music is therefore based on what Augustine referred to as *occulta familiaritas* and what Plato investigated according to the characteristics of different musical modes: "So there can be no doubt that the order of our soul and body seems to be related somehow through those same ratios by which ... sets of pitches, suitable for melody, are joined together and united."[141] The conclusion of the first chapter is that music is so naturally united with humans that they cannot be free from it even if they so desired. Therefore the power of intellect is needed in order to comprehend and master an art that is innate. Nevertheless, it is not sufficient to a musician to find pleasure in

---

depicted in numerical ratios, which ultimately lead to the existence of seven concentric circles or spheres. This pattern is eternal, but the universe created according to it is time-bound. The earth, moon, sun, and five stars are now moving along the seven spheres. One of the main concepts in Timaeus is harmony, which is the principle of creation, the way the model imitates its creator.

139 Inst. Mus. 1, 1 (PL 63, 1168BC): "Unde fit, ut cum sint quatuor matheseos disciplinae, caeterae quidem ad investigationem veritatis laborent; musica vero non modo speculationi, verum etiam moralitati conjuncta sit. Nihil est enim tam proprium humanitati, quam remitti dulcibus modis astringique contrariis. Idque non modo sese in singulis vel studiis vel aetatibus tenet, verum per cuncta diffunditur studia, et infantes ac juvenes, necnon etiam senes, ita naturaliter affectu quodam spontaneo modis musicis adjunguntur, ut nulla omnino sit aetas quae a cantilenae dulcis delectatione sejuncta sit."

140 Inst.Mus. I,1 (PL 63, 1170AB): "Uulgatum quippe est. quam sepe iracundias cantilena represserit. quam multa uel in corporum. uel in animorum affectionibus miranda perfecerit."

141 Inst.Mus. I, 1 (PL 63, 1171 A): "Quia non potest dubitari, quin nostrae animae et corporis status eisdem quodammodo proportionibus uideatur esse compositus. quibus armonicas modulationes posterior disputatio coniungi copularique monstrabit."

melodies without the knowledge of how they are structured internally by means of ratio of pitches.[142]

The second chapter presents the most lasting contribution by Boethius to the medieval theory of music. He makes a distinction between three types of music:

1. **World music** (*musica mundana*), which means the movement of stars and heavenly bodies, the fluctuation of seasons, and the harmony of elements.
2. **Human music** (*musica humana*), which means the consonance of the parts of human body as well as the harmonious relation between soul and body and the harmony of mind.
3. **Instrumental music** (*musica instrumentalis*), which is divided to music made by plucking strings, blowing air, or striking an object.

In the end of the first book, Boethius determines who *musicus* is, and in doing so, he draws the same conclusion as Augustine in *De Musica*. The conclusion is that a musician is not a player of a musical instrument, and Boethius draws a sharp distinction between instrumentalists and music theorists. A professional playing *kithara* is a *citharedus*, and a player of an aulos is an *auleodus*. Instead, *musicus* " … is one who has gained knowledge of making music by weighing with the reason, not through the servitude of work, but through the sovereignty of speculation." A musician is one who can form judgements according to speculation or reason concerning music.[143] Boethius' definition of music could as well be *facultas secundum speculationem*. In his treatise *De Arithmetica*, Boethius defined music as a science of numbers in relation, whereas arithmetic is the discipline of numbers *per se*.[144]

---

142 Inst. Mus. I, 1 (PL 63, 1171C): "Ut ex his omnibus perspicue nec dubitanter appareat. ita nobis musicam naturaliter esse coniunctam: ut ea ne si uelimus quidem carere possimus. Quocirca intendenda uis mentis est. ut id quod natura est insitum. Scientia quoque possit comprehensum teneri. Sicut enim in uisu quoque non sufficit eruditis colores formasque conspicere. Nisi etiam quae sit horum proprietas inuestigauerint: sic non sufficit cantilenis musicis delectari. Nisi etiam quali inter se coniunctae sint uocum proportione discatur."

143 Inst. Mus. I, 34 (PL 63, 1139C): "Isque est musicus. cui adest facultas secundum speculationem rationemue propositam ac musicae conuenientem. de modis ac rithmis. deque generibus cantilenarum. ac de permixtionibus ac de omnibus de quibus posterius explicandum est ac de poetarum carminibus iudicandi."

144 Arithmetica I, 1: "Musica vero quam prior sit numerorum vis, hinc maxime probari potest, quod non modo illa natura priora sunt, quae per se constant, quam illa, quae ad aliquid referuntur. Sed etiam ea ipsa musica modulatio numerorum nominibus adnotatur, et idem in hac evenire potest, quod in geometria praedictum est."

The musical cosmology of antiquity plays a prominent role in Boethius' *chef-d'oeuvre, The Consolation of Philosophy*.[145] Although the book does not directly deal with music, the personified Philosophy sings recurrently during the course of the work. The songs of Philosophy are aimed at rescuing Boethius from an irrational love of Fortune, as he feels himself wretched when unjustly imprisoned. These songs manifest the moral power of music. In general, the *Consolation* may contain more reflection on music than *De institutione musica*.[146] Perhaps the most celebrated part of the *Consolation* is the poem *O qui perpetua* (Book III, poem 9), which deserves to be analyzed from the standpoint of music.

> Thou everlasting law, founder of earth and heaven alike, who hast bidden time stand forth from out Eternity, for ever firm Thyself, yet giving movement unto all.[147]

The law (*ratio*) that governs heaven and earth is none other than *musica mundana,* a God-given order that sets the universe in motion. The musical cosmology of *Timaeus* is discernible throughout the poem, as the world is created out of unstable matter (*materia fluitans*) according to the eternal idea (*ab exemplo*) in God's mind, of which the visible world is but a picture (*in imagine*). This all happens through a musical pattern.[148] Boethius states that God binds the first principles of nature by the orders of numbers (*tu numeris elementa ligas*). That the harmony of the universe is a matter of numbers is a chief indication of its musical character. In *De Arithmetica*, Boethius defined harmony as "unifying of many

---

145 Chadwick 1981, 101: "It is not surprising that De institutione musica anticipates many themes which are restated in the Consolation of Philosophy: the harmony of the heavens and the seasons, the 'love' that produces concord out of the warring elements of the world, the binding of the elements by numbers, and the 'consonant members' of the world-soul. Arithmetics directs the mind towards immutable truths unaffected by the contingencies of time and space. But music advances even further towards that 'summit of perfection' for which the quadrivium is a prerequisite. The theory of music is a penetration of the very heart of providence's ordering of things. It is not a matter of cheerful entertainment or superficial consolation for sad moods, but a central clue to the interpretation of the hidden harmony of God and nature in which the only discordant element is evil in the heart of man."
146 "The 'Consolatio' is more than saturated with world music [musica mundana]; it goes far beyond 'De Musica' in developing the philosophic purposes of that music" Chamberlain 1984, 392.
147 Cons.Phil. III, m. IX: "O qui perpetua mundum ratione gubernas, / terrarum caelique sator, qui tempus ab aeuo ire iubes stabilisque manens das cuncta moueri." (transl. Cooper).
148 Cons. Phil III, m. IX: "quem non externae pepulerunt fingere causae / materiae fluitantis opus uerum insita summi / forma boni liuore carens, tu cuncta superno / ducis ab exemplo, pulchrum pulcherrimus ipse / mundum mente gerens similique in imagine formans / perfectasque iubens perfectum absoluere partes."

things and the concord of separate things" (*plurimorum adunatio et dissidentium consensio*).[149] The readers of Boethius' *Consolation* have discerned a fourth species of music in addition to *mundana, humana* and *instrumentalis*. This is *musica divina*, which exists in God, and by which he first creates and thereafter maintains *musica mundana*. God himself is the *ratio*, to whom the poetic prayer *O qui perpetua* is addressed. This eternal law that is God himself is the same as *love:* "All these are firmly bound by Love, which rules both earth and sea, and has its empire in the heavens too."[150] Thus, with his thorough knowledge of Boethius, Dante Alighieri may later speak of *l'amor che muove il sole e l'altre stelle*, "love that moves the sun and other stars."[151]

Boethius' close contemporary, Cassiodorus (c.485–585), saw music as being connected to Christian doctrine. Besides the movements of the stars and the pulsation of our veins, the right moral behavior is "music." The Bible itself is musically arranged: the Ten Commandments make a "decachord" and the Psalter is named after a musical instrument since "the exceedingly sweet and grateful melody of celestial virtues is contained within it."[152] Cassiodorus' definition of music is overtly mathematical, reiterating that of Boethius' *De Arithmetica:* "Musical science is the discipline which treats of numbers in their relation to those things which are found in sounds, such as duple, triple, quadruple, and others called rel-

---

149 Cons.Phil III m IX: "Tu numeris elementa ligas, ut frigora flammis,/ arida conueniant liquidis, ne purior ignis / euolet aut mersas deducant pondera terras" Arithm. II, 32. Conveniently for the compilatory authorship of Boethius, it is a commune bonum of classical philosophy. The same definition is found in Greek by Philolaos: εστι γαρ αρμονια πολυμιγεων ενωσις και διχα φρονεοντων συμφρονησις. Tatarkiewicz 1970, 86.
150 Cons.Phi. II m.8: "Hanc rerum series ligat / Terras ac pelagus regens, / Et coelo imperitans amor."
151 Chamberlain (1984, 403) sums up the significance of Boethius' Consolatio for theology of music:"Divine music is the source of all the others, directly of world music and physical human music, and indirectly, through world music, of moral human music and of instrumental music. World music is a visible sign of divine music, a visible pattern for the human music of the soul and also for the instrumental music of man. Instrumental music, in turn, serves to maintain and regain human music. And finally, human music of the soul leads man back to divine music, from which he began. Music in Boethius is not only, therefore, the substance as well as the instrument of ethics ... but it is also the substance as well as the instrument of metaphysics. In the realm of pure being, music is; and the visible music of the universe is the means or instrument by which we know that it is. Boethius has not presented this body of ideas for its own sake, explicitly identified, but what he has embodied in the 'Consolatio' is a full ideology of music and a much clearer one than that of 'De Musica' and a fuller one than that of other Latin writers on philosophic aspects of music, except St. Augustine."
152 De Artibus V (PL 70, 1208–1209).

ative that are similar to these."[153] Music therefore has a therapeutic value, as when David expelled the unclean spirit from Saul and Asclepiades restored a madman to his sanity by using music. Music also has both intellectual and emotional advantages: "This branch of learning is most pleasing and useful. It leads our understanding to heavenly things and soothes our ears with sweet harmony."[154]

Another author of late antiquity, Isidore of Seville (560–636) wrote his encyclopedic *Etymologiae* in the seventh century. This work, or rather set of works, encompasses nearly everything inherited in the civilization. In the third book, Isidor deals with liberal sciences. Although representative of the Boethian mathematical understanding of music, Isidore concedes the sensuous character of music when he defines music as *peritia modulationis sono cantuque consistens.*[155] The emphasis here is noteworthy, especially when compared to Augustine's *scientia bene modulandi* or Boethius' *facultas secundum speculationem.* First, Isidore selects the word *peritia* instead of *scientia*. Whereas both words can be used for an art or a science, *peritia* carries more practical connotations. Second, Isidore speaks in terms of the voice (*sonus*) and song (*cantus*) in the definition of music. Isidore acknowledges both the cosmic dimensions and psychological power of music and argues that no science can be perfect without music because it pertains to everything.[156]

2.3.2 High medieval ideas: Bernard of Clairvaux and Thomas Aquinas

Bernard of Clairvaux (1090–1153) is not generally regarded as a major figure in the history of music. Nonetheless, being one of the classics of Western spirituality and an influential theologian for Luther, the few remarks he makes concerning music are instructive. As a theologian, Bernard's emphasis was on experi-

---

153 De Artibus V (PL 70, 1209): "Musica est disciplina vel scientia quae de numeris loquitur, qui ad aliquid sunt his qui inveniuntur in sonis; ut duplum, triplum, quadruplum, et his similia, quae dicuntur ad aliquid."

154 De Artibus V (PL 70, 1212B): "Gratissima ergo nimis utilisque cognitio, quae et sensum nostrum ad superna erigit, et aures modulatione permulcet."

155 Etym III, 15 (PL 82,162).

156 Etym III, 17 (PL 82, 163–164): "Itaque sine musica nulla disciplina potest esse perfecta, nihil enim est sine illa. Nam et ipse mundus quadam harmonia sonorum fertur esse compositus, et coelum ipsum sub harmoniae modulatione revolvitur. Musica movet affectus, provocat in diversum habitum sensus." Sometimes the sentence "without music no knowledge is perfect" is attributed to Hrabanus Maurus, who reiterates it nearby verbatim in his De Universo XVIII,4 (PL 111, 494–500).

ence and emotion.[157] Instead of Anselm of Canterbury's celebrated *credo ut intelligam*, Bernard would have used the term *credo ut experiar*.[158] In other words, experience is the way to attain knowledge of God. The Song of Songs, to which Bernard devoted most of his literary output, is primarily a book of experience. By religious experience Bernard refers to the knowledge of divine things through direct contact, as experiental knowledge is the equivalent to love – or in the words of Gregory the Great – *amour ipse notitia est*.[159] In religious experience all the capacities of the human mind are needed, not intelligence alone. Bernard comments on the nuptial song, the Song of Songs:

> Let those who have experienced it enjoy it. Let those who have not burn with desire, not so much to know it as to experience it. It is not a noise made aloud, but the very music of the heart. It is not a sound from the lips but the stirring of joy, not a harmony of voices but of wills. It is not heard outwardly, neither does it sound in public. Only he who sings it hears it – the Bride and the Bridegroom.[160]

At first sight, Bernard seems to promote the idea of singing "in the heart" instead of "with all the heart." Bernard explicitly states that this nuptial music is not heard outwardly. However, the experiential nature of his theology does not allow music to remain within the heart, and Bernard was actively reforming the chant of the Cistercian order. In a letter reflecting on the music of the order, Bernard observes that the reason music should please the ear is that it could move the heart (*sic mulceat aures, ut moveat corda*). Furthermore Bernard did not adhere to the scruples of Augustine concerning the relation between words and music. To Bernard, music does not annul the word but makes it fruitful (*sensum litterae non evacuet, sed fecundet*).[161] Music is the language of expe-

---

157 On the experiental character of both Bernard's and Luther's theology, see Manns 1987, 104 – 154.

158 Stiegman 2001, 130.

159 Hom.in Ev. XXVII (PL 76, 1207).

160 PL 183, 789: "Experti recognoscant, inexperti inardescant desiderio, non tam cognoscendi, quam experiendi. Non est enim strepitus oris, sed jubilus cordis; non sonus labiorum, sed motus gaudiorum; voluntatum, non vocum consonantia. Non auditur foris, nec enim in publico personat: sola quae cantat audit, et cui cantatur, id est sponsa et sponsus."

161 PL 182, 610 – 611: "Cantus ipse, si fuerit, plenus sit gravitate; nec lasciviam resonet, nec rusticitatem. Sic suavis, ut non sit levis; sic mulceat aures, ut moveat corda. Tristitiam levet, iram mitiget; sensum litterae non evacuet, sed fecundet." Chrysogonus Waddell (1992,305 – 306) writes: "La fonction de la musique ètait donc, pour Bernard, d'ajouter profondeur et intensité à notre expérience des mots de l'Epouse, mots de l'Eglise, mots de la Liturgie. Grâce à la musique, ce mot resonné avec une plus grande douceur, adoucit les passions de l'âme plus efficacement, et, par-dessus tout, fertilise ce mot."

rience, and were Bernard to offer a definition of music, it would be *scientia recte canendi*.[162] This definition involves no speculation of musical cosmology, but an expression of the joy of a loving heart. Bernard's theology itself can be depicted in musical terms, as Jean Leclercq recommended reading Bernard in Latin, aloud, so as to appreciate the music of his words. All of Bernard's theology applies to what he said about Song of Songs: *sola quae cantat, audit*; only the voice that sings can understand.[163]

Thomas Aquinas (1226–1274) summarizes most of the previous thought about theology and music in his *Summa theologiae* (IIa IIae, quaestio 91). Aquinas inquires into the text of Col 3:16, asking whether God should be praised by song (*utrum in laudibus Dei sint cantus adhibendi*). He also quotes Jerome and Gregory the Great as authorities who appeared to be suspicious of singing. Aquinas acknowledges both the use of music introduced by Ambrose and the qualms Augustine had concerning it. He is also indebted to the Aristotelian and Boethian theory of harmony.

First, Aquinas asks whether it is appropriate to praise God aloud at all. Aristotle says in *Nicomachean Ethics*, "The best of men are accorded not praise, but something greater." If that is true about the best of men, what about God? He is above everything and would deserve far more than praise, being "above all praise," as Sirach says (Sir 43:33). Furthermore, God should be worshipped by one's mind (*mente/corde*) rather than by one's lips, since the Lord himself quotes Isa 29:13: "This people … honors me with their lips, but their heart is far from me." Praise urges humanity to better action, but God does not need praise. Being unchangeable and the supremely good, God does not need to grow better, nor is it possible at all (*non habet quo crescat*).

The answer is that we do not praise God *propter Deum* but *propter nos*. This is because God does not need our praise as it does not give him any information that he would not already know. Our praise also does not increase his greatness. Humanity instead needs to praise God, and in praising God our devotion (*affectus*) toward God is awakened. Outward praise is also beneficial to others by inciting their affections toward God.[164] To say that God is above all praise is true

---

162 PL 182, 1122.

163 Leclercq 1987.

164 S.Th. II-II q.91 a.1 co: "Et ideo necessaria est laus oris, non quidem propter Deum, sed propter ipsum laudantem, cuius affectus excitatur in Deum ex laude ipsius, secundum illud Psalm., sacrificium laudis honorificabit me, et illic iter quo ostendam illi salutare Dei. Et inquantum homo per divinam laudem affectu ascendit in Deum, intantum per hoc retrahitur ab his quae sunt contra Deum, secundum illud Isaiae XLVIII, laude mea infrenabo te, ne intereas. Proficit etiam laus oris ad hoc quod aliorum affectus provocetur in Deum."

when we speak about God in his essence (*quantum ad eius essentiam*). In that regard, our praise to God can be speechless reverence, while he is incomprehensible and ineffable. But we can speak of God in terms of his works, which are ordained for our good (*secundum effectus ipsius, qui in nostram utilitatem ordinantur*). We are obliged to praise God for his gifts, and Aquinas states that outward praise alone is of no avail because praising God has to happen *cum affectu*. On the other hand, outward praise can help arouse inner devotion (*ad excitandum interiorem affectum*), both for the one who praises and others who hear it.[165]

The latter part of *quaestio 91* is dedicated to music, posing the question: Is God to be praised with song? It seems to be a reasonable question. First, Col 3:16 speaks about *cantica spiritualia*, which can be understood as the opposite of *cantica corporalia*. Aquinas quotes Jerome's commentary on Eph 5:19, where Jerome says that we should sing to God more with our hearts than our voices. Singing also seems to hinder the praise of the heart, since the singer may pay more attention to the melody than what he/she is singing about. Another point is that the hearers may understand the text better when it is not sung.

In answering these doubts about music, Aquinas recalls the conclusion in the previous article: voice is needed (*necessaria est*) to arouse human devotion toward God.[166] Everything that can help the human *affectus* move toward God is useful to Christian worship. Besides, "it is evident," says Aquinas, "that the human soul is moved in various ways according to the various melodies of sound."[167] Therefore the use of music in worship is a "salutary institution" (*salutari fuit institutum*), especially for the weaker minded. Augustine is an example of the power of music, as he was moved by music and wept after hearing the chants of the church. Moreover, it is necessary to note that in Christianity, spirituality is not tantamount to immateriality. Interestingly, Aquinas does not say that a spiritual song is a song that has spiritual words. The spirituality of a song is therefore judged by its *effect*:

---

165 S.Th II-II q.91 a.1.ad 2: "Ad secundum dicendum quod laus oris inutilis est laudanti si sit sine laude cordis, quod loquitur Deo laudem dum magnalia eius operum recogitat cum affectu. Valet tamen exterior laus oris ad excitandum interiorem affectum laudantis, et ad provocandum alios ad Dei laudem, sicut dictum est."

166 Moreover, in S.Th. II-II q.81 a7, Aquinas deals with religion and says about the usefulness of the corporeal signs that the human mind is in need of corporeal things so that the human mind may be aroused by them to the spiritual acts by means of which he is united to God. The internal acts of religion take precedence over the others and belong to religion essentially, while its external acts are secondary, and subordinate to the internal acts.

167 S.Th. II-II q.91 a.2 co: "Manifestum est autem quod secundum diversas melodias sonorum animi hominum diversimode disponuntur." Aquinas refers to Aristotle's Politics, book VIII and the Boethius' Inst.mus. I, 1.

canticles are spiritual "inasmuch they arouse spiritual emotion."[168] Aquinas admits that singing is not good for mere pleasure (*propter delectationem*). Jerome and Augustine are right when they condemn singing ostentatiously or for pleasure. Perhaps the most interesting part of Aquinas' discussion about music is the issue of whether singing hinders the praise of the heart:

> The soul is distracted from the meaning of a song when it is sung merely to arouse pleasure. But if one sings out of devotion, he pays more attention to the content and meaning, both because he lingers more on the words, and because, as Augustine remarks (Confess. x, 33), "each affection of our spirit, according to its variety, has its own appropriate measure in the voice and singing, by some hidden affinity wherewith it is stirred." The same applies to the hearers, for even if they do not understand what is sung, yet they understand why it is sung, namely, for God's honor, and this is enough to arouse their devotion.[169]

Aquinas appeals to the Augustinean notion of *occulta familiaritas* between music and the movements of the soul. Furthermore, the benefits of singing can be apprehended from the standpoints of the singer and hearer. For example, the singer is twice as attentive to the text as the reader, because the singer lingers more on it (*diutius moratur super eodem*) and singing a word usually takes longer than reading it. Considering that the style of singing that Aquinas had in mind was most likely the Gregorian chant, it makes this comparison even more understandable. The second point is that the affective power of music – the hidden affinity – influences the singer as well as the hearer. The hearers can benefit from singing even if they do not comprehend the words being sung. Nevertheless, they can understand the purpose of singing (*propter quid cantantur*) and it will be sufficient to arouse their devotion, although they do not understand the content of the song (*quae cantantur*).[170] In this passage, Aquinas assigns music a place that is superior to words – something rather rare both in his works and in Christian theology in general.[171] For Aquinas, the use of music is meant *ad excitandam devotionem*. He reads Eph 5:19 *psallentes in cordibus vestris*, but does not understand it as referring to the silent music of the heart. As a matter of fact, Aquinas renounces the entire notion as heretical. Instead, he emphasizes the fact that the

---

168 S.Th II-II q.91 a.2 ad 1: "Ad primum ergo dicendum quod cantica spiritualia possunt dici non solum ea quae interius canuntur in spiritu, sed etiam ea quae exterius ore cantantur, inquantum per huiusmodi cantica spiritualis devotio provocatur."

169 S.Th. II-II 91, a2, ad 5.

170 S.Th II-II q.91 a.2 ad 5: "Et eadem est ratio de audientibus, in quibus, etsi aliquando non intelligant quae cantantur, intelligunt tamen propter quid cantantur, scilicet ad laudem Dei; et hoc sufficit ad devotionem excitandam."

171 Burbach 1966, 80 – 81.

songs of the church are aimed at inciting our inner devotion (*ut mens nostra incitetur ad devotionem interiorem*). There are no doubt abuses of music, but the basic intention of church music is to arouse devotion, especially that of the uneducated.[172]

Good music has three characteristics: joy (*hilariter*), attention (*attentive*), and devotion (*devote*).[173] That joy is a characteristic of true music is obvious, given the treatment of music in *Summa theologiae* precisely at the *locus* of praise. Moreover, praising God is an expression of joy, and gratitude of the heart turns to the *jubilus* of the mouth.[174] The word *jubilus* has traditionally (since Augustine) been used for singing praise without words. For Aquinas, it is an expression of ineffable joy, with no words but voice only.[175] Attention means to be attentive both to the words of the chant and to the reason for singing (i.e., the praise of God). As was mentioned previously, the feature that can make music a tool for God even when the words are not understood is devotion. In short, music has to move the whole being of a person: emotion (*hilariter*), intellect (*attentive*), and the will (*devote*).[176]

2.3.3 Fifteenth century musical theology: Jean Gerson and Johannes Tinctoris

One reason why these two figures, a French theologian and a Flemish music theorist, deserve to be chosen from all fifteenth-century musical thinkers is that

---

172 Super Eph. Cap. 5 l. 7: "Ex hoc error haereticorum confunditur dicentium quod vanum est cantare domino cantica vocalia sed spiritualia tantum. Nam in laudibus Ecclesiae est aliquid per se considerandum, et hoc est quod apostolus dicit in cordibus. Aliquid vero propter duo, scilicet propter nos, ut mens nostra incitetur ad devotionem interiorem; sed si ex hoc aliquis commoveatur ad dissolutionem, vel in gloriam inanem, hoc est contra intentionem Ecclesiae. Item, propter alios, quia per hoc rudes efficiuntur devotiores."
173 Burbach 1966, 82–86.
174 In Ps 12:4, "Exulta: Hic ponitur exhortatio ad exultationem: et primo ut sit gaudium in corde, Exulta; secundo ut sit jubilus in ore."
175 In Ps 32:3, "Est autem jubilus laetitia ineffabilis, quae verbis exprimi non potest, sed voce datur intelligi gaudiorum latitudo immensa." For Augustine's definition of jubilus, see CCL 38,254.
176 As a later exponent of the Thomistic approach to music, one could mention Gabriel Biel, whose Canonis Missae Expositio Luther was thoroughly familiar with. Biel acknowledges the usefulness of music to delight the soul, arouse the devotion and promote attentiveness. Biel, Can. Miss. Expositio, Lectio LXII B: "Proficit etiam cantus attentioni, dum animus diutius moratur circa sententiam verborum que cantantur. Profundius quippe intelligere possunt ea, et mastigare quam si raptim ac celerius sine cantu proferantur propter quod supra dixit Augustinus [Conf X,33], quod voces influebant in aures, et veritas eliquebatur in cor eius."

they are often regarded as being the forerunners of Luther's view on music. According to scholarly consensus, Gerson's poem, *De laude musice*, and Tinctoris' treatise, *Complexus effectuum musices*, are of special importance in investigating the sources of Luther's musical thought.[177]

Theologian, church politician and chancellor of the University of Paris, Jean Gerson (1363–1429) considered the method of true theology to be more of penitential affection than intellective investigation.[178] Theology is, for *Doctor Consolarius*, an affective and practical science. Apart from *Consolatio Theologiae*, which is composed in the same fashion as Boethius' *Consolation of Philosophy*, Gerson's literary output (ca. 600 works) has for the most part remained in oblivion. Among the least known of his works – rarely mentioned in dictionary entries about him – are his three treatises on music, which are referred to under the title *Tractatus de Canticis*.[179] These treatises were written during the last decade of Gerson's life (approximately 1420–1425). The first of them is *De canticorum originali ratione*, which discusses sensible, rational and divine song. Sensible song deals with the history and origin of music, the classification of sound production and musical genres, as well as musical instruments. Rational music amounts to the philosophical treatment of music (the music of the spheres) and discussion about love as the principle of universal harmony. Divine song is the song of union of the soul with God, which is also called the nuptial song (*epithalamium*).

The middle treatise, *De Canticordo*, is also divided in three parts. The first part speaks about the differences between the song of the heart (*canticordum*) and the song of the mouth. The second part examines more closely the *canticordum*, which is the numeral voice that only the ear of the heart can perceive (*sola cordis aure perceptibiles*). The last part is about the mystical scale, which provides both the most original and the most inaccessible musical contribution by Gerson, as the notes of this musical scale consist of human emotions. The last treatise, *Carmina et Centilogium*, is a compilation of poems (*Carmina*) and regulations about music. The second *Carmen*, *De Laude musice*, is the best known of Gerson's musical output.

---

177 Guicharrousse (1995, 62) supposes that the course of music in the university of Wittenberg consisted of the treatises of both Tinctoris and Gerson. Veit (1986, 23–24) sees the possible connection between Gerson's de laude musice and Luther in Adam de Fulda's De Musica, where the poem is cited. Beginning in 1502, Adam de Fulda was a professor of music in Wittenberg and Luther's closest musical collaborator, Johann Walter, was his pupil. Veit sees a possible influence of Tinctoris' complexus effectuum musices in Gabriel Biel's Sacri canonis missae expositio's Lect. 62 B. See also Söhngen 1967, 91; Bader 1996, 183–184; Leaver 2007, 71–73.

178 Ozment 1969, 49–54.

179 Abbreviated below TC I-III. I use the new edition of Isabelle Fabre (2005) instead of the more commonly used Glorieux' Œuvres Completes (OC).

It is easy to discern the Neo-Platonic and speculative emphasis in Gerson's musical thought. The technical term is *canticordum*, the song of the heart that is the purpose of the entire literary endeavor. The song of the mouth (*canticum oris*) is, however, not to be scorned. Gerson defends some musical practices in the church against spiritualist judgment, one example being the singing of children in the church. Gerson concedes that little children neither have the understanding of the heart nor reason, asking whether it would therefore be right that children did not sing at all, especially not in the church. Relying on Ps 8:2, "From the lips of children and infants you have ordained praise" and the point that John the Baptist leapt in his mother's womb when Mary greeted Elizabeth (Luke 1:41), Gerson concludes that the song of children is also pleasing to God.[180]

The definition of music in Gerson's mystical theology is *numerosa vox amoris*, the numerical voice of love. Other possible definitions might be "numerical love" (*amor numerosus*) or "loving number" (*numerus amorosus*); all include *vox, numero,* and *amor.*[181] Gerson defines song in *Centilogium* as the "numerical voice arranged to honor God" (*vox numerosa ad Dei gloriam ordinata*).[182] Here the definition has three essential aspects: first that it is vocal; secondthat it is numerical; and third that it be aimed at the glory of God. This definition has a strong biblical basis: that song is voiced is based on the Vulgate reading of 1 Cor 14:10, "*nihil sine voce est.*" As for being a number, Gerson turns to Wis 11:20, according to which God created everything "in number, measure and weight." Gerson does not count the number sufficient to call something musical, as music is about sounding number, *numerus sonorus.* This means that there is no music without sound, although this sound may be imperceptible to human ears.[183] Finally, God is the creator of song, the source of its nature and the aim to which music strives.[184] The proportions of numbers in a song have to meet the aesthetic stand-

---

180 TC II, 2, 24.

181 TC I, 3, 7: "[u]t canticum in sua generalitate sumptum describi poterit, quod est numorosa vox amoris vel amor numerosus vel numerus amorosus." Gerson gives a more physical definition for music in TC I, 2, 1:"sonus causatus ab aere repercusso, pulchros suavesque numeros."

182 TC III, 2, 1. Another combination of vox, amor, numero and Gloria Dei is in TC I,2,16: "[q] uod omnis creatura cantat, psallit, modulatur et iubilat Deo, quoniam est amor naturalis numerosus in Dei gloriam ordinatus. "

183 TC I, 2, 5: "Omnia quipped fecit Deus in numero; quo pacto musice colligimus exinde rationem? Grata fatemur dignaque scitu consideratio. Neque enim solus sufficit numerus ad musice rationem, sed ut sonorous sit opportet: est itaque subiectum musice numerus sonoros."

184 TC III, 2, 2–3: "Canticum in sua generalitate descriptum accipit vocem consone ad Apostolum dicentem nichil esse sine voce. Et attendit quod omnia fecit Deus in numero et propter se ipsum, et sic in omnibus est vox numerosa ad Dei gloriam ordinata. Canticum habet ex Deo agente modum, per Deum exemplantem speciem, in Deo finiente ordinem."

ards of beauty, elegance, sweetness, joyfulness, usefulness, and salubrity.[185] Everything created by God sings, and one is invited to sing through one's natural instinct or through one's intellect.[186] Music originates from the union of nature and love.[187] Indeed, the whole universe is a monochord of divine wisdom and the one string in this monochord is love.[188] Moreover, the harmony of the universe is ultimately derived from the inner music of the Holy Trinity. Gerson is somewhat reluctant to speak about this mystery of intra-Trinitarian music, as scripture tells nothing about it. Nevertheless, Gerson clearly refers to it, arguing that the voice of the Father is the Son as his Word, and the Spirit is the bond of love between them. This produces the sweetest music (*musica suavissima*) and is the song of the highest sweetness and the joy (*canticum summe suavitatis et letitie*) of *amor numerosus*.[189]

The song of the heart, *Canticordum*, is not to be understood as an opposite of the outward song of the mouth, but rather as its fulfillment. The song of the heart is ecstatic and eschatological music that can be executed already *in via*.

> That voice is the voice of a God-formed (*deiformis*) and pious soul, who shouts, after contemplation or meditation, directed upwards and downwards, through everything and to everywhere, since heaven and earth is full of God's glory, to all creatures together, exulting and jubilating with an expanded mouth of the spirit (*dilatato mentis ore*): "Praise the Lord in his holiness![190]

---

185 TC III, 2, 4: "Canticum redditur ex numerosa proportione hoc pulchrum et decorum, hoc suave et iocundum, hoc utile et salutiferum, et oppositos disproportio parit effectus."

186 TC III, 2, 5.

187 TC I, 1, 7: "Vides quomadmodum musica suum cepit a natura et ab amore unitateque primordium."

188 TC I, 2, 8: "Metaphysicalis demum ratio concludit totum istud universum recte dici monocordum divine sapientie, in quo delectatur ludens ab initio, cuis monocordi amor est unica corda."

189 TC I,3,5: "Desinamus insuper querere si convenienter possumus in illa Trinitate gloriosissima ponere canticum summe suavitatis et letitie, sicut illic ponimus Verbum numerosissimum plenum rationibus et ydeis absque termino. Ponimus et amorem iocundissimum Spiritum Sanctum, quo Verbum tendit in Patrem et Pater in Verbum tenore gratissimo;" TC I,2,10: "Qualiter porro sit in divina Trinitate vox Patris ipse Filius, Verbum eius, qualiter amor amborum Spiritus Sanctus cum quodam numero, ut consequenter ponatur illic musica suavissima quae est amor numerosus, nec audemus nec volumes aliquam in vebis novitatem aperie que non a Sacris Litteris sit expressa; nobis quippe ad solam hanc regulam loqui fas est."

190 TC I, 1, 15; "Vox ista vox est anime deiformis ac devote, que post contemplationem vel meditationem, sursum directam et deorsum – per omnia videlicet quaquaversum, quoniam pleni sunt celi et terra gloria Domini –, tunc dilatato mentis ore iubilat, exultat et exclamat ad omnem generaliter creaturam: 'Laudate Dominum in sanctis eius.'"

This praise is perfect *in patria*. The only duty of the beatified is to praise God with their voices (*vox laudis*).[191] The use of the word *vox* is not an accident. Gerson thinks in accordance with Aristotle that the movements of the heavens do not bring forth sound, but resurrected humans may have vocal music when they praise God.[192] Nevertheless, Gerson writes that Christians should practise singing praise already *in via*: "Let us exercise already here on earth the voice of praise, that we shall continue in heaven."[193]

The only duty of the blessed in heaven and the best work of humans on earth is praise. *Propria et finalis operatio hominis est cognitio summi Domini cum frui-tione et laude sua.* Therefore the office of singing is not a minor one. As a man with a great ecclesiastical and scientific career, Gerson posits the question of what use it is to praise God. Would there be something more urgent to do, some-thing more meritorious, perhaps? Gerson replies that when a person praises God, that person should not think that he/she is doing nothing, nor should a person think that there is no merit or reward for it. Praise is a great reward in itself, and it is an even greater reward because it is free.[194]

The deepest meaning of the song of the heart is *Epithalamium*, the nuptial song. By and large epithalamium refers to the Song of Songs, which speaks about the union between the Bride and the Bridegroom. Strictly speaking, Ger-son understands epithalamium as being the nuptial song *in via*, not *in patria*.[195] The root of music is therefore the love of God. To understand the nuptial song in Song of Songs, one profits more from anointing (*unctio*) than reading (*lectio*), more from praying (*devotio*) than explanation (*demonstratio*), and more from burning affectual desire (*desiderium fervens in affectu*) than from eager intellec-

---

191 TC I, 1, 26: "Quid enim viri beati dicimus officium quam vox laudis ad Dominum iuxta illud:'Beati qui habitant in domo tua Domine; in secula seculorum laudabunt te.'[Ps 84:5]."
192 TC I, 2, 4: "Aristoteles, qui post et inter ceteros plenius assecutus est veritatem de quinta essentia celesti que incorruptibilis impartibilisque est, ponit consequenter neque sonum neque auditum proprie sensibiles illic esse … Sic intelligetur Apostolus de linguis angelorum; de hominibus bero, macime post corporum resumptionem, non est improbabile musicam vocalem illis esse."
193 TC I, 1, 16. "Exerceamus hic igitur in terris vocem laudis que nobis perseveret in celis."
194 TC I, 1, 17: "Quoniam propria et finalis operatio hominis est cognitio summi Domini cum fruitione et laude sua. Vivis igitur, o homo, quamdiu et quantum laudat anima tua Dominum; est et istic iter quo ostendit Dominus salutare suum. Quare noli conqueri dum laudas quasi nichil agas, quasi nondum premia capias. Laus est magnum, crede michi, pretium sibi, magnum valde etiam dum gratis sit, ymo maius dum gratis sit."
195 TC I, 2, 21, 34.

tual scrutiny (*studium vehemens in intellectu*).[196] The emphasis of affect in Gerson's theology is clearly discernable in his view of *Canticordum*.

Gerson's poem for the praise of music, *De laude musica*, begins as follows:

> New music that comes about through the impulse of divine love cannot be adequately exalted by any praise. It refreshes the spirit, drives away cares, and soothes ennui, and is a congenial companion to the travellers whom it bears along. Through the midst of snows and through [blazing] suns, in reliance on son I shall go, patient in hope, happy, eager and cheerful. For miserable cares flee at [the sound of] song through the empty air, and every hostile plague that might lie in wait is dispelled.[197]

Unlike in the speculative writings of *Canticordum*, Gerson begins here with the effects of music in the human spirit and soul. There is a striking resemblance with the second poem of the first book of *Consolatio Theologiae*, which speaks about the power of theology. Theology makes cares flee and gladdens the mind (*cure fugiunt mens hilarescit*). Gerson also employs musical imagery on the same occasion. Theology is said to "lighten life's boredom and gloom and comfort by echoing Zion's songs" (*ac vite relevat tedia mente / dolat resonans cantica Syon*). Music is also present with the figures of Orpheus and David, who used their songs to conquer death and to expel demons, and Gerson praises theology and music as having the same manner.[198] David and Orpheus also play a part in *De laude musice:*

> On encountering the string-players Saul is turned as it were into another man, he plays the strings and becomes a new prophet. While the evil spirit torments him the shepherd David who sings to the cithara forces it to depart through song.[199]

---

196 TC I, 3, 47: "Deterret nos hec consideratio pleniorem de Canticis Canticorum temptare sermonem in hoc opusculo tertie partitionis, quo theologia post historiam et philosophiam assumpsit originem cantici divinalis in caritate radicati, non completam dare cognitionem que nec magnis voluminibus expletur; addito quod unctio plus in hac docet quam lectio, plus devotio quam demonstratio, plus desiderium fervens in affectu quam studium vehemens in intellectu."

197 TC III, 1, II, 1–9. "Musica diuini noua pulsu que fit amoris / extolli nulla laude satis poterit, / Cor recreat. curas abigit. falstidia mulcet / Fitque peregrinis quos vehit apta comes. / Per medias hiemes per soles carmine fisus / Ibo spe paciens, letus, alacris, ouans. / Nam fugiunt tristes cantu per inania cure / Omnis et insidians hostica pestis hebet."

198 Cons. Theol I m.2 (OC IV, 28).

199 TC III,1, II, 10–13: "Vertitur occursu psallentum Saul velut alter. / Factus homo psallit fitque propheta nouus./ Exagitat nequam dum spiritus hunc, cytharedus / Pastor per numeros cogit abire David."

The first sentence refers to Saul's prophetic ecstasy in 1 Sam 10 and the latter to the well-known incident in 1 Sam 16. Gerson relates the biblical figures to Greek mythology in describing the power of music: Amphion, Arion, Pythagoras, and Pan are mentioned,[200] together with Elisha, who was filled with the Spirit with the help of music. From the history of the church, Gerson mentions St. Ignatius, who – according to the legend – heard angels sing antiphonally and then wrote down the antiphonary of the church. The martyrs Agnes and Cecilia are also mentioned, the first because she is said to have heard angels playing when she was burned to death and the latter because she came to be honored as the patroness saint of church music. Music is beneficial in many ways: it can heal bodies, it rejoices, soothes, and relieves the spirit.[201] The silent song of St. Cecilia leads Gerson to recall the words of the Apostle Paul:

> You instructed us, Paul, to sing psalms to God in our hearts, for such action brings blessing in twofold way. Here and now begins heaven, and dwells in exile with the custom and manner of the blessed life. Death comes in time that loses the bonds of the flesh and victoriously raises the singer of psalms aloft.[202]

The same distinction *in patria/in via*, which is so important in *epithalamium* occurs again here. The Pauline singing in the heart is not understood as opposing the singing of the mouth. Rather, the song of heart means the eschatological dimension of the Christian song. Furthermore, song is a matter of a loving heart, not of a scrutinizing intellect. The mystical music of Gerson has moral overtones, and in a Boethian manner, he states that the only aspect of God's creation not in concord in the cosmic harmony is the evil will. Yet, the new music is able to set even that in concord:

---

200 TC III, 1, II, 41–44: "Amphion ac Orpheus cantu mouisse feruntur /Hic lapides diras hic furias Herebi./ Moribus hec duris si transfers instituendis / Mutandique bona dogma salubre canunt;" 65–66: "Prebe fidem grecis delphinus Ariona vexit. / Fluctus per medios dum lira mulcet eum."; 71–72: "Fistula Pan Phebi cythare certauit agrestis / Iudice te Mida victus Appollo fuit;" 15–16: "Pithagoras motus fuerat componere cordis /Adiectis cythare compositis numeris."
201 TC III, 1, II, 31–32: "Quid quod corporibus curandis musica prodest. / Dum cor letificat, lenit et alleuiat."
202 TC III, 1, II, 93–98: "Cordibus vt nostris psallamus Paule monebas /Actio nam talis iure beat duplici./ Inchoat hic et nunc celum, viteque beate. /Moribus et ritu degit in exilio /Mors venit in terra que carnis vincula resoluit /Cantantem in psalmis victor in alta vehit." In the Salzburg manuscript of Carmina there is a note in the margin: "Collige sex causas quare vocaliter oras. Vt torpor cede mentis deuocio crescat. Vt cor mundetur et proximus edificetur. Lingua laudetur opifex, demonque fugetur."

Bodies are organs consonant with spirits; the world is a single choir with which the mind (*Nous*) loves to play. With the harmony of the world the evil will, at discord with itself, becomes concordant with the whole under God's direction.[203]

One is not necessarily open to God's effects (or to those of music). Therefore Gerson makes a pun: *ut sis sub molle, molle cor adde tibi*, "that you may be under a soft tone, take on a soft heart."

Gerson's theology of music had little impact on posterity. According to Joyce Irwin, this is due to the inconsistency of Gerson's thought. Gerson did not scorn outward music, but oriented himself nevertheless toward inward, inaudible music. Although appreciating church music, he did not provide a theological basis for cultivating elaborate polyphonic music. That music can arouse emotions was not sufficient for him, since it cannot penetrate further than the exterior senses, meaning the interior senses must generate their own music. Without a stronger theological basis for music, later thinkers who emphasized the interior at the expense of the exterior (e. g. Zwingli) drew the logical conclusion to abandon church music.

The Franco-Flemish music theorist and composer Johannes Tinctoris (1435 – 1511), who spent most of his creative years in Italy, was one of the leading writers on music in his day. His writings illustrate what had happened to the theory of music in late medieval times; the Pythagorean-Boethian mathematical order of music had yielded to a new kind of aesthetic perception. The prologue of his *Liber de arte contrapuncti* (1477) contains the ruthless refutation of the *music of the spheres:*

> Before carrying out this project, I cannot pass over in silence the opinion of numerous philosophers, among them Plato and Pythagoras and their successors Cicero, Macrobius, Boethius, and our Isidore, that the spheres of the stars revolve under the guidance of harmonic modulation, that is, by the consonance of various concords. But when, as Boethius relates, some declare that Saturn moves with the deepest sound and that, as we pass by stages through the remaining planets, the moon moves with the highest, while others, conversely, ascribe the deepest sound to the moon and the highest to the sphere of the fixed stars, I put faith in neither opinion. Rather I unshakeably credit Aristotle [De Caelo, II] and his commentator [Aquinas], along with our more recent philosophers, who most manifestly prove that in the heavens there is neither actual nor potential sound.[204]

---

203 TC III, 1, II, 21–14: "Corpora spiritibus sunt organa consona. mundus / Est chorus vnus quo ludere noys amat. Carmine mundano sibi dissona praua voluntas / Concordans toti, fit moderante deo."
204 Tinctoris (ed.Seay) 2:11.

Tinctoris argued that instead of looking at the stars and meditating on *musica mundana*, one should listen to *musica instrumentalis*, which is the only way to learn music – through one's ears, not through one's reasoning. It is the earthly instruments that produce the concords of sounds and melodies, not heavenly bodies.[205] The old times were not best, for after leveling pitiless judgment against old music, Tinctoris praises the music of his contemporaries, such as Johannes Ockeghem, Antoine Busnois, John Dunstable, and Guillaume Dufay, saying, "Nearly all the works of these men exhale such sweetness (*suavitutinem redolent*) that in my opinion they are to be considered most suitable, not only for men and heroes, but even for the immortal gods."[206]

Complexus effectuum musices is not among Tinctoris' great theoretical treatises, but it is a praise of music. Its form resembles more a compilation of authoritative quotations about the power of music: quotes from the Bible, from Augustine, Isidor, Bernard, and Aquinas as well as from Aristotle, Quintilian, Ovid, Virgil, and Cicero. All the classical figures are presented: Pythagoras, Orpheus, Saul, David, Elisha, Asclepios, the tears of Augustine, and the hymns of Ambrose. It details twenty effects of music, which according to Tinctoris are:

> 1. Music delights God. 2. Music embellishes the praises of God. 3. Music intensifies the joys of the blessed. 4. Music joins the militant Church to the triumphant Church. 5. Music prepares for the reception of the Lord's blessing. 6. Music encourages souls to piety. 7. Music drives away sadness. 8. Music releases the anxiety of the heart. 9. Music puts the devil to flight. 10. Music causes ecstasy. 11. Music elevates the earth-bound mind. 12. Music revokes the evil will. 13. Music delights humans. 14. Music heals the sick. 15. Music tempers work. 16. Music incites the soul to combat. 17. Music encourages love. 18. Music increases the joy of conviviality. 19. Music glorifies those skilled in it. 20. Music makes the soul blessed.[207]

---

205 Tinctoris (ed.Seay)2, 12: "Concordantiae igitur vocum et cantuum quorum suavitate, ut inquit Lactantius, aurium voluptas percipitur non corporibus caelestibus, sed instrumentis terrenis cooperante natura conficiuntur." Before the refutation of the music of the spheres at the dawn of the new era, there had emerged a middle alternative of Pythagorean and Aristotelic theory of musica mundana in the 13th century. The anonymous tract Philosophica disciplina (ca.1245) followed by Arnoul de Provence's Divisio scientiarum (1250), tries to accommodate the Boethian music of the spheres with Aristotle's rejection of it by supplying an alternative theory: that there does exist a "musica mundana" albeit unsuitable for our ears, generated by the light rays emanating from heavenly bodies as there rays strike each other and cut through the air. Although unheard, the effects of this "music" are similar to those produced by the sounds of perceptible music: their effect refreshes and stimulates nature (Dyer 2007, 54–55).

206 Transl. Strunk.

207 Tinctoris (ed.Seay) 2, 165–166: "Deum delectare, / Dei laudes decorare, / Gaudia beatorum amplificare, / Ecclesiam militantem triumphanti assimilare, / Ad susceptionem benedictionis divinae praeparare, / Animus ad pietatem excitare, / Tristitiam depellere, / Duritiam cordis resolvere,/ Diabolum fugare,/ Extasim causare, / Terrenam mentem elevare,/ Voluntatem malam

The treatise is not a serious theological survey, but it reveals a clear shift of emphasis away from the speculative, Boethian tradition. The cosmic dimensions of music are not mentioned at all. The treatise concentrates on the effect that music has on humans, notably the psychological and emotional effects (nos. 7, 8, 12, 13). In addition to the therapeutic value of music (no. 14), the military use of music (no. 16) is also appreciated, not to mention the erotic dimension (no. 17). Music even has a meaning in social cohesion (no. 18) and the professional integrity of musicians (no. 19).

The theological effects of music are of special interest. The first effect, *Musica Deum delectat,* is based on the notion that music is an artifact (*artificium*) of God. God, like any craftsman, is delighted with his perfect work. Moreover, God desires to hear the music of his beloved spouse, the church. In Song 2:14, God proclaims: "Let me hear thy voice."

As if he were saying: "Because your voice is sweet, that is, melodious, I desire you to let me hear it." And God would not desire to hear the sweetness of the voice (*vocis dulcedinem*), if it did not delight him in any way.[208]

The religious use of music is witnessed both by the examples of pagan antiquity and by the history of the Bible and the church. Although Tinctoris distinguishes between true and false religion, the pagan examples are also valid examples of the power of music. The most profound theological point is in the last effect, *musica animas beatificat.* In a scholastic fashion, using a conscious allusion to Thomas Aquinas, Tinctoris makes the audacious conclusion that music can be a means of salvation:

> No one doubts that people can be brought to repentance by hearing a song. For this reason the Church has introduced the singing of God's praises. And, since the soul attains redemption through repentance, it follows that music is in this case the cause of salvation. But this salvation is the highest bliss, attained not only, as mentioned above, by those who hear music but especially those who have knowledge of it. That is why the prophet says: Blessed is the people that know the joyful sound."[209]

This paragraph reveals that, in Tinctoris' thinking, there is a difference between the mere hearing of music and understanding of it. Tinctoris distinguishes between two ways of how music gives joy to humans, both the internal and the ex-

---

revocare, / Homines laetificare, /Aegrotos sanare, / Labores temperare, / Animos ad praelium incitare, / Amorem allicere, / Iocunditatem convivii augmentare, / Peritos in ea glorificare, /Animas beatificare." Leaver's (2007, 71) English version differs from the one here presented in two points: 16. incites the soul to [spiritual?] combat; 20. makes [our] spirits glad.

208 Tinctoris (ed.Seay) 2, 166 – 167.

209 Tinctoris (ed. Seay) 2, 177. The allusion to Aquinas is to S.Th II-II q.91 a.2, co.

ternal. One takes delight in music internally by a *virtus intellectiva*, which provides one an understanding of the apposite composition and performance. In contrast, the outward delight of music is provided by *potentia auditiva*, in which one perceives the sweetness of the harmonies. The delight one takes in hearing music without understanding it, however, is no less, even though the perfect enjoyment of music consists of both hearing and understanding.[210]

2.4 Medieval theological aesthetics

2.4.1 Theological treatment of beauty

The theological treatment of music is a part of theological aesthetics. Although the word "aesthetics" is of later origin,[211] and although there is no such academic discipline as "theological aesthetics," the question of beauty has always been a part of theology. According to Aquinas, the aesthetic perception is characteristically human. Unlike other animals, humans take pleasure in the beauty of a sensory object for its own sake.[212] This is what Kant later called "disinterested pleasure" in the aesthetic contemplation, of delight as an end in itself and not based on the usefulness or existence of its object.[213] Mindful of its Kantian origin, I adopt the expression "disinterested pleasure" for aesthetic perception in this study.

In medieval thinking, beauty was primarily an attribute of God. The beautiful (*pulchrum*) belongs with the *transcendentals:* the being (*ens*), the one (*unus*), the true (*verum*), and the good (*bonum*). They are in the very structure of being,

---

210 Tinctoris (ed. Seay) 2,173: "Namque quanto plus in hac arte perfectus est, tanto plus ab ea delectatur, eo quod naturam ipsius et interius et exterius apprehendat. Interius quidem virtute intellectiva, qua intelligit debitam compositionem ac pronuntiationem, et exterius potentia auditiva, qua percipit concordantiarum dulcedinem ... Musica vero minus illos laetificat qui nihil ex ea penitus quam sonum percipiunt, extrinseco etenim sensu tantummodo delectantur."
211 Alexander Gottlieb Baumgartner's Aesthetica (1750) first introduced the academic discipline of aesthetics.
212 S.Th. I, 91q, a.3."Solus homo delectatur in ipsa pulchritudine sensibilium secundum seipsam;" S. Th. I-II q. 27 a. 1 ad 3 "Ita quod bonum dicatur id quod simpliciter complacet appetitui; pulchrum autem dicatur id cuius ipsa apprehensio placet." Eco (1988, 58) explains this: "The term apprehension in this passage may be defined as a kind of seeing or looking which is mediated by the senses but is of an intellectually cognitive order, and which is both disinterested and yet produces a certain kind of pleasure."
213 Kant 1790, 204–205. For the imminent problems of Kant's aesthetics, see Zangwill 2008.

something that is common to all creatures.[214] This approach to beauty is thus quite different from modern aesthetics, where the emphasis is on the human perception and aesthetic judgment of an individual. Moreover, the medieval notion of beauty was not associated with the arts, or works of art, as it is in modern aesthetics, but with God, the soul, and nature. Augustine discussed the question concerning the objective and subjective side of beauty in *De Vera Religione*. He asked: Are things beautiful because they give delight or do they give delight because they are beautiful? Augustine concludes beyond doubt that beautiful objects give delight because they *are* beautiful.[215] There are two distinct ideas of beauty in the medieval aesthetics. First, the Platonic-Pythagorean tradition mediated by Augustine and Boethius saw mathematical proportion or harmony as an essential condition of beauty. The biblical basis for this line of thought was found in Wis 11:20, "You have ordered all things according to measure, number, and weight." The world was created by "divine art" as an ordered whole, and therefore it is beautiful. The second tradition that informed the medieval views of beauty was traced from Pseudo-Dionysius the Areopagite back to Neoplatonism. Characteristic of this tradition is that it regards not only harmony but also brightness and light as essential to beauty. These approaches may be called the "aesthetics of proportion" and the "aesthetics of light," and the complete idea of beauty includes them both. In the words of Augustine, all beauty is a matter of proper proportions and pleasant color.[216]

---

214 Whether beauty actually is one of the transcendentals is a debated issue. Jan A. Aertsen (1991) argues that unlike Etienne Gilson, Jacques Maritain and Umberto Eco suggest, Aquinas never adds pulchrum to the list of the transcendentals. The place of the beautiful among the transcendentals is between the true and the good. Beautiful adds a cognitive component to the good. When Aquinas defines good as that which simply pleases the appetite ("simpliciter complacet appetitui") beautiful is that which pleases when apprehended ("id quius ipsa apprehension placet"). To sense beauty is a cognitive act. Aertsen sees the beautiful as the connection between the true and the good, when true is related to the intellectual and the good to the appetitive. Beauty is to see the true as good. It is an "affective" understanding.

215 De Vera Rel. 32 (PL 34, 148): "Et prius quaeram utrum ideo pulchra sint, quia delectant; an ideo delectent, quia pulchra sunt. Hic mihi sine dubitatione respondebitur, ideo delectare quia pulchra sunt."

216 PL 33,65: "Omnis pulchritudo est partium congruentia cum quadum suavitate coloris." This distinction is propagated by the medievalist Edgar De Bruyne (1969, 48 – 61).

2.4.2 The aesthetics of proportion

The answer to Augustine's question of what makes things beautiful lies is their harmonious proportions – beauty is harmony, the right proportions and relationships. Ultimately, as can be seen in *De Musica*, the principle of beauty is "numberliness" (*numerositas*).[217] This principle limits the realm of the aesthetic. It makes the perception of beauty a matter of sight and hearing, since other senses lack the ability to perceive relationships. Ultimately, harmony consists of numbers. In *De Libero arbitrio*, Augustine presents numbers as the key to understanding the whole of creation:

> Behold sky and earth and sea, and all in them that shines above, or creeps below, or flies, or swims; all these things have forms, because they have numerical dimensions. Remove these, and the things will be nothing. From whom do they derive their being but from him who created number? And number is a condition of their existence. And the human artists, who make material objects of all forms, use numbers in their works. So if you seek the strength which moves the hands of the artist, it will be number.[218]

Although Augustine promoted aesthetic objectivism (things please because they *are* beautiful), he maintained that beauty must to some extent also be in the eye of the beholder. There must be a harmony in the soul as well, because without harmony the soul could not respond to beauty. Of the five kinds of numbers presented in *De Musica*, only the first, *numerus sonans*, is outside the soul. The other four are the soul's perceptions, actions, and judgments. In all beautiful things, be they colors, sounds, or smells, it is the equality of number (*aequalitas numerosa*) that pleases.[219] There is also a different kind of beauty, which Augustine calls *suavitas* to distinguish it from *pulchritudo*. *Suavitas* portrays the beauty of hearing and of the lower senses (smelling, tasting, touching), whereas *pulchritudo* applies to vision and moral judgment.[220] The reason for this distinction is that the pleasure we receive from musical sounds lies less in their harmonious proportions than in their direct charm.[221] For smells, the case becomes even clearer: a smell pleases or displeases us before one can analyze its proportions – if such an analysis is indeed possible. Another important distinction between *pulchrum* and *aptum* was made

---

217 De Ordine II 15, 42: "Hinc est profecta in oculorum opes, et terram coelumque collustrans, sensit nihil aliud quam pulchritudinem sibi placere, et in pulchritudine figuras, in figuris dimensiones, in dimensionibus numeros."
218 De Lib.Arb. II, 16, 42.
219 De Musica VI, 13, 38.
220 De Ordine II, 11, 33–34; Eco 1986, 66.
221 Thus Tatarkiewicz 1970, 51.

by Augustine in his first published work as a young rhetorician, *De pulchro et apto*. This treatise has since been lost, but its central thought can be traced from Augustine's extant writings. Most beautiful objects are called beautiful because they are suitable or useful (*aptus*) for another purpose. This applies, for example, to the beauty of a shoe, which is unrelated to its usefulness for the foot. Appropriate responses to the beauty of creation are praise, awe, jubilation, and love. Jubilation (*jubilus*) has deeply musical overtones as the word means the wordless song of praise. The praises of human beings do not find expression in rational propositions, but rather in wordless jubilation before the indescribable beauty of creation.[222] Despite his scruples with outward beauty, Augustine sees the beauty of creation as a divine revelation. In *Confessions* he writes, "I said to all the things that throng the gateways of the senses: 'Tell me of my God, since you are not He.' They cried out in a great voice: 'He made us.' My question was my gazing upon them, and their answer was their beauty (*interrogatio mea intentio mea et responsio eorum species eorum*)."[223]

Thomas Aquinas' definition of beauty in its most concise form is *pulchra enim dicuntur quae visa placent*, "things that cause pleasure when seeing them are called beautiful."[224] The act of calling something beautiful requires both the object and someone to perceive its beauty. In this regard, Aquinas diverges from the view of his teacher, Albert the Great. For Albert, the beauty of a thing is its resplendence of form (*claritas*), which makes it beautiful even if there is no one to see it.[225] As referred earlier, beauty is an attribute of God. Within the Holy Trinity beauty is ascribed to the Son. Following the teaching of Hilary of Poitiers, Aquinas ascribes eternity as a feature of the Father, beauty (*species*) of the Son and *usus* of the Holy Spirit. He then describes three characteristics that are required for something to be beautiful:

1. *Integritas sive perfectio*. Nothing incomplete or insufficient is regarded as beautiful.
2. *Proportio sive consonantia*. Orderly proportion and harmony of the parts is required.
3. *Claritas*. Brightness in colors is generally seen as beautiful. Light itself is beautiful.[226]

---

222 Harrison 1992, 130–133. De Civ.Dei XI, 29.
223 Conf. X 6, 10.
224 S.Th. I, q5, a4.
225 Eco 1986, 24–27.
226 S.Th I, 39 q, a.8, co. The beauty of the Son is accordingly as follows: 1. He has in Himself fully and truly the nature of the Father (*habens in se vere et perfecte naturam patris*). 2. He is the express image of the Father. We call pictures that depict their object perfectly beautiful even if

For the most part, considering something as beautiful (*pulchrum*) contains a functional viewpoint (*aptum*). An object is beautiful because it is apt for the purpose it is intended for. The celebrated example given by Aquinas is that when someone makes himself a saw for the purpose of cutting, he makes it of iron, which is a suitable material for the purpose, instead of making it of glass, even though that would be the more beautiful material. Considering the purpose, iron is more "beautiful" than glass on this occasion.[227] The beauty of a human being, however, may indicate the beauty of the body or the beauty of the spirit. Both consist of the proportionate brightness related to the purpose of their existence. Therefore, honesty can be called spiritual beauty.[228]

For Bonaventure, all things form a stairway to God. All that is created is either a vestige or an image of God.[229] Bonaventure's *Journey of the Soul to God* (*Itinerarium mentis in Deum*) begins with the outer traces of God; we must pass through the vestiges of God in the outer world and enter the image of God in our own soul and, finally, transcend to the eternal, spiritual First Principle – God.[230] Bonaventure suggests that creation testifies to God's power, wisdom and goodness in its many properties, one of which is beauty. *Pulchritudo* in this context implies "the variety of lights, figures and colors in simple, mixed or complex bodies."[231] Another aesthetic property of creation is *fullness* (*plenitudo*), because it requires

---

the object were ugly in itself (*si perfecte repraesentat rem, quamvis turpem*). 3. He is (as John of Damascus says) the light and splendor of the intellect (*lux et splendor intellectus*).

227 S.Th. I, 91q, a3, co.

228 S.Th. II. II. q,145.a. 2 co; "pulchritudo corporis in hoc consistit, quod homo habeat membra corporis bene proportionata cum quadam debiti coloris claritate, et similiter pulchritudo spiritualis in hoc consistit, quod conversatio hominis sive actio eius sit bene proportionata secundum spiritualem rationis claritatem.Hoc autem pertinet ad rationem honesti, quod diximus idem esse virtuti, quae secundum rationem moderatur omnes res humanas. Et ideo honestum est idem spirituali decori."

229 Itin. I, 2: "Cum enim secundum statum conditionis nostrae ipsa rerum universitas sit scala ad ascendendum in Deum; et in rebus quaedam sint vestigium, quaedam imago." In Breviloquium II, 12, Bonaventure makes a further division between vestigium, imago and similitude, of which the latest is possible only for the deiform beings.

230 Itin. I, 2: "[O]portet, nos transire per vestigium, quod est corporale et temporale et extra nos, et hoc est deduci in via Dei; oportet, nos intrare ad mentem nostram, quae est imago Dei aeviterna, spiritualis et intra nos, et hoc est ingredi in veritate Dei; oportet, nos transcendere ad aeternum, spiritualissimum, et supra nos aspiciendo ad primum principium, et hoc est laetari in Dei notitia et reverentia maiestatis."

231 Itin. I, 14: "Pulchritudo autem rerum secundum varietatem luminum, figurarum et colorum in corporibus simplicibus, mixtis et etiam complexionatis, sicut in corporibus caelestibus et mineralibus, sicut lapidibus et metallis, plantis et animalibus, tria praedicta evidenter proclamat."

form and *order.* Bonaventure's definition of beauty is a slightly modified version of Augustine's in *De Musica: "pulcritudo nihil aliud est quam aequalitas numerosa."*[232] The macrocosm of the world enters the microcosm of the soul through the five senses. This entry occurs through the threefold process of perception (*apprehensio*), enjoyment (*oblectatio*), and judgment (*diiudicatio*). For the present study, it is interesting to see how Bonaventure defines the function of *oblectatio*. He follows Augustine's distinction of *pulchritudo* and *suavitas,* but adds a third class of sensuous enjoyment, which he calls *wholesomeness* (*salubritas*). For Bonaventure, beauty (*speciositas*) is exclusively a matter of sight, whereas *suavitas* belongs to hearing and smelling, and *salubritas* to tasting and touching.[233] Bonaventure summarizes, "Since all things are beautiful and in a certain manner delightful, and beauty and delight are not apart from proportion, and proportion is first in numbers, it is necessary that all things be measured."[234]

2.4.3 The aesthetics of light

In the above examination of proportional aesthetics, factors appeared that are not strictly proportional, such as the Augustinean *suavitas,* which appeal to us immediately without (or prior to) any sense of proportion. The element of light (*claritas*) is also a part of the proportional aesthetics. Speaking of "the aesthetics of light" does not suggest that there were two different aesthetic schools in medieval philosophy. A better expression would be that there were two complementary views of beauty. To elaborate on the difference between proportion and light, proportion presupposes a composite structure. It consists of parts. In contrast, light is a simple entity and has a more immediate effect on our mind than harmony. The charm of light is not in its harmony, nor in its weight, nor in any other physical attribute, but simply in the direct perception of it.[235] Treatment of "light" precedes the treatment of "beauty" in Pseudo-Dionysius' *The Divine Names:*

---

232 Itin. II, 5. Here Bonaventure quotes *De Musica* VI,13,38, and also *De Civitate Dei* XXII,19,2: "Omnis enim corporis pulchritudo est partium congruentia cum quadam coloris suavitate."

233 Itin. II, 5: " Delectatur autem sensus in obiecto per similitudinem abstractam percepto vel ratione speciositatis, sicut in visu, vel ratione suavitatis, sicut in odoratu et auditu, vel ratione salubritatis, sicut in gustu et tactu, appropriate loquendo."

234 Itin. II, 10: " Cum igitur omnia sint pulcra et quodam modo delectabilia; et pulcritudo et delectatio non sint absque proportione; et proportio primo sit in numeris: necesse est, omnia esse numerosa"

235 Ambrosius, Hexaemeron: "Lucis natura hujusmodi est, ut non in numero, non in mensura, non in pondere ut alia, sed omnis eius in aspectu gratia sit." (PL 14, 143 A). For a closer account on the aesthetics of light see De Bruyne 1969, 55–61.

> Light comes from the Good, and light is an image of this archetypal Good ... The goodness
> of the transcendent Good reaches from the highest and most perfect forms of being to the
> very lowest ... It gives light to everything capable of receiving it, it creates them, keeps them
> alive, preserves and perfects them. Everything looks to it for measure, eternity, number,
> order. It is the power which embraces the universe.[236]

In the last sentence, light is presented as the source of measure and order. Therefore, the aesthetics of light precedes the aesthetics of proportion. Light is the
source of everything, that is, beauty is the source of everything (αρχη παντων
το καλον).[237] We call things "beautiful" that have their share in "beauty,"
which is God himself. God is the Beautiful (καλον), the Good (αγαθον), and
the One (εν). Beauty belongs to Dionysius' list of the transcendentals, and the
longing for beauty is what actually brings everything into being.

> Beauty unites all things and is the source of all things. It is the great creating cause which
> bestirs the world and holds all things in existence by the longing inside them to have beau-
> ty. And there it is ahead of all as Goal, as, the Beloved, as the Cause toward which all things
> move, since it is the longing for beauty which actually brings them into being.[238]

If beauty is an attribute of all beings, it follows that even ugly things embrace
beauty, inasmuch as they exist. For them, beauty is a goal and a desire. If beauty
is light, even that which is unharmonious can have its share of beauty when it is
enlightened.

Among medieval theologians, the aesthetics of light is attributed to Robert
Grosseteste (1168–1253). According to him, the brilliance of gold is beautiful,
not because of its proportions, but because of its light. Likewise, the beauty of
the stars is not based on the harmony of their elements, but on their joyous radiance. Light is beautiful, even without the harmonious proportions of physical
figures. Grosseteste concedes that beauty means the harmony of proportions
(*proporcionum autem concordia pulchritudo est*), however, the beauty of light
consists in unity with itself. Referring to the authority of St. Basil, Grosseteste
continues that the nature of light is simple and united with everything and therefore it is also the most proportionate.[239] The utmost simplicity and unity of light
means that light is the source of all proportionality. Without light, nothing can
manifest beauty. Light is the source and the essence of all corporeal things;

---

236 De divinis nominibus IV 4 (PG 3, 697C)
237 PG 3, 704 A.
238 PG 3, 702 A.
239 Hexaemeron p. 2. 4: "hec per se pulcra est, quia eius 'natura simplex est sibique per omnia
similis;' quapropter maxime unita, et ad se per equalitatem concordissime proporcionata."

they exist insofar as they participate in light.[240] The aesthetics of light emphasizes the immediate pleasure of beauty. God's words, "*fiat lux*," created the world out of light, drove away the darkness (*tenebras dispulit*), destroyed sorrow (*meroremque dissolvit*), and rendered all things joyful and delightful (*letam iucundamque*). Thus, light itself is beautiful and pleasing to sight (*visui iocundissima*). To employ such words indicates that aesthetic perception is a matter of joy and pleasure more than of understanding and moral judgment.[241] That light is something more immediate than harmony is also Aquinas' opinion. The brightness (*claritas*) of God is nothing else than his substance. God shines not through another light, but through himself.[242]

2.4.4 Some traits of Renaissance aesthetics

Similar developments that were previously noticed in music occurred in other areas of aesthetic thinking during the Renaissance, while appreciation of a purely aesthetic dimension emerged.[243] In Renaissance aesthetic thinking there were speculative Neoplatonists on the one hand, and the more empirically minded theorists on the other. Marsilio Ficino (1433–1499) ranks among the Neoplatonists. He claimed that when one says "love," one actually means, "desire for beauty" (*pulchritudinis desiderium*). If love is desire for beauty, one might fear that it reduces love to a physical attraction. The question resolves with the distinction between "sensuous" and "absolute" beauty. According to the Platonic formula *per corporalia ad incorporalia*, those who are addicted to the former will be kept away from the latter, whereas those who approach the lower, sensuous beauty in the right spirit may use it as a stepping-stone to loving the higher, ab-

---

240 "Corporeitas ergo aut est ipsa lux, aut est dictum opus faciens et in materiam dimensiones inducens, in quantum participat ipsam lucem et agit per virtutem ipsius lucis ... Lux vero omnibus rebus corporalibus dignioris et nobilioris et excellentioris essentiae est, et magis omnibus corporibus assimilatur formis stantibus separatis, quae sunt intelligentiae. Lux est ergo prima forma corporalis." (De luce, Philos. Werke 51–52.)

241 Hexaemeron p. 2 X 3–4: "Prima vox Domini naturam luminis fabricavit ac tenebras dispulit, meroremque dissolvit et omnem speciem letam iocundamque subito produxit' ... quapopter eciam sine corporearum figurarum armonica proporcione ipsa lux pulchra est et visui iocundissima." Light is the basic concept of Grosseteste's philosophy as a whole, see McEvoy 1982.

242 Super Ioannem 1.11 "Claritas Dei non est alius quam eius substantia: non enim est lucens per participationem luminis, sed per ipsam."

243 For the decline of the ancient idea of pulchrum in favor of artistic bellum, see Tatarkiewicz 1972.

solute beauty.[244] Accordingly, Ficino's view of beauty is not something corporeal. As a matter of fact, even when we love something that we see, it is not the external appearance (*materia*) that is pleasing, but rather its *imago*, which occurs through the sight and enters the soul, and is thus non-corporeal. Beauty is more a matter of spiritual image (*res spiritualis*) than of corporeal appearance (*corporea species*). Consequently, there is no such thing as "corporeal beauty," because the beauty in the virtues of the soul, bodies, and sounds is non-corporeal. Beauty is in the *mind* of the beholder. Ficino concludes that the idea of beauty refers more to sight than hearing, because sight and light are more similar to thought than to hearing and sound. The right dispositions (*habitus*) of the soul are not just beautiful, they are beauty itself. Hence, whatever beauty we encounter is already within us, "Beauty – wherever it appears – is pleasing and meets with praise since it conforms to the idea of beauty innate in us and is consistent with it in every respect."[245]

Leonardo da Vinci (1452–1519) represents a more practically oriented view of beauty. In his unfinished *Treatise on Painting*, da Vinci points out that the art of painting is a practical science because it needs both practical observation and formal speculation to succeed. It exceeds both medieval artisanship and the Platonic contemplation on beauty. Considering this, it is quite natural that a Renaissance artist like da Vinci should have been an artist, scientist, and inventor, all at the same time. To picture an arm in motion requires a close observation of actual arms and their movements. This leads the artist to discover the muscles and joints of the arm, and dissect and penetrate the hidden secrets of nature.[246]

Wittenberg was far from the heart of Italian art, and was probably little affected by it. However, the aesthetic thinking of the Renaissance had an important exponent writing in German. Albrecht Dürer (1471–1528) was not only one of the greatest artists of his time and later an adherent of the German Reformation, but also a remarkable aesthetic thinker. Dürer promoted proportional aesthetics, which defines beauty as moderate and well proportioned. As a Renaissance artist, Dürer did not use mathematical ratios to calculate the proportions for his paintings, but rather based his calculations on experience. Dürer's aesthetic judgment is ultimately based on sense perception, not unchanging numbers. An interesting detail in Dürer's aesthetic is his perplexity over the concept of beauty: *Was aber die Schönheit sei, das weiss ich nicht*. "What beauty might be, I do not know."[247] To illustrate the perplexing nature of beauty, Dürer imagined

---

244 See Beardsley 1966, 118–121.
245 Tatarkiewicz 1974, 108–109.
246 Beardsley 1966, 124–128.
247 A sentence put to Dürer's mouth.

two persons quite unlike in every detail yet equally pleasing in the eye of the beholder, and difficult to judge either one as more beautiful than the other. Aesthetic judgment is often very uncertain. This, however, was not Dürer's only argument. What disentangles him from any kind of relativism is his pointing out that, while our judgment on beauty may be arbitrary, beauty itself is not. Dürer argued that ultimately only God could judge what is beautiful.[248] Nevertheless it is possible for humans to discover the salient features of beauty. In addition to proportionality, there are some other artistic standards, as good art must be in accordance with life and nature.[249] This qualification could be called *verisimilitude*. This notwithstanding, art is not a mere imitation of nature, but also involves artistic skill and imagination. To become an artist, one needs innate talent, love, enthusiasm, practice, and education.[250] Therefore, the second qualification of good art is *skill*. The third qualification is *pleasure*. "We like to see a beautiful thing because it gives us delight," states Dürer in *Course in the Art of Measurement* (1525).[251] In what is referred to as the *aesthetic excursus* of his *Four Books on Human Proportion*, written shortly before his death in 1528, Dürer summed up the purpose of art, "to honor God and to be useful, good and lovely to humans."

---

248 Dürer, Schriften, 146: "Es lebt auch kein Mensch auf Erd, der sagen noch anzeigen kann, wie die schönest Gestalt des Menschen möchte sein. Niemands weiss das dann Gott, die Schön zu urteilen."

249 From the "aesthetic excursus" (1528): "daraus kummt, wer etwas Rechts will machen, dass er der Natur nichts abbrech und leg ihr nichts Unträglichs auf."(Schriften, 225); "Aber je Genäuer dein Werk dem Leben gemäss ist in seiner Gestalt, je besser dein Werk erscheint, und dies ist wahr, darum nimm dir nimmermehr für, dass du etwas besser mügest oder wellest machen, dann es Gott seiner erschaffnen Natur zu würken Kraft geben hat, dann dein Vermügen ist kraftlas gegen Gottes Geschöff."(Schriften, 233)

250 Course in the Art (1525):"Item wer ein Moler will werden, der muss van Natür dorzu geschick sein. Item die Kunst des Malens würd bass durch Lieb und Lust gelernt dann durch Zwang. Item aus welchem ein grosser künstreicher Moler soll werden, der muss ganz van Jugend auf darbei erzogen werden. Item er muss van guter Werkleut kunst viel abmachen, bis dass er ein freie Hand erlangt."(Schriften, 143)

251 Schriften, 154. Beardsley (1966, 128) translates the three properties of Dürer's aesthetics: "verisimilitude, skill, and beauty."

2.5 The Medieval theory of affects

2.5.1 The problematic affectivity

The theological significance of music, as well as its theological perplexity, is closely related to the overall view of emotions. Christian theologians' reaction to music more or less reflects their attitude toward affectivity. There are a number of English translations for the Latin word *affectus:* "emotion, inclination, disposition to something, or affection." These words do not convey the depth of *affectus* in theology. Therefore the word "affect" will in this study stand for the non-rational side of human nature, including affections and emotions.[252]

The affective side of the soul has always been a source of trouble for Christian theologians; in fact, Greek philosophers even thought it dubious. Suspicion was primarily aroused by the corporality of emotions. Being emotionally affected involves physical reactions, such as heartbeat, blood pressure and speed of breath. For a philosopher these reactions would hardly seem appropriate. Because of their physical character, emotions were thought to represent the lower parts of the soul. In Western thinking, Cicero's choice of the Latin equivalent for the Greek πάθος turned out to be ominous; instead of *passio* or *adfectio*, he chose *perturbatio*, which literally means confusion and disorder. In his *Tusculan Disputations*, Cicero taught that passions are irrational disorders of the soul that follow from misunderstanding.[253] This view of Cicero reflected the Stoic notion of *apatheia*, which regards emotions as being dispensable for the wise man. Another way to view emotions, *metriopatheia*, was promoted by Plato and Aristotle. According to this stance, emotions are essential to the soul, although they should be subdued and controlled by reason. Some Stoics strived for the complete extirpation of emotions from the soul.[254]

---

252 The philosophical vocabulary concerning affects/emotions is somewhat unsteady. In the French Enlightenment philosophy, the habitual ("long-term") desires were called "passion," and acute, instant feelings "émotion," whereas Kant named "Affekt" the sudden emotional stroke and "Leidenschaft" a dominating habitual desire. Lanz 1971, 94–95. According to Petri Järveläinen (2000, 43–70), Emotions involve an affective feeling component and an evaluative cognitive component, the feeling component being a pleasant or an unpleasant feeling about what is expressed by the propositional evaluation. Emotions also involve paradigm-scenarios that are learnt socially. In Järveläinen's view, it is characteristic of a religious emotion that 1) there is a cognitive object condition: religious emotions essentially involve a thought of the divine, 2) the thought of the divine is existentially significant to the subject, and 3) the thought of the divine is associated with religious cults and practices such as worship, prayer or meditation.
253 Tusc. Disp. III, 24–27.
254 Knuuttila 2004, 5–6; Hengelbrock 1971, 89, 91.

By and large, emotions have been treated in Western philosophical and theological tradition either as cognitions or as volitions, which implies emotion to be a kind of inchoate understanding or an imperfect form of will.[255] Relatively seldom have the faculties of the soul been seen conversely: that emotion is perhaps the first and elementary act – or dimension – of the soul, and is followed by will and understanding.[256]

2.5.2 Defining affects

A good starting point for the discussion on theological usage of the word *affectus* in the medieval thinking is *Benjamin minor* or *Twelve Patriarchs* of Richard of St. Victor (d.1173).[257] Richard presents the two wives of Jacob, together with their handmaids and sons, as tokens for the different aspects of the human mind. Rachel and Leah represent the two powers of mind that are given to every rational spirit: reason and affection.[258] Out of the former, right counsels (*consilia recta*) arise, and out of the latter, holy longings (*desideria sancta*). Both wives have their own handmaid. Rachel's handmaid is Bilhah, who represents imagination, whereas Leah's handmaid Zilpah epitomizes sensuality. Both are necessary; without imagination, reason would know nothing, and without sensation, affection would have no object. Bilhah tends to be loquacious because of all the visual things she perceives, and Zilpah is depicted as intoxicated by the pleasurable things she encounters. There is a reason why Leah is said to have poor eyesight – affection is unable to judge between desirable and despicable things and is thereby easily drawn toward pleasurable things by her handmaid, sensation. Leah, the basic *affectio*, gives birth to seven sons, i.e. seven principal emotions (*affectus*): hope, fear, joy, grief, hatred, love, and shame.[259] These are *ordered*

---

255 On emotions as cognitions or value judgments in ancient literature see Sorabji 2000, 17–155.

256 The latter view is, to the best of my knowledge, promoted by thinkers that do not belong to the time-span of this study. The most notable are the theologian Friedrich Schleiermacher and the philosopher of art Susanne K. Langer.

257 For a further analysis of this text see Knuuttila 2004,201– 203.

258 PL 196, 2– 3: "Omni spiritui rationali gemina quaedam vis data est ab illo Patre luminum, a quo est omne datum optimum, et omne donum perfectum. Una est ratio, altera est affectio: ratio, qua discernamus, affectio, qua diligamus; ratio, ad veritatem, affectio, ad virtutem." It is worth noting that the exact word here is affectio. In medieval literature, other words meaning the emotional side of human person are passio, affectio, affectatio.

259 PL 196, 6: "Principales ergo affectus septem sunt qui ab una animi affectione alternatim surgunt. Spes videlicet et timor, gaudium et dolor, odium, amor et pudor."

emotions, the same as virtue. What makes the ordering of emotions virtuous is the great self-discipline required. Richard notes that the affection is not drawn from pleasurable things without great effort. As Leah's name indicates, this is truly "laborious," and makes it understandable why Leah is so despised among men, whereas Rachel, "wisdom," is universally desired.

In Thomas Aquinas the medieval theory of emotions is fully developed. According to him, emotions (passions) are "acts of the sensitive appetite, inasmuch as they are united to some bodily change."[260] Emotions belong to the appetitive, intentional powers of the soul, in contrast to the apprehensive, receptive ones. Moreover, they are acts of the sensitive appetite since they belong to the non-rational part of the soul. Aquinas called the four principal passions joy, sorrow, hope, and fear, drawing these into further distinctions.[261] First, there are *passiones virtutis concupiscibilis,* which are directed toward attaining something good. According to Aquinas, these are love, hatred, desire, delight, sorrow, and flight. Second, there are the fighting emotions, *passiones virtutis irascibilis,* either in the sense that the desired good is difficult to achieve (*bonum arduum*) or that the unwanted evil is arduously avoided (*malum arduum*). These fighting passions are hope, despair, fear, courageousness, and anger.[262] They may be further divided according the presence or absence of the desired/disagreeable object.[263]

Table 1. The basic emotions (passions) according to Aquinas.

	DESIRED	DISAGREEABLE
GENERAL	love	hatred
PRESENT	delight	sorrow
ABSENT	desire	flight
DIFFICULT TO AVOID		courageousness/fear
DIFFICULT TO ACHIEVE	hope/despair	

---

260 S.Th I, q.20, 1, ad 1: "actus appetitus sensitivi, inquantum habent transmutationem corporalem annexam."

261 S.Th I.II q.25 a 4.

262 S.Th. I-II q. 26–48. There are many lines of thought involved in medieval theory of emotions. A distinction can be made between neoplatonic-Augustinean and Aristotelist-Thomistic approach, where the affect is identified with the will in the former or seen as a controller of drives of the soul in the latter. The platonic vision sees affects (or emotions) related to appetitus intellectivus and the Aristotelians to appetitus sensitivus. For theory of emotions in Pierre d'Ailly, Jean Gerson and Luther's Erfurt professors Usingen and Trutfetter, see Knuuttila 2006, 282–286. A short introduction to the medieval affect theory can be found in zur Mühlen 1992, 93–101.

263 Knuuttila 2004, 245–246.

Besides the Aristotelian view promoted by Aquinas, there was also the Augustinean-Neoplatonic vision of emotions, in which it is possible to claim that emotions or affects belong to the intellectual appetite. In this view, the affect is the basic directedness of the will and that knowledge of God attainable in this life is affective. Although it is impossible for human understanding to grasp God, it is possible for the affect to experience him.[264]

2.5.3 Evaluating affects

The affects belong to the non-rational part of human personhood. As involuntary movements, something that is common with humans and animals, they are not morally right or wrong as such.[265] Their moral value depends on how far the will consents with them and how far reason directs them. In evaluating affects, temptation to sin is a case in point.

The first step to sin is *suggestio* – something is suggested to a human mind that is tempting. The suggestion alone has been argued to be not a sin at all (as Augustine thought), or a venial sin (as Gregory the Great said). What is important at this point is whether one finds pleasure (*delectatio)* in the suggestion or not. If the pleasure felt is fought against, the sin committed is a venial one. If *delectatio* leads one to consent (*consensus*) to the sinful suggestion, one commits a mortal sin. The culmination of the process is the sinful act (*opus*), where consent leads. Thus in Adam's and Eve's sin the serpent made a suggestion, Eve felt pleasure in it and Adam consented. This was captured in a pattern that the devil suggested, the flesh takes pleasure and the spirit consents to the sin.[266] In medieval times

---

264 This view was promoted among others by Bonaventure. See zur Mühlen 1992, 96–101.
265 S.Th. I-II q.24, a 1.
266 A typical account by Gregory the Great states the fourth and fatal step of sin is to refuse to confess the sin: Mor. IV, 27 (PL 75, 661BC): "Quatuor quippe modis peccatum perpetratur in corde, quatuor consummatur in opere. In corde namque suggestione, delectatione, consensu, et defensionis audacia perpetratur. Fit enim suggestio per adversarium, delectatio per carnem, consensus per spiritum, defensionis audacia per elationem. Culpa enim, quae terrere mentem debuit, extollit, et dejiciendo elevat, sed gravius elevando supplantat. Unde et illam primi hominis rectitudinem antiquus hostis his quatuor ictibus fregit. Nam serpens suasit, Eva delectata est, Adam consensit; qui etiam requisitus, confiteri culpam per audaciam noluit. Hoc vero in humano genere quotidie agitur, quod actum in primo parente nostri generis non ignoratur. Serpens suasit; quia occultus hostis mala cordibus hominum latenter suggerit. Eva delectata est; quia carnalis sensus, ad verba serpentis mox se delectationi substernit. Assensum vero Adam mulieri praepositus praebuit; quia dum caro in delectationem rapitur, etiam a sua rectitudine

there was also discussion about pro-passions, the involuntary movements of the soul prior to making any judgment on the suggestion. It was questioned whether sin is to simply have a thought of a sinful act, or whether it became sin only when passions were delighted.[267] According to Peter Lombard, any positive reaction to a forbidden thing is a sin, however involuntary it might be. Augustine had operated with a distinction between an unavoidable initial stage of a movement toward sin and its continuation, which could be prevented by the controlling will, but Lombard did not make this distinction.[268]

Affects are thus related to the question of weakness of the will. If one acts against one's better judgment, what is the reason for such behavior? Either something is missing in the reasoning itself or the will does not act according to it.[269] Emotions are well known to make humans act against their will, "for I do not do what I want, but I do the very thing I hate."[270] Augustine speaks about the inner conflict of two wills in the soul, a conflict not between two different subjects but within the one ego, who is both willing to do good and at the same time turning away from it. This latter will preventing good actions is obviously an affective one, consisting of various desires. Augustine's account on emotions is strongly

---

spiritus infirmatus inclinatur. Et requisitus Adam confiteri noluit culpam, quia videlicet spiritus, quo peccando a veritate disjungitur, eo in ruinae suae audacia nequius obduratur."

267 Sorabji (2002, 8–13) observes how the Stoic notion of first movements of the soul was transformed to the Christian doctrine of venial and mortal sins. "These degrees of sin go with all sorts of new questions which it is possible to ask about thoughts. Did you put yourself in the way of the thought? Did you let it linger? Did you enjoy it? Did you enjoy the mere thinking about sin, or were you enjoying the sin itself about which you were thinking?"

268 Knuuttila 2006, 177–191. "Anselm [of Laon] says that unpremeditated, inevitable pleasure is an infirmity, and that it is also called a pre-passion (propassio). Because of the fall of Adam and Eve, human beings suffer from the infirmity that evil suggestions and pre-passions take place in them against their will. Even though sinful pre-passions are not wholly under one's own control, they are counted as venial sins, and one has to shoe that one is sorry for them – not doing so would mean that they have been accepted" (179). Much of the medieval discussion on emotions was focused on these pre-passions and their voluntariness. John of La Rochelle described the voluntariness of the first movement with the terms "permitting will" (voluntas permittens) or "permitting consent" (consensus permittens) He thought that when a first movement is not prevented, it is somehow accepted.

269 Saarinen 1993 distinguishes between three heuristic models of weakness of the will in medieval discussion. First is that something is wrong in the premises of the logical syllogism. The second alternative is that the conclusion of the syllogism is grasped properly, but temporarily neglected for some reason. The third model includes a strong view of the freedom of the will: the reason (or virtue) does not rule the will but merely recommends an action to it. There may be other forces (like desire) that affect to the decision of the will, or – in the most extreme version – the will is free to choose whatever it wants.

270 Romans 7:15.

a volitional one. Although the will is the choice to do something, all dynamic acts of the soul are somehow under the controlling power of the will. Even if emotions in their initial state are uncontrolled movements, the will can react to them either by consenting to emotional suggestions, or by refusing them.[271]

Even though emotions were mostly regarded as a problematic subject of study, there was an issue that had to be discussed exclusively in affective terms: the human relationship to God, and especially the enjoyment awaiting Christians in heaven.[272] The idea of beatific enjoyment involves a positive assessment of feeling pleasure (*fruitio, delectatio*). That notion may seem slightly contradictory with Augustine's statement about emotions belonging exclusively to the present life. In heaven, where no sin exists, *apatheia* will prevail.[273] However, it is precisely Augustine's concept of enjoyment that contributed to the affective view of blessedness – Augustine stated that to enjoy (*frui*) something means to rest in it with satisfaction, for its own sake, whereas to use something (*uti*) means to employ it to obtain what is desired.[274] The proper object of enjoyment is the Holy Trinity, and the supreme joy is to enjoy the triune God in whose image humanity is created.[275] Furthermore, to enjoy something meant for use is a sin. The delights of the passing world are constantly charming our hearts and becoming the objects of our enjoyment, and are mainly treated as temptations.[276] Augustine remarks that this does not mean that any creature ought not to be loved. The question pertains to the kind of love that is required. If a creature is loved on account of itself, love amounts to desire (*cupiditas*). In *On the Trinity*, Augustine distinguishes between the ways we should love inferior things, equals, and God:

> Since the creature is either equal or inferior to us, we must use the inferior for God and enjoy the equal, but in God. For just as you ought to enjoy yourself, but not in yourself but in Him who made you, so you ought also to enjoy him whom you love as yourself.[277]

---

271 On emotions and the will in Augustine, see Knuuttila 2004, 168–172. On two wills in Augustine, see Saarinen 1993:32–43.

272 On the beatific enjoyment discussed in this section, see Kitanov 2006, 149–167.

273 De Civ.Dei XIV, 9.

274 Doct. Christ. I, 4 (PL 34, 20): "Frui enim est amore alicui rei inhaerere propter seipsam. Uti autem, quod in usum venerit ad id quod amas obtinendum referre, si tamen amandum est."

275 Doct. Christ. I, 5; De Trin, I, 8: "Hoc est enim plenum gaudium nostrum quo amplius non est, frui trinitate Deo, ad quius imaginem facti sumus."

276 Doct. Christ I, 4 (PL 34,21): "[Q]uod si amoenitates itineris, et ipsa gestatio vehiculorum nos delectaret, et conversi ad fruendum his quibus uti debuimus, nollemus cito viam finire, et perversa suavitate implicati alienaremur a patria, cujus suavitas faceret beatos."

277 De Trin. IX, 8. transl. Matthews.

Considering the different functions of the human mind (memory, understanding, will) Augustine posits enjoyment as a matter of will. This is indicated in his definition of enjoyment (*fruitio*), "for we enjoy the things we know when the will rests by rejoicing in them for their own sake" (*fruimur enim cognitis, in quibus voluntas ipsis propter se ipsa delectata conquiescit*).[278] Enjoyment is therefore volitional, but pleasure (*delectatio*) is not. One can choose to enjoy something that causes one to feel pleasure, but one cannot choose whether or not to be pleased by something.[279] One could ask, concerning beatific enjoyment, where pleasure comes from? For instance, John Duns Scotus asks whether the word *frui* should be used only for the perfect act of pursuing something for its own sake, or for the pleasure resulting from the act, or for both. Even Augustine himself seems to use *frui* as a synonym for both delight (*gaudium*) and pleasure (*delectatio, voluptas*). In addition, Augustine uses the word *frui* as an aggregate of an act of the will and the resulting pleasure. Scotus analyzes Augustine's definition of enjoyment as follows: If enjoyment were the same as pleasure, the words *fruimur cognitis* would be superfluous, and if enjoyment were the same as the act of will, why bother to say *voluntas delectata conquiescit?*[280] In addition to delight (*gaudium*) and pleasure (*delectatio*), love (*dilectio*) is also involved in enjoyment. Scotus sees love and enjoyment as being separate, since delight can be an object of love, but love itself cannot be its object.[281] Unlike love, pleasure is not a free act. Peter Aureoli saw pleasure as an act of free will. Accordingly, the beatific enjoyment was essentially pleasure. "The act of the supreme love is to be pleased with God."[282] William of Ockham disagreed with Aureoli at this point, arguing that love is superior to pleasure. This is because love is an act of free will that is possible only for rational creatures, whereas pleasure can be experienced by irrational beings as well. Moreover, like distress, pleasure is not an act, but a passion of the will. As Scotus argued, loving is possible without pleasure. More-

---

278 De Trin. X, 10, 13.

279 See 2.2.3. above.

280 Lectura I, d.1, pars 2, q.1, n.80: "Idem, aliquae auctoritates volunt quod frui includat utrumque, et ita est unum per accidens, dicente Augustino X De Trinitate: 'Fruimur cognitis , in quibus voluntas delectata conquiescit.' Si autem esset tantum delectatio, non oporteret dicere:'fruimur cognitis'; si autem tantum action, non esset dicendum: 'voluntas delectata conquiescit.'"

281 Reportatio I-A d.1, pars 2, q.2., a.1, n.73: "Item, delectatio est per se obiectum alicuius fruitionis vel dilectionis, cuius dilectionis ipsa dilectio non potest esse obiectum, ergo ipsa different realiter."

282 Script.sup.Sent. d.1, sect.7C, a.1e, n.63: "Praeterea, amor ille est beatificus et fruitio patriae, qui est actus potissimus caritatis. Sed, actus potissimus caritatis est complacere ultimate in Deo. Igitur ultimata delectatio et complacentia boni divini est amor beatificus et fruitio beatorum."

over, the acts of will generate the passion of pleasure or distress, which cannot exist separately, but the acts of love, hope, fear, or joy can all occur without concomitant pleasure or distress. Therefore pleasure is *passio*, not *actus voluntatis*.[283] Walter Chatton approved of Aureoli's argument that ultimate enjoyment is essentially pleasure. Chatton concluded that if beatific enjoyment were to be distinct from pleasure, it follows that an individual could enjoy God without pleasure and be unhappy. Since that is not possible, ultimate enjoyment is pleasure.[284] Contrary to Ockham, Robert Holcot argued for a different causality between pleasure and love so that love does not cause pleasure, but pleasure causes love. This happens when the awareness of the beatific vision of God causes pleasure and the pleasure causes love of God as the source of pleasure.[285] To summarize, there is a perfect pleasure in heaven, something surpassing the capacities of the will.

Besides scholastic determinations, there is also the strong mystical tradition of medieval theology that cultivated an affective way of talking about God. *Gerson* defined mystical theology as the knowledge located in affectivity, while all other forms of knowledge are found in the intellect. For Gerson, mystical theology could be referred to as "the art of loving," and all emotions arise from love. From this perspective, when one loves God, one also hates all things opposite to God. Accordingly, the experience of God's presence brings joy and in God's absence, sadness. In Gerson's system, virtues as well as vices originate in affectivity, and a major difference is attributed to carnal and spiritual affections.[286] Carnal affections must be purified or extirpated from the soul or changed into spiritual affections in the state of blessedness. Bernard of Clairvaux took advantage of carnal emotions in a mystical way. In *De diligendo Deo*, Bernard puts forward a four-stage account of love. The first stage is that a human being loves him/herself selfishly. The adversities of life lead then to the second stage, where one needs God and thus loves God for selfish reasons. Needing God and tasting his goodness leads one's soul to the third step – which is most often the highest possible in this life – where one loves God for God's sake. This is, however, not the highest

---

283 Quodlib. II, q.17, a.2. On Ockham's theory of passions of the will and whether he understood Auriol's position correctly, see Hirvonen 2004, 140–170.
284 Rep.sup.Sent I, d.1, q.2, a.2, n.69: "Nullo enim modo volo concedere quod per quamcumque potentiam Dei aliquis posset esse perfecte beatus per fruitionem beatificam, et tamen non delectari."
285 In Sent. I, q.3, a.8, d.5: "[d]ato quod delectatio aliqua sequatur naturaliter cognitionem alicuius delectabilis, sicut poniunt aliqui quod ad claram dei visionem sequitur naturaliter delectatio: et ad istam delectationem sequitur volitio."
286 OC VIII, 32–35.

stage of divine love. The highest stage occurs when one loves oneself for the sake of God. That is to say that both the *imago* and *similitudo Dei* have been perfected in a human person. At this point, one has become united with God. The human affects merge in God, willing nothing but God's will, which leads to deification: *sic affici, deificari est.*[287] Without a doubt, human emotions go through a complete transformation on this mystical path. Nevertheless, emotions are needed as the material upon which God acts and our way to God is depicted entirely in affective terms.[288] In short, in Christian mysticism affection has the upper hand. Recalling Richard of St. Victor's Old Testament imagery in the *Twelve Patriarchs*, it is important to realize that Rachel, "the wisdom," passed away at the birth of Benjamin, who stands for the loving contemplation of God.[289]

3 Optimum Dei donum – the essence of music

Luther's most recurrent statement about music is that it is a gift of God. That claim may not seem surprising on its surface, but is worth a closer examination. In *"On Music,"* Luther states that music is a gift of God, not of men (*donum Dei non hominum est*)[290] and in *"Encomion musices,"* he praises music as the excellent gift of God (*donum Dei excellentissimum*).[291] *Table Talk* includes even bolder statements: that music is a great gift and divine indeed (*Musica maximum, immo divinum est donum*),[292] or a distinctive gift of God and close to theology (*Musica est insigne donum Dei et theologiae proxima*),[293] and finally, the greatest gift of God (*optimum Dei donum*).[294]

---

287 De dil. Deo 10, 38.

288 As Knuuttila (2004, 198) summarizes Bernard's position, "Affective experience is the medium of understanding biblical texts and also the source of the certainty of faith."

289 PL 196, 52CD: "Dei est hoc donum, non hominis meritum. Sed absque dubio talem, tantamque gratiam accipit nemo, sine ingenti studio et ardenti desiderio. Novit haec Rachel, et idcirco studium multiplicat, et desiderium suum quotidianis incrementis acrius inflammat. In tanta namque quotidiani conatus anxietate, in hujusmodi doloris immensitate, et Benjamin nascitur, et Rachel moritur, quia cum mens hominis supra seipsam rapitur, omnes humanae ratiocinationis, angustias supergreditur. Ad illud enim quod supra se elevata, et in extasi rapta, de divinitatis lumine conspicit, omnis humana ratio succumbit. Quid est enim Rachelis interitus, nisi rationis defectus?"

290 WA 30 II, 696, 5.

291 WA 50, 368, 4–5.

292 WA Tr 1, 968.

293 WA Tr 3, 3815.

294 WA Tr 5, 4441, 21: "Musica optimum Dei donum." WA Tr 2, 2387: "Musica est optimum donum et divinum."

It is tempting to interpret these kinds of expressions as a music-lover's enthusiasm, yet this is hardly tenable for Luther. He is not likely to use the word gift (*donum*) loosely or in a vague manner. As a theologian, the notion of a gift is essential to him, and in short, Luther's theology could be depicted as a theology of giving. God is, to use the idiom of Oswald Bayer, categorically giving.[295] Therefore an investigation must first seek to show how Luther understands the word *gift*. After that, it is possible to elucidate the question of what kind of gift music is and what is so special about it.

3.1 Gift (donum) in Luther's theology

3.1.1 To be God is to give

To call something a gift of God implies no more than that God has created it. However, for Luther, a gift is much more. One would not exaggerate in saying that a gift (*donum*) is the key to Luther's theology as a whole.[296] In *Dictata super Psalterium,* Luther defines God: *hoc est esse Deum: non accipere bona, sed dare,* "this is what it means to be God: not to take good, but to give it."[297] This establishes a relational definition of God. More than all-knowing and omnipotent, God is all-giving, the attribute perceived in God's gifts. To begin with the most popular texts, Luther explains in *The Small Catechism* what the "daily bread" is of the Lord's Prayer. It consists of "everything included in the necessities and nourishment for our bodies, such as food, drink, clothing, shoes, house, farm, fields ... upright spouse ... good friends, faithful neighbors, and the like."[298] Luther defines the daily bread in *The Large Catechism* more concisely as "everything that belongs to our entire life in the world."[299] This includes

---

[295] Bayer 2008, 254: "God is categorically the one who gives: the Father does not just give some particular things – namely, life and the world: he gives us himself in this creation. In the same way the Son gives himself to us – and at the same time gives us the Father once again in a new way, whose face was obscured from our view because of sin. The Spirit finally is nothing other than the opener and distributor of this self-giving of Christ – and thereby that of the Father as well."

[296] Therefore Wetzel's argument "Donum ist ja für Luther ein Allgemeinbegriff ohne spezifischen Inhalt" (Wetzel 1954, 160) is inadequate.

[297] WA 4, 269, 21. For the implications of this quote, see Mannermaa 2010, 23.

[298] BC 357, 14; WA 30 I, 253, 8 – 15.

[299] BC 450; WA 30 I, 204, 10 – 14: "Und das wirs kürtzlich fassen, so will diese bitte mit eingeschlossen haben alles was zu diesem gantzen leben ynn der welt gehöret, weil wir allein umb des willen das tegliche brod haben müssen."

food and clothes, as well as the realms of society, culture, and economy. All this is a gift of God, which he provides out of his goodness "even to the godless and rogues." The Lord's Prayer affirms that we receive all this from God's fatherly goodness. For Luther, to speak about God is to speak about what he gives, and this emphasis is discernable in all Luther's works. His hymns, condensed musical expressions of his thought, are particularly rife with it. They tell of the Triune God who is everything, does everything and gives everything for the benefit of humanity.[300] The creedal hymn, "*Wir gleuben all an einen Gott*" is a case in point.

> Wyr gleuben all an eynen Gott, / schepfer hymels und der erden, /der sich zum vater geben hat, / das wyr synen kinder werden. / Er will uns allzeyt erneren / leyb und seel auch wol bewaren./ Allem unfal will er waren; / Kleyn leyd soll uns widerfaren. /Er sorget fur uns, hutt und wacht / es steht alles ynn seyner macht.[301]

God is portrayed in the first stanza as one who has given himself to us as Father. God is not a father in some immovable, detached way, but his being Father is a self-giving act, *sich-zum-Vater-Geben*. The eternity and omnipotence of God are also described solely from the standpoint of our benefit: "He both soul and body feedeth, all we need he doth provide us; he through snares and perils leadeth, watching that no harm betide us. He careth for us day and night, all things are governed by his might."[302] God the Father is a giver, not just in the beginning, but constantly. God as creator is not merely a first cause or a shipbuilder, who makes a ship and leaves it sailing alone. Instead, creation is also conservation, which is not a separate act of God but the continuation of creation. Furthermore, everything on heaven and earth is "daily given, sustained, and protected by God."[303] The earth does not produce fruit on its own, the sun does not rise, nor do women give birth out of mechanical or biological causality. Luther does not deny that there is a certain order that all creatures obey, but maintains

---

300 Veit 1986, 161–162: "In der soteriologischen Atmosphäre der geistlichen Lieder Luthers steht der Mensch absolut im Mittelpunkt, es geht hier einzig und allein um die Dinge, die dem Menschen zugute kommen und ihn zu seinem Heil führen. Die dem Menschen gewidmete Aufmerksamkeit, die die Lieder noch viel stärker zum Ausdruck bringen als seine anderen Werke – was vielleicht auf das Wesen dieser Literaturgattung zurückzuführen ist, in der der Gläubige sich in allem, was ihn betrifft, seinem Gott gegenüber äussert – zeigt sich in einem betont personalen Zug: das Werk Gottes ist ganz auf das ,pro me', mehr noch auf das gemeinschaftliche ,pro nobis' ausgerichtet."

301 AWA 4, 238–241.

302 English trans. Leaver 2007, 122.

303 BC 433, 19; WA 42, 233: "apud Deum idem est creare et conservare."

this order is not a law of mechanical necessity but a gift of God's mercy.[304] The keyword here is blessing (*benedictio*), which gives all living things the ability to grow and procreate.[305] That all species produce appropriate descendants is possible due to God's creating and conserving activity.[306] As the Catechism states, "God daily and abundantly provides shoes, clothing … along with all the necessities and nourishment for this body and life. God protects me against all danger and shields and preserves me from all evil."[307]

That there is anything at all is a sign of God's love for his creation. The Christian view of how the world began is *creatio ex nihilo*, and Luther sees this not only as the state of affairs in the beginning, but as currently applicable. God is constantly creating "out of nothing," and in an early sermon, Luther even speaks of a threefold *nihil*. The first is nothing in the literal sense, that is, related to being (*ens*), the second is nothing as an equivalent of being false, which is in opposition to truth (*verum*), and finally, nothing in the sense of evil, which is in opposition to good (*bonum*). To save the humankind from this triplex *nihil*, God sent his Son and gave his Spirit. This is an act of the Triune God, and in accordance with medieval theology, Luther states that the Father is the source of being (*essentia*), the Son himself is truth (*veritas*), and the Spirit is goodness (*bonitas*). Moreover, the redemption and sanctification of human beings is *creatio ex nihilo*, as it was on the first day of creation.[308]

---

304 Thus this order should not be thought as "Schöpfungsordnungen" in the sense of 19th century theology, Lohse 1995, 262–264.

305 WA 14, 108, 13–109, 4:"Hic dat benedictionem quod antea non fecit, hoc est: hanc naturam dedit piscibus et volucribus ut crescant. Primum opus est, ut ex aqua fecit volucres et pisces. Ultra hoc adiecit, ut multiplicarentur, sicut supra item fecit: primum creavit, postea iubet, ut fructum ferat, quod ita multiplicantur, est opus maiestatis divinae."

306 WA 42, 27, 31–40: "Quod igitur terra profert frumentum, arbores et omnis generis herbas huius diei opus est. Nunc quidem omnia nascuntur ex sui generis semine. Sed prima creatio sine semine simpliciter ex virtute verbi est facta. Quod autem nunc semina proveniunt, Id quoque est creationis opus plenum admiratione. Nam singularis virtus est, quod granum in terram cadens suo tempore surgit, et fert fructum secundum speciem suam. Illud autem certum est indicium non fortuitam creationem, sed praecipuum divinae providentiae opus esse, quod similia a similibus perpetuo ordine enascuntur. Sic ex tritico non fit nisi triticum, ex ordeo non nisi ordeum, ex siligine siligo. Perpetuo eadem singularum specierum ratio, ordo, conditio servatur."

307 BC 354, 2.

308 WA 4, 600, 22–31; Löfgren 1960, 26; Sammeli Juntunen's dissertation (1996) on nihil in young Luther's thought has shown that when Luther says that a human is "nothing", he means that every human, both in his/her natural and spiritual existence is totally dependent on God. On the transcendentals ens, verum, bonum (and pulchrum) relating to the Trinity, see WA 43, 276, 29–40 (discussed in section 6.1.3. below).

When singing about the second person of the Trinity, it is impossible to avoid the word "give," as the Son is the supreme Gift. Luther incorporates very powerful, categorically giving pictures of salvation in his hymns as well as in his sermons. The hymn *Nun freut euch lieben Christen gmeyn* portrays salvation as a drama that God has lived. God had mercy on humans and "gave his dearest treasure" (*es liess seyn bestes kosten*) to save them.[309] The Christmas hymn *Gelobet seist du, Jesu Christ* likewise praises Christ who has done "everything for us" – becoming a stranger in the world in order to lead us from the valley of death to heaven, being himself poor to make us rich, all motivated by his love.[310]

The obvious point here is that justification through faith is a gift that can be understood in the same vein as *creatio ex nihilo*. The exposition of the first article of faith in *The Small Catechism* is revealing: "I believe that God has made me together with all that exists ... and all this is done out of pure, fatherly, divine goodness and mercy, without any merit or worthiness of mine at all."[311] The words "merit" and "worthiness" used here are more easily connected to the doctrine of justification. To use them in speaking about creation may sound absurd. Of course no one can "merit" one's existence or be "worth" being. As a matter of fact, that is precisely what the Lutheran doctrine of justification is pointing at. The *loci* of creation and redemption are inseparable. It is as absurd to argue that one can merit salvation (or a bit of it), as it is to claim that one can earn existence.[312]

The Holy Spirit is also approached from the view of *pro nobis*. The Spirit is defined, rather than in doctrinal terms, as a comforter and giver of gifts. As with the other persons of the Trinity, Luther always speaks more about the work of Holy Spirit than its essence. The most frequent word for Holy Spirit in Luther's hymns is *Tröster*, "comforter."[313] The Holy Spirit maintains the unity of a Christendom in which sins are forgiven and prepares for us (*ist bereyt uns*) the eternal life after this life.[314]

---

309 AWA 4, 154 – 157; Leaver 2007,161 – 167; Veit 1986, 91 – 92.
310 AWA 4,166: "Der son des vatters, Got von ardt / ain gast in der welt ward / Und fürt uns auss dem yamer tal;/ er macht uns erben in seym saal ... Er ist auff erden kommen arm/ das er unser sich erbarm / Und in dem hymel machet reych. / unde seynen lieben engeln gleych ... Das hat er alles uns gethan / seyn gross lieb zu zeygen an."
311 BC 354, 2.
312 See also Bayer 2008, 95 – 100.
313 Veit 1986, 188.
314 AWA 4, 240: "Wyr gleuben an den heylgen geyst,/ Gott mit vater und dem sone / Der aller blöden tröster heyst/ und mit gaben ziehet schone./ Die gantz Christenheyt auff erden / hellt ynn eynem synn gar eben. / Hie all sund vergeben werden, /das fleysch soll auch widder leben. / Nach diesem elend ist bereyt /uns eyn leben ynn ewigkeit." AWA 4, 224: "Du hochster troster

A pivotal concept in Luther's theology is the gift (*donum, Gabe*). Everything that is, is a gift of God the Father. In Christ, God gives himself wholly and completely to us. This giving happens not only for us (*pro nobis*), but also in us (*in nobis*), as the Holy Spirit who is both God himself and his gift to us.[315] In *The Supper of Christ* (1528) the idea of the Trinity as an endlessly giving Deity is fully elaborated:

> These are the three persons and one God, who has given himself to us all wholly and completely with all he is and has. The Father gives himself to us, with heaven and earth and all the creatures, in order that they may serve us and benefit us. But this gift has become obscured and useless through Adam's fall. Therefore the Son himself subsequently gave himself and bestowed all his works, sufferings, wisdom, and righteousness, and reconciled us to the Father, in order that restored to life and righteousness, we might also know and have the Father and his gifts. But because this grace would benefit no one if it remained so profoundly hidden and could not come to us, the Holy Spirit comes and gives himself to us also, wholly and completely. He teaches us to understand this deed of Christ, which has been manifested to us, helps us receive and preserve it, use it to our advantage and impart it to others, increase and extend it. He does this both inwardly and outwardly – inwardly by means of faith and other spiritual gifts, outwardly through the Gospel, baptism and the sacrament of the altar, through which as through three means or methods he comes to us and inculcates the sufferings of Christ for the benefit of our salvation.[316]

To be God is to give. This does not merely mean that God likes to give or that it is natural to him. Ultimately, there is no way of speaking about God except through the language of giving. The righteousness of God, *iustitia Dei*, is a good and a crucial example. As Luther himself reported in 1545, the words "God's righteousness" in Rom 1:17 caused him a spiritual crisis and eventually led him to his reformatory breakthrough.[317] The problem was solved when Luther realized that the words "God's righteousness" do not refer to a property of God's majesty, but the power with which he makes us righteous. This involves a peculiar theological grammar, for which Luther found support from Augustine and developed further. In *Lectures on Romans*, Luther draws the conclusion that if something is

---

aller not / hilff, das wyr nicht furchten schand noch tod, / Das ynn uns die synnen nicht verzagen, / wenn der feind wird das leben verklagen."

315 On the Holy Spirit as both God and gift, see Kärkkäinen 2003, 162–171.

316 StA 4, 251, 22–252, 5. The teaching about the Holy Trinity in the Large Catechism is the same; BC 439, 63–440, 65.

317 WA 54, 185–187. I choose not to enter to the discussion of the date and details of Luther's "reformatory turn." For that, see Lohse 1995, 97–110.

said to be in God, it is a thing that he gives us.[318] In his autobiographical note, Luther tells that he began to apply the same grammatical rule to other attributes of God, such as power and wisdom. "The power of God" is that which God uses to make us strong, and "the wisdom of God" is how God makes us wise.[319] The only sensible way to talk about God is to speak in terms of what he gives us.

3.1.2 To receive is to participate

God gives his goodness to all creatures, even the godless and rogues. God's gift is in this sense a unilateral act of giving, with no presuppositions from the recipient's side. Yet it is not the purpose of God's giving to remain unnoticed. Luther's *The Large Catechism* states:

> Thus, you see, God wishes to show us how he cares for us in all our needs and faithfully provides for our daily sustenance. Although he gives and provides these blessings bountifully, even to the godless and rogues, yet he wishes us to ask them so that we may realize that we have received them from his hand and may recognize in them his fatherly goodness toward us.[320]

To analyze the concept of a gift, let us assume that a gift is not a gift in the full sense when the intention of the giver is not realized. In other words, something is not a gift by merely being there. On the contrary a gift requires a giver whose intention is to give it. Moreover, the act of giving presupposes a recipient to whom the gift is given and who receives it.[321] These two acts of the recipient,

---

318 WA 56, 173, 24–25: "Dicuntur autem haec omnia Dei, non quod in ipso sint, sed quod in nobis ex ipso sint."

319 WA 54, 186, 10–13: "Discurrebam deinde per scripturas, ut habebat memoria, et colligebam etiam in aliis vocabulis analogiam, ut opus Dei, id est, quod operatur in nobis Deus, virtus Dei, qua nos potentes facit, sapientia Dei, qua nos sapientes facit, fortitudo Dei, salus Dei, gloria Dei."

320 BC 451, 82–83.

321 Saarinen 2010, 17–24, observes in the act of giving, besides the giver, the gift, and the recipient, a fourth role, which is the beneficiary. This distinction, originating from Augustine's idea of sacrifice, is useful in determining Luther's position in the discussions about Holy Supper as a sacrifice. Nonetheless, the Eucharistic sacrifice is a concept that seems inappropriate for Luther's theology. However, Wolfgang Simon (2003, 288–302) has detailed three legitimate concepts of sacrifice in Luther's thought. The first one is "social ethical": the outward person gives gifts of the Creation to a neighbor. The second and the third are the "inner" sacrifices – a person gives thanks to God in praise; Christ gives the believer to the Father in justification.

to recognize the giver's intention and to receive the gift, are clearly indicated here. God wishes us to recognize his fatherly goodness toward us.

Receiving God's gifts includes more than simply accepting his goodness. In the preface to *Christmas Postil* (1522), Luther warns the reader not to think of Christ as a Moses figure, as Christ is neither a lawgiver nor primarily even an example. Before one looks at Christ as an example, one should recognize him as a gift and present (*gabe und geschenck*) from God. This gift should not only be accepted or received, as one should be perfectly certain that Christ's suffering becomes one's own, "as you were Christ himself."[322] The circle of giving is completed when God, besides giving us everything we need, gives himself to us in order that he makes us one with himself. Christ's presence in faith is a gift. In his *Commentary on Galatians* (1535) Luther writes, "The Christ who is grasped by faith and who lives in the heart is the true Christian righteousness, on account of which God counts us as righteous and grants us eternal life."[323]

Finnish studies on Luther have promoted the thought of *unio* in the Lutheran doctrine of justification. The basic insight has been that the later view of justification as a purely forensic imputation of righteousness fails to understand how Luther related forensic justification to the ontological justification achieved through union with God in Christ. In brief, to believe is to participate in God. The forensic and ontological sides of justification have been called *favor* and *donum*, respectively.[324] Christ himself is the righteousness of a Christian, and this righteousness embraces both the forgiveness of sins based on the merit of Christ (*favor*) and the saving presence of Christ that renews the believer (*donum*), for "it is no longer I who live, but Christ who lives in me" (Gal 2:20). This means that Christ is the essence of our faith. By remaining in us, Christ abolishes sin, kills death, and carries us to his kingdom of grace, righteousness, and joy. Here the *commercium admirabile* takes place, where sin belongs to Christ and his righteousness becomes ours.[325]

---

322 WA 10 I 1, 11, 12–18: "Das hewbtstuck und grund des Euangelij ist, das du Christum tzuuor, ehe du yhn tzum exempel fassist, auffnehmist unnd erkennist alß eyn gabe und geschenck, das dyr von gott geben und deyn eygen sey, alßo das, wenn du yhm tzusihest odder hoerist, das er ettwas thutt odder leydet, das du nit tzweyffellst, er selb Christus mit solchem thun und leyden sey deyn, darauff du dich nit weniger muegist vorlassen, denn alß hettistu es than, ia alß werist du der selbige Christus."

323 WA 30 I, 229, 28–30: "Ergo fide apprehensus et in corde habitans Christus est iustitia Christiana propter quam Deus nos reputat iustos et donat vitam aeternam."

324 Peura 1998. For fuller treatment see Mannermaa 2005; Vainio 2008, 19–53.

325 WA 40 I 283, 26–284, 19: "'Iam non Ego, sed Christus in me vivit'; Is est mea forma ornans fidem meam, ut color vel lux parietem ornat. (Sic crasse res illa exponenda est; Non enim possumus spiritualiter comprehendere tam proxime et intime Christum haerere et manere in

This union with Christ that Luther speaks about could, of course, be understood in strictly relational terms, as a way to understand the meaning of Christ's work. Moreover, to attribute an ontological view of faith to Luther seems to compromise the essential Lutheran tenet that faith is not a *habitus* in a human person.[326] Christ's dwelling in a believer can be understood as the believer's personal property or as an abiding position, whereas the Lutheran doctrine of justification emphasizes the foreign righteousness (*justitia aliena*) of a believer. This foreign righteousness means that the righteousness imputed to the sinner is coming from outside and can never be internalized or pass into a believer's own possession.[327] Against this view it is maintained that the real and ontological participation in Christ amounts to the opposite of the scholastic *habitus* of grace. Christ is both the object and the subject of faith and faith is a work of God through the Word. In addition, there is nothing in the human person that could act as a basis for justification. God creates the new reality of faith in the human heart and thus remains there – to receive Christ is to become one with him.[328] According to Lutheran theology, the gift (*donum*) is often seen as a consequence of grace (*favor*). This means the presence of Christ in a Christian results from the forgiveness of sins and the act of forensic justification.[329] As a corrective to this view, the ontological union with Christ guards the *sola gratia* principle so

---

nobis, quam lux vel albedo in pariete haeret.)Christus ergo, inquit, sic inhaerens et conglutinatus mihi et manens in me hanc vitam quam ago, vivit in me, imo vita qua sic vivo, est Christus ipse. Itaque Christus et ego iam unum in hac parte sumus. Vivens autem in me Christus abolet legem, peccatum damnat, mortem mortificat, quia ad praesentiam ipsius illa non possunt non evanescere. Est enim Christus aeterna pax, consolatio, iustitia et vita; His autem cedere oportet terrorem legis, moerorem animi, peccatum, Infernum, mortem. Sic Christus in me manens et vivens tollit et absorbet omnia mala quae me cruciant et affligunt. Quare haec inhaerentia facit, ut liberer a terroribus legis et peccati, eximar e cute mea et transferar in Christum ac in illius regnum, quod est regnum gratiae, iustitiae, pacis, gaudii, vitae, salutis et gloriae aeternae; in illo autem agens, nihil mali potest nocere mihi." In this significant passage, Luther employs the image of color and wall (albedo in pariete) which is quite unfortunate, as he tries to portray how Christ is the forma, i.e. the true reality of the faith.

326 Siirala 1956, 152 presents a traditional position: "Der Glaube als Hören ist nicht ein 'habitus', den der Mensch zu seiner Verfügung und als eine Sicherheit für sein Leben haben könnte. Das Hören' bedeutet keine bestimmte Position, die der Mensch zu finden und vor dem Worte einzunehmen versuchen soll. Das rechte Hören, der rechte Glaube ist die Situation, die Gott geschaffen hat, indem er sein Wort in Jesus Christus Fleisch werden liess."

327 Thus Jüngel 2001, 204–207.

328 WA 40 I, 233, 16–24: "Est et hic notandum, quod ista tria, Fides, Christus, Acceptio vel Reputatio, coniuncta sunt. Fides enim apprehendit Christum et habet eum praesentem includitque eum ut anulus gemmam. Et qui fuerit inventus cum tali fide apprehensi Christi in corde, illum reputat Deus iustum."

329 Solid Declaration III, 17–24 (BC 564–566).

that grace and the gift mutually presuppose each other. Without Christ dwelling in human beings, God cannot be pleased with them. Therefore to receive Christ is to participate in Christ, or more precisely, to be one with Christ.

3.1.3 To be given is to give back

The anthropological usage of the word "gift" may also elucidate the notion of "gift of God." At first sight, these two seem to be mutually exclusive. Anthropologists like Marcel Mauss have noticed that giving a gift always involves exchange, which can also be viewed as the economic notion of gift.[330] For example, when I give a gift to someone, I expect something in return. This is not necessarily a material reward, but perhaps it is gratitude or a rise in the social status of the giver. In this sense then, there are no "free" gifts, and a gift includes the acts of giving and receiving.[331] By merely receiving a gift, the recipient performs a reciprocal act, a kind of counter-gift. Moreover, there are prerequisites for something to be a gift. For instance, if a gift is immediately returned, this is not a counter-gift, but a refusal of that gift. On the other hand, if something of the same value is given in return, it is an act of commerce. If the same gift is returned later, this is a loan. Only when something else is given later can it be called a gift. In addition, the act of giving back need not, as John Milbank has shown, be aimed toward the giver of the (first) gift. Giving back can be giving further.[332] The Lutheran view of the categorically giving God is not completely disjointed from the anthropological concept of gift. Bo Kristian Holm has even argued that Luther's view of the justification and of a new life is closely dependent on his view of mutuality and reciprocity.[333] Luther's thought would otherwise be difficult to understand, for example, in the following passage of *Sermon on the Good Works (1520)*:

---

330 Mauss 1990.

331 Milbank (1995, 125) outlines a minimum of return in giving a gift as follows: "[I]t seems that a good, a sensible gift, always does receive something back; if not the gratitude of another and delight in her pleasure, plus the sense that we have benefitted her, then at least the self-awareness that we have sought to do so, such that the thwarting of the gift is outside our control, and need not deprive us of our 'present' status of generosity of heart. This, at least, comes back to us, as a compensation for what should return."

332 Saarinen 2005, 17–25. Interestingly, Begbie (2000, 246–270) makes use of Milbank's idea of a gift in explaining the theological significance of musical improvisation. In musical improvisation, the theme is received from another and given back or given further, in a different form.

333 Holm 2006, 4.

When this faith is rightly present, the heart must be made joyful by the testament, and grow warm and melt in God's love. Then will follow praise and thanksgiving with a pure heart, from which the mass is called in Greek Eucharistia, that is, "thanksgiving," because we praise and thank God for this comforting, rich, blessed testament, just as he gives thanks, praises and is joyful, to whom a good friend has presented a thousand and more gulden. Although Christ often fares like those who make several persons rich by their testament and these persons never think of them, nor praise or thank them. So our masses at present are merely celebrated, without our knowing why or wherefore, and consequently we neither give thanks nor love nor praise.[334]

If no response were expected from humans, this passage would become utterly inconceivable. On the other hand, is it not true that salvation "by grace, through faith" excludes all giving from humans to God? Does this not make the ideas of "Gift of God" and "economic gift exchange" incompatible? Does Luther's vehement denial of all counter-gifts to God really mean there is no possibility to give anything back to God, or does it mean that the true counter-gift to God is to admit that one cannot give anything to God in return?[335] Non-identical giving to someone other than the (first) giver, however, is less problematic. That a receiver of God's grace becomes a giver to his/her neighbor is highly compatible with Luther's theology. Indeed, the motivation of Christian love for one's neighbor is the abundance of God's self-giving. God does not need anything from me, but my neighbor needs my help. As I have such a gracious God, I can give of my own for my neighbor's benefit. However, this does not happen as a calculated act to receive a reward.[336] The reciprocity of a gift is present both in faith and in love.

---

334 StA 2, 44, 14 – 19: "Wan nu disser glaub recht gehet / so musz das hertz von dem testament frolich werde(n) / vnd in gottis liebe erwarmen und tzurschmeltzen. Da folget dan lob vnd danck / mit sussem hertze(n). davon heisset die mesz auff krichsch Eucharistia / das ist / dancksagung / das wir got loben vnnd dancken / fur solch trostlich / reich /selig testament /gleich wie der danckt /lobt / vnd frolich ist / dem ein gut freund / tausent odder mer gulde(n) bescheiden hat. Wie wol es Christo vil mal geht / gleich wie denen / die mit yhrem testament etlich reich mache (n) / die yhr nymmer gede(n)cke(n) / noch lob / noch da(n)ck sagen / alszo gehn itzt vnsere meszsenn / das sie nur gehaltenn werdenn / wissenn nit / wotzu odder worumb sie diene(n). drumb / wir auch widder dancken /noch lieben noch loben / bleyben durr vnd hart da bey / lassens bey vnsern gebetlin bleybenn."
335 Holm 2006, 16. Actually, the commercium admirabile is explicitly depicted in *The Christian Freedom* (1520) in the terms of a gift-exchange, where faith is seen as a wedding ring, a nuptial gift. StA 2, 275, 19 – 277, 9.
336 Holm 2006, 122. See also Raunio (1998, 114):"Only when the Christian possesses such a God who continually gives him good things and whom he considers always the font of everything good, can he love the neighbor without searching for anything from him as reward. If faith as a divine gift is the 'organ' that receives good things from God and lets God be the Giver, then love is

In faith, God gives his word and his righteousness to the believer and the believer gives his/her sinfulness to God. In love, a Christian gives him/herself to Christ and to his/her neighbor.[337] Moreover, by confessing that God is the giver, the believer participates in the responsive act of praise and thanksgiving. The "categorical giving" of God does not exclude the response of humanity, although the reciprocity between God and humans is asymmetric. After all, a human never gives back as much as God gives to him/her. Christ's death on the cross is the first gift, which functions as a starting mechanism for the gift-exchange. Justification as participation in Christ's righteousness makes the genuine giving possible so that a person, as a receiver, participates in the act of giving.[338]

3.1.4 The gifts of humans as the gifts of God

To call music an excellent gift of God may also sound striking because music pertains to the realm of human culture. The question contains a certain anachronism – early sixteenth century culture was not an independent realm distinct from religion as in today's sense. However, this emphasis is noteworthy since simultaneously at the turn of the sixteenth century the idea of the composer as a creative genius was emerging in Western music, which is to say that music was increasingly understood as a product of human creativity. Luther is particularly clear in emphasizing that music is a gift of God and *not* of human beings (*quia donum Dei non hominum est*),[339] although Luther himself has been regarded as an early proponent of the idea of creative genius. According to the music historian Walter Wiora, Luther's laudatory appraisal of Josquin is due to his *ingenium*. The freedom Luther experiences in Josquin's music is the hallmark of a genius composer. Furthermore, musical freedom mirrors free will in that "others do what they can, Josquin does what he wants."[340] Or, to be more precise, the sec-

---

the 'substance' that always gives itself to others. Through the gift of the divine nature or love the Christian gives himself continually to God and his neighbor."

337 Holm 2006, 117, 123.

338 Saarinen 2005, 49. "Praise and service witness to the productivity and fruitfulness of the faith of Christians. The believer thus participates in circulating the gift given."Holm 2006, 67, 136: "Der Glaube ist ... sowohl 'Gabe' von Gott als auch ,Gabe' für Gott."

339 WA 30 II, 696, 5.

340 Wiora 1988, 130–131: "So hat Luther an Josquin Desprez das Wesen des Ingenium hervorgehoben und aus dem Gegensatz zwischen Gesetz und Gnade begründet. Wo nur das Gesetz herrscht, da seien die Arbeit und ihre Ergebnisse sauer und lustlos, wo aber Begnadung, Gratia, Charisma wirken, da gehe die Arbeit gut vonstatten. So habe Gott die Frohe Botschaft auch durch die Musik gepredigt: An Josquin werde die Überlegenheit der Gnade und Begnadung

ond-hand report states that Luther said, "Josquin is the master of the notes, which must do as he wishes, while other composers must follow what the notes dictate."[341] However Luther's admiration of Josquin is to be interpreted, as Luther is consistent in arguing that music is not a human achievement even if it were an elaborate polyphonic setting of a master composer. Actually, as will be seen in due course, Luther would say the more skillfully composed the music, the more God makes it. At this point, let us examine some remarks on Luther's theology of culture.

In 1524 Luther commented on Psalm 127:2 (In vain you rise early and stay up late, toiling for food to eat – for while they sleep he provides for those he loves) by saying that a man must always work and do something. At the same time, he must remember that it is not his work that gives him a living, but God's blessing. It merely looks as if he earns his living by his work, since God does not give him anything unless he works. As Jesus said, "The birds do not sow or reap or store away in barns," but they too would die of hunger unless they fly after their food. A bird finds food not due to the work it does but to God's goodness. Who then has put the food where the bird finds it other than God? This is Luther's view of cooperation between God and his creation.[342]

Human labor and human agency is needed for God's purposes. The idea of a *vocation* is also important in understanding Luther's view of musicianship.[343] Luther uses the German word *Beruf* to refer not only to an occupation, but also to a

---

sichtbar; seine Kompositionen fliessen fröhlich und frei aus dem vollen, nicht durch Regeln genötigt und gezwungen." Josquin gained the official position as the canonical master composer soon after Luther's death in *Heinrich Glarean*'s textbook of musical theory, *Dodecachordon* (1547). Hoelty-Nickel 1960, 147: "According to Glarean, a work of art requires two prerequisites, *ars* ans *ingenium*. *Ars* he interpreted as the laws and rules of music that can be taught and learned. To him, *ingenium* means the original and creative impulse of the musician, which is purely a gift." An interesting detail is, that Nicolas Listenius' *Musica* (1537), a Lutheran textbook on the rudiments of music, is generally considered to be the first to record the new concept of a musical work. A prerequisite for such a conception was the recognition of musical composition as an independent endeavor. Lippman (1992, 23 – 24).

341 Not found in WA, but from Johann Mathesius' book entitled *Martin Luthers Leben* (227– 228)
342 WA 15, 368, 9 – 16: "Also soll und mus der mensch auch erbeyten und ettwas thun, Aber doch daneben wissen, das eyn ander sey der yhn neere denn seyne erbeyt, nemlich Goettlicher segen, wiewol es scheynet, alls neere yhn seyne erbeyt, weyl Gott on seyne erbeyt yhm nichts gibt. Gleych wie wol das voeglin nicht seet noch erndtet, Aber doch muest es hungers sterben, wo es nicht nach der speyse floehe und suchte. Das es aber speyse findet, ist nicht seyner erbeyt, sondern Gottes guete. Denn wer hat seyne speyse dahyn gelegt, das es sie findet? on zweyffel Gott alleyne."
343 A classical study concerning Luther's idea of vocation is Wingren 1948. See also a more concise treatment of Froehlich 1999.

spiritual calling. So Luther spiritualized all professions or occupations, such that all human work, as lowly as it may appear, is a vocation from God. The criterion of whether the work is good is not its alleged spirituality, but the way it benefits one's neighbor. This idea was directed against the monastic understanding of a meritorious life. Works of love are therefore not directed toward God, but toward neighbors who need help. This all is God's work. He could act according to *potentia absoluta* without human efforts, but has chosen differently. God acts through human masks (*larva Dei*); he raises children through the toil of their parents, milks cows through the farmers, and protects the state through soldiers. Whoever works regardless of its seeming unworthiness does the work of God. The aim of a vocation is always for the benefit of one's neighbor.[344]

Vocation is a completely earthly thing, existing for the temporary benefit of others. The earthly vocation also has a spiritual significance, since living according to one's vocation leads ultimately to praying for God's help and trusting in him. A comparison between a monk's and a husband's life is a good example for Luther. A monastic life can mean a lifestyle where one tries to avoid all everyday trouble and to rise above the struggles of ordinary life to achieve divine contemplation. For Luther, this means that a monk has no real opportunity to believe. A married life instead teaches us to look at God and forces us to pray and believe.[345] Therefore one might say that the vocation is an act of love, since it works for the benefit of others. This is also a work of faith, since it forces us to trust in God. Without vocation, God loses his grasp on humans and can no longer use humans as his hands and feet, nor can he be their God and the source of ultimate trust.

---

344 WA 31 I 436, 7–19:"Was ist aber alle unser erbeit auff dem felde, im garten, jnn der stad, im hause, im streit, im regiern anders gegen Gott, denn ein solch kinderwerck, dadurch Gott seine gaben zu felde, zu hause und allenthalben geben wil? Es sind unsers herrn Gotts larven, darunter wil er verborgen sein und alles thun. Hette Gideon nicht dazu gethan und were zu felde gezogen widder Midian, so weren die Midianiter nicht geschlagen, Und Gott hette sie doch wol on Gideon koennen schlahen. Er kunde wol kinder schaffen on man und weib. Aber er wills nicht thun, sondern gibt man und weib zu samen, auff das scheine, als thu es man und weib, und er thuts doch unter solcher larven verborgen. Man spricht: 'Dat deus omne bonum, sed non per cornua taurum', Gott bescheret alles gut, aber du must zu greiffen und den ochsen bey den hoernern nemen, das ist, du must erbeiten und damit Gotte ursachen und eine larven geben." Potentia Dei absoluta and potentia Dei ordinata are definitions used in the nominalist philosophy for the power of God according to his unreserved omnipotence vs. his actual operations.
345 WA 12, 106, 24–27: Nymbstu aber eyn weyb und wirst ehlich, so ist das der erste stoss: Wo willtu nu dich, deyn weyb und kind erneren? und das weret deyn lebenlang. Also das der ehliche stand von natur der artt ist, das er auff gottis hand und gnade leret und treybt zu sehen, und gleich zum glauben zwinget

In faith, all Christians have a similar position before God. As for their earthly calling, Christians differ from one another. As vocation is not *imitation* in the medieval sense of *imitatio Christi,* all Christians have different vocations. This does not divide Christendom, but is a sign of the richness of creation. We may learn from the lives of the saints regarding their faithfulness in their *own* mission and may imitate their faithfulness, though not their works, because our task is different. Besides solidarity, vocation, or *Beruf,* also adapts itself to individualism and makes room for artistic creativity in the modern sense.[346]

3.2 Music as a gift of God

3.2.1 The four-stage division of music

To say that music is a gift of God means, according to the above examination of *donum* in Luther's theology, that God demonstrates his loving goodness through music. God also wants us to appreciate this gift and receive it with joy. So God is intimately present to us in music. In return, we can praise God with the gift of music. That Luther calls music the best gift of God (*optimum Dei donum*) encompasses all this.

The most systematic account of music by Luther is provided by *Encomion musices,* or the preface to Georg Rhau's motet collection *Symphoniae iucundae* (1538).[347] As the largest extant text and also as the most reliable source on the subject, its analysis is indispensable in order to determine Luther's understanding of *donum illud divinum et excellentissimum,* as he defines music at the outset of the preface.[348] In this particular text, Luther analyzes music according to the following schema:

1. The phenomenon of sound
2. Music in the nature, birdsong in particular
3. Human voice
4. Art music[349]

---

346 For Luther's ideas concerning vocatio and imitatio, see Wingren 1948, 184–196.
347 For the history of this text, see introduction 1.3.
348 WA 50, 368, 4–5.
349 I adopt the division made by Söhngen 1967, 85–86. Other ways to conceive the structure of Encomion musices are Blankenburg (1972, 99) 1. Die Musik als ein Teil der Schöpfung 2. das Geheimnis der menschlichen Stimme, 3. die Wirkungsmacht der Musik, 4. der usus musicae, d.h. die Zusammengehörigkeit vom Wort Gottes und der Musik, 5. das Lob der musica artificialis, 6. Warnung vor dem Missbrauch der Musik; Bader (1996, 184): I res ipsa (WA 368, 10–

In all these stages, music is a gift of God. To be exact, the status of music as a gift of God increases when we move upwards to the more complicated and cultivated forms of music. Indeed, the salient features of music as a gift of God become more apparent in music as art.

3.2.1.1 The phenomenon of sound

The first stage of music is the phenomenon of sound, and Luther observes:

> Music has been instilled and implanted in all creatures, individually and collectively. For nothing is without sound or harmony. Even the air, which of itself is invisible and imperceptible to all our senses, and which, since it lacks both voice and speech, is the least musical of all things, becomes sonorous, audible, and comprehensible when it is set in motion Wondrous mysteries are here suggested by the Spirit.[350]

This passage reflects Luther at his nearest position to the Pythagorean theory of music. Literally, Luther states that nothing is without sound or "sounding number" (*Nihil est sine sono, seu numero sonoro*), and this means that the connection between music and mathematics is essential. From this, some scholars have drawn the conclusion that Luther's conception of music is Pythagorean.[351] Regardless of its historical prominence, except for that single sentence, the *harmony of the spheres* is conspicuous in its absence in Luther's theology of music. Although the mathematical understanding of music was most likely a part of his university education, Luther neither expounds on music using numbers, nor does he men-

---

370, 12) II vsus tantae rei (370, 13 – 372, 10) III Musica naturalis et musica artificialis (372, 11–363,6), and Block (2002, 45): 1. Wesen der Musik (368, 10 – 370, 12) 2. Ergehen und Verstehen der Musik (370, 13 – 373, 6).

350 WA 50, 369, 1– 6: "Primum, si rem ipsam spectes, inuenies Musicam esse ab initio mundi inditam seu concreatam creaturis vniuersis, singulis et omnibus. Nihil enim est sine sono, seu numero sonoro, ita vt et aer ipse per sese inuisibilis et inpalpabilis, omnibusque sensibus inperceptibilis, minimeque omnium musicus, sed plane mutus et nihil reputatus, tamen motus sit sonorus et audibilis, tunc etiam palpabilis, mirabilia in hoc significante spiritu mysteria, de quibus hic non est locus dicendi."

351 Brian L. Horne (1985, 27) states that for Luther, music is a world, "in which every note and rhythm finds its proper place in the whole," an order, which is, "a sure indication of the stability of God in a shifting and unstable world." The reason why music is so appropriate to indicate this is that it is "entirely non-figurative, non-representational and non-verbal" art. Horne's article has been very influential in the Anglo-Saxon world and has probably led to Jeremy Begbie's article on Calvin and music (2003), to depict Luther's view on music as "Pythagorean." Hermann Abert (1924, 105) proposed quite the opposite reason for Luther's proximity to music: it is precisely the most subjective of all arts.

tion Pythagoras when speaking about music.[352] Instead, Luther refers incidentally to Pythagoras. In his sermon from the same year (1538), Luther comments that Pythagoras claims that the movement of the stars begets a sweet harmony, but people are unable to perceive it because they are accustomed to it. This likewise portrays humanity – we have many beautiful creatures, but we do not appreciate them because they are so common.[353] According to Oswald Bayer, this "Pythagoreanism" may refer to Luther's "natural theology." In other words, the wonders of creation surround us, but we are deaf and blind to them until faith opens us to the creation.[354] One may suppose that Luther does not deny there is a *harmony of the spheres*, but this is of little interest to him and does not relate to music. In this sense, Luther is closer to Tinctoris, who taught that in order to know music, one should play musical instruments rather than look at the stars.[355]

In this concise treatment of musical cosmology, Luther moves swiftly on to a more concrete and, for him, meaningful connection – the dependence of music and physics. Compared to the speculative tradition, this is clearly a realistic trait. The physiological nature of sound, while self-evident, is nonetheless wondrous. Furthermore, all creatures are involved in music. Universal music does not refer to the planetary orbits or the harmony of the spheres, but simply the physical phenomenon of sound that anyone can perceive. In the German version

---

352 According to Kleineidam (1992, 64) the textbook of music in Erfurt University was Johannes de Muris' mathematical treatise entitled *Musica speculativa* (1323). On the other hand, Junghans (1984, 38–39) argues that the music instruction at Erfurt was influenced by the more practical approach of Johannes Tinctoris.

353 WA 46, 493–495. The same thought is expressed in Lectures on Genesis: "Pythagoras fabulatus est de motu Sphaerarum coelestium, sive id ex se ipso, sive ex patribus habuit: quod motus isti assiduo suavissimum concentum edant: Sed mortalium animos et aures ista assiduitate stupefactos, ut non exaudiant eos amplius." (WA 43, 444, 13–17).

354 Bayer 2008, 106–112.

355 At this point I must disagree with Paul Helmer, who claims, "'Sounding number' is a concept fundamental to Luther's understanding of music and one that seems to have eluded Luther scholars to this day." The truth underlying Helmer's position is that the contemporary English translations have failed to render *numero sonoro* accurately. In other respects, Helmer places too much weight on numerus as the sole principle of Luther's musical thought, conjecturing that Luther "would definitely have been exposed to such ideas" as the numerical symbolism in Dufay's motets. (Helmer 2009, 153–154, 159–160) I agree with Guicharrousse (1995, 245–246): "Officiellement, la musique est toujours enseignée à l'université dans le cadre des mathématiques, mais cette tutelle et de plus en plus perçue comme un anachronisme. Les quelques restes de l'ancienne conception repérables dans l'œuvre de Luther sont tout au plus des vestiges d'un passé déjà révolu."

of the text, Luther suggests the example of a stick struck through the air.[356] This is not only a realistic but also a "democratic" approach to music, as one does not need to be an expert to understand music. Furthermore, the physical explanation of music, of vibration of airwaves, is for Luther not a reductionist notion, that is, not to say that music is *just-a-vibration-of-airwaves*. Rather, the vibration is an awe-inspiring fact, a good starting point for a theology of music. In other words, how can vibration of air produce the world of sound and harmony even though air itself is the least musical of all things? It is a miracle, and it is music in the status of potentiality. As such, it is a gift and the creation of God. This is similar to the matter without form in the beginning of creation. Formless matter was not something prior to God's creation, as Augustine believed. For Augustine, the formless matter was almost nothing (*paene nihil*) out of which God created heaven and earth.[357] By contrast, Luther believed that God created the world absolutely out of nothing. Though initially formless, by the force of its mere being it was a creation of God. Being and sounding forth this chaotic matter shows that music is implanted in everything that is. In short, music is not an enigma, but a gift.[358]

3.2.1.2 Music of nature: birdsong in particular

It is possible to argue that God created the components of musical phenomena: sound, pitch, rhythm, and timbre. Living creatures then make music from these components. However, this does not apply to Luther's idea of music, for concomitant with his view of continuous creation, Luther sees God as the agent in all music. The next stage of music introduces the living beings as well as the notion of beauty:

---

356 "Ja auch die Lufft/so doch unsichtbar und unbegreifflich ist/wenn man darein schlegt mit einem stabe/so klinget sie." Leaver 2007, 320.

357 Confessiones XII 8, 8: "tu enim, domine, fecisti mundum de materia informi, quam fecisti de nulla re paene nullam rem … terra autem ipsa quam feceras informis materies erat, quia invisibilis erat et incomposita, et tenebrae super abyssum. de qua terra invisibili et incomposita, de qua informitate, de quo paene nihilo faceres haec omnia quibus iste mutabilis mundus constat." Juntunen (1996, 63 n. 95) reads paene nihil as not totally nothing, but a lower way of being. According to Schwanke (2004, 52–53) Luther says of this tohu-wa-bohu, that it is already distinguished out of nothing by God and that it does not have the ability to take a form of its own (eigengeschöpfliches Gestaltungsvermögen).

358 Wetzel (1954, 159–165) compares Luther's position to that of Adam of Fulda, who was a full-fledged exponent of harmonia mundi. Luther approves Fulda's numerical position but makes it theological. Adam believes that God has created the harmony of the world and now it is the task of a musician to find it out. That is, God has caused, rather than created it. For Luther, instead, from the beginning to the end, music is the work of God.

> Music is still more wonderful in living things, especially birds, so that David, the most musical of all the kings and minstrel of God, in deepest wonder and spiritual exultation praised the astounding art and ease of the song of birds when he said in Psalm 104, "By them the birds of the heaven have their habitation; they sing among the branches."[359]

What is especially delightful for Luther in birdsong is its "art and ease" (*peritia et certitudo*), which are also the standards of musical craftsmanship. The German version describes a nightingale at length, which is Luther's favorite among the musicians of nature:

> This noble art has its image in all creatures Ah with what delightful music the Almighty Lord has blessed his song-master, the dear nightingale, together with his young scholars and many thousands of birds in the air, that each kind has its own mode and melody, its delightful sweet voice and fantastic coloratura, that no one on earth can comprehend.[360]

Several strophes of praise also occur in *Frau Musica*, especially to the song of the nightingale. "For our dear Lord she sings her song / In praise of him the whole day long." For Luther, birdsong was therefore a kind of musical ideal. The song of the nightingale is characterized as sweet (*lieblich*) and its effect is that it makes everyone happy (*macht alles froelich uberal*).[361]

The best human music recalls this cheerfulness of birdsong. The excellence of the music by Josquin des Prez was precisely in its freedom and joyfulness, which was akin to the song of a finch.[362] The sense of freedom in Josquin's music made it possible for Luther to state that God has also preached the Gospel through music, *Sic Deus praedicavit euangelium etiam per musicam*. Birdsong is the paragon of creation's praise to its creator. So exemplifying the reciprocity of

---

359 WA 50, 369, 6 – 11: "Sed mirabilior est Musica in animantibus, praesertim volucribus, vt Musicissimus ille Rex et diuinus psaltes Dauid cum ingenti stupore et exultante spiritu praedicit mirabilem illam volucrum peritiam et certitudinem canendi, [Ps 104, 12] dicens Psalmo centesimo tertio, 'Super ea volucres coeli habitant, de medio ramorum dant voces.'"

360 Leaver 2007, 315, 320: "Das also diese edle Kunst in allen Creaturen ihr bildnus hat. Ach wie eine herrliche Musica ists / damit der Allmechtige HERR im Himel seinen Sangmeister / die liebe Nachtigal / sampt jren jungen Schülern / und so viel tausend mal vögel in der Lufft / begnadet hat / do ein jedes geschlecht seine eigene ahrt und Melodey / seine herrliche süsse stim und wünderliche Coleratur hat / die kein Mensch auff Erden erlangen noch begreiffen kann."

361 WA 35,484,11 – 16: "Die beste zeit im jar ist mein, / Da singen alle Voegelein, / Himel und erden ist der vol, / Viel gut gesang da lautet wol. / Voran die liebe Nachtigal / Macht alles froelich vberal."

362 WA Tr 2,1258: "... des alles composition frolich, willig, milde heraus fleust, ist nitt zwungen und gnedigt per regulas, sicut des fincken gesang." For a closer discussion of this Table Talk, see chapter 6.2.2. below.

the gift, birdsong is a both a gift *of* God and gift *to* God. Furthermore, the birds give instruction to humans and embarrass them by their singing. This is particularly true in the light of Matt 6:26, "Consider the birds of the sky." In his commentary on the *Sermon on the Mount,* Luther wants us to be embarrassed by the greed (*geitz*) and concern (*sorge*) we exhibit to support ourselves. In short, birdsong is a living reminder of God's endlessly giving goodness. Compared to humans – who would despair when they do not have a food store for at least two weeks – birds continue to sing though they do not necessarily know where they'll get food tomorrow. God has made birds our masters, to teach us to trust in God and to cast all our troubles on him. And they teach us to recall the words of *The Small Catechism*, "God provides me with all I need, daily, without any merit of my own." Whereas humans should be wiser than all other creatures, they have become sufficiently deranged to believe no creature could teach them, yet a little bird would be their master, although it has neither the Bible nor reason as a guide.[363] Luther's favorite bird, the nightingale, is depicted in this text as nearly singing itself to death out of joy. Besides, the nightingale characteristically can only live freely. A nightingale would be safe in a cage and would not have to toil for its food, but it prefers freedom and trusts God's protection. "It sings all night and practically shrieks its lungs out. It is happier in the woods than cooped up in a cage."[364]

3.2.1.3 The human voice

Despite all Luther's appreciation of birdsong, compared to the human voice it is an incomplete form of music. From the standpoint of theology of culture, it is useful to notice that human action makes God's creation even more perfect. Compared to the human voice the music of nature is almost unmusical.

> And yet, compared to the human voice, all this hardly deserves the name of music, so abundant and incomprehensible is here the munificence and wisdom of our most gracious Creator. Philosophers have labored to explain the marvelous instrument of the human voice: how

---

363 WA 32 I, 461, 5 – 462, 19.

364 WA 32 I, 462, 26 – 35: "Darumb Wenn du eine nachtgal hoerest, so hoerestu den feinsten prediger, als der dich dieses Euangelij vermanet, nicht mit schlechten blossen worten sondern mit der lebendigen that und exempel, weil sie die gantze nacht singet und gellet sich schir zu tod und ist viel froelicher im wald denn wenn sie im vogelbawr gefangen ist, da mans mit allem vleis warten mus und doch selten gedeiet odder lebendig bleibt, als solt es damit sagen: Jch wolt viel lieber jnn des Herrn kuchen sein, der himel und erden geschaffen hat und selbs koch und hauswirt ist und teglich unzelich viel vogelin speiset und erneret aus seiner hand und nicht ein sack vol sondern himel und erden vol kornlin hat."

can the air projected by a light movement of the tongue and an even lighter movement of the throat produce such an infinite variety and articulation of the voice and of words? And how can the voice, at the direction of the will, sound forth so powerfully and vehemently that it cannot only be heard by everyone over a wide area, but also be understood? Philosophers for all their labor cannot find the explanation; and baffled they end in perplexity; for none of them has yet been able to define or demonstrate the original components of the human voice, its sibilation and (as it were) its alphabet, e. g., in the case of laughter – to say nothing of weeping. They marvel, but they do not understand. But such speculations on the infinite wisdom of God, shown in this single part of his creation, we shall leave to better men with more time on their hands. We have hardly touched them.[365]

The German (Figulus) version is remarkably shorter here, as it reduces the phonetic and language theoretical excursus of the Latin preface:

> Heathen philosophers have labored to explain how the human tongue can wonderfully express the thoughts of the heart, both in speaking and singing, but without success. Truly they have come no further than establishing the 'abc' of music, namely, that of all known creatures only humans can use it to express the joy of their hearts on laughter and their afflictions in weeping.[366]

This is what Luther has to say about the nature of human voice (*vox humana*), in which there are five aspects in this passage to single out. Vox humana is: (1) a gift of God's generosity (*munificentia*) and wisdom (*sapientia*). It consists of (2) the physical phonetic sound producing (*motus linguae/gutturis*), which is (3) under human decision (*pro arbitrio animae gubernantis*) and strives to become (4) not only heard, but also understood (*non solum audiri sed et intelligi*). The source of this activity is (5) the thoughts of the heart (*die gedancken des Hertzens*).

The possibility of human speech organs producing audible and understandable sound is also perceived as a miracle elsewhere in Luther's Works. In a 1544 sermon on the Holy Trinity, Luther compares our ignorance of the mystery of

---

365 WA 50, 369, 12–370, 12: "Verum ad humanam vocem omnia sunt prope immusica, tanta est optimi Creatoris in hac vna re supereffusa et incompraehensibilis munificentia et sapientia. Sudarunt Philosophi, vt intelligerent hoc mirabile artificium vocis humanae, quo modo tam leui motu linguae leuiorique adhuc motu gutturis pulsus aer funderet illam infinitam varietatem et articulationem vocis et verborum, pro arbitrio animae gubernantis, tam potenter et vehementer, vt per tanta interualla locorum circulariter ab omnibus distincte non solum audiri, sed et intelligi possit. Sed sudant tantum, nunquam inueniunt, et cum admiratione desinunt in stuporem, Quin nulli adhuc reperti sunt, qui definire et statuere potuerint, quid sit ille sibilus et alphabetum quoddam vocis humanae, seu materia prima, nempe Risus (de fletu nihil dicam). Mirantur, sed non complectuntur. Verum haec speculabilia de infinita sapientia Dei in hac vna creatura relinquamus melioribus et ociosioribus, nos vix gustum attingimus."
366 Leaver 2007, 316.

the Trinity to our ignorance of matters in general. He argues that little as we understand how a seed becomes a plant, or how a human body grows, so little we understand how the human tongue produces so many different sounds that can be heard and understood by so many people.[367] This notion also has bearing on sacramental theology. In *the Supper of Christ* (1528), Luther expounds on Christ's real presence in the Eucharist. When a preacher speaks, his voice is a single voice, although dozens, hundreds, or thousands of ears might simultaneously hear it. If God can do this with a physical voice (Luther uses an expression that is typical to him, and of importance below, *mit eyner leiblichen stymme*), why could he not make the body of Christ be in several places at the same time? After all, Christ's risen body passed through stone much more easily than any voice.[368]

It is worth noting that the issue at stake in this passage is the understanding of music (*vox*) and not of words. This has not been generally noticed, due to the scholarly emphasis that has focused more on the relationship of music and text. Moreover, the fact that this text is a preface to a motet collection – in other words, music with text – has prevented scholars from seeing that words are not an issue here.[369] Luther makes a subtle move in language philosophy and presents music as the primary language. Here, music is not derived from spoken language, but vice versa, *speech is a species of music*. Music is therefore the basic

---

367 WA 21, 522, 14 – 20: "Wer hat je ersehen oder sagen koennen, wie es zugehet, das ein bletlin aus einem bawm wechset oder ein koernlin zur wurtzel wird, und eine kirschen aus der bluet durch holtz und kern wechset? Item, wie eines Menschen Leib und Glieder zusehens wachsen und zunemen, Oder was doch ist das sehen der augen, Wie es zugehet, das die Zunge so mancherley unterschieden stimme und wort machet, welche in so viel Ohren und Hertzen unterschiedlich gehen?"

368 StA 4,98, 25 – 99,14: "Es stehet da ein prediger / vnd predigt / Seine stym ist ein einige stymme, die aus seinem munde gehet und ynn seinem munde gemacht wird vnd ist / Noch kompt die selbige einige stym / so an einem ort ist / nemlich ynn seinem munde / ynn vier, funfftausent odder zehen tausent oren ynn einem augenblick / Vnd ist doch kein andere stym ynn den selbigen viel tausent oren / denn die ynn des predigers munde ist / vnd ist zu gleich ynn einem augenblick ein einige stym / ym munde des predigers / vnd allen oren des volcks / als were sein mund vnd yhr ohren on alles mittel ein ort / da die stymme were. Lieber / kan Gott solchs thun mit einer leiblichen stymme / warumb solt ers nicht viel mehr thun konnen mit dem leibe Christi / ob er gleich an einem ort were (wie sie sagen) vnd dennoch zugleich an vielen orten warhafftig ynn brod vnd wein sein als ynn zweyen ohren? weil sein leib viel geschwinder und leichter ist denn keine stymme / vnd ist yhm alle creatur durchleufftiger denn die lufft der stymme ist / wie er das ym grabe stein beweiset hat / Sintemal kein stym so leicht durch einen stein faren kan / als Christus leib thet."

369 This holds at least for the following commentaries of this text: Leaver 2007, Begbie 2007, Block 2002, Krummacher 1997, and Bader 1996. Only quite recently has Britta Emrich (2010, 69 – 80) dedicated several pages to the ideas expressed in this paragraph.

language of humanity, which includes speech, laughter, and weeping as well. Music is also comprehensive; while the spoken language is proper to express matters of understanding, music can express and understand the human will and emotions.

According to Luther, philosophers have come no further than realizing that only humans can use their voice to express their joy or affliction. One could ask Luther, what exactly makes the use of human voice so different from birdsong that these two forms could not even be compared (*sunt prope immusica*)? Furthermore, are not euphoric and dysphoric sound signals found among animals? The key to the answer is the mental vocabulary used here, the decision (*arbitrium*), to understand (*intelligi*), and the human heart (*Hertz*). Human laughter or weeping is not merely a sensory response to outward impulses, as joy or affliction is a state of the heart, a frame of mind, or an affect. The text continues with the concept of music as the ruler of human affects (*domina et gubernatrix affectuum humanorum*), which is the subject of the next chapter of this study. Somewhat later in the *Encomion*, Luther claims that the gift of language combined with the gift of voice was given to humans to let them know they should praise God *verbo et Musica*. Thereafter, Luther makes the following observations on the diversity of human voices:

> For even a comparison between different men will show how rich and manifold our glorious Creator proves himself in distributing the gifts of music, how much men differ from each other in voice and manner of speaking so that one amazingly excels the other. No two men can be found with exactly the same voice and manner of speaking, although they often seem to imitate each other, the one as it were being the ape of the other.[370]

That God has given humans different kinds of voices and musical talents illustrates Luther's idea of vocation. That all human beings have a voice of their own is a sign of the creator's prolific goodness and is also the source of artistic creativity. People need not imitate one another, as everyone has a genuinely unique voice of his or her own.[371] To know someone by voice is also a theolog-

---

370 WA 50, 372, 5–10: "Iam si comparationem feceris inter ipsos homines, videbis quam multiplex et varius sit Creator gloriosus in donis Musicae dispertitis, quantum differat homo ab homine in voce et verbo, vt alius alium mirabiliter excellat, negant enim posse duos homines inueniri similis per omnia vocis et loquelae, etiam si saepius imitari alii alios videantur, velut alii aliorum simiae."

371 Guicharrousse (1995, 99–100) mentions – not directly quoting this paragraph – that the ape was a diabolical animal in medieval symbolism, which was also used by Luther in that sense; WA 47, 686, 20. If the allusion to apes is understood in a negative sense, one could hear the echo of Plato's Republic, where the philosopher forbids all musical instruments and tonoi which imitate something. Plato: Republic, Book X, 603a-607a.

ically significant matter. For example, Jesus said of the good shepherd, "the sheep follow him, for they know his voice" (John 10:4), and after the resurrection, Mary Magdalene recognized the Lord not by his appearance but by his voice when he called her name (John 20:16).[372]

3.2.1.4 Art music

The particular benefit of music is its ability to move and express human emotions. That is the reason why the human voice (*vox humana*) is a higher form of music than birdsong. This becomes even more apparent in the nearly ecstatic manner in the fourth and highest stage of music, *musica artificialis*. To Luther, the best example of this is a four-voice motet, where other voices dance around the tenor:

> But when (musical) learning is added to all this and artistic music which corrects, develops, and refines the natural music, then at last it is possible to taste with wonder (yet not to comprehend) God's absolute and perfect wisdom in his wondrous work of music. Here it is most remarkable that one single voice continues to sing the tenor, while at the same time many other voices play around it, exulting and adorning it in exuberant strains and, as it were, leading it forth in a divine roundelay, so that those who are at least bit moved to know nothing more amazing in this world.[373]

Natural music is corrected (*corrigat*), developed (*excolat*), and refined (*explicet*) by art music. In other words, the skills of musical composition improve the gifts of creation. It is noteworthy that Luther does not proclaim that music is a work of God (*opus Dei*) until he speaks about art music. Here the presence of God is revealed in the immediate delight of music, and a good composer can make the goodness of natural music perceivable. Luther uses the same type of expressions when describing how he himself composes and arranges music. In a letter to Johann Agricola (May 1530) Luther wrote:

---

372 WA 11, 409, 20 – 28; WA 28, 455, 14 – 27. Emrich (2010, 84) concludes that those who listen to a sermon are the only ones to decide whether that sermon is the voice of Christ or not. The criterion is, whether the sermon awakens the listeners' faith and trust in Christ.

373 WA 50, 372, 11–373, 4: "Vbi autem tandem accesserit studium et Musica artificialis, quae naturalem corrigat, excolat et explicet, Hic tandem gustare cum stupore licet (sed non comprehendere) absolutam et perfectam sapientiam Dei in opere suo mirabili Musicae, in quo genere hoc excellit, quod vna et eadem voce canitur suo tenore pergente, pluribus interim vocibus circum circa mirabiliter ludentibus, exultantibus et iucundissimis gestibus eandem ornantibus, et velut iuxta eam diuinam quandam choream ducentibus, vt iis, qui saltem modice afficiuntur, nihil mirabilius hoc seculo extare videatur."

> I chanced to find a piece of paper on which was written this old song arranged for three voices. I cleansed (*expurgavi*), corrected (*correxi*) and improved (*emendavi*) it, added a fourth voice, and also quickly prepared a text for the music.[374]

To purify music is not to reduce it to a simple unison chant, as Karlstadt and Zwingli preferred to do. Instead, the objective is to adorn and to exult music, and to make it flourish through many voices.

Musica artificialis in the sixteenth-century context does not necessarily pertain to "art music" in the modern sense. Instead, *musica artificialis* can be music produced by humans, "artistic" or not. As Hermann Abert emphasized, in the sixteenth-century world, there were neither "musicians" nor the "public" in today's sense. There were undoubtedly professionals and craftsmen of music, but all people were creatively active in music, in a manner that is hard to perceive today. Many beautiful melodies of the time – hymn tunes and others – have no known composer. Music was a matter of social cohesion rather than artistic self-expression.[375] However, Luther's wording in *Encomion musices* suggests deliberately artistic music.[376] Moreover, this is a preface to a polyphonic motet collection and Luther is praising precisely that type of music.

Theologically, there is no doubt that Luther considered a composer such as Josquin des Prez to be "gifted" (in the sense of "talented"). But at the same time, Luther maintains that music is a gift of God and not of men. A composer's activities, as well as that of a musician, are works of God. For Luther, human work contradicts God's work when concerning the question of justification. In other matters, the phrase holds, *omnia nostra opera tu agis in nobis,* "all that we have accomplished you have done in us" (Isa 26:12). Commenting on these words, Luther observes that all true teaching and moral behavior in the Church, as well as all spiritual gifts, are the works of God and not our own, and this is the true pride of the church.[377] Needless to say, music is also one of our works that God performs through us. God gives gifts to us in order that we could benefit others. In *Table Talk* Luther refers to the communal character of music by saying that the task of a composer is to bear the fruits of his/her work for someone else to enjoy:

---

374 WA Br 5, 321, 8–10.
375 Abert 1924, 108–110.
376 Söhngen 1967, 85, note 186.
377 WA 30 II 146, 16–21: "'Quoniam omnia nostra opera tu agis in nobis.' Haec est gloriacio nostra firma, quia omnia opera ecclesiae in verbo et moribus sunt [non] propria sua, sed dei ipsius, ideo perdurabunt, quia confidit in deo et non in seipso. Lege sich der Tewffel wider sie. Omnia enim dona spiritus, Verbum, fides, Charitas, potencia, iusticia, opulencia non est sua, sed divina et ipsius dei, quis impiorum illos impugnabit? quia non sunt scilicet nostra, sed dei."

When a musician composes and works, others benefit of it. The same happens in everything else: The one preaches and the other is edified, one sows and the other harvests
(says Christ).[378]

According to the above stated model of reciprocity, as receivers of God's gifts, humans become givers to others. This act of giving does not want anything in return. The sower and the harvester are different persons (John 4:37). The composer is thus depicted as an unselfish giver because someone else benefits in terms
of enjoyment from his/her efforts. There is no mention of payment or artistic recognition, although these are not excluded. The work of a composer is to serve
his/her neighbors with the gift of music.

3.2.2 The excellence of music as a gift of God

Luther expressed some puzzling statements, namely that music is "the greatest"
or "an excellent" gift of God. These could easily be dismissed as rhetorical moves
bearing no theological import. Moreover, the *optimum donum* quotes are from
Table Talk, which are relatively untrustworthy as sources. As necessary as it is
to be cautious against over-interpreting Luther's personally positive attitude toward music, considering *Musica optimum Dei donum* merely as a product of a
music-lover's enthusiasm is not a valid claim. The idea of music as an excellent
gift of God is consistent throughout Luther's works. It is certainly true that music
cannot be regarded as "the best gift of God" in an absolute sense. That kind of
solution would result in insuperable difficulties. For example, how could music
be better than the Son of God, who has been given on our behalf, or the Holy
Spirit that the Father sends, or the Father, who has given himself to us as Father?

A tenable way to understand music as the best gift of God is to see it as the
most *paradigmatic* gift. Music therefore conveys the idea of gift in an optimal
way – it is something that God gives us out of his fatherly goodness. Furthermore, it is something that is not merely given, but also received in the sense
that it becomes ours. Music is also a gift that is given further when we praise
our God with music. When Luther expounds what kind of gift music is in *Encomion*, it does not suffice for him to make only a scholarly definition. If that were
the case, "there is nothing without a sounding number" would suffice. That
music is a gift of God means that it has an impact on us; it causes a response
and makes a change in our behavior. The nature of music as a gift of God be-

---

378 WA Tr 1, 555: "Sicut musicus componit et laborat, alius fruitur, sic fit in omnibus aliis. Alius
praedicat, alius fruitur. Alius seminat, alius metit (ait Christus)."

comes more readily apparent only when the ecstatic "divine roundelay" is experienced in an elaborate motet. Luther's concern in music is its beauty and its power to move and to comfort humans, and this emphasis is related to his view on God. Luther does not depict God with detached scholastic terminology, but always in terms of what God gives. Music is for Luther *theologiae proxima*,[379] something compared in strength to nothing else than the Word of God. Explaining what is common between theology (or Word of God) and music, Luther states that they both create a calm and joyful disposition, thus expelling the devil.[380] In short, music and the Word of God have the same kind of *modus operandi*. Recalling Luther's comments on how faith works in our heart in the *Sermon on the Good Works*, it is instructive to look how similarly he writes about the role of music in the church in his *Hymnal Preface* of 1545:

> Sing to the Lord a new song [Ps 96:1]. For God has cheered our hearts and minds through his dear Son, whom he gave for us to redeem us from sin, death, and the devil. He who believes this earnestly cannot be quiet about it. But he must gladly and willingly sing and speak about it so that others also may come and hear it. And whoever does not want to sing and speak of it shows that he does not believe and that he does not belong under the new and joyful testament, but under the old, lazy, and tedious testament.[381]

The circle of giving is initiated in God's act of salvation, which in turn affects the human heart. As a result of the joy experienced in the heart, a song arises both as an expression of gratitude to God and as an invitation to others to participate in the gifts of God.

Music has certain characteristics that closely connect it to theology. An effortless way to understand how music and theology are *coniunctissima* is to

---

379 WA Tr 3, 3815: "Musica est insigne donum Dei et theologiae proxima"; WA 30 II, 696, 12: "Proximum locum do Musicae post Theologiam."

380 WA BR 5, 639, 12–17: "Et plane iudico, nec pudet asserere, post theologiam esse nullam artem, quae musicae possit aequari, cum ipsa sola post theologiam id praestet, quod alioqui sola theologia praestat, scilicet quietem et animum laetum, manifesto argumento, quod diabolus, curarum tristium et turbarum inquietarum autor, ad vocem musicae paene similiter fugiat, sicut fugit ad verbum theologiae. WA 50, 371, 1–2: Musicam esse vnam, quae post verbum Dei merito celebrari debeat, domina et gubernatrix affectuum humanorum. "

381 LW 53, 333; WA 35, 477, 5–12: "Singet dem HERRN ein newes lied, Singet dem HERRN alle welt. Denn Gott hat unser hertz und mut froelich gemacht, durch seinen lieben Son, welchen er fuer uns gegeben hat zur erloesung von sunden, tod und Teuffel. Wer solchs mit ernst gleubet, der kans nicht lassen, er mus froelich und mit lust dauon singen und sagen, das es andere auch hoeren und herzu komen. Wer aber nicht dauon singen und sagen wil, das ist ein zeichen, das ers nicht gleubet und nicht ins new froeliche Testament, Sondern unter das alte, faule, unlustige Testament gehoeret."

say the Word of God turns easily to music. Besides that, there is a paradigmatic affinity between them, and several aspects are common to music and the word of God, as Luther understands it. These aspects are to be investigated further in this study:

1. Music is a completely outward, physical phenomenon. In contrast to the spiritualist reformers, Luther wanted to emphasize the importance of the physical world as the bearer of spiritual reality. There is no inner word without the outer word. There is no inner meaning of baptism without the outward sign of baptizing.

2. Music is an aural and auditory phenomenon. To Luther, the Word of God is foremost the word that is proclaimed and heard. He mentions often the fact that Christ himself wrote nothing and even the apostles did not write extensively. This means that the word of God proceeds through hearing.

3. Music moves human emotions. When the word of God is sung, it moves both human intellect and emotions (*affectus*). Faith grasps the whole personhood. The depths of the human will are inaccessible except to music and the word of God.

4. Music is a tool to be used against the devil. The devil wants people to lose faith and become insecure and sad. Music, among other earthly pleasures and the Word of God, is one of the most powerful tools against "the spirit of sadness."

3.2.3 The reciprocity of the gift of music: Praise.

3.2.3.1 Singing praise as Christian service

The categorically giving goodness of the Triune God evokes a response of praise in us. Whereas there are few texts concerning music in Luther's Works, the problem with the theme of praise (*laus*, *Lob*) is that it is an embarrassment of riches. Praise and music are nevertheless mutually interconnected. First, praising God is the lot of humans in paradise. In his *Lectures on Genesis*, Luther outlines what the Sabbath service would have been like in a state of innocence:

> This tree of the knowledge of good and evil, or the place where trees of this kind were planted in large number, would have been the church at which Adam, together with his descendants, would have gathered on the Sabbath day. And after refreshing themselves from the tree of life he would have praised God and lauded Him for the dominion over all the creatures on the earth which had been given to mankind. Psalms 148 and 149 suggest a kind of liturgy for such thanksgiving, where the sun, the moon, the stars, the fish, and the dragons are commanded to praise the Lord. Yet every one of us could have composed a better and more perfect psalm than any of these if we had been begotten by Adam in innocence. Adam

would have extolled the greatest gift, namely, that he, together with his descendants, was created according to the likeness of God.[382]

Liturgy in paradise would have consisted mainly, if not exclusively, of singing praise. However, the situation did not completely change after the Fall. Commenting on Cain and Abel's sacrifice (Gen 4:3, 4), Luther notices that Adam and Eve taught their children to offer praise. However, the first sacrifices were not meant to propitiate God or atone for sins, but they were sacrifices of thanksgiving in advance for the coming of Christ.[383] Subsequently, Luther explains Gen 4:26, "At that time calling upon the name of the Lord was begun" to mean that calling upon the name of the Lord is an excellent definition of what it means to worship God. Calling upon the name of the Lord is the work of the First Table (of Ten Commandments). This includes fear of God, trust in God, confession, prayer, preaching, and thanksgiving. From the work of the First Table follow spontaneously the works of the Second Table.[384] All aspects of life became involved in the circle of praise. Praising God and calling upon his name is the fountain from which all good works flow. In *The Beautiful Confitemini* (1530), Luther determines the two sacrifices and "divine services" of the New Testament. They are both thanksgiving to God, which means "preaching, teaching, singing, and confessing." The first is our humiliation, which is great, broad, long, and unending sacrifice. It is offered when God corrects us through his Word in all our works and reduces our holiness, wisdom, and strength to nothing so that by the time we die, our pride, trust, and confidence in our own efforts and knowledge is dead. Only then one can truly sing, "I thank thee that thou hast humbled me" (Ps 118:21). The other sacrifice

---

382 LW 1, 105 – 106; WA 42, 80, 19 – 28; "Haec igitur arbor scientiae boni et mali, seu locus, in quo magno numero huiusmodi arbores fuerunt consitae, fuisset Ecclesia, ad quam Adam cum posteritate sua die Sabbato convenisset, et post refectionem ex arbore vitae praedicasset Deum, et laudasset eum pro tradito dominio omnium creaturarum super terram. Sicut Psalmus 148. et 149. quandam formam talis gratiarum actionis proponunt, ubi sol, luna, stellae, pisces, dracones iubentur laudare Dominum. Quanquam nullus tam eximius est Psalmus, quo non unusquisque nostrum meliorem et perfectiorem potuisset componere, si in innocentia ab Adamo propagati essemus. Praedicasset Adam summum beneficium, quod esset cum posteritate sua conditus ad similitudinem Dei."

383 WA 42,183,36 – 40: "Quia enim Spiritu sancto pleni sunt et illuminati cognitione venturi Christi, hanc ipsam spem futurae liberationis liberis suis proponunt et hortantur eos ad gratitudinem tam misericordi Deo praestandam. Nullum enim alium finem traditorum sacrificiorum fuisse statuendum est."

384 WA 42, 242, 15 – 18: "Hoc cum fit, sequentur quasi sua sponte etiam secundae tabulae cultus seu opera. Est enim impossibile, ut, qui primae tabulae cultus praestat, non etiam praestet secundam tabulam."

is that God comforts and helps us so that we can rejoice before him and in him, completing the psalm verse "... and become my salvation." This is the Christian thanksgiving offering[385] Thanksgiving is the true Christian sacrifice. This is the only gift we can give to God.[386] From the viewpoint of gift exchange, it is important to note that, according to Luther, honor (*ere*) is the only thing God holds for him-self. Everything else is given to us. There is nothing else for us to give to God than honor, which means to "confess, say, sing, live, act, and suffer in a manner that attests that everything belongs to God."[387]

Luther connects "praise" with "preaching" and "confessing." For the present study, the connection to "singing" is important because praising God is irrevocably musical. In the preface to the New Testament, Luther notes that *euangelion* is a Greek word for good news that one sings and speaks of and is happy about. Note-worthy is the word "order" (*davon man singet, saget und frölich ist*). It is hardly arbitrary, since Luther takes as a biblical witness the Israelites who "*sungen und sprungen und frölich waren*" out of joy when David defeated Goliath. Accordingly, in the next paragraph, Luther presents the human response to the salvific action of God as "singing, thanking, praising God and being happy forever" (*Dauon sie singen, dancken, Gott loben vnd froelich sind ewiglich*). Thus music is mentioned

---

385 WA 31 I 169, 24 – 171, 2: "Das sind die opffer und Gottes dienst, die jm newen Testament jm thor des HERREN geuebt werden von den gerechten und Christen, Nemlich das sie Gott dancken und loben mit predigen, leren, singen, bekennen. Und der selbigen opffer sind zwey: Eines ist unser demuetigen ... Das ander opffer ist, Wenn uns Got dagegen auch widderumb troestet und hilfft, das der geist und newer mensch so viel zu neme, so viel das fleisch und allter mensch abnimpt, gibt uns jhe lenger, jhe groesser und reicher gabe und hilfft uns jmer siegen und obligen, das wir froelich fuer jhm und jnn jhm sind ... Wer das thut, der singet diesen vers: Jch dancke dir, das du mein heil, helffer und heiland bist. Dis ist auch ein ewiges, grosses, teglichs opffer bey den gerechten ym thor des HERRN Vnd hie mit verwirfft er vnd hebt auff alle opffer des alten testaments, welche sind bilder vnd figur gewesen dieser danckopffer vnd haben beide von frumen vnd bosen geschehen mugen, Aber diese danckopffer kan niemand thün, denn allein die frumen, gerechten odder Christen."

386 WA 40 II, 609. 7 – 9: "In novo testamento non cultus quam unicus, praestantissimus, quam celebrare, laudare filium illum dei, manifeste cantemus, praedicemus, legamus"; WA 10 I 2, 80, 20 – 24: "Alle das gutt, das wyr gott thun mugen, das ist: lob unnd danck, wilchs auch der recht eynige gotisdienst ist, wie er selb sagt p̄s. 49: Das opffer des lobs preysset mich, und das ist der weg, durch wilchen ich yhm weyße die selickeyt gotis. Alle ander gutter empfahen wyr von yhm, auff das wyr solch opffer des lobs dafur geben."

387 WA 2, 94, 18 – 22: "Dan gottis ere das erst, letzt, hochst ist, das wyr im geben kunnen, und er auch nichts meher sucht und fordert. Wir konnen im auch sunst nichts geben, dan alle ander guter gibt er uns, die ere aber behelt er ym allein, das wir erkennen, sagen, singen, leben, wircken, und alles thun unnd leydenn betzeugenn, das gottis alle dinck seynd."

three times in a concise text where Luther wants to depict the very essentials of the Gospel.[388]

As a language of praise, music belongs to the essence of the church. Luther's definition of the true Christian church is found in *On the Councils and the Church* (1539). He establishes seven hallmarks of the church (*notae ecclesiae*), of which the sixth has a musical character:

> Sixth, the holy Christian people are externally recognized by prayer, public praise, and thanksgiving to God. Where you see and hear the Lord's Prayer prayed and taught; or psalms or other spiritual songs sung, in accordance with the word of God and the true faith … The psalms too are nothing but prayers in which we praise, thank and glorify God … However, we are now speaking of prayers and songs which are intelligible and from which we can learn and by means of which we can mend our ways. The clamor of monks and nuns and priests is not prayer, nor is it praise to God.[389]

The church is recognized by prayer, praise, and thanksgiving in public (*gebet, Gott loben und dancken oeffentlich*). Where psalms and spiritual songs are sung, there is the holy, Christian church. The concern at this point is not only singing, but also singing with understanding (*verstentlich*), singing in order to learn to know God, and to become better persons (*daraus man lernen und sich bessern kan*). Besides the happy noise, the subject matter and the moral behavior

---

388 WA DB 6, 3, 23–4, 11: "Denn Euangelion ist eyn kriechisch wortt, vnd heyst auff deutsch, gute botschafft, gute meher, gutte newzeytung, gutt geschrey, dauon man singet, saget vnd frolich ist, gleych als do Dauid den grossen Goliath vberwand, kam eyn gutt geschrey, vnd trostlich newtzeyttung vnter das Judisch volck, das yhrer grewlicher feynd erschlagen, vnd sie erloset, zu freud vnd frid gestellet weren, dauon sie sungen vnd sprungen vnnd frolich waren, Also ist dis Euangelion Gottis vnnd new testament, eyn gutte meher vnd geschrey ynn alle wellt erschollen durch die Apostell, von eynem rechten Dauid, der mit der sund, tod vnnd teuffel gestritten, vnd vberwunden hab, vnnd damit alle die, ßo ynn sunden gefangen, mit dem todt geplagt, vom teuffel vberweldiget gewesen, on yhr verdienst erloset, rechtfertig, lebendig vnd selig gemacht hat, vnd da mit zu frid gestellet, vnd Gott wider heym bracht, dauon sie singen, dancken Gott, loben vnd frolich sind ewiglich, ßo sie des anders fest glawben, vnd ym glawben bestendig bleyben."

389 LW 41, 164;StA 5, 604, 13–24: "Zum sechsten erkennet man eusserlich das heilige Christliche Volck am gebet, Gott loben vnd dancken o(e)ffentlich. Denn wo du sihest und ho(e)rest, das man das Vater vnser betet vnd beten lernet, auch Psalmen oder Geistliche lieder singet, nach dem wort Gottes vnd rechtem glauben, Jtem den Glauben, Zehen gebot vnd Catechismum treibet o(e)ffentlich, Da wisse gewis, das da ein heilig Christlich volck Gottes sey / Denn das gebet ist auch der theuren heilthumb eins, dadurch alles heilig wird, wie S(ankt) Paulus sagt / So sind die Psalmen auch eitel gebet, darin man Gott lobet, dancket und ehret, … Aber wir reden vom gebet und gesenge das verstentlich ist, daraus man lernen und sich bessern kann / Denn der Mu(e)nche, Nonnen, Pfaffen lo(e)ren ist kein gebet auch kein Gotts lob." –

are also involved. Being a sign of the true church, song should not cease for a moment, because a response to the categorical giving of God is the categorical praise of the church. That idea has consequences for the liturgical changes introduced during the Reformation. In *Formula missae* Luther urges the congregation to sing *halleluja* even during Lent since it is the *vox perpetua ecclesiae* and the praise of the Lord's victory that is continuous.[390]

The close connection between singing and believing is indicated in the 1545 hymnal preface, where Luther declares that whoever does not want to sing about the salvation that God has prepared shows that he does not believe at all but is still under the law. This preface is dedicated to the song of the New Testament. Luther begins by depicting the Old Testament service, which was tedious and reluctant and not a good starting point for music because the "heart and mind must be willing if one is to sing."[391] However, the New Testament is different.[392] In his polemic writing *Against Hanswurst* (1541), Luther uses the music in evangelical churches as a proof of their being genuine Christian assemblies, as congregations of the Reformation "hold, believe, sing, and confess" the Apostolic Creed of the ancient church. Thus the close connection becomes apparent between singing and confessing: "We sing the same psalms and praise and thank God with united heart and voice according to the teaching of Christ, the practice of the apostles and the ancient church, and their command to us to follow their example."[393] Although it may seem audacious to include music as one of the hallmarks of the church (*notae ecclesiae*), it has a sound basis in the way the praise and proclamation of the Gospel is portrayed in *On Councils and the Church*.

3.2.3.2 Critical comments on music

There has been sufficient evidence to demonstrate the connection between *laudare* and *canere*, or *loben* and *singen* thus far. Nonetheless, to state that music is *nota ecclesiae* requires that one take into account those texts where Luther seems to state the opposite. There are several places where Luther adopts a critical tone when he speaks about music and musical phenomena such as singing, organ,

---

390 WA 12, 210, 11–12: "Alleluia enim vox perpetua est Ecclesiae, sicut perpetua est memoria passionis et victoriae eius."
391 WA 35, 476, 25–26: "Froelich und lustig mus hertz und mut sein, wo man singen sol."
392 WA 35, 477, 5–12.
393 LW 41, 196; WA 51 ,481, 17–482, 11.

and bells.[394] For example, a case in point is *A Sermon on the New Testament* (1520). The core idea of this sermon is that the closer we are to the way Christ celebrated the Holy Supper with his disciples, the better our service is. Luther explicitly declares that the first Eucharist had no "chasubles, *singing*, or pretentiousness, but solely thanksgiving to God and the use of the sacrament."[395] At this point Luther includes "singing" along with organ, bells, and liturgical vestments as part of the outward traditions and habits that have obscured the meaning of the sacrament. Luther's advice for understanding the Eucharist was to relinquish everything that stimulates our senses, be it clothes, songs, prayers, or gestures. The true meaning of the sacrament is in the words of Christ himself: "Take, eat: this is my body." Without these words, there is nothing in the Eucharist. A noteworthy detail is that Luther admonishes Christians to let go of all outward habits, *until* they understand these words of Christ (*biß das wir zuvor die wort Christi fassen*). At the outset, this criticism toward singing is not meant to be a permanent position. Luther merely wants to increase the status of the words of institution and to focus attention on them.[396] The removal of music is undoubtedly a rhetorical move in this context. Later in the sermon, Luther concedes the meaning of the outer signs to faith, of which the Eucharist is the highest example. God has always connected his word to outer signs, as many incidents of the Old Testament testify. The Eucharist is an outward sign in order that we should be drawn to the inner, spiritual understanding through it, or in Augustinian words, *per corporalia ad incorporalia*.[397] Eventually music serves

---

394 e.g. WA 5, 652, 15–19 (voices, organ); WA 2, 84, 25–31 (singing):WA 6, 452, 11–15 (choirs, organ); WA 10 I 1, 75, 1–5 (bells, singing); WA 10 I 1, 625, 2–10 (organ, bells); StA 1, 338 (musical phenomena in general).

395 StA 1, 290, 22–26: "Dan do Christus selbst / vnd am ersten / diß sacrament einsetzt vnnd die ersten meß hielt und u(e)bet / da war keyn platten / kein casell / kein singen / kein prangen / ßondern allein dancksagung gottis vnd des sacrame(n)ts prauch."

396 StA 1, 291, 12–18: "Wo(e)lle(n) wir recht meß halten vn(d) vorstahn / ßo mussen wir alles faren lassen / was die augen vnd alle synn in dißem handel mugen zeygen vn(d) antragen, es sey kleyd / klang gesang / tzierd / gepett /tragen / heben / legen /odder was da geschehen mag yn der meß / biß das wir zuuor die wort Christi fassen und wol bedencken / damit er die meß volnbracht und eyngesetzt vnd vns zuvolnbringen bevolhen hatt / dan darynnen ligt die meß gantz / mit all yhrem weßen / werck / nutz vnd frucht / on wilche nichts von der meß empfangen wirt."

397 StA 1, 294, 13–18: "Dan wir arme menschen / weyl wir in den funff synnen leben / mu(e)ssen yhe zum wenigsten / ein eußerlich zeychen haben neben den worten, daran wir vns halten und zusammen ku(m)men mugen / doch alßo / das das selb zeychen ein sacrament sey / das ist / das es euserlich sey / und doch geystliche ding hab und bedeut / damit wir / durch das euserliche / in das geystliche getzoge(n) werden / das euserlich mit den augen des leybs / d(as) geystliche, ynnerliche mit den augen des hertzen begreyffen."

to emphasize the words of institution: "May God grant us that we read the Mass in German and *sing* most loudly its most secret words."[398] Moreover, Luther's use of the sacrament is meant to take place within a congregation, where the people "encourage, move, and warm" each other. Although he does not mention singing at this point, singing together is a prominent way to achieve the sense of belonging together. Luther concludes that as long as we stay in this physical existence, we are in need of coming together so that we may kindle in others this faith by our "example, prayer, thankfulness, and praise."[399] In this text, which on the surface treats "singing" as something not belonging to the essence of faith, song as a medium of the Word and as a way to exhort one another is fully acknowledged. On a closer examination, the same position is espoused in other similar passages in Luther's works. His critical comments on music are often aimed at reluctant, superficial singing, to music that does not rise from the bottom of the heart, which he identifies in *On Councils and the Church* as "the clamor of monks and nuns and priests."[400]

3.2.3.2 Eschatological and ecstatic dimensions of praise

Luther considered praise a hallmark of the church and not something to be confined to humans. To Luther, praising God is what the everlasting life is about. In the *Lectures on Hebrews* Luther writes:

> Hell is hell not because punishment is there but because praise of God is not there. Likewise, heaven is not heaven because joy is there, but because praise of God is there, as Ps 84:4 states: 'Blessed are those who dwell in Thy house, ever singing Thy praise. For God gives them pleasure and for this reason they rejoice. Therefore a Christian, as a child of God, must always rejoice, always sing, fear nothing, always be free from care, and always glory in God.[401]

---

398 StA 1, 297, 1–2: "Aber wolt Gott / das wir deutschen meß su deutsch leßen / vn(d) die heymlichsten wort auffs aller hohist sungen."

399 StA 1, 307, 2–7: "So ist auch das vorteyl da / das wir noch ym fleysch leben / vnd nit alle ßo volkomen sein, vns ym geyst zu regiren, Ist vns nodt / das wir leyplich zu sammen kummen / eynis der ander mit seynem exempell / gepeet / lob / vn(d) danck zu solchem glauben entzu(e) nden / wie ich droben gesagt vnd durch leyplich sehen oder empfahen des sacraments vnd testaments / bewegen / mehr vnd mehr pesseren den selben glauben."

400 Block (2002, 50–68) analyzes the places where Luther seems to be critical towards music and discovers that they consider everything other than music itself (like his critique of music in Papal worship).

401 LW 29, 177; WA 57, 176.

The position here is that there is no doubt concerning music being in heaven. Singing is a duty of the angels that the blessed share. Furthermore, singing praise is caused by the ineffable pleasure God gives in heaven. Therefore praise constitutes heaven itself. If one believes in an everlasting life, one *must* sing. Perhaps a consoling notice should be made in favor of those who feel themselves to be non-musical. In the preface to the 1545 hymnal Luther says that those who do not *want* to sing or speak about the faith are still under the old covenant. In other words, it is not about the musical performance, but about the willingness.

As the language of praise, music has the benefit suggested above in discussing the *vox humana* – music can express joy beyond words. Singing is an ecstatic way to praise God. In the First Psalm Commentary, Luther explains Ps 45:1 *Eructavit cor meum verbum bonum:*

> "Augustine says that, in the opinion of some, it was understood in this way: 'My heart uttered a good word, that is, a hymn and praise to Christ, as blasphemy is an evil word.' (And this opinion is not absurd, because the saints cannot 'pour out' the joy of their heart: they can scarcely 'utter' it.)'I speak my works,' that is to say, 'my praises'. For the highest works of man are the praise of God. We cannot pay back anything but praise and confession."[402]

Praising God naturally turns to music because the joy in the saints' hearts transcends all words and music expresses these feelings. Luther begins expounding on this very psalm by saying, "Whenever the word 'song' is used in psalm titles, it must always be understood that such a psalm is one of joy and dancing and is to be sung with a feeling of a rejoicing heart."[403] In a likewise manner, Luther tells about the ecstatic character of music in *Magnificat-commentary (1521)* when he comments on the phrase "my soul magnifies (*magnificat*) the Lord" (Luke 1:46). When we feel the goodness of the Lord, our heart is overwhelmed by joy, so that no words or thoughts seem to be enough. "All words and thoughts fail us, and our whole life and soul must be set in motion, as though all that lived within us wanted to break forth into praise and singing (*singen und*

---

[402] LW 10, 220; WA 3, 261, 38 – 262, 4: "Augustinus autem sic secundum quosdam dicit accipi: Eructavit cor meum verbum bonum, i. e. hymnum et laudem Christo. Sicut blasphemia est verbum malum. (Et hec sententia non est absurda, quia sancti gaudium cordis non possunt effundere, sed vix eructare.) Dico ego opera mea, i. e. laudes: quia summa opera hominis sunt laus Dei, nec possumus aliquid retribuere nisi laudem et confessionem tantum."

[403] WA 3, 253, 6 – 8. "Ubicunque 'Canticum' in titulis habetur, semper debet intelligi, talem psalmum esse gaudii et tripudii et cum affectu exultandi cantandum. Nam Canticum et cantus ex abundantia gaudentis cordis oritur."

sagen)."[404] When the soul experiences the presence and goodness of God it feels more than it can express. Luther says, in accordance with the mystical tradition, that praising God is not a human work at all but "a happy suffering" (*frolich leyden)*.[405] In the *Magnificat commentary* Luther judges church music critically because of claims that some sing without true devotion. On the contrary, when Mary contemplates God's works in her heart she is more sighing than speaking; the few words she utters in her song are full of life, burning with spirit.[406] Although at the top of the ecstatic experience may be complete silence, music expresses ecstatic joy better than words.[407]

Ecstasy is a concept that is rarely combined with Luther's theology.[408] He does not encourage Christians to pursue mystical experiences. Lutheran spirituality is attached to the faithful use of the Word and sacraments, Catechism and hymns. However, he presents the Catechism as a means to attain ecstasy in *A Simple Way to Pray* for the barber Peter (1535). The problem dealt with in this tract is the unwillingness to pray. At the beginning, Luther tells his friend Peter that when he has noticed his own unwillingness to pray, he takes his Psalter, utters aloud the Ten Commandments, the Creed, or other texts. In this respect, it is noteworthy that Luther expressly states that he utters these words aloud (*mündlich*).[409] Although he does not use the word "sing," considering his monastic background, it is highly likely that he sings the psalms. The aim of uttering psalms and Catechism chapters is to warm the heart to prayer.[410] After that, he prays the Lord's Prayer (that Luther presents in the form of a paraphrase). Whenever the heart becomes willing to pray, the exact words are not im-

---

404 LW21, 307, StA 1, 324, 9–13: "Wie viel mehr wirt solch lebendig bewegu(n)g sich regen / szo wir gottes gutte empfinden / die uberschwenglich grosz seind ynn seinen wercken(n) / das vnsz alle wort und gedancken zu wenig werdenn / vnd das gantz leben vn(d) Seele mussen sich bewegen lassen / alsz wolts allisz gerne singen vnd sagen, was ynn vnsz lebet."
405 StA 1, 319–220.
406 StA 1, 339.
407 WA 3, 372, 23–24: "Et hec in disputatione et multiloquio tractari non potest, sed in summo mentis ocio et silentio, velut in raptu et extasi."
408 On Luther and ecstasy, see Ruokanen 1986. For ecstasy in Magnificat, see Ghiselli 2005, 132–137.
409 WA 38, 358, 5–359,3: "ERstlich, wenn ich fuele, das ich durch frembde geschefft oder gedancken bin kalt und unluestig zu beten worden, wie denn das fleisch und der teuffel allwege das gebet wehren und hindern, Neme ich mein Pselterlein, lauffe jnn die kamer oder, so es der tag und zeit ist, jnn die kirchen zum hauffen und hebe an, die Zehen Gebot, den Glauben und, darnach ich zeit habe, ettliche sprueche Christi, Pauli oder Psalmen muendlich bey mir selbs zu sprechen, aller ding, wie die kinder thun."
410 WA 38,360, 1–2: "Wenn nu das hertz durch solch muendlich gesprech erwarmbt und zu sich selbs komen ist [...]"

portant. Luther then advises to listen to the voice of the Holy Spirit. At that point, he is astonishingly close to the spiritualist notion of the "inner word." The implication is that one should stop praying aloud and instead let the Holy Spirit preach in the soul, giving rich and good thoughts. The major difference is that Luther's ecstatic prayer is immediately attached to the Catechism and to the outwardly spoken word.[411] Catechism is nevertheless suggested as a medium for ecstasy. Luther continues with the Commandments and treats them as doctrine, song, confession, and prayer (*lerebüchlin, sangbüchlin, beichtbüchlin, betbüchlin*). After the abounding meditation of the Catechism, the heart – at least – should be concentrated on and warm for prayer. One could ask, if that is the preparation for prayer, then what is prayer? It is not possible to postulate a higher stage of prayer here, for to pray and meditate on the Catechism is real prayer. According to *A Simple Way to Pray*, this is also the Lutheran way to attain ecstasy. Speaking and singing psalms and prayers aloud is emotionally effective, and that shall be the next characteristic of music to be examined more closely.

4 Domina et gubernatrix affectuum humanorum – the power of music

The property of music that makes it God's best gift is its ability to move the human heart. Music is the "mistress and governess of human emotions" (*domina et gubernatrix affectuum humanorum*). This is much more than to merely suggest that music is a device for arousing a pious mood. Furthermore, moving the human *affectus* to love God is the work of Holy Spirit. In order to understand the depth of this issue, the role of affects in Luther's theology should be examined first. Then it is possible to ask how music moves human affects. For Luther, the affective power of music is related to the power of the word, which is primarily the spoken word (*verbum vocale*). This discussion on the musical character of the word is the final analysis presented in this chapter.

---

411 WA 38, 363, 9–16: "Kompt wol offt, das ich jnn einem stuecke oder bitte jnn so reiche gedancken spacieren kome, das ich die andern Sechse lasse alle anstehen, Und wenn auch solche reiche gute gedancken komen, so sol man die andern gebete faren lassen und solchen gedancken raum geben und mit stille zuhoeren und bey leibe nicht hindern, Denn da predigt der Heilige geist selber, Und seiner predigt ein wort ist besser denn unser gebet tausent, Und ich hab auch also offt mehr gelernet jnn einem gebet, weder ich aus viel lesen und tichten hette kriegen koennen."

4.1 The affects in Luther's thinking

4.1.1 The affectivity of Luther's theology

There are various expressions for the affectivity of Luther's theology. Lennart Pinomaa spoke of the *existential* character of Luther's theology, claiming that it is a theology of troubled conscience.[412] In a different sense, Gerhard Ebeling called Luther's hermeneutics existential, meaning that the understanding of the Bible occurs through being moved by the word (*Ergriffenwerden*).[413] Oswald Bayer has written about Luther's *experiential* theology using the key words *oratio, meditatio,* and *tentatio.*[414] In addition, Antti Raunio has emphasized Luther's idea of theology as a *practical* discipline.[415] Lately, Birgit Stolt has paid attention to the "intense emotional undercurrent" of Luther's Bible translation.[416] All these different approaches tend to say that affects play an important part in Luther's theology.

To attest to the affectivity of Lutheranism, *The Small Catechism* expounds on the meaning of the Ten Commandments always beginning with the words, "we must thus fear and love God." The most celebrated account of Lutheran theology is organized emotionally, according to the concupiscible and irascible affects.[417] In the same fashion, *The Large Catechism* is equally affective when it explains the meaning of the word "god":

> A 'god' is the term for that to which we are to look for all good and in which we are to find refuge in all need. Therefore, to have a god is nothing else than to trust and believe in that one with your whole heart. As I have often said, it is the trust and faith of the heart alone that make both God and an idol. If your faith and trust are right, then your God is the true one. Conversely, where your trust is false and wrong, there you do not have the true God. For these two belong together, faith and God. Anything on which your heart relies and depends, I say; that is really your God.[418]

---

412 Pinomaa 1940.

413 Ebeling 1951, 175.

414 Bayer 2007, 32–37. Moreover, Bayer asserts that "Luther does not separate the academic disputation that seeks to ascertain truth from comforting the troubled conscience. Intellectual knowledge about faith is not separated from the affective experience of faith; the art of disputation serves the task of caring for souls" (p. xvi).

415 Raunio 1997.

416 Stolt 2009, 141–147.

417 On fearing and loving God in Luther's catechisms see Beutel 1998, 45–65.

418 BC 386, WA 30, I, 133, 1–8: "Ein Gott heisset das, dazu man sich versehen sol alles guten und zuflucht haben ynn allen noeten. Also das ein Gott haben nichts anders ist denn yhm von hertzen trawen und gleuben, wie ich offt gesagt habe, das alleine das trawen und gleuben des

It is remarkable that "god" here is not the one who is understood to be the first and greatest, but the one on which one's heart relies and whom one trusts. Certainly the intellectual side is involved, but the emphasis is strongly on the affective. For Luther, trust (*[ver]trawen*) was the basic affect. It is the alternative word for faith, which is a focal concept beyond dispute. Without faith, unbelief reigns in the human heart. It is the basic affect of a sinner that is prior to any activity of will or reason.[419] Thus, in place of the basic scholastic pairing of affect as *amor – odium*, there is Luther's theology that postulates the antithesis between *faith* and *unbelief*. In previous scholarship, it is generally taken for granted that Luther's faith is not an opinion of a merciful God. Surprisingly, the deep affectivity of faith has not often been properly grasped.

The affectivity of faith does not refer only to the fact that Luther may explicitly call faith an affect[420] and define unbelief as the affect of self-love, *diligere seipsum*.[421] Knowing God, making theology, and living as a Christian are all affective affairs for Luther. In *Lectures on Hebrews* (1518), Luther makes a division between intellect and affect in relationship with the Word of God (presented here as law). His emphasis is undoubtedly on the affect:

> For by 'mind' and 'heart' (for this is how we are speaking now) it means intellect and affect. For to be in the mind means to be understood; to be in the heart means to be loved. Thus to say that the Law is in the mouth means that it is taught; to say that it is in the ear means that it is heard; to say that it is in the eyes means that it is seen. Therefore it is not enough for the Law to be in the soul and to state objectively that it is there. No, it must be in the soul formally [formaliter], that is, the Law must be written in the heart out of love for the Law.[422]

The law of God is not formally, that is, truly in the heart unless it is affectively grasped. That faith is a matter of heart, not a mere intellectual understanding, is a constant theme throughout Luther's career. In a sermon during the 1540 s

---

hertzens machet beide Gott und abeGott. [Glaube und trawen machet ein Gott.] Jst der glaube und vertrawen recht, so ist auch dein Gott recht, und wideruemb wo das vertrawen falsch und unrecht ist, da ist auch der rechte Gott nicht. Denn die zwey gehoeren zuhauffe, glaube und Gott. Worauff du nu (sage ich) dein hertz hengest und verlessest, das ist eygentlich dein Gott."
419 Mühlen 1992, 105.
420 WA 5,460, 30 – 31: "Nam fides potens affectus est, exerceri vult et quiescere non potest nec sinitur."
421 WA 57, 41, 17: "Nihil est profundius in homine quam ille affectus: diligere seipsum."
422 LW 29, 198; WA 57, 196, 14 – 19: "Nam per 'mentem' et 'cor' intellectum et affectum (ita enim nunc loquimur) accipit. Esse enim in mente est intelligi, esse in corde est diligi. Sic esse in ore legem est eam doceri, esse in aure est audiri, esse in oculis est videri. Proinde non sufficit legem esse et obiective dictam in anima, sed formaliter, id est per dilectionem legis inscriptam in corde esse legem oportet."

Luther ridicules the notion of faith as knowledge of historical facts as "inexperienced and unintelligent" talk. Luther states that when some have once heard or read the Gospel, they have understood and believed it sufficiently, but if there is no change in their hearts, it proves the opinion false. The Gospel is preached and heard repeatedly because it should be fruitful for us, awakening and moving us so that we would have new courage and new joy. Luther says that there will also be new thoughts and new understanding so that intellect is not ruled out, but the most important is that the heart must experience (*erfaren*) and taste (*schmecken*) the resurrection of Christ.[423]

A recurrent word considering affectivity is "heart." Luther states in the *Large Catechism* that trust and faith of the heart makes both God and an idol. Accordingly, he states in *Lectures on Hebrews*, the law must be written in the heart. Luther's theology could well be labeled as "theology of the heart."[424] Yet, there are some preconditions for such an interpretation. First, "heart" today refers simply to "feelings." This kind of understanding immediately makes Luther's theology narrower and renders Christian faith as a mere emotive attitude with no cognitive content. Luther also uses the word "heart" differently. Commenting on Ps 51:10, "Create in me a clean heart, o God," Luther explains that the German word *Herz* stands for a number of Latin terms: soul (*anima*), mind (*intellectus*), will (*voluntas*), and emotion (*affectus*).[425] It is therefore necessary to bear in mind that for Luther, as in Christian theology in general, the heart (*cor, Herz*) is the innermost being of a person as well as the source of thoughts, volitions, and feel-

---

423 WA 21, 224, 19 – 225, 1: "Und nicht so gering noch leicht ding ist umb den Glauben, wie die unverstendigen und unerfarnen Geister wehnen… so da meinen, Glaube sey nichts anders denn die Historia und geschicht gehort haben und wissen, und darnach sich duencken lassen, sie haben alles, was das Euangelium von Christo sagt, wenn sie es ein mal gehort oder gelesen, flugs rein und gar aus verstanden und ausgegleubt, das sie nichts mehr beduerffen daran lernen und gleuben. Aber das solches nichts sey denn ein loser, nichtiger gedancken, beweiset, das sie selbs muessen bekennen, das solche erkendnis der Historien im hertzen gar still, kalt und faul bey jnen ligen bleibt … So doch je dis grosse hohe werck der Aufferstehung Christi darumb geschehen und dazu sol gepredigt werden und also gehoeret und erkand, das es in uns frucht schaffe, unser hertz erwecke und anzuende, new gedancken, verstand und mut, leben und freude, trost und stercke in uns wircke … Und darffest dich keines Glaubens rhuemen, ob du gleich den schaum auff der zungen oder den dhon in den ohren und den traum im gedechtnis von der Historien behalten hast, davon das hertz nichts erferet noch schmecket."
424 As the names of Bengt Hoffman's monograph (1989) and Birgit Stolt's article (2009) suggest.
425 WA 40 II 425, 18 – 20: "Nam quod Latine dicimus 'Animam, Intellectum, Voluntatem, Affectum', haec fere omnia Germani vocabulo Cordis reddunt."

ings.[426] Luther's vocabulary concerning the soul is not fixed. The affect is synonymous sometimes with *voluntas* ("the will") or *motus* ("movement"). When *affectus* is synonymous with *cor* ("heart"), it embraces the innermost being of a human person. However, the innermost being is by no means separable from the human "self." When the affect refers to the "heart," it is not a function of the soul, but instead the source of the soul's functions.[427]

Luther occasionally speaks of the intellect as an affect. In medieval discussion, affection was treated as a separate kind of knowledge, an inchoate understanding that is subordinate to the intellect. Luther states it conversely – the intellect has an affective character. In a Christmas sermon in 1514, Luther discusses at length how we become one with God. To portray how our intellect and affect desire their Object (that is, God), he uses the Aristotelian concepts *materia* and *forma*; our search for God is like matter seeking its form. In themselves, the affect and intellect are nothing, and they become being (*ens*) only when they reach their object, which actually is their being (*esse*) and action (*actus*).[428] This passage has been often analyzed, particularly by Finnish Luther scholars. This Christmas sermon illustrates Luther's thoughts concerning deification as well as the ontological traits of his theology.[429] Besides this, there is one significant feature that has not gained equal attention. Luther presents here intellect as a desire, an appetitive force – in a word, as an affect. The allusion to the affectivity of the intellect is not a haphazard idea of an early sermon but has specific im-

---

426 In Dictata Luther says: "Cor autem voluntatem et affectum significant" WA 4, 7, 22. Later, Luther praises the Book of Psalms for letting us to see in the heart of the saints, involving not just their feelings but thoughts also: "...das wir ynn den grund vnd quelle yhrer wort vnd werck, das ist, ynn yhr hertz, sehen koennen, was sie fur gedancken gehabt haben, wie sich yhr hertz gestellet vnd gehalten hat" (WA DB 10 I 101, 22–24)

427 Metzger 1964, 221: "Menschsein ist für Luther immer ‚Affekt'; der Begriff meint die irrationale Wirklichkeit des Menschen, die Personmitte (vgl. die Vertauschbarkeit von affectus, cor, conscientia etc) nicht als fixierbare autarke Instanz, sondern als der Ort, auf den hin alle Lebensäusserungen gesehen werden können, durch die wir mit Begegnengem in Kommunikation stehen." Mühlen (1992, 106–107) also adds to the synonyms for affect the concept of experientia.

428 WA 1, 29, 18–27: "Sic enim Aristoteles ait: Intellectus impossibilis est nisi eorum, quae intelligit, sed potentia est ipsa omnia, et ipse est quodammodo omnia. Sic etiam appetitus et appetibile sunt unum, et amor et amatum, quae omnia substantialiter intellecta falsissima sunt. Sed sic quia intellectus et affectus dum desiderant sua Obiecta, in quantum sic desiderantes, habent se velut materia appetens formam, et secundum hoc, i.e. in quantum desiderantes, non autem in quantum subsistentes, sunt pura potentia, imo quoddam nihil et fiunt quoddam ens, quando obiecta attingunt, et ita obiecta sunt eorum esse et actus, sine quibus nihil essent, sicut materia sine forma nihil esset."

429 See Mannermaa 1994; Peura 1990, 103–105.

plications in Luther's later reflections. In other words, affectivity contributes to the rightness of reason and is a remarkable statement in light of the Stoic opinion of affects that mainly disturb the intellect. Furthermore, wisdom (*sapientia*) is not solely a matter of intellect or reasoning. Luther may state that *Omnia secundum spiritum seu secundum affectum intelligenda*, "everything must be understood according to the spirit, that is, according to the affect."[430] This means that to understand something with affect is the spiritual way to understand it, as it is also the most intelligent way to understand it, and the affect then becomes the basis of human understanding. In *Operationes in Psalmos*, Luther observes that the affect (which on this occasion he also refers to as love, will, or devotion) is the primary source from which all opinions are formed. If the affect is wrong, the opinions become instantly false (*mox*).[431]

If the primacy of affect is understood to mean affect is a higher (or better) power of the soul, or a more suitable psychological faculty, and thus more capable of grasping faith, then the main point of Luther's argument is lost. Luther's purpose is not to show in a mystical vein that although our intellect does not grasp God our desiring love does. On the contrary, one of the crucial points in Luther's doctrine of justification was that love as a *habitus* in the soul does not justify us before God. Against the scholastic doctrine of love as the *forma* of faith, Luther states that Christ is the form of faith and, moreover, he wants to put faith in the place of love in the doctrine of justification.[432] The 1514 Christmas sermon provides a clue to the right understanding of the affectivity of Luther's theology – human intellect and human affect are nothing without God as their object. Only in God do they find their being. This means that one attains God through passionate love as little as with one's understanding. God is *incomprehensibilis* as well as *superamabilis*, beyond the capacities of our intellect and affect.[433] Recalling the etymology of the word *affectus* reveals the Lutheran affective theology. The root of affect is the verb *afficio*, which means, "to exert an influence on something," or "to be affected." Affective faith means a faith that is passive, in the position of a receiver. This very character of affects was suspect

---

430 WA 3, 90, 35–36.

431 AWA 2, 177, 12–14: "Primum est enim omnium affectus ipse, seu amor, seu voluntas, seu studium, qui si perversus et impius est, mox opiniones parit impias, falsas et mendaces." In his early notes on Gabriel Biel's Collectorium Luther comments the distinction between apprehensive and appetitive faculties of the soul: "Quia qualis amor, talis notitia. Sicut autem in rebus corporalibus pondus est Amor, ita figura et quantitas est Notitia, quia per hanc suo modo cognoscit, quis locus ei idoneus sit, quo cadat" (WA 59, 41, 26–29).

432 Especially in the 1535 commentary on Galatians, see WA 40 I 225–229.

433 WA 3, 124, 8; Kärkkäinen 2003, 100–101.

for rational philosophers; affects move us in a way we do not understand or even want. Similarly, another word for emotions, *passio*, has the same connotation, especially when associated with the passion of Christ. Passiveness in this respect does not mean being empty or immovable, but on the contrary, to be filled and moved by something. The affectivity of Luther's theology means that it is concentrated on the Word of God. In other words, pondering reason and emotion as psychological factors is of no avail. Our affects tell us that we are *affected* by something we neither choose nor understand, whereas our intellect pretends to be an independent agent. In that regard, the affects are right. On the contrary, in terms of knowing God, our affect is as blind as our intellect and needs to be enlightened by the Word of God. Until then, both the apprehensive and appetitive parts of our soul resemble the Aristotelian matter anticipating the form.

Often Luther treats affect and intellect not as psychological capacities, but aspects of a human's turning against or toward God.[434] The point of departure is that God dwells in the spirit, in faith, through his Word, and the Word operates through hearing. Moreover, hearing is theocentric affectivity. In *Lectures on Hebrews*, Luther says that hearing (*audire*) transcends both human understanding and desiring.[435] It is necessary to point out that Luther speaks here about all *active* capacities of a human being, both intellectual and emotional. This means that hearing the word surpasses the highest intellectual thoughts and strongest emotional desires. To hear the word is to be under the influence of the word, to be *affected* by it.

> This is the glory of faith, namely, hot to know where you are going, what you are doing, what you are suffering, and after taking everything captive – perception and understanding, strength and will – to follow the bare voice of God and to be led and driven rather than to drive.[436]

---

434 Mühlen 1992, 102.
435 WA 57, 139, 4–9: "Utrumque enim verbum hoc loco ponitur absolute, scil. 'audi' et 'contestabor', q. d. tu esto auditor et ego ero predicator, quia non nisi auditu capiuntur, que Christus locutus est de celo et futura vita, cum non solum superent omnem intellectus altitudinem, sed eciam omnem desiderii latissimam capacitatem"; see Joest 1967, 226–227.
436 WA 57, 236, 1–3: "Atque haec est gloria fidei, nescire scilicet, quo eas, quid facias, quid patiaris, et captivatis omnibus, sensu et intellectu, virtute et voluntate, nudam Dei vocem sequi et magis duci et agi quam agere."

In this sense, faith is *passio*.[437] Faith is also born through hearing the word, beyond human activity, and it is God alone who can see and change the basic *affectus* of a human person, which is the same as to create faith.

4.1.2 The affect and emotions

Despite the inconsistency of Luther's vocabulary, it is possible to make a distinction between the affect (singular) and occasional emotions (or affects plural). "The affect" refers to the hidden, inner will and to "emotions," to the particular affections of humans.[438] This basic affect is either love/faith or hatred/unbelief. To state that the human heart is ruled by the affect means that God alone can comprehend the human heart and change the way it is directed. Luther discusses some of the affects or emotions in particular in his Psalter preface (1528/1545):

> A human heart is like a ship on a wild sea, driven by the storm winds from the four corners of the world. Here it is stuck with fear and worry about impending disaster; there comes grief and sadness because of present evil. Here breathes a breeze of hope and of anticipated happiness; there blows security and joy in present blessings.[439]

---

437 WA 40 I 43, 1–2: "Christiana iusticia est mere contraria, passiva, quam tantum recipimus, ubi nihil operamur sed patimur alium operari in nobis scilicet deum."

438 Mühlen 1992, 105:" Dieser innere verborgene Affekt, der affectus occultus, bestimmt die gesamte Erfahrung des Menschen. Er kann in seinem Wesen nicht durch die Vernunft, sondern nur durch den Glauben erkannt werden, der dass Herz des Menschen von der sich selbst begründenden Eigenliebe befreit und sich als ein durch den Heiligen Geist neu ermöglichtes Grundvertrauen auf Gott gründet. Liebe und Hoffnung werden zum lebendigen Ausdruck jener affektiven Existenzbewegung des Glaubens." Furthermore, Mannermaa (1991, 2) uses the term affectus/voluntas occultus, "A human person is governed by hidden inner will (voluntas occulta et intima). This will is hidden from man himself in the sense that it is not an object of his straight and objectional knowledge. Man can not grasp it with his immediate reflection. Nevertheless it is in a most intimate way a part of man himself – if not the most profound essence of man indeed. This hidden inner will is always directed to something, that man considers as good – even if this good should be actually bad. This will and its directedness constitutes the basic tone of man. If the will is in repose in its end, the tone of man is joy. If the will is, instead, deprived of the real or imagined good that it is directed to, the overall affect is sadness. In the case man is in danger of losing the object of his will, his world is constituted by fear, whereas the will that is directed to the desirable good through adversities is hope etc. Thus the hidden inner will constitutes how man is tuned and what forms his basic affect at any moment. It defines what is a person's world like" (transl. mine).

439 WA DB 10 I, 101, 33–37: "Denn ein menschlich hertz ist wie ein schiff auff eim wilden meer, welches die sturmwinde von den vier orten der welt treiben, Hie stoesst her furcht vnde sorge fur zukuenfftigem vnfal, Dort feret gremen her vnd traurigkeit von kegenwertigem vbel. Hie webt

Without providing a detailed account of emotions, Luther adheres to the traditional taxonomy concerning them.[440] The four basic emotions that Luther proposes are the same as those of Aquinas. In *Dictata*, Luther explains "the chariots of God" (Ps 68:17), stating that God's chariots have two wheels on both sides, meaning two of them are directed to good with love (concupiscible) and two of them to evil with hate (irascible). These basic affects are hope *(spes, Hoffnung)*, joy *(gaudium, Freude)*, fear *(timor, Furcht)*, and sorrow *(dolor, Traurigkeit)*.[441] The advantage of the Book of Psalms among the books of the Bible is its affectivity. It does not merely tell about the acts of the saints, but portrays their hearts in a way that is beneficial to all Christians. Although joy and hope are positive affects and generally considered (in Luther's thought) as precisely "Christian" affects, Luther does not treat fear and grief as something that should be extirpated. The Psalter as a Christian *gnothi seauton* is a mirror for human emotions. These emotions are not separate psychological movements under detached self-observation, but are those related to God. To feel emotions toward *(gegen)* God and with *(mit)* God renders them doubly powerful.[442] The communion of saints in the Psalter preface is a community of those who share the same affections. The Psalter "teaches you in joy, fear, hope, and sorrow to think and speak as all the saints have thought and spoken."[443]

A Christian's emotions differ from those of a non-Christian. In his great *Commentary on Galatians*, Luther states that when God sends the Holy Spirit into the hearts of the believers, it evokes new opinions *(iudicium)*, sensations *(sensus)*,

---

hoffnung vnd vermessenheit von zukunfftigem glueck. Dort bleset her sicherheit vnd freude ynn gegenwertigen guetern."

440 Elenius (2005, 51–64) discusses Luther's records of emotions and their relatedness to the medieval taxonomies. Elenius notes that Luther may describe affectively also attitudes, virtues, and vices: WA 40 II, 26, 16–21; WA 43, 308, 29–31; WA 1, 14, 17–19.

441 WA 3, 404, 25–29: "Cuius quattuor rote sunt quattuor affectus spes, timor, gaudium, dolor. In utroque latere due, scilicet duo ex amore boni et duo ex odio mali." Later in Dictata Luther establishes that these four emerge from love and hatred. WA 4, 102, 7–10: "Omnes enim quattuor affectus carnis evacuat istis motivis, qui sunt timor, spes, gaudium, tristitia. Qui oriuntur ex amore et odio: ex quolibet duo. Amor spem futuri et gaudium presentis boni facit. Odium timorem futuri et tristitiam presentis mali parit." Luther does not use the words irascibilis or concupiscibilis.

442 WA DB 10 I 102, 19–22: "Vnd (wie gesagt) ist das das aller beste, das sie solche wort gegen Gott vnd mit Gott reden, welchs macht das zweifeltiger ernst vnd leben in den worten sind. Denn wo man sonst gegen Menschen in solchen sachen redet, gehet es nicht so starck von hertzen, brennet, lebt, vnd dringet nicht so fast."

443 WA DB 10 I 104, 1–4: "Aber der Psalter helt dich von den Rotten zu der heiligen Gemeinschafft, Denn er leret dich in Freuden, Furcht, Hoffnung, Trawrigkeit, gleich gesinnet sein vnd reden, wie alle Heiligen gesinnet vnd geredt haben."

and affections (*motus*) in them. It is worth noting that the work of the Holy Spirit includes sensual or corporeal existence as well. In the realm of intellect, faith as the gift of the Holy Spirit means the ability to have certain opinions about God's will. Without the Word, no one can be certain about anything.[444] Certainty is not just the correctness of logical reasoning because this is also an emotion.[445] The Psalter preface portrays the emotions belonging to the present good as joy and certainty (*sicherheit vnd freude*). The affect of joy is a sign of faith. As it is impossible to be certain of anything without faith, it is also impossible to sincerely rejoice without faith.

Since faith includes the whole personhood and evokes new understanding, sensations, and emotions, Luther describes the saints as deeply emotional persons. In *Lectures of Genesis*, Luther presents the patriarchs as examples for Christians precisely because they had warm feelings and were capable of both mourning and rejoicing. Luther states that the saints are "the tenderest people."[446] Luther also explicitly refutes the Stoic notion of wisdom that is not moved by emotion. For instance, Mary the Mother of God was anxious about her son; Psalms tell recurrently how David was mournful and tempted to sin; Paul felt fear, was worried and then relieved when Epaphroditus recovered. Emotions belong to the full life of a Christian. To Luther, the Stoic teaching of *apatheia* is not

---

444 WA 40 I 572, 16–28: "Altera est, qua Spiritussanctus per verbum mittitur in corda credentium, ut hic dicitur: 'Misit Deus Spiritum filii sui in corda' etc. Illa fit sine visibili specie, Quando videlicet per verbum vocale concipimus ardorem et lucem, qua alii et novi efficimur, qua novum iudicium, novi sensus et motus in nobis oriuntur. Ista mutatio et novum iudicium non est opus humanae rationis aut virtutis, sed donum et effectus Spiritussancti, qui cum verbo praedicato venit, qui fide purificat corda et spirituales motus in nobis parit. Ideo maxima differentia est inter nos et inter hostes et depravatores verbi. Nos, gratia Dei, certo statuere et iudicare possumus ex verbo de voluntate Dei erga nos, de omnibus legibus et doctrinis, de vita nostra et aliorum. Contra Papistae et phanatici spiritus de nulla re certo iudicare possunt. Hi enim depravant et pervertunt, Illi vero persequuntur et blasphemant verbum. Sine verbo autem nihil certi de ulla re iudicari potest." In the Advent Postil Luther warns to understand "heart" or "thoughts" in Phil 4,7 as natural emotions and thoughts: "Hertz und synn soll hie nicht verstanden werden von naturlichem willen und verstentniß, sondern, wie sich Paulus selbs deuttet, hertz und synn ynn Christo Jesu, das ist: den willen und verstand, den man ynn Christo und von Christo und unter Christo hat und furet" (WA 10 I 2, 187, 20–23).

445 According to Järveläinen (2000, 100–102) Luther thought that salvific faith is realised as supernaturally caused, because natural human beings are unable to regard themselves as unworthy of divine acceptance. It is this awareness combined with the experience of grace that together form the affect fiducia.

446 WA 43, 276, 17–18: "Sancti patres fuerunt tenerrimi homines, et natura puriores, ideoque στοργας excellentiores habuerunt, quam alii insensati."

only wrong but drives people to despair.[447] In contrast to the restrained attitude to emotions, Luther could state that the peculiarity of a Christian's emotions is not their correctness, but their warmth and tenderness. In that respect he also does not promote *metriopatheia*. In other words, affectivity is a part of the mission of the church and the Holy Spirit praises natural human emotions. Although the Fall destroyed genuine emotions, God wants to heal them, which occurs, according to Luther, in marriage and in the church.[448] No doubt, music is also a part of this divine affective therapy. The way the Word of God applies to our emotions occurs through our auditory perception. With a living voice it is possible to touch the human affects, whereas a written text does not convey its author's emotions. The Apostle Paul expressed this concern in his words to the Galatians, writing, "How I wish I could be with you now and change my tone!" (Gal 4:20). In short, vocality advances the power of the Word, and music has a peculiar influence on emotions.[449]

---

447 WA 40 II 102, 17–103, 1: "Et hic locus, ut etiam supra obiter monui, gravissimam consolationem nobis affert, quia admonet, quod sine concupiscentia et tentationibus carnis, imo etiam sine peccatis vivere non possimus. Admonet igitur nos, ne faciamus, ut quidam, de quibus Gerson scribit, qui eo nitebantur, ut prorsus nihil tentationum et peccatorum sentirent, hoc est, ut plane saxa essent. Talem imaginationem habuerunt Sophistae et Monachi de Sanctis, quasi fuerint meri stipites et trunci et plane caruerint omnibus affectibus. Certe Maria sensit maximum dolorem animi amisso filio, Luc. 2. Conqueritur David passim in Psalmis, se immodica tristicia propter magnitudinem tentationum et peccatorum suorum concepta pene absorberi. Conqueritur et Paulus se 'foris pugnas, intus pavores' sentire, Se 'carne servire legi peccati', Ait se 'solicitum esse pro omnibus Ecclesiis', Et 'Deum misertum esse sui, quod Epaphroditum vicinum morti restituerit vitae, ne dolorem super dolorem haberet'. Itaque Sophistarum Sancti similes sunt Sapientibus Stoicorum, qui tales finxerunt sapientes, qualis nullus unquam fuit in rerum natura. Et hac stulta et impia persuasione, quae nata est ex inscitia huius Paulinae doctrinae, adegerunt Sophistae seipsos et alios infinitos ad desperationem."
448 Forsberg 1984, 101–105; WA 43, 277, 2 "Spiritus sanctus laudat naturales adfectus."
449 WA 40 I 651, 21–32: "Vulgo dicitur Epistolam esse mortuum nuntium, quia non plus potest dare, quam habet. Et nulla Epistola tum accurate scripta est, in qua non desideretur aliquid. Variae enim sunt circumstantiae, et momenta temporum, locorum, personarum, morum et affectuum varia sunt, quae Epistola nulla potest exprimere. Ideoque varie afficit lectorem, iam contristat, iam exhilarat, prout lector affectus est. Viva autem vox, si quid asperius aut intempestivius dictum est, potest illud interpretari, mitigare et corrigere. Itaque optat Paulus se potius praesentem esse, ut vocem suam temperare et mutare posset, prout videret circumstantias affectuum hoc requirere, Ut, si videret quosdam nimium perturbatos, sic moderaretur sermonem, ne nimis contristaret eos, Si econtra elatos, saevervius obiurgaret, ne nimium securi et tandem contemptores fierent."

4.2 The affective power of music

4.2.1 Music moves the human heart

The masters of the human heart are, according to the *Encomion musices*, emotions (*affectus*), inclinations (*impetus*), and spirits (*spiritus*). A closer scrutiny of the Latin passage is useful here:

> Siue enim velis tristes erigere, siue laetos terrere, desperantes animare, superbos frangere, amantes sedare, odientes mitigare, et quis omnes illos numeret dominos cordis humani, scilicet affectus et impetus seu spiritus, impulsores omnium vel virtutum vel vitiorum? Quid inuenias efficatius quam ipsam Musicam?[450]

These three Latin words, *affectus*, *impetus*, *spiritus*, are uniquely connected in this preface. Spirit (*spiritus*) refers to the Holy Spirit or the devil. The spiritual dimension of emotions is that they are originated in the current spirit. As with the Holy Spirit, the devil has an emotional impact on human beings. To equate the affect with the spirit emphasizes the fact that we are not in control of our hearts. The middle word, *impetus*, is also a word referring to a violent attack of emotion, an uncontrollable movement of the soul. Luther uses the word sometimes referring to the Holy Spirit (whose *impetus* is that of consolation and encouraging)[451] as well as Satan (whose attacks are to be conquered with the Word of Christ),[452] to St. Paul (who vehemently attacks false apostles in the Epistle to the Galatians),[453] as well as Luther himself (he speaks of *impetus responendi* after reading Erasmus' *Diathribe*).[454] *Affectus*, *impetus*, and *spiritus* are nearly synonymous for the innermost part of a human person. Whereas affect represents the basic orientation of the person, spirit denotes that either God or Satan reigns in the heart, and impetus is a word for the movements of the soul that are beyond the control of the will. The words chosen suggest that the effects of music are

---

450 WA 50, 371, 5 – 9. Neither of the German versions of Encomion musices render *affectus et impetus seu spiritus*. Walter's translation speaks only of the movements of the human heart (bewegung des Menschlichen hertzen) and Figulus's edition omits it altogether. Leaver 2007, 322.
451 WA 55 II, 811, 338 – 341: "Cum spiritus exuberans semper nouis Ecclesiam aquis irriget, Quia 'fluminis impetus (non autem stagni quies) letificat ciuitatem Dei'. Non enim fastidium et nauseam vult, Sed consolationem in scripturis suis dare fidelibus."
452 WA 29, 160, 27 – 30: "ut probe discamus verba Christi, quae nobis robur, arma et praesidia suffitientia adeoque invicta erunt adversus omnes diaboli impetus et insanias quibus adversus hoc sacramentum sevit."
453 WA 40 I, 62, 5.
454 WA 18, 601, 32. Another good translation for impetus as an impulse (Sorabji 2000, 42 – 43).

of utmost significance, something more than merely raising sentiments. The power of music to move the affect is second only to (or comparable to) the Word of God.[455]

The way music moves the affects has a property that Luther does not discuss but that has significance for the philosophical theories of emotion – music touches the affects directly. Usually emotions have a cognitive component: I am happy or sad about something because something happened. An emotion is therefore a response to a fact, thing, or incident (real or imagined) that constitutes its cognitive content. Musical emotions are exceptional in that respect because the cognitive component of an emotion caused by music is difficult to determine. It seems that music addresses the human affectivity immediately, omitting cognitive faculties. In the case of instrumental music (which I claim Luther's view of music comprises), this feature becomes particularly apparent. While it is possible to postulate cognitive content to a piece of music, to demonstrate it amounts to one of the most difficult problems within the philosophy of music.[456] Music challenges the theories of emotion that consist of both a cognitive component and a behavioral suggestion. Listening to music is a deeply emotional experience without clearly defined cognitive content and with no necessary behavioral response. Although Luther does not discuss the effects of music in these terms, he appears to suggest an immediate power of music on the affects.[457]

---

455 WA Br 5, 639, 12–15: "Et plane iudico, nec pudet asserere, post theologiam esse nullam artem, quae musicae possit aequari, cum ipsa sola post theologiam id praestet, quod alioqui sola theologia praestat, scilicet quietem et animum laetum."

456 On the problems of how music may express some cognitive content or how its relationship to emotions is understood, see Kivy 1989; 1999; Robinson 1994; Scruton 1999, 140–170. According to Kivy's widely discussed theory, music "is expressive of" (Kivy refuses to say "expresses" or "arouses") feelings because it has the same "contour" as human behavior expressive of emotions. As example of this is the "weeping" figure of Monteverdi's Arianna. Certain musical gestures or elements are expressive of emotion by virtue of convention, like the "sadness" of the minor triad. One of the disadvantages of the theory is that it is hardly applicable to others than "garden-variety" emotions (as Kivy refers to them) such as joy and grief. Robinson aspires to treat more complex emotions such as "cheerful confidence turning into despair" but has to concede that she cannot show how these emotions and their expressions can occur in music. The result of this philosophical discussion is that the most accurate explanation of the feeling I have when listening to Sibelius' Tapiola is "the feeling I have when listening to Sibelius' Tapiola."

457 Elenius (2005, 25–50) divides Luther's concept of emotion in four parts: the cognitive component, the affective dimension, bodily changes, and a behavioral suggestion. This position is amply substantiated by Luther quotes. Nevertheless, music does not fit in there, as Elenius acknowledges in passing. (p. 86) Elenius is dependent on Järveläinen (2000, 43–44), who promotes the componential theories of emotion. Emotions involve an affective feeling compo-

4.2.2 Music raises a variety of emotions

As the ruler of human affects, music has the ability to generate a variety of emotions. According to the *Encomion,* it is possible for music "to comfort the sad, to terrify the happy, to encourage the despairing, to humble the proud, to calm to passionate and to calm those full of hate."[458] Music can arouse terror, humility, and tranquillity. To ascribe this kind of power to music suggests that there are both harmful and useful possibilities in the use of music. Although Luther concentrates on the God-pleasing effects of music, he does not deny that music may have an undesirable influence on a person. For example, he is well aware of lascivious and bad music and is concerned about the youth, wishing that they could have better music with pious words to practice.[459] Luther's address to the young reader at the end of *Encomion musices* is illustrative:

> Take special care to shun perverted minds which prostitute this lovely gift of nature and art with their erotic rantings; and be quite assured that none but the devil goads them on to defy their very nature which would and should praise God its Maker with this gift, so that these bastards purloin the gift of God and use it to worship the foe of God, the enemy of nature and of this lovely art.[460]

As are all God's great gifts, music is polluted in the Fall, and that pollution has affected its use rather than its essence. Whereas music was once suited for sacred things, states Luther in *Operationes in Psalmos,* in the course of time it became a tool for lust and luxury.[461] That notwithstanding, Luther has great difficulties in understanding "enthusiasts" – even Augustine – who see the power of music as being problematic.[462] According to that view, to be emotionally affected by music is dangerous for one's spirituality. Luther would instead state the opposite, that to *not* enjoy the delight of music would be an act of unbelief and to

---

nent and an evaluative cognitive component, the feeling component being a pleasant or unpleasant feeling about what is expressed by the propositional evaluation.

458 WA 50, 371, 5 – 7.

459 WA 35, 473, 19 – 474, 1.

460 WA 50, 373, 11 – 374, 5: "Et deprauatos animos, qui hac pulcherrima et natura et arte abutuntur, ceu impudici poetae, ad suos insanos amores, et summo studio caueto et vitato, certus, quod Diabolus eos rapiat contra naturam, vt quae hoc dono vult et debet Deum solum laudare autorem, isti adulterini filii, rapina ex dono Dei facta, colunt eodem hostem Dei et aduersarium naturae et artis huius iucundissimae." The Figulus version is more graphic in listing carnal desires as "gluttony, drunkenness and unchastity."

461 AWA 2, 162, 15 – 17: "Usum musicae fuisse olim sacrum et divinis rebus accommodatum, successu temporum (ut omnia) in luxus et libidinis servitutem redactum."

462 WA 30 II, 696, 3; WA Tr 5, 4441.

not be moved by music would be inhuman. Wickedness does not extend to the essence of music. The fact that even music can be twisted to the devil's purposes attests only to the devil's deceitfulness, not to anything inherent in music itself. In fact, Satan is the enemy of God, nature, and this lovely art (*hostis Dei et adversarius naturae et artis huius iucundissimae*). In this, God, nature, and art are connected in a way that excludes all contrariety between them, because both the nature and the art of music witness to their creator. Undoubtedly, people may utilize music for their carnal desires. Nonetheless, Luther's attitude to music is unreservedly positive, and to state that music belongs to *adiaphora* and is therefore neither good nor bad as such would be a complete misinterpretation.[463] Luther considered music to be of divine origin and its very nature is to praise its maker. Any resulting bad music is the devil's acting against nature (*Diabolus eos rapiat contra naturam*). In short, the fundamental note of the ultimate goodness of creation is well heard.[464]

4.2.3 Above all, music delights the human heart

Without a doubt, Luther saw the most important effect of music to be joy. Looking at the few extant lines of Luther's *On Music* suffices to clarify the salient feature of music that makes it an outstanding gift of God:

μουσικην εραω
Eciam damnantes non placent Schwermerii
Q u i a
1. Dei donum non hominum est
2. Quia facit letos animos

---

[463] Music as an adiaphoron became a controversy in later Lutheranism. There were two traits of Luther's thought to be important for the development. First, external ceremonies were matters of Christian freedom. On the other hand, Luther had emphasized the God-given character of music and elevated it to a place next to theology. Therefore two approaches existed side by side in Lutheranism: an adiaphoristic and an obligatory understanding of music. The latter meant to interpret Luther's position in an extremely positive way. In contrast to Calvinism, it was maintained that the use of music is an obligation in the church. Irwin 1993, 11–22.

[464] Hubert Guicharrousse dedicates an entire chapter to attest that Luther sees the devil's role in music as very strong (diabolus in musica, Guicharrousse 1995, 83–106). What makes his attempt less convincing is that his argument is based on Luther's idioms that use musical imagery, such as "the Pope is playing the old tune" or "devil's fiddlers." Emblematic to Guicharrousse's approach in this chapter is that when describing Luther's attitude toward dance as prohibitive (which is approximately correct), he neglects the reference to the "heavenly roundelay"(divinam choream, WA 50, 373, 3) of Encomion musices altogether.

3. Quia fugat diabolum
4. Quia innocens gaudium facit.[465]

Music is a gift of God and not human beings. It makes souls happy, it drives away the devil, and it creates an innocent joy. The centrality of delight becomes apparent when Luther reiterates the same idea from slightly different angles three times in a row. What is the difference between "facit l[a]etos animos" and "innocens gaudium facit"? *Laetitia* and *gaudium* are both words meaning "joy."[466] In the middle there is the notion of the exorcising power of music. To Luther, the devil is primarily the spirit of sadness who cannot tolerate music. The outcome of the analysis is that Luther states in *On Music* nothing more than that music is a source and an expression of joy. Furthermore, the exorcisng power of music almost elevates it to a sacramental status:

> The Holy Ghost himself honors her as an instrument for his proper work when in his Holy Scriptures he asserts that through her his gifts were instilled in the prophets, namely, the inclination to all virtues, as can be seen in Elisha (2 Kgs 3:15). On the other hand, she serves to cast out Satan, the instigator of all sins, as is shown in Saul, the king of Israel (1 Sam 16:23)[467]

In light of all the power Luther ascribes to music, is not surprising that he argues that the Holy Spirit honors music as his proper instrument (*Honorat eam ipse Spiritus sanctus, ceu sui proprii officii organum*). The biblical examples Luther cites are illuminating. For Luther, the biblical basis for the use of music is above all the incident in 1 Sam 16:23, "And so it was, whenever the spirit from God was upon Saul, that David would take a harp and play it with his hand. Then Saul would become refreshed and well, and the distressing spirit would depart from him." In Luther's Bible translations, there is a subtle alteration in this episode between the versions of 1524 and 1545. For example, verse 14 reads, "But the Spirit of the Lord departed from Saul, and an evil spirit from the Lord troubled him." In the 1524 translation the word "troubled" is *blehet*, or "afflicted,"

---

465 WA 30 II 696, 2–8.

466 The possible difference between them is treated in Section 6.2.4.

467 WA 50, 371, 9–13: "Honorat eam ipse Spiritus sanctus, ceu sui proprii officii organum, dum in scripturis suis sanctis testatur, dona sua per eam Prophetis illabi, id est omnium virtutum affectus, vt in Eliseo videre est, Rursus per eandem expelli Satanam, id est omnium vitiorum impulsorem, vt in Saule rege Israel monstratur."

and in 1545, *macht jn seer vnrügig,* "made him unsettled."[468] The evil spirit is the spirit of discomfort and sadness, and music has exorcising power comparable to the Word of God. It can therefore drive away "the creator of saddening cares and disquieting worries," *spiritus tristitiae.*[469] It is necessary to understand that for Luther, sadness was not primarily a state of mind, a blue mood, or something psychologically explicable. *Tristitia* is an affect contrary to *gaudium* and reflects one's position before God (*coram Deo*). The work of the devil is to make one doubt the goodness of God and lose one's joy. In short, the devil tries to annul the work of God. Satan is the spirit of sadness and cannot tolerate the joyful song of faith, as witnessed by the examples of Saul and Elisha.[470]

The other biblical basis for the use of music is 2 Kgs 3:15, "Then it happened, when the musician played, that the hand of the Lord came upon Elisha." The prophet was given *omnium virtutum affectus,* which in this context is tantamount to the Holy Spirit, as the devil is *impulsor omnium vitiorum.* In a way reminiscent to this incident, Luther recounts in *Table Talk* that he himself has gained the willingness to preach with the help of music.[471] If the evil spirit is driven away by music and the Holy Spirit is given to prophets by music, to ascribe to music a sacramental status would not be far-fetched. Indeed, to be delighted means to have received the gift of salvation. That music can delight humans and be also

---

468 WA DB 9 I, 238, 14: "Der geyst aber des HERRN weych von Saul, vnd eyn boser geyst von dem HERRN blehet yhn"; WA DB 9 I, 241, 14: "Der Geist aber des HERRN weich von Saul, vnd ein boeser Geist vom HERRN macht jn seer vnruegig."

469 WA 30 II, 696, 7; WA Br 5, 639,16; WA Tr 1, 968:"Musica maximum, immo divinum est donum, ideo Satanae summe contrarium, quia per eam multae et magnae tentationes pelluntur. Diabolus non expectat, cum ea exercetur." Perhaps the most thorough study in Luther's view of the devil is that of Hans-Martin Barth (1967, 146) where he says: "Er ist der 'spiritus tristitiae', er neidet uns die Freude; alle Traurigkeit kommt demnach von ihm, selbst schwermütige Träume. Denn Gott ‚hasst die Traurigkeit und liebt ein fröhliches … Herz.'"

470 WA 54, 33, 39 – 34, 10: "Doch hilfft die Musica, oder noten, als ein wunderliche Creatur und gabe Gottes seer wol dazu, sonderlich wo der hauffe mit singet, und fein ernstlich zu gehet. Denn so lesen wir vom Propheten Eliseo 4. Re. 3. das er durch das Psalterspiel (da man freilich Psalmen auff gespielet hat, nach der ordenung Davids) den Geist der weissagung in sich erwecket, Wie auch David mit seinem Psalter spiel offt den boesen geist Saul veriaget, oder doch hindert oder schwechet, lesen wir j. Re. 16. Denn dem boesen geist ist nicht wol dabey, wo man Gottes wort im rechten glauben singet oder predigt. Er ist ein geist der traurigkeit, und kan nicht bleiben, wo ein hertz Geistlich (das ist, in Gott und seinem wort) froelich ist, Davon auch S. Antonius sagt, das geistliche freude dem Teuffel wehe thue."

471 WA TR 5, 4441: Canebatur passio, quam attentissime observabat suis legibus dicens: Musica optimum Dei donum. Saepius ita me incitavit et acuit das ich lust zu predigen gewonnen habe.

an expression of joy is a serious and deeply theological mission. Joy is the gift of the Holy Spirit and sadness the work of the devil.

Luther's preface to the burial hymns (1542) is highly instructive concerning faith and joy in music. At first sight, one might say that if anywhere, sad music is appropriate at a funeral. Yet Luther argues quite the opposite. He notes it a small wonder that those who are sad at a funeral have no hope. For Christians, death is but a deep, strong, and sweet sleep while one awaits resurrection. Therefore Christian churches are not houses of wailing or mourning. Luther recalls the word *Koemiteria* ("dormitory, resting place"), from which the word "cemetery" is derived.

> Accordingly, we do not sing any dirges (*Trawrlied*) or doleful songs over our dead at the grave, but comforting hymns of the forgiveness of sins, of rest, sleep, life, and of the resurrection of the departed Christians so that our faith may be strengthened and the people be moved to true devotion.[472]

Luther also expresses his approval of the outward decorum and festivities concerning funerals. He reminds readers how the patriarchs of Israel conducted their burials with pomp and splendor. To Luther, there is nothing wrong with decorating tombs, erecting tombstones, and singing beautiful songs for the departed. "All this is done so that the article of the Resurrection may be firmly implanted in us. For it is our lasting, blessed, and eternal comfort and joy (*trost und freude*) against death, hell, the devil, and every woe (*traurigkeit*)."[473]

The delight of music may not always be readily apparent. Indeed, many psalms appear to be frightful and sad, but when examined more closely are found to be joyful and full of consolation. Although concerning mainly the words of the psalms, the notion is applicable to music broadly as well. As an ex-

---

472 WA 35, 478, 31–479, 2; LW 25, 326.
473 WA 35, 479, 3–18: Denn es auch billich und recht ist, das man die Begrebnis ehrlich halte und volbringe, Zu lob und ehre dem froelichen Artickel unsers Glaubens, nemlich von der aufferstehung der Todten, Und zu trotz dem schrecklichen Feinde, dem Tode, der uns so schendlich dahin frisset, on unterlas mit allerley scheuslicher gestalt und weise. Also haben (wie wir lesen) die heiligen Patriarchen, Abraham, Jsaac, Jacob, Joseph, &c. jre Begrebnis herrlich gehalten, und mit grossem vleis befohlen. Hernach die Koenige Juda gros geprenge getrieben uber den Leichen, mit koestlichem Reuchwerg allerley guter edler Gewuertz. Alles darumb, den stinckenden schendlichen Tod zu dempffen, und die aufferstehung der Todten zu preisen und bekennen, Damit die Schwachgleubigen und Traurigen zu troesten Dahin auch gehoert, was die Christen bisher und noch thun, an den Leichen und Grebern, Das man sie herrlich tregt, schmueckt, besinget und mit Grabzeichen zieret. Es ist alles zuthun umb diesen Artickel von der aufferstehung, das er feste in uns gegruendet werde, Denn er ist unser endlicher, seliger, ewiger trost und freude wider den Tod, Helle, Teuffel und alle traurigkeit.

ample, Luther cites Ps 51, which as a psalm of repentance looks anything but joyful. Yet, because it speaks of the forgiveness of sins, it is particularly effective to comfort an anxious mind.[474] The song of the church is also not always joyous. For instance, the "new song" of Isa 42:10 does not necessarily refer to merry jumping but resembles more the complaining and sighing of wretched people (*eiulatui et fletui gementium et afflictorum*). This song nevertheless comforts the saddened singers.[475]

4.2.4 *Canticum novum* as the song of joy

An idea that betrays the development of the Reformer's thought perhaps better than other musical expressions is the new song (*canticum novum*). It has been noticed that Luther's thinking concerning music, although always positive, does not remain the same throughout his career but undergoes a slight change that reflects his reformatory theology.[476] In *Dictata super psalterium*, Luther interprets *canticum novum* as reflecting the spiritual state of an individual:

> Only a new man can sing a new song. But the new man is a man of grace, a spiritual and inner man before God. The old man, however, is the man of sin, the carnal and outer man before the world. The newness is grace, the oldness, sin.[477]

There are three traits discernible in this quotation that are typical of young Luther. First, the antithesis is between *sin* and *grace*. Old songs are carnal and worldly songs and new songs are spiritual and holy songs (psalms in particular). The second trait is the sharp distinction between the *inner* and *outer* song. This division is not applicable to the later position adopted by Luther. The view of

---

474 WA 40 II, 473, 25–29: Sicut econtra alii Psalmi in speciem horridi et tristes sunt, quos tamen, si diligencius introspicias, laetissimos et plenissimos consolatione invenies, Qualis superior Psalmus fuit 'Miserere', de poenitentia et remissione peccatorum, de sacrificio Dei et cultu Dei, mire efficax ad consolandas afflictas mentes

475 WA 25, 273, 7–10.

476 Söhngen (1967, 100–112) gives the most profound account available on the young Luther's position on music. According to Söhngen, it is typical of young Luther to emphasize that a) music is a psychological device for devotion (andachtspsychologisches Hilfsmittel); b) the contemporary music is somewhat suspicious; c) music is a matter of psychology instead of theology; and d) in the first Psalm commentary Luther uses still much of the allegorical reading of musical instruments. It is noteworthy that Söhngen's picture of young Luther is dependent on Ernst Bizer's *Fides ex auditu*, where the breakthrough of Luther's reformatory theology is dated under the writing of Operationes in Psalmos, that is, in 1519.

477 WA3, 182, 24–27.

contemporary music is also remarkably bleak in young Luther, who remarks, "The songs of our time are surely extremely old, even though in point of time they are the latest." Here Luther seems to harbor some moralistic suspicion toward music outside the Church.[478]

At the breakthrough of his reformatory theology, Luther presents a version of *canticum novum* in the light of *theologia crucis*. In 1519 he wrote:

> Singing to the Lord does not always mean to be happy and to rejoice. On the contrary, the new song is song of the cross, which is, praising and carrying God in the midst of afflictions and up to death.[479]

The new song manifests the paradox of Christian existence – God delights our heart by making us sad, and the glory of God is hidden in the cross. At this point the new song can be understood as something that we are naturally unwilling to hear.[480]

In the course of time, the antithesis shifts to the *grace-law* or Old and New Testament. In the Isaiah lectures (1532/34), the new song is seen as being contrary to the worship of the old covenant. Luther states succinctly that the New Testament has no outward worship of God besides thanksgiving (*nullus alius Dei cultus externus in novo Testamento sit quam gratiarum actio*). This means that true religion is no longer bound by place, time, or person. In the new covenant, all Christians are priests offering a spiritual sacrifice, which is to sing, praise, preach, write, and read the good deeds of Christ.[481]

---

478 WA 3, 182, 33–36: "Cantica vetera sunt omnes turpes et scurriles et carnales et mundiales cantilene, etiam si hodie primum cantentur aut componantur. Cantica autem nova sunt omnes psalmi, cantica honesta, sancta, pia et spiritualia, etiam si a tempore primi hominis fuissent: immo illa sunt novissima."

479 WA 2, 333, 25–27: "Deinde cantare domino non semper est letari et gaudere, immo canticum novum est canticum crucis, hoc est laudare et portare deum in mediis tribulationibus, atque adeo in morte."

480 Söhngen (1967, 102) states that crux here is still understood from the standpoint of humilitas theology. It is not the cross by which God saves us, but the cross he gives us to bear. That interpretation is due to his dating of Luther's reformatory breakthrough (see note 60 above).

481 WA 25, 27, 24–35: "'Cantate Domino canticum novum.' Agit iam infirmo illi et stulto Deo coram mundo gratias pro tantis beneficiis, quae hactenus praedicavit. Simul indicat, quod nullus alius Dei cultus externus in novo Testamento sit quam gratiarum actio. Et quia dicit 'Cantate NOVUM canticum', abrogat omnem illum veterem cultum Dei, qui in lege fuit. Finium autem terrae et Insularum ideo meminit, ut reprehendat Iudaeos, qui putabant Deum nusquam nec debere nec posse coli quam in Hierusalem. Quasi dicat: Religio non est amplius ulli vel loco vel tempori vel personae alligata. Euangelion enim praedicabitur in omnem terram et Christiani

The song of Moses and the song of Christ are juxtaposed in Luther's third psalm commentary (1532–1535). Although the terms *canticum novum/ cantica vetera* are not used here, they are nevertheless implied. Luther comments on Ps 45:1, "My tongue is like the pen of a scribe that writes swiftly" by saying, "I will not sing of servitude or of a physical kingdom but of a spiritual and most joyful kingdom." Moses could not sing this type of song. The well-known slowness of Moses' speech (Exod 4:10) signifies that the kingdom of the law could not be delightful. Moses was unable to sing well, which is implied by stating that he was a slow and stumbling speaker. By comparison, Christians instead have a joyful spirit and a joyful heart, and sing[482] of the sweet promises and the good news of certainty of conscience. In *Summaries of the Psalms* of the early 1530 s this view of the new song encompasses the whole creation. When Luther describes the new song in Ps 96, he emphasizes that it is a song of praise, to which all pagans, peoples, waters, and forests are invited to join. It is a thanksgiving to God who helps us against sin, the devil, hell, and all evil. It is the new song of a new kingdom, new creation, and new humanity, not a song of law or of works.[483]

Finally, in the 1545 preface to the Bapst Hymnal, the new song (*newe lied*) is used to announce that faith, joy, willingness, and music belong together:

> The 96ᵗʰ Psalm says "Sing to the Lord a new song. Sing to the Lord all the earth" For in the Old Covenant under the law of Moses, divine service was tedious and tiresome as the people had to offer so many and varied sacrifices of all they possessed, both house and field. And since they were restive and selfish, they performed this service unwillingly or only for the sake of temporal gain ... Now with a heart as lazy and unwilling as this, nothing or nothing good can be sung. Heart and mind must be cheerful and willing if one is to sing ... Thus there is now in the New Testament a better service of God, of which the Psalm

---

omnes erunt sacerdotes et sacrificabunt oblationes spirituales, sicut dicit Psal. 110., hoc est sacrificium laudis. Id enim est canere, laudare, praedicare, scribere, legere beneficia Christi."
482 Literally "teach" (doceo). Matthias Mikoteit's study on Luther's third psalm lecture (2004, 102–141) has shown that Luther uses words such as "laudare","docere", and "gratias agere" almost synonymously. "Das Verschmelzen der Begriffe des Lobens und des Verkündigens in der dritten Psalmenvorlesung zeigt ... dass das Loben für Luther in diesen Zusammenhängen eine kerygmatische Gestalt besitzt."(p. 119) Although Mikoteit does not mention "canere" it obviously belongs to the same series of words. One needs only to look at a passage such as "In novo testamento non cultus quam unicus, praestantissimus, quam celebrare, laudare filium illum dei, manifeste cantemus, praedicemus, legamus" (WA 40 II, 609, 7–9).
483 WA 38, 51, 1–7: "Hie wird allen Heiden, landen, leuten, welden, wassern, bewmen aufgelegt zum Gottes dienst, das sie loben und dancken sollen, Darumb, das er richtet und regieret mit gerechtigkeit und warheit, das ist, Er hilfft von sunden und allem das sunde mit bringet, als tod, helle, Teuffels gewalt und alles ubel. Das ist das newe lied vom newen Reich, von newen Creaturen, von newen menschen, nicht aus dem gesetz noch wercken, sondern aus Gott und Geist geboren, und die eitel wunder sind und thun jnn Christo Jhesu, unserm Herrn."

here [speaks]. For God has cheered our hearts and minds through his dear Son, whom he gave for us to redeem us from sin, death, and the Devil. He who believes this earnestly cannot be quiet about it. But he must gladly and willingly (fröhlich und mit lust) sing and speak about it so that others also may come and hear it.[484]

Luther's fully developed position on the new song defines *canticum vetus* in a new way. The old song is not so much understood as worldly or carnal music – something other than religious music. It is rather the unwilling and cheerless music under the law. It is the service of God under punishment and reward. The source of the new song is the cheerful message of the New Testament. That message makes the heart glad, which in turn makes one sing aloud. It is not just a matter of an individual's devotion, but also carries a missionary character. "He must sing and speak about it so that others also may come and hear it" (*das es andere auch hören und herzu komen*).

The theological significance of joy deserves to be treated as a topic of its own in the next chapter. A peculiar affinity between the Word of God and music has been mentioned several times in this study. Luther proclaims that music is second only to the Word of God in creating joy and driving the spirit of sadness away. Moreover, music makes the human heart ready and willing to receive the Word of God.[485] For these reasons, the relationship between music and the Word of God will be discussed next.

4.3 Music combined with the Word of God

4.3.1 Verbum vocale as the primary form of the Word

Music has two advantages that make it theologically valuable. The first is its affectivity, its ability to move human emotions. The second is that it occurs through hearing. These features link it closely to the Word of God, which for Luther is orally delivered, *verbum praedicationis*. Luther argues in *On Councils and the Church*, "whenever you *hear* or see the word *preached*, believed, confessed, and lived, you can believe that there is *ecclesia sancta Catholica*."[486] The reality of the Word is depicted in exclusively auditory (and experiential) terms with si-

---

484 WA 35, 476, 17–477, 9.
485 WA 35, 484: "Zum Goettlichen Wort und warheit / Macht sie das hertz still und bereit."
486 StA 5, 591, 16–18: "Wo du nu solch wort hoerest odder sihest predigen / gleuben / bekennen vnd darnach thun / da habe keinen zweivel /das gewislich / daselbs sein mus ein **rechte** Ecclesia sancta Catholica, ein Christlich heilig Volck."

lent reading of the Bible not mentioned. Accordingly, the explanation of the third commandment in *The Large Catechism* asserts that, besides rest, the purpose of Sunday is to offer the opportunity to "assemble to hear and discuss God's Word and then to offer praise, song, and prayer to God."[487] As for the work of the Holy Spirit, the Catechism states, "Where Christ is not preached, there is no Holy Spirit to create, call, and gather the Christian church, apart from which no one can come to the Lord Christ."[488] The primary problem in the papacy was not that there was no scripture, but that there was failed preaching. The Gospel is a sermon and a voice of God's mercy. Luther differentiates it from the written text and states that it is primarily oral preaching and living word (*mundliche predig und lebendig wortt*).[489] Indeed, orality is the proper nature of Gospel. Luther also makes the observation that writing books is contrary to the essence of the New Testament, for Christ himself wrote nothing and the apostles wrote little. Instead, they proclaimed the Gospel with a physical voice (*mit leyplicher stymme*).[490] Instead of the Holy Writ, Luther calls the Gospel "good clamor" (*gute geschrey*), an idiom that perhaps falls short of musicality but presents well the vocal quality of the Gospel.[491] Since there is no other way to know God than through his Word, and since the Word comes to us through preaching, the best service is to hear and believe God's *voice* (*summum cultum esse audire vocem Dei et credere*).[492] In a sermon in 1534, Luther explains why Jesus put his fingers in a deaf man's ears and touched his tongue (Mark 7:33):

> "He takes under special treatment two organs, ears and tongue, because he knows that the kingdom of Christ is grounded on the word. It can not be understood or comprehended oth-

---

487 BC 397, 84.

488 BC 436, 45.

489 WA 12, 259, 8 – 13: "Evangelion aber heysset nichts anders, denn ein predig und geschrey von der genad und barmhertzikeytt Gottis, durch den herrren Christum mit seynem todt verdienet und erworben, Und ist eygentlich nicht das, das ynn buechern stehet und ynn buchstaben verfasset wirtt, sondernn mehr eyn mundliche predig und lebendig wortt, und eyn stym, die da ynn die gantz wellt erschallet und offentlich wirt außgeschryen, das mans uberal hoeret."

490 WA 10 I 1, 626, 6 – 9, 19 – 21; 627, 1 – 3: "Darumb hatt auch Christus selbs seyn lere nitt geschrieben, wie Moses die seyne, ßondern hatt sie mundlich than, auch mundlich befollhen tzu thun und keynen befelh geben sie tzu schreyben. Item die Apostolln haben auch wenig geschrieben ... Denn ehe sie schrieben, hatten sie tzuuor die leutt mitt leyplicher stymme bepredigt und bekeret, wilchs auch war yhr eygentlich Apostolisch und new testamentisch werck. Das man aber hatt mussen bucher schreyben, ist schon eyn grosser abbruch und eyn geprechen des geystis das es die nott ertzwungen hatt, und nit die artt ist des newen testaments."

491 WA DB 6, 4, 23 – 5, 5.

492 WA 40 I 361, 29.

erwise than with these organs: ears and tongue, and it reigns solely through word and faith in human heart. The ears comprehend the word, the heart believes it, and the tongue then speaks and confesses what the heart believes."[493]

In the lecture on Hebrews, Luther observes that the ears are a Christian's proper organs (*aures sunt organa Christianae hominis)*, because their work – hearing – is one required in Christianity. One becomes a Christian through ears alone, that is, by faith.[494] In his lectures on Isaiah (1527), Luther declares the interconnectedness between the Word, ear, heart, and affect. The ears and heart are the organs that God wants to have in his service. All other parts of us exist so that they can serve our neighbor.[495] The Word is the power and essence of Christianity. This Word is not some propositional knowledge that someone might master once having heard it. The daily exercise of the Word is needed, not just that we hear it, but that we apply it affectively.[496] Christianity is not about knowledge but affect (*neque enim consistit Christianismus in scientia sed in affectu).*[497] Owing to the

---

493 WA 37, 512, 36 – 513, 20: "Er nimpt aber hie sonderlich die zwey gelied fur sich, Ohren und Zungen, denn jr wisset, das das Reich Christi gegruendet ist auff das wort, welchs man sonst weder fassen noch begreiffen kan on durch diese zwey gliedmas, ohren und zungen, und regiret allein durch das wort und glauben im hertzen der menschen. Das wort fassen die ohren, und das hertz gleubets, Die zunge aber redets oder bekennets, wie das hertz gleubet."

494 WA 57, 222, 1– 9: "Verum eximia est in verbo 'aures' emphasis et energia, quod in nova lege omnia illa coeremoniarum infinita onera id est peccatorum pericula ablata sunt, nec iam pedes aut manus nec ullum aliud membrum Deus requirit praeter aures. Adeo sunt omnia in facilem vivendi modum redacta. Nam si quaeras ex Christiano, quodnam sit opus, quo dignus fiat nomine Christiano, nullum prorsus respondere poterit nisi auditum verbi Dei id est fidem. Ideo solae aures sunt organa Christiani hominis, quia non ex ullius membri operibus, sed de fide iustificatur et Christianus iudicatur."

495 WA 25, 99, 12– 16: "'Et dicent: Venite.' Hic vides cultum, opera, studia et sacrificia Christianorum. Non iactant se haec vel alia opera facturos, Non instituunt novos vitae modos, novam vestiendi rationem &c.., Sed hoc unum opus habent, ut eant ad audiendum et discendum, non requiruntur manus, non oculi &c.. sed aures et cor, reliqua omnia membra debent servire proximo. Haec duo, aures et cor, uni Deo servire debent." Note that I use both the manuscript version of WA 25 and the printed edition of WA 31 I when referring to Luther's explanation at this point.

496 WA 25, 99, 16– 17: "Regnum enim hoc in solo Verbo consistit et illi soli ad hoc Regnum pertinent, qui in perpetuo usu Verbi sunt et perpetuo manent discipuli verbi"; WA 31 I 21, 13 – 18: "Euangelion est vis, potencia et opus Christianorum, et ii sunt veri Christiani, qui de die in diem idem magis magisque discunt nec cito fastidientes nauseant. Contra sectarii sunt, qui semel auditum mox, mox putant se plene intelligere. Christiano opus est, ut semper discat dicere: 'Fiat voluntas tua.' Verba quidem facile eloqui, sed affectum apponere nunquam hic perfecte fiet, sed post mortem, ergo nunquam satis disci potest."

497 WA 25, 99, 24; WA 31 I 21, 22– 23: "Nam res Euangelii non consistit in sciencia, sed in affectu."

weakness of our flesh, we need the constant exercise (i.e. hearing) of the Word so that this affect would prevail in us. The Word, ear, heart, and affect belong together because hearing the Word ignites the affect of our heart. In short, to believe means to have that heartfelt affect caused by the Word.[498] The musicality of the Word is also apparent in Luther's comments on Col 3:16.[499] The Word of Christ "dwells in us richly" when we sing and hear the Word continuously.

The emphasis on the vocal and external character of the Word was important in Luther's confrontation with the spiritualists who promoted the inner word, spiritual guidance without outer means.[500] Compared to that, the physical word (*leibliches wort*) provided a source of certainty. "The wind blows where it wills, and you hear the sound of it," (John 3:8) sounds like a spiritualist's motto, "You cannot bind the Holy Spirit to outer religious rituals." Luther, however, has a completely different understanding of the matter. That the wind blows where it wills does not mean that one cannot know where it is. Instead, the words, "you hear the sound of it" mean a certainty based on the physical reality. Physically stated, the blowing of the wind of the Spirit is true because one senses its vibrations. As in a sacrament one feels with one's senses the water, the bread, or the wine, so one also feels the Word in one's ears.[501] Here

---

498 WA 31 I 21, 26–27: "Necesse igitur est semper audire verbum dei, semper annunciare mortem Christi, semper ruminare, ut illustrentur affectus nostri"; WA 25, 99, 25–30: "Quare perpetuo manent discipuli et reminant Verbum, ut subinde nova aliqua flamma exsuscitetur cor, ne torpeat aut fastidiat Verbum. Huc facit, quod quotidie labimur, neque enim cessant nos impetere caro, mors, peccatum, mundus et Sathan, mundi princeps. Ab his hostibus nullo momento tuti sumus. Nisi igitur in perpetuo Verbi usu sumus, quod in tentatione positi obvertamus insultanti Sathanae, actum de nobis est."

499 WA 31 I, 21, 19.

500 StA 5, 427, 15–429, 2; BC 322, 3: "In these matters, which concern the spoken, external Word, it must be firmly maintained that God gives no one his Spirit or grace apart from the external Word, which goes before. We say this to protect ourselves from the enthusiasts, that is, the "spirits", who boast that they have the Spirit apart from and before contact with the Word." (The Smalcald Articles) Mühlen (1972, 232–264) attests that verbum externum was Luther's most important weapon against Erasmus, Karlstadt, Müntzer, Zwingli, Oekolampadius, and the Pope. In addition, the Augsburg Confession condemns "Anabaptists and others who teach that we obtain the Holy Spirit without the external (leiblich) word"(BC 40, 4).

501 WA 47, 33, 16–28: "Und deutet der herr, was das sausen sej, nemlich das leibliche wortt, so man horet, das zeugkniss oder die reden, so prediger fhuren, das ist: die predigt des gottlichen wortts. Den im gantzen Christentumb haben wir nichts hohers noch grossers denn das wortt. Das sausen des windes hoeret man, und die heilige schrieft helt uns allenthalben das wortt fhur, als in der Tauffe, do ist das wortt das Heubtstucke, denn man hoeret das wortt und fhulet das wasser, und ohne das wort ist die Tauffe nichts. Denn was kan wasser ohne das wortt gottes thun? Also auch im abendmal ist das brodt und der wein nichts ohn das wortt. Denn do bliebe brod fur und fur brod, auch wein bliebe wein, aber wen das wortt an das Sacrament der Tauffe

the physicality of the sound is theologically important to Luther. Unlike Biel or Mauburnus, his mentors in spirituality who considered reading aloud as a helping device for beginners that could be later discontinued, Luther made vocality a proof of certainty.[502]

If the ecclesiological article of the Augsburg Confession, "the church is the assembly of saints in which the Gospel is taught purely and the sacraments are administered rightly," is interpreted through the continuousness and physicality of the Word, it follows that purity of doctrine is not the only thing that should be cherished in Lutheran proclamation. Preaching should be pure as well as abundant. Elsewhere, Luther expressly states that "the beautiful music of the Gospel" must fill our ears so that we hear nothing else. The Word is compared to a giant bell or horn that fills the air so that nothing else is heard, so our ears would be blessed and know no other consolation or righteousness than that of the Gospel.[503] According to Luther, the word is a physical, auditory phenomenon, like music.[504]

---

und des abendmals gefasset wirt, das thuts, dan fhulet mans, wie man das Sausen des windes fhulet, den wenn das wort gehort wirt, so fulen wir den schall des wortts fur unsern ohren."
502 Nicol 1984, 53–81; concerning Luther's idea of meditation, Nicol says that it is not just linguistic but melodious phenomenon (p. 52–53).
503 WA 22, 242, 12–22: "Des gleichen sol auch der schoene klang und die liebliche Musica des Euangelij von Christo also die ohren einnemen und fuellen, das man dafur auch kein anders nicht hoere, Gleich als eine grosse glocken oder Heer paucken und bosaunen die lufft so vol schallet und dohnet, das man nicht dafur hoeret, was man sonst redet, singet und schreiet, Also, das in alle unserm leben und thuen allezeit dis Wort die oberhand habe im hertzen durch den Glauben und von keinem andern trost, gerechtigkeit und heil wisse. Das weren wol selige augen und ohren, die der seligen zeit des Euangelij kuendten also brauchen und erkennen, was jnen darin Gott gegeben, Denn solch auge und ohre helt Gott selbs fur einen trefflichen teweren schatz und heiligthum, mit aller welt nicht zubezalen, wenn sie auch viel mehr und heller liecht und Sonnen hette"; WA 10 I 1, 679, 13–18: "Nu sihe, ists nit feyn geordnet, der Herodische gottisdienst hatt eherne glocken, und der viel und groß, damit man tzu solchem gottisdienst das volck locket; wie der gottisdienst ist, ßo sind auch die glocken odder reytzungen. Dem rechten gottisdienst hatt gott andere unnd rechte glocken geben, das sind die prediger, die solchen gottisdienst ynn das volck lautten unnd klingen sollen."
504 Albrecht Beutel (1998, 114) speaks about the thoroughly communicative and vocal quality of Luther's language. "Das Kommt bereits in dem sprechsprachlichen Duktus seiner Schriften und Briefe unüberhörbar zum Ausdruck. Sie sind voller Musik und verlangen danach, laut gelesen und also gehört zu werden. Natura verbi est audiri [WA 4, 9, 18] gilt auch hier."

4.3.2 *Das Wort im Schwang:* Singing as the optimal form of verbum vocale

Singing the Word is more effective than merely reading it aloud. *Encomion musices* proclaims the following:

> It was not without reason that the fathers and prophets wanted nothing else to be associated as closely with the Word of God as music. Therefore we have so many hymns and Psalms where the Word and music join to move the listener's soul, while in other living beings and physical bodies music remains a language without words.[505]

The particular benefit of music is that it moves the human affect, which is also the work of the Gospel. When the Word and music join together, they complete each other's mission. The statement *simul agunt sermo et vox in animo auditoris* means that in singing psalms, word and music – or message and voice – act simultaneously. That combination of music and word is not possible for any creatures other than humans. Luther stresses their connection often. To the composer Ludwig Senfl, Luther wrote:

> Except for theology there is no art that could be put on the same level with music, since except for theology it alone produces a calm and joyful disposition (*quietem et animum laetum*) ... This is the reason why the prophets did not make use of any art other than music: when setting forth their theology they did it not as geometry, not as arithmetic, not as astronomy, but as music, so that they held theology and music most tightly connected (*coniunctissimas*).[506]

That theology and music share affectivity and vocality is obvious here. In fear of *natural theology*, scholars have been inclined to interpret the *coniunctissima* proximity of music and the Word on a hierarchical scale of arts, where astronomy, arithmetic, etc. are below and theology is on the top, with music being in the

---

505 WA 50, 371, 14–372, 2: "Vnde non frustra Patres et Prophetae verbo Dei nihil voluerunt esse coniunctius quam Musicam. Inde enim enim tot Cantica et Psalmi, in quibus simul agunt et sermo et vox in animo auditoris, dum in caeteris animantibus et corporibus sola musica sine sermone gesticulatur."

506 WA Br 5, 639, 9–10, 12–21; LW 49, 427–429. "Neque dubium est, multa semina bonarum virtutum in his animis esse, qui musica afficiuntur ... Et plane iudico, nec pudet asserere, post theologiam esse nullam artem, quae musicae possit aequari, cum ipsa sola post theologiam id praestet, quod alioqui sola theologia praestat, scilicet quietem et animum laetum, manifesto argumento, quod diabolus, curarum tristium et turbarum inquietarum autor, ad vocem musicae paene similiter fugiat, sicut fugit ad verbum theologiae. Hinc factum est, ut prophetae nulla sic arte sint usi ut musica, dum suam theologiam non in geometriam, non in arithmeticam, non in astronomiam, sed in musicam digesserunt, ut theologiam et musicam haberent coniunctissimas, veritatem psalmis et canticis dicentes."

middle.[507] The question, however, is not which one of the *artes liberales* is the best, but what is the optimal form of the Word. Music is the best form of the Word due to its auditory and affective character.[508] Liberated from the strictly text-based understanding of the Word, music does not compromise the primacy of the Word. Word is for Luther *verbum efficax*, the word of creation, which induces that which it announces. In God's Word, *dictum* and *factum* are the same.[509] This is the basis for Lutheran sacramental realism. When Christ said of the bread on the Last Supper "this is my body," the bread is his body by the virtue of his word. It is not his body after some kind of philosophical interplay between essence and accidence. Neither is this change dependent on the recipient's faith or attitude. The Word of Christ makes Christ's words happen. The Word as the promise of the Lord makes both baptism and Eucharist sacraments. Ultimately, the preached Word has a sacramental character. It does not merely refer to the fact of salvation, but mediates it, becoming *Verbum efficax*.[510]

The Word is not a theological category of revelation, but a living reality that comprehends our whole existence. In singing, liturgy, prayer, preaching, and reading aloud, the Word is "in motion" (*ym schwang*).[511] In his first draft for the service order *Concerning the Order of Public Worship (1523)*, Luther reiterates this phrasing:

---

507 This hierarchical order is behind the opinion of Blankenburg (1957, 19), who maintains that when Luther says that he gives to the music the next place after theology, it means "It is certainly not considered equal, but yet closely related."

508 Block 2002, 129 shares this conviction: "Das Ausloben der Musik als ars proxima Theologiae gründet in ihrer auditiv-affektiven Wirkkraft, zielt also auf eine parallele Qualifikation und weniger auf eine abgrenzende Nachordnung."

509 WA 40 II, 230, 4.

510 Bizer 1961, 178:"Hat Luther zuerst vom Sakrament aus der Predigt aus angesehen, so sieht er jetzt die Predigt vom Sakrament aus an und begründet ihren besonderen Charakter wieder mit Röm. 1,17 ... das Sakrament wird vom Wort aus verstanden, und das Wort selbst bekommt sakramentalen Charakter. Der Ausgangspunkt für beides ist das neue Verständnis von Rom. 1,17: 'Im Evangelium wird die Gerechtigkeit Gottes offenbart', d.h. sie wird durch der Wort geschenkt." In Bernice Sundkvists dissertation the sacramental character of preaching in Luther's theology is displayed in three events of the Bible history. In the beginning (Gen 1), God is one with His Word. The Word is Christ himself, the Hebrew dabar, through which the world was created. In the incarnation (John 1), the Word became flesh and thus accessible to us. In the ascension (Mark 16), the word of God was released from its local state to an unrestricted presence. Christ is no longer seen as being physical. Therefore preaching is needed. The preached Word is a sacrament, not just a human testimony but the Word of God itself. The Word of Creation gives the identity to preaching, incarnation gives the content and ascension (and Pentecost) gives the efficacy to the Word preached. Sundkvist 2001, 200 – 205.

511 On this concept, see Vajta 1953, 118 – 122. Martin Brecht (1986, 126) interprets "dass das Wort im Schwang gehe" to mean the same as "ausgelegt werden."

... it is not our intention to do away with the service, but to restore it again to its rightful use (*ynn rechten schwang zu bringen*) ... For all that matters is that the Word of God be given free reign (*ym schwang*) to uplift and quicken souls so that they do not become weary ... Let everything be done so thath the Word may have free course (*ym schwang gehe*) ... For all the Scripture shows that the Word should have free course (*ym schwang gehe*) among Christians.[512]

Luther wrote this tract because some order was needed after Karlstadt's violent liturgical reform in Wittenberg during Luther's absence. Luther could not simply return to the traditional order, but was forced to articulate the basic principles of the evangelical reform of the liturgy. The guiding principle was the free reign of the Word. The tract distinguishes three abuses: 1) The Word of God had been silenced; 2) Non-Christian fables, hymns,[513] and sermons were introduced instead; and 3) The service was performed as a meritorious work to attain God's grace. Luther believed that the free reign (*ym schwang gehen/bringen*) of the Word would amend the situation itself, concluding, "We can spare anything but the Word." Earlier, in the *Invocavit- sermons* (1522), Luther exhibited strong confidence in the power of God's Word. He argued that no coercion is needed against the abuses prevailing in the church. Instead, Luther believed that one should trust to God's Word and let it work without one's own efforts. In other words, the preacher does not have power over human hearts; only God can convert or harden them. Furthermore, the preacher can enter no further than to one's ear, as God alone can move human hearts how and when he wants. Therefore the Word must be allowed to operate freely (*frey gehen lassen*) without one's own works. The pastor's duty is to proclaim, but the consequences of listeners' hearts belong to God's power.[514]

---

512 WA 12,35–37; LW 53,11–14.

513 This is one of the texts where Luther uses the word "sing" in a critical tone (cf. Section 3.2.3.2.): In the beginning of the tract, he states that "God's word has been silenced, and only reading and singing remain in the chuches" (das man gottis wort geschwygen hat, und alleyne geleßen und gesungen ynn den kirchen). A little later he admonishes that "when God's Word is not preached, one had better neither sing nor read, or even come together." (Darumb wo nicht gotts wort predigt wirt, ists besser, das man widder singe noch leße, noch zu samen kome) WA 12, 35, 11–12, 24–25.

514 WA 10 III 15, 18–31: "Aber niemand sol man mit den Haren dauon reissen, sondern man sol es Gott heim geben und sein wort allein wircken lassen one unser zuthun oder wercke. Warumb? Darumb, denn ich hab nicht in meiner Hand die Hertzen der Menschen als der Toepffer den Thon, mit jnen zu schaffen nach meinem gefallen, wie Gott aller Menschen Hertzen hat in seiner Hand, sie zubekeren oder zu verstocken. Ich kan mit dem worte nicht weiter komen denn in die Ohren, ins Hertz kan ich nicht komen. Weil man denn den Glauben ins hertze nicht giessen kan, so kan noch sol auch niemands darzu gezwungen noch gedrungen werden, denn Gott thut

Luther suggested in *On Councils and the Church* that the Word is not only heard but also believed and executed. The advantages of music are involved in the Word's becoming flesh in Christian life and in music's natural power to enter our hearts. In *Concerning the Order of Public Worship,* Luther wanted to avoid tedium, constraint, and seeking for reward during a service. Instead, preaching and hearing the Word of God should happen alone to the glory of God and for the neighbor's good.[515] The virtue of music is introduced with the question: how does one listen to God's Word willingly, not only by one's ears but also with one's heart? The answer is "through music." Singing psalms, antiphons, and responsories is useful in avoiding tedium and letting the Word of God be *ym schwang,* so that it can uplift and refresh souls.[516] It is possible to read this in a very practical and superficial way – people just cannot listen to preaching for a long time. Therefore it is good to sing occasionally in order to avoid tedium.[517] Whereas the question at stake has practical and pedagogical implications, it contains a profoundly theological insight as well. Luther's hymnal prefaces illustrate both pedagogical and theological aspects.

In *Preface to the Wittenberg Hymnal* (1524), Luther notes that St. Paul himself instituted the ancient custom of the church to sing psalms in Col 3:16, so that God's Word and Christian teaching might be instilled and implanted in many ways. That is what the first Lutheran hymnal is aiming at, "so that the holy Gospel which now the grace of God has risen anew, may be noised and spread

---

solchs alleine und macht das Wort lebendig in der Menschen Hertzen, wenn und wo er wil nach seinem Goettlichen erkentnis und wolgefallen. Darumb sol man das Wort frey gehen lassen und nicht unsere wercke dazu thun, Wir haben Ius verbi und nicht executionem, Das ist, das Wort sollen wir predigen aber die folge Gott heimgestalt sein."

515 WA 12, 36, 32–34: "Und das man sie ermane, solchs frey, nicht aus tzwang odder unlust, nicht umb lohn tzeytlich noch ewig, sondern alleyne gott tzu ehren, den nehisten tzu nutz tzu thun."

516 WA 12, 36, 11–26: "Wenn nu die Lection und auslegung eyn halb stund odder lenger geweret hatt, soll man drauff yn gemeyn got dancken, loben und bitten umb frucht des worts &c.. Dazu soll man brauchen der psalmen und ettlicher gutten Responsoria, Antiphon, kurtz also, das es alles ynn eyner stund ausgerichtet werde, odder wie lange sie wollen, denn man mus die seelen nicht uberschutten, das sie nicht mude und uberdrussig werden, wie bis her ynn klostern und stifften sie sich mit esels erbeyt beladen haben.Desselben gleychen an dem abent umb sechs odder funffe widder also tzu samen ... Aber weyl nu das newe Testament auch eyn buch ist, las ich das alte Testament dem morgen, und das newe dem abent, odder widderrumb und gleych also lesen, aus legen, loben, singen und beten, wie am morgen, auch eyn stund lang. Denn es ist alles zuthun umb gottis wort, das dasselb ym schwang gehe und die seelen ymer auffrichte und erquicke, das sie nicht lassz werden."

517 As Luther states in Formula missae (StA 1, 374, 2–3): "In Ecclesia nolumus tedio extingui spiritum fidelium."

abroad" (*zu treyben und ynn schwanck zu bringen*). The first Lutheran hymnal was artistically very ambitious. The hymns were polyphonic settings in four or five parts, and Luther emphasized that this is no coincidence. "All these songs were arranged in four parts to give the young something to wean them away from love ballads and carnal songs and to teach them something of value in their place, thus combining the good with the pleasing, as is proper for youth."[518]

First, to combine good with pleasing (*das güte mit lust*) is a pedagogical point. An efficient way to learn is to sing beautiful and pleasing songs. However, this combination of being good and pleasing is simultaneously difficult. To do right with pleasure is exactly what humans are incapable of doing before God. It is not a question of whether humans can perform outwardly righteous acts. The problem is whether they are doing it willingly, without coercion, without fear of punishment or without hope for reward. If music can make humans willing to hear the Word, it is of an utmost theological significance, as suggested in *Frau Musica*: "*Zum Goettlichen Wort und warheit / Macht sie das hertz still und bereit.*"[519] Music is also reciprocal in this respect. Music can both make us willing, and through music we perform our willingness. For example, it is common for all lovers to readily talk, sing, and listen about their love. Therefore those who love God want to have his Word always on their lips and in their ears. The most perfect way to stay under the influence of the Word is to sing it.[520] Music promotes theological understanding, and it can move the affect better than words alone. The Word needs and uses music in order to establish and nourish faith. In his *Preface to the Burial Hymns* (1542) Luther declares:

> We want the beautiful art of music to be properly used to serve her dear Creator and his Christians. He is thereby praised and honored and we are made better and stronger in faith when his holy Word is impressed on our hearts by sweet music.[521]

---

518 WA 35, 474, 18 – 475, 1: "Und sind dazu auch ynn vier stymme bracht, nicht aus anderer ursach, denn das ich gerne wollte, die iugent, die doch sonst soll und mus ynn der Musica und andern rechten kuensten erzogen werden, ettwas hette, damit sie der bul lieder und fleyschlichen gesenge los werde und an derselben stat ettwas heylsames lernete, uns also das guete mit lust, wie den iungen gepuert, eyngienge."

519 WA35, 484, 7 – 8.

520 AWA 2, 44, 21 – 54, 4: "Mos est natura omnibus amantibus de suis amoribus libenter garrire, cantare, fingere, componere, ludere, item libenter eadem audire. Ideoque et huic amatori, beato viro, suus amor, lex domini, semper in ore, semper in corde, – si potest – in aure est."

521 WA 35, 480, 5 – 9: "Das also solcher schoener schmuck der Musica in rechtem Brauch jrem lieben Schepffer und seinen Christen diene, Das er gelobt und geehret, wir aber durch sein heiliges wort, mit suessem Gesang jns Hertz getrieben, gebessert und gesterckt werden im glauben."

If "sweet music" (*süsser Gesang*) advances our faith and morality, it is obvious that the sweetness of music does not pose a problem to Luther. On the contrary, sweetness is the key to the theological significance of music. What else can move hearts without coercion, persuading with its sweetness alone, besides music and the Gospel? That the pleasure music affords is entirely time-embedded and sensuous is not a threat to the faith but something that belongs to its essence. This in turn necessitates the analysis of the concept of pleasure in Luther's thought.

5 Joy (gaudium) and Pleasure (voluptas) in Luther's theology

In the previous chapters it has become clear that the Gospel is a message "that one sings, speaks, and is happy about" (*davon man singet, saget und frolich ist*). Joy has also established itself as the quality of music that makes it *optimum Dei donum*, "the best gift of God." Music offers us joy and is the expression of our happiness. Joy is the affect of faith. Granted, spiritual joy is distinct from the usual, worldly joy, but it is not completely another matter. If it were, there should be other words describing it.[522] Although the words *Freude/gaudium* and their derivatives (*froh, fröhlich* etc.) are among the most frequent in Luther's works,[523] there has been remarkably little scholarly interest in Luther's notion of joy.[524] Luther is not often regarded as a thinker who is preoccupied with joy

---

[522] Wetzel's (1954, 194–197) notion of joy displays the tenets of the dialectical theology. He argues that, for Luther as well as Augustine, to make music out of joy is not an expression of emotion (Gefühlsausdruck). Wetzel considers psychological joy to be rejoicing over something good given to us, whereas faith rejoices in the Giver. It is clear, says Wetzel, "dass die Glaubensfreude und die natürliche Freude schlechterdings nichts miteinander zu tun haben." (p. 196).

[523] Search for word "freude" has 1184 hits in Luther's works (WA 1–54). That word seldom occurs alone. The most frequent combinations (biblical quotations excluded) are "freude und lust" (54 hits, e. g. WA 19, 313, 29–30; 314, 13; 402, 2; 427, 2; WA 30 I 151, 17; 163, 13; WA 45, 57, 30), "freude und trost" (37 hits e. g. WA 19, 314, 16; 660, 18; WA 36, 130, 9), "freude und friede/ruhe" (18 hits e. g. WA 45, 165, 21), "freude und wonne" (16 hits e. g. WA 10 II, 413, 20) and "freude und seligkeit/ewige leben/herrlichkeit" (11 hits e. g. WA 7, 548, 19; WA 45, 45, 8).

[524] Günther Metzger (1964,94–96) is reviewing joy – among other affects – in Dictata super psalterium. There Metzger distinguishes the following features of joy: it is a sign of faith, mark of the new creation and an eschatological phenomenon. Joy does not remain inside, but "sie drängt nach aussen, will sich 'äussern'." Ulrich Asendorf (1998, 206–212) has dedicated a chapter of his study on Lectures on Genesis to affects and eschatological joy. There he notices in

and pleasure. Lutheran theology is commonly understood as being a theology of the cross, a teaching about justification through faith alone. That type of theology does not naturally estimate sensuous pleasure highly. Yet I claim that this connection is essential in order to understand Luther's thinking. Music can indeed advance our understanding of Luther's theology by uncovering its joyous nature. This chapter explores the theological depths of pleasure and joy. The first point is that the source basis differs from the previous chapters. The texts discussed here will no longer directly deal with music. Instead, the more central and better-known works of Luther will be examined, such as *The Bondage of the Will*, *On Christian Freedom*, and the *Postils*. For if the theological horizon of music – a theology of pleasure – is of some value in Luther's thought, it needs to be discernible in Luther's main works and not just in the few pages he dedicated to music.

5.1 Joy

5.1.1 The Gospel is good news

The theological significance of joy is most obviously derived from Gal 5:22, "The fruit of the Spirit is love, *joy*, peace, patience ..." The fact that joy immediately follows the greatest of all – love – is a signal of its central position in Christian life. The passages on this verse in Luther's commentaries on Galatians are useful in examining his teaching of joy. Another instructive Bible verse is Phil 4:4, "Rejoice in the Lord always, I will say it again: Rejoice!" Luther's sermon on this text in 1521 is also illuminating.

In his advent sermon, Luther proclaims that joy is a fruit and consequence of faith (*frucht und folge des glawbens*) that can be read in two ways. First, if one does not rejoice, then that person does not properly believe. Second, it is indeed not possible to rejoice at all without faith. However, an important adjustment must be made at this point, as apparently it is possible to rejoice in passing pleasures, "in silver or gold, in eating or drinking, health or wisdom." This kind of joy is not real but deceptive, which cannot move or fill the depths of the heart (*des hertzen grund rhuren noch fullen*). True joy is rejoicing in God, and is not possible when there is sin and fear of God's punishment in one's conscience. Luther claims that one might as well try to burn water as to talk to such

---

passing that the older Luther often uses the image of drunkenness when speaking about spiritual joy. Birgit Stolt (2000, 147–172) has also discussed the role of humor in Luther's writings.

a person of joy in God. Luther also refers to the good conscience as the joy over all joys on earth.[525] Accordingly, preaching the Gospel of the forgiveness of sins is equal to teaching people how to rejoice. The road to true joy runs through the valley of despair when, in order to obtain a good conscience, one must be discouraged (*vortzagen*) from one's own works, apprehend God in Christ, and believe the promises of the Gospel.

> But what does the Gospel promise other than that Christ is given for us; that He bears our sins; that He is our Priest, Mediator, and Advocate before God, and that thus only through Him and His work is God reconciled, are our sins forgiven and our consciences set free and made glad? When this sort of faith in the Gospel really exists in the heart, God is recognized as favorable and pleasing (*suss und lieblich*). The heart confidently feels His favor and grace, and only these. It fears not God's punishment. It is secure and in good spirit because God has conferred upon it, through Christ, superabundant goodness and grace.[526]

The superabundant joy in God is something ever-present in Christian life, and the adversities of life do not make it cease. If one has a gracious God, what can harm one? Neither sin nor hell can damage the person trusting God, let alone lesser adversities. Although it is true that a Christian cannot be entirely without sin, and that sin brings naturally with it sadness and a burdened conscience, joy in Christ should always prevail in people's hearts. Ultimately it is not a matter of choice or a heroic manifestation of the power of one's will, but simply letting Christ be greater than our sin (*Christus grosser lassen seyn denn unser sund*).[527]

5.1.2 Characteristics of Christian joy

The musical character of joy is obvious in Luther's 1531 commentary on Galatians. Joy is the *voice* of the bride and bridegroom (*gaudium est vox sponsi et sponsae*). This nuptial image introduces physical expressions of joy, such as singing and dancing, as well as:

---

525 WA 38, 113, 5–16: "freude uber alle freude ist ein gut gewissen"; AWA 2, 205, 1–9: "Fides enim in deum seu 'lumen vultus dei' laetificat cor et intima hominis stabili et vera laetitia imbuit, dum pacem remissis peccatis et securam fiduciam in deum facit, etiam in mediis passionibus. Neque enim est ullum gaudium, ulla pax, nisi conscientia pura."
526 WA 10 I 2, 170,23–172,8.
527 WA 10 I 2, 173, 13–25.

Sweet cogitations of Christ, wholesome exhortations, *pleasant songs of praise and thanksgiving*, whereby the godly do instruct, stir up and refresh themselves. God loves not heaviness and doubtfulness of spirit. He hates unsound doctrines and sorrowful cogitations; and he loves cheerful hearts. He has not come to oppress us but to cherish our hearts.[528]

There is a distinction between *gaudium carnis* and *gaudium Spiritus*. Nevertheless, that distinction is not made according to the outward expression of joy but according to its source. Spiritual joy is rejoicing in Christ and the source of this joy is the certitude of faith that Christ is our Savior. As stated above, joy and certainty belong together. Therefore any uncertain teaching about God is *tristis doctrina*. To emphasize this certitude, Luther teaches that believers already have the things they anticipate in faith through the joy of their heart.[529]

Pertaining to the innermost place of the human soul, Christian joy does not remain inside, but inevitably bursts out in proclaiming and expressing itself by words and behavior (*verbis et gestibus*).[530] In *Christmas Postil* (1522), the joy of the shepherds in the night serves as an example. Joy makes one willing to speak and hear about what faith has received in the heart. Accordingly, the shepherds became loquacious in saying, "Let us go to Bethlehem and see this thing that has happened, which the Lord has told us about" (Luke 2:15). They could have uttered the more succinct, "Let us go to Bethlehem to see what God has done there." That is a characteristic of spiritual joy. It bursts out in abundant words, and even that does not appear sufficient. Luther quotes Ps 45:1, "my

---

528 WA 40 II, 117, 24–28: "Est vox sponsi et sponsae, hoc est, iucundae cogitationes de Christo, salubres exhortationes, laeta carmina, laudes, gratiarum actiones, quibus sese mutuo adhortantur, exercent et exhilarant pii. Aversatur ergo Deus tristiciam Spiritus, odit tristem doctrinam, tristes cogitationes et verba et delectatur laeticia. Non enim venit, ut contristaret, sed ut exhilararet nos." ##Emphasis mine.##??##

529 AWA 2, 207, 8–9: "Voluerunt onstensilia bona increduli, iam habent; voluerunt invisibilia creduli, iam in laetitia cordis ea habent."

530 WA 40 II, 117,33–118,14: "Ubi hoc gaudium non carnis, sed Spiritus est, ibi cor intus laetatur per fidem in Christum, quia certo statuit, eum esse Salvatorem et pontificem nostrum, et foris hoc gaudium verbis et gestibus ostendit." In Operationes in Psalmos Luther contests the opinion of Augustine (and Cassiodorus) about that the words "voce mea" (Ps 3:5) do not mean outer voice. We ought to use our voice in joy as in sorrow – as our Lord did on the cross: "Voce mea' B. Augustinus et post eum Cassiodorus putant non de corporea voce, sed de voce cordis dictum esse, nec de ea ipsa nisi purissima, propter pronomen mea, quod sua vox non sit, quae impuris orantis cogitationibus interpelletur. Quae vera esse credo, non tamen vocem corpoream exclusam esse puto, quod vox affectus, quando vehemens est, se continere non possit, quin erumpat in vocem corpoream. Nam et Christus in Cruce utique corporea voce clamavit et nobis clamandum esse docuit in angustia, ut sic totis viribus intus et foris dominum invocemus. AWA 2, 138,30–139,6.

heart is overflowing with a good matter," by stating that it means what one wants to say is much greater than what one is able to utter. In Ps 51:14 it is stated, "my tongue shall sing aloud (*eraushupffenn*) of thy righteousness," which according to Luther means to "speak, *sing* and tell about it rejoicing and jumping" (*mit freuden und sprungen dauon reden, singen und sagen*). The phrase Luther uses for Ps 119:171, "My lips will pour forth praise" (*erausschewmen*), depicts the state of the heart, which is like a boiling pot that bubbles up (*schewmet*).[531] This indicates that Luther conceives of Christian joy not as silent joy within the heart, but as a rather noisy phenomenon. To describe the nature of this joy, Luther repeatedly uses musical expressions, particularly the word *singen*. Another outward expression of joy that Luther talks about is laughter. Christian theologians have traditionally had a reserved attitude toward laughter, and abstaining from laughter has severed spiritual joy from earthly amusement. In his 1522 preface to the New Testament, Luther argues that if one believes in the Gospel one must be happy and laugh from the bottom of one's heart. It is not possible to understand "the laughter of the heart" (*lachen des hertzens*) as something remaining in the secrecy of the soul.[532] Laughter in God is an expression of our

---

531 WA 10 I 1, 135,12–136,9: "Das funfft ist frewd, wilche sich ertzeygt ynn de wortten, das man gernn dauon redet und hoeret, das der glawbe ym hertzen hat empfangen. Alßo hie die hirtten schwetzen mitteynander frolich und freuntlich von dem, das sie gehoertt und gleubt hatten, und machen fast viel wort, alß wollten sie unnutz schwetzen; sie haben nit gnug, das sie sagen: last uns gehen gen Bethlehem und sehen das wort, das da geschehen ist, thun dazu und sagen: Wilchs gott gethan hatt unnd unß kund gethan; ists nit eyn ubrig geschwetz, das sie sagen: das da geschehen ist, das gott gethan hatt? Hetten sie es doch wol mit kurtzen worten geredt: Alßo last unß sehen das wort, das gott alda than hat. Aber die freud des geystis geht alß ubir mit frolichen worten, und ist doch nichts ubrig, ia, noch alleß tzu wenig, unnd kunnen es nit ßo erauß schutten, wie sie gernn wollten, wie ps. 44. sagt: Meyn hertz schluckt erauß eynn guttis wort, alß sollt er sagen: Ich wollts gern erauß sagen, ßo kan ich nit. Es ist grosser, denn ichs sagen kann, das meyn sagen kaumet eyn schlucken ist; daher kompt die rede ps. 50. und an mehr ortten: Meyn tzung wirt eraußhupffenn deyn gerechtickeyt, das ist, mit freuden und sprungen dauon reden, singen und sagen &c.. Und ps. 118: Meyn lippen werden dyr eyn lob eraußschewmen, gleych wie eyn siedend topffenn quillet und schewmet" Cf. the discussion of ecstasy in 3.2.3.3.

532 WA DB 6, 5, 20–23: "Nu kan yhe der arme mensch, ynn sunden, todt vnd zur helle verstrickt, nichts trostlichers horen, denn solch thewre lieblich botschafft von Christo, vnd mus seyn hertz von grund lachen vnd frolich druber werden, wo ers glewbt das war sey." The same idea appears in a Christmas sermon in 1520, WA 7, 190, 5–7:"Wie koent ein mensch nit lachen und freude vol sein, so er gantzlich in seinem hertzen glaubt und darfuer hielt, das das kind sein sey?" Also a sermon on St. Michael's day 1544 (WA 49, 584, 33–39) teaches: "O wer das gleuben koende (sage ich aber mal) und gewislich in seinem hertzen schliessen, das unser wort nicht unser, sondern Christi wort, unser teuffen Christi Tauffe, unser absolviren und Sacrament reichen Christi sey, der muste doch zum wenigsten einen tag oder zween frolich werden, Gerne wolt

trust in God's *philanthropia* (Titus 3:4). Therefore, the absence of laughter challenges the presence of faith.[533]

The earlier commentary on Galatians (1519) adds another aspect to spiritual
joy. It could be called the social character of joy in Christ. Rejoicing in Christ is
not only joy in God but also joy in one's neighbor. Joy is directed toward God and
one's neighbor in the same manner as love. Luther explains what it is to rejoice
in one's neighbor in the same terms as he later clarifies the seventh commandment in his catechisms. In other words, one rejoices in one's neighbor when one
does not envy one's neighbor's goods, but instead congratulates the neighbor as
if they were one's own. Thus one praises God's gifts in one's neighbor.[534]

5.1.3 Joy and love

Joy is the affect of faith and faith is also love. The relation between faith, love,
and joy could be presented according to following formula:

FAITH > LOVE > JOY [> MUSIC]

Love as the basic affect is inaccessible to a person. This implies more than it is
not under one's own control to decide to love. It is equally difficult even to *become aware* of one's love. In an early sermon (1514), Luther tells what Zacchaeus'
joy (Luke 19:8) indicates:

---

ichs selbs gleuben und also predigen, das es andere auch gleubten, Aber das wir nicht hertzliche
freude und lust hievon empfinden, das ist ein zeichen, das es uns nicht zu hertzen gehet, wie es
solt."

533 WA 10 I 1, 101, 13 – 19: "Glewbistu aber, ßo ists nitt mueglich, das dauon deyn hertz nitt sollt
fur freuden ynn gott lachen, frey, sicher und muetig werden. Denn wie mag eyn hertz trawrig
odder unlustig bleyben, das da nit tzweyffellt, Gott der sey yhm fruntlich und hallte sich gegen
yhm als eyn gutter frund, mit dem er sich alß mit yhm selbs alliß dings wol vormuege? Es muß
solch freud und lust folgen; folget es aber nit, ßo ist gewißlich der glawb noch nit recht da."
534 WA 2, 593, 24 – 28: "Gaudium, secundus fructus, aeque ut charitas, in deo et proximo est: In
deo, quando de divina misericordia laeti sumus, etiam in mediis mundi procellis laudantes et
benedicentes dominum in camino ignis die ac nocte, In proximo vero, quando illius bonis non
invidemus, sed congratulamur tanquam nostris propriis, laudantes dona dei in illo." In this
early commentary there is also an emphasis not found in "mature" Luther, to praise God in the
midst of the fire of hell (in camino ignis). This idea of praising God even when condemned to
hell is not unheard of in devotio moderna mysticism. Later, Luther saw hell as completely out of
question for a Christian, as something that can not concern him/her at all. See WA 10 I 2, 173.

Zacchaeus did not long for Christ to come, and yet longed for it. That he did not, becomes apparent of the fact that he climbed to the tree in order to see Christ passing by but did not presume or want to expect that he would go that way. It is obvious that he did not consider himself worth for it and was content with seeing him and hiding thereafter. After all, he did not have anything to boast of before Christ who was coming, and he knew that he is not worthy compared to other people. That he nevertheless longed for Christ is apparent because he received him with joy. Joy is a sign of preceding love and longing. If someone had asked him, does he not want to have Christ, he would have answered: "I do not venture to wish or want it." The love and longing would answer instead: "Certainly, I hope that will happen." Look at the profundity of the human heart. Its truth is so intimate and its will so hidden, that it does not know itself and does not even rejoice in willing. The willingness is only sensed and lived, not elicited. That is the proper heart, these [i.e. love and longing] are the innermost of a human person.[535]

It is difficult to determine what Zacchaeus felt concerning the coming of Christ. The only indication that he already loved Christ was his joy when he received Christ. The affect of love is hidden, even when the joy of the heart may not always be apparent. Nevertheless, joy is an expression of this longing of the heart. That the innermost heart is hidden and known by God alone does not mean that it is entirely imperceptible, because faith and love in the heart expresses itself through joy. Therefore joy is *signum praecedentis amoris et cupiditatis*, a sign of the precedent love and longing. God's love is not unnoticed in the soul. Unlike what Aquinas and Duns Scotus (according to Luther) taught, the grace of God is not a divine ornament of human works but a powerful force that acts continuously in one's soul. Grace is God's love, with Christ himself living in faith. Although love itself may not be known, its effects are perceived.[536]

---

535 WA 1, 97,29 – 98,1: "Zachaeus autem non cupiebat Christi adventum, et tamen cupiebat. Quod non cupiebat, patet, quia adscendit tantum ut videret transiturum, non autem praesumebat nec audebat cupere ingressurum. Patet enim manifeste, quod non se dignum putavit, quia voluit esse contentus eo viso et latere postea: non enim habuit, unde gloriosum sibi foret Christum advenisse, sciebat sese non mereri prae caeteris omnibus. quod autem cupiebat, patet, quia accepit illum gaudens Gaudium enim est signum praecedentis amoris et cupiditatis. Si enim quis ipsum interrogasset, velletne Christum habere, Respondisset 'non audeo optare nec velle'. Illi autem respondissent 'Utique, et spero sic futurum'. Videte ergo profunditatem cordis humani, cuius veritas tam intima est et tam secretum velle, ut nesciat sese nec gaudeat velle, solummodo sentitur et vivitur hoc velle, non autem elicitur. Hoc est rectum cor, haec sunt interiora hominis."

536 WA 10 I 1, 104,20 – 105,11: "Es ist gar eyn groß starck, mechtig unnd thettig ding umb gottis gnade, sie ligt nit, wie die trawmprediger fabuliern ynn der seelen und schlefft odder lessit sich tragen, wie eyn gemallt brett seyne farbe tregt. Neyn, nit alßo, sie tregt, sie furet, sie treybett, sie tzeucht, sie wandellt, sie wirckt allis ym menschen und lessit sich wol fulen und erfaren; sie ist vorporgen, aber yhr werck sind unuorporgen, werck unnd wortt weyssen, wo sie ist, gleych wie die frucht unnd bletter des bawmß artt unnd natur außweyßen. Darumb wirtt tzu wenig und tzu

Within the Augustinean tradition there is nothing problematic in stating that to love God is to be pleased in God and to rejoice in him. However, rejoicing in creatures is another thing. According to the *ordo caritatis*, God is the supreme goal of love and one should love things that are above one's self. Humans are superior to other creatures and should therefore not love creatures but God, and themselves, as *imagines Dei*.[537] Luther disavowed the *ordo caritatis* in his theology.[538] To love God does not mean to abandon lower things and to strive toward God above. By contrast, loving God means to receive God's endless and continuous goodness in the visible world. To love creation does not obstruct but advances the love of God, because creation reveals the essence of God as self-giving love, as has become obvious in the section dealing with Luther's concept of "gift." Indeed, not to rejoice in the gifts of creation would be an expression of ingratitude.

In the *Heidelberg Disputation*, Luther declares that divine love is love that creates its object. That means that God's love is directed to those who are sinful, insane, and sick and that his love makes them righteous, wise, and healthy. On the contrary, human love is directed to that which it finds pleasing.[539] Christians are called to partake in the divine love, "being Christ" to each other.[540] The source of love is always God. Only when one has such a God who continually gives everything good can one love one's neighbor selflessly. In accordance with divine love, Christians should relate to others as if the infirmity and sin of others belonged to themselves. Therefore it is possible to maintain that it is an act of disbelief not to delight in that which does not appear delightful. "From faith flow forth love and joy in the Lord, and from love a cheerful, willing, free life that serves our neighbor without charge."[541] Thus, Luther believed that a Christian is not merely allowed but obliged to delight in the creation of God. In particular, one should be pleased to see God in one's neighbor, regardless of his/her sin.

---

gering von yhr gepredigt, ßo man yhr nitt mehr gibt, denn das sie die werck schmucke und helffe vollnbringen, wie die Sophisten Thomas, Scotus und das volck yrren und vorfuren. Sie hilfft nit alleyn die werck thun, sie thutts alleyn, ia, nit alleyn die werck, sie wandellt und vornewet die gantz person."

537 See the quote of Augustine's De Trinitate in 2.5.3.

538 For Luther's theology of love, see Raunio 1998, 113–122; 2001, 154–180; Mannermaa 2010; Kopperi 1997, 161–172.

539 StA 1, 365, 4–10: "Amor Dei non inuenit, sed creat suum diligibile, Amor hominis fit a suo diligibili ... Prima pars patet, quia amor Dei in homine uiuens, diligit peccatores, malos, stultos, infirmos, ut faciat iustos, bonos, sapientes, robustos, (et) sic effluit potius, (et) bonum tribuit."

540 Notably in the latter part of *On Christian Freedom* (StA 2, 285, 19–299, 22).

541 StA2, 299, 16–17: "Sih also fleusset auss dem glauben die lieb vnd lust zu gott / vnd ausz der lieb / ein frey / willig / frolich lebenn dem nehsten zu dienen vmbsonst."

The good things of God must flow from one another and become common, so that everyone accepts his neighbor as if he was Christ himself. From Christ they flow to us, since he has accepted us into his life as if he were what we are. From us the good things of God shall flow to those who need them; even in such a perfect manner, that I have to set my faith and righteousness in behalf of my neighbor before God to cover his sins.[542]

The Lutheran *ordo caritatis* opens from above. To love God is to participate in God's categorical giving. This does not result to despising inferior things but in recognizing God's bountiful grace even where it appears ostensibly as something opposite.[543]

---

542 WA 7,37, 32–38: "Sihe also mussen gottis gutter fliessen auß eynem yn den andern und gemeyn werden, das ein yglicher sich seynis nehsten also annehm, als were erß selb. Auß Christo fliessen sie yn uns, der sich unser hatt angenommen ynn seynem lebenn, als were er das gewesen, das wir sein. Auf uns sollen sie fliessen yn die, so yr bedurffen, Auch so gar, das ich muß auch meynenn glaubenn und gerechtickeyt fur meynenn nehsten setzen fur gott, seyne sund zu decken."

543 Matthias Zeindler (1993, 399–400) calls Luther's approach in Heidelberg disputation the aesthetics of the cross, aesthetica crucis: "Nicht nur das Mächtige und das Starke geniesst unter den Menschen Ansehen, sondern auch das Schöne. Schönheit hat die Kraft, dem Blick auf sich zu ziehen. Dagegen gehört es zum Niedrigen, dass es ästhetisch unbedeutend ist und das Sehen gleichgültig lässt. Und erst recht ist das Elend hässlich und stösst den Blick sogar ab. Was unten ist, wird deshalb auch aus ästhetischen Gründen nicht angesehen, die fehlende Schönheit ist ein Element der Marginalisierung. Der Blick der Kirche wird an dieser Stelle ein anderer sein. Da sie sich durch Gottes schöpferisches Sehen die Blickrichtung hat umkehren lassen, übersieht sie weder das ästhetisch Unbedeutende, noch wendet sie die Augen vom Hässlichen ab. Es gehört zu ihrer Aufmerksamkeit für und zu ihrer Solidarität mit den Schwachen, dass sie hier aufmerksam ist und gegebenenfalls dem Abstossenden standhält. Nicht nur geniesst das Schöne Ansehen, dass Angesehene gilt auch oft als schön. Der Mensch empfindet in der Regel das Gute, Gesunde und Intakte als schön. Ist sein Blick nach oben orientiert, dann wird er vor allem demjenigen Schönheit zusprechen, was Macht, Stärke und Reichtum repräsentiert, demjenigen also, das ihn in seinem Drang zur Selbstkonstitution und Eigenmächtigkeit bestätigt. Auch hier unterscheidet sich die Kirche. Nicht auf das Angesehene fixiert, gewinnt sie eine neue Freiheit in der Wahrnehmung. Sie findet Schönheit nicht mehr allein an dem, was den allgemeinen Massstäben gemäss wertvoll ist, sondern auch an dem, was dem nach oben orientierten Blick verborgen bleibt. Auch am vordergründig Unbedeutenden kann sie Schönheit entdecken. Durch ihren erneuerten Blick eröffnet sich der Kirche ein weites Feld neuer Schönheit."

5.2 Pleasure

5.2.1 Pleasure and will

Pleasure (*voluptas*, *Lust*) is closely connected to the notion of joy and to some extent is synonymous with it. To feel joy in something is to feel pleasure in it. However, *voluptas* implies some connotations that *gaudium* does not. Pleasure is a more sensuous feeling than joy. One can rejoice in hope, in something not yet there, while pleasure is more overtly directed to something present. *Lust* is the German word that is most often connected to *freude* in Luther's works.[544] If one does something with joy (*freude*), one does it willingly, with pleasure (*lust*). This applies equally to earthly delights, to Christian joy, and to God himself, whose *lust und freude* is to give without reward.[545] One of the basic convictions of Luther's theology is that humans are completely unable to fulfil the requirements of the divine law willingly and with happiness. In the original state of creation, Adam delighted in obeying God. However, after the Fall, people followed the devil with joy.[546] To regain the pleasure requires an act of God's mercy. To obey God with joy is possible only because God has sent his Son to redeem us and has poured the Holy Spirit into our hearts through faith. In faith we know that we have a merciful God and our heart obeys God with love and willingness (*lust und liebe*).[547]

One of the most central and opaque works of Luther is *Bondage of the Will* (*De Servo Arbitrio*). Without the notion of pleasure, Luther's argumentation in this book is impenetrable. The major problem is how it is possible for a human person to rejoice in God's commandments. The editor of Luther's complete works, Georg Rörer, inserted into both the Wittenberg and Jena editions of *De servo arbitrio* the following paragraph:

> I could wish indeed that another and better word had been introduced in our discussion than this usual one, "necessity," which is not rightly applied either to the divine or the human will. It has too harsh and incongruous a meaning for this purpose, for it suggests

---

[544] See note 519 above.

[545] WA 21, 482, 33–35: "ein solcher Herr, der gerne gibt, und seine lust und freude ist zu geben, lauter umbsonst, on alles gesuche." For wordly joys see e.g. WA 34 II, 114, 10–11.

[546] WA 47, 661,39–662,24: "Adam hatte lust und freude gott gehorsam zu sein. Iam gaudemus, wenn wir gott zuwider dem Teuffel solle folgen."

[547] WA 22, 256,37–257,3: "Er zeigt aber auch, woher die Christen solche krafft haben, das sie des Fleisches luesten koennen widerstehen, Nemlich, das sie haben den Geist empfangen durch den Glauben und wissen, das sie einen gnedigen Gott haben, daher jr hertz lust und liebe gewinnet, Gotte gehorsam zu sein und sich fur suenden zu hueten."

a kind of compulsion, and the very opposition of willingness, although the subject under discussion implies no such thing. For neither the divine nor the human will does what it does, whether good or evil, under any compulsion, but from sheer pleasure and desire, as with true freedom.[548]

It is highly possible that this addition is authentic. Luther did reconsider his choice of words in this work later and probably discussed this with Rörer.[549] Nevertheless, the addition is compatible with the argumentation in *The Bondage of the Will*. Perhaps a more suitable title for the work would be *The Bondage of the Delight*, since it is the delight of the will that remains impossible for us to change.

Luther states that, unless God gives his Spirit, humans do evil not out of compulsion (*coacte*) but out of necessity of immutability (*necessitate immutabilitatis*). Necessity of immutability refers to one's inability to change the direction of his/her will (the affect). This applies both to the human and divine will. The Rörer addition continues to say that God's will is immutable and infallible. His will cannot change, and God's will governs our will, which is mutable but unable to do good by itself and hence also immutable. There is thus a two-level immutability. God's will is immutable, since it is eternal and infallible and the human will is mutable, but nevertheless the human will is not under the control of human decision. As far as it depends on human powers, the basic directedness of the human will is immutable.[550]

An important distinction can be made between compulsion and necessity. The human will does not do evil unwillingly and under coercion, for, "a man void of Spirit of God does not evil against his will as by violence ... but he does it spontaneously, and with desiring willingness" (*sponte et libenti voluntate*). When a person is forced to do something contrary to this evil will, the will continues to resist and to be averse to what it is forced to do. Just think of how difficult it is to persuade those who insist on their own opinion (*affecti*

---

548 StA 3, 191 note 107: "Optarim sane aliud melius vocabulum dari in hac disputatione quam hoc usitatum Necessitas, quod non recte dicitur, neque de divina, neque humana voluntate. Est enim nimis ingratae et incongruae significationis pro hoc loco, quandam velut coactionem, et omnino id, quod contrarium est voluntati, ingerens intellectui, cum tamen non hoc velit causa ista quae agitur. Voluntas enim sive divina sive humana nulla coactione, sed mera lubentia vel cupiditate quasi vere libera facit quod facit, sive bonum sive malum."
549 Kolb 2005, 26 – 28.
550 StA 3, 191, note 107: "... sed tamen immutabilis et infallibilis est voluntas Dei; quae nostram voluntatem mutabilem gubernat, ut canit Boethius: Stabilisque manens das cuncta moveri; et nostra voluntas, praesertim mala, se ipsa non potest facere bonum." The quotation of Boethius' O qui perpetua is an interesting detail, cf. section 2.3.1.

aliqua re haerent). They may succumb only under coercion or for something more advantageous – that is, for punishment or reward. Nevertheless, their hearts remain unaffected. The same holds for the justified. After our will is changed by God, it remains immutable, for "when God works in us, the will, being changed and sweetly breathed on by the Spirit of God, desires and acts, not from compulsion, but responsively, from pure willingness, inclination, and accord (*mera lubentia et pronitate ac sponte*)." That being the case, the renewed, God-oriented will is also not free in the absolute sense. It is bound to God and its basic directedness is not under the power of human decision, "so that neither is there here any willingness, of free-will, to turn itself into another direction, or to desire anything else, while the influence of the Spirit and grace of God remain in the human person."[551] This makes a human a horse – or a mule – on which God or Satan rides. In other words, it is not in its power to choose which rider it will bear, or which it will seek.[552]

At the end of the book, Luther employs the image of birth to capture that faith is in no way an accomplishment of the human will. Luther quotes John 1:13, "Which were born, not of blood, nor of the will of the flesh, nor of the will of man, but of God." The word "blood" in this case, according to Luther, refers to Jews; "the will of the flesh" is carnal desires and "the will of man" is the best part of personhood, the free will. None of these is capable of making one a

---

551 StA 3, 207, 10 – 33: "Necessario vero dico, non coacte, sed ut illi dicunt, necessitate immutabilitatis, non coactionis, hoc est, homo cum vacat spiritu Dei, non quidem violentia, velut raptus obtorto collo, nolens facit malum, quemadmodum fur aut latro nolens ad poenam ducitur, sed sponte et libenti voluntate facit. Verum hanc libentiam seu voluntatem faciendi non potest suis viribus omittere, cohercere aut mutare, sed pergit volendo et lubendo, etiam si ad extra cogatur aliud facere per vim, tamen voluntas intus manet aversa et indignatur cogenti aut resistenti. Non autem indignaretur, si mutaretur ac volens vim sequeretur. Hoc vocamus modo necessitatem immutabilitatis, id est, quod voluntas sese mutare et vertere alio non possit, sed potius irritetur magis ad volendum, dum ei resistitur. Quod probat eius indignatio. Hoc non fieret, si esset libera vel haberet liberum arbitrium. Interroga experientiam, quam sint impersuasibiles, qui affecti aliqua re haerent. Aut si caedunt, vi vel maiore alterius rei comodo caedunt, nunquam libere caedunt. Si autem affecti non sunt, sinunt ire et fieri, quecunque eunt ac fiunt. Rursus ex altera parte, si Deus in nobis operatur, mutata et blande assibilata per spiritum Dei voluntas iterum mera lubentia et pronitate ac sponte sua vult et facit, non coacte, ut nullis contrariis mutari in aliud possit, ne portis quidem inferi vinci aut cogi, sed pergit volendo et lubendo et amando bonum, sicut antea voluit et lubuit et amavit malum. Quod iterum probat experientia, quam invicti et constantes sint viri sancti, dum per vim ad alia coguntur, ut magis inde irritentur ad volendum, sicut ignis a vento magis inflammatur quam extinguitur, ut nec hic sit ulla libertas vel liberum arbitrium alio sese vertendi aut aliud volendi, donec durat spiritus et gratia Dei in homine."
552 . StA 3, 208, 2 – 7.

child of God. That is possible only through being born of God. Even as it is impossible for someone to decide to be born, it is also impossible to decide to want to love God.[553]

The question of the free will is therefore a question of love. When God changes human will, it desires, craves after, and loves (*volendo, lubendo et amando*) that which is good, as before it sought after evil. In *The Christian Freedom*, Luther argues that out of faith flows love and pleasure (*lieb und lust*) to God and willingness to serve the neighbor.[554] Pleasure appears to be an essential part of will and love. If the problem of free will were to be a simple matter of decision, it should not be impossible to decide to believe in God. It is possible to convince oneself logically that there is a God, or at least to witness sufficient evidence for the possibility of God's existence. If faith is understood more in terms of love toward God, it becomes much more difficult. Even then it is possible to consider love as a matter of decision more than of emotion. This is an important emphasis in marital love, for instance. Love can be viewed as faithfulness, a decision to act lovingly. The problem is that love toward God is not the same as the patient tolerance between spouses. The commandment is, "Love the Lord your God with all your heart and with all your soul and with all your mind" (Matt 24:39, Luke 10:37). Luther cannot understand this otherwise than that the deepest emotions of the heart, pleasure (*lust*), love (*liebe*), and joy (*freude*), are involved.[555] If faith essentially involves pleasure in God's will, it is inevitably beyond human decision. This implies that one cannot decide to feel pleasure for something. Sometimes it is possible and necessary to reluctantly do good in front of humans. Yet before God, that which is done unwillingly is not done at all.[556] This is why *liberum arbitrium* does not lead to faith.

Luther regards this ultimate dependency on God's decision as liberating. At the end of his treatise, Luther admits that even if it were possible he would not want to make a free decision in the matters of salvation. He proclaims that if there was free will or anything left in his hands by which he might strive toward salvation (*aut quippiam in manu mea relinqui, quo ad salutem conari possem*), his

---

[553] StA 3, 344,25 – 345,14.

[554] StA2, 299, 16 – 17: "Sih also fleusset auss dem glauben die lieb vnd lust zu gott / vnd ausz der lieb / ein frey / willig / frolich lebenn dem nehsten zu dienen vmbsonst."

[555] WA 10 I 2, 359, 30 – 35: "Es saget nicht von der zungen noch von der hand noch von den knien, sondern es redet von dem gantzen leybe und von allem, das du hast und bist. Sol ich keinen frembden Got haben, so můß ich warlich den einigen rechten Got mit dem hertzen haben, das ist: ich můß jm von hertzen holdt sein, ymmerdar an jm hangen, mich auff jn verlassen, jm trawen, lust, liebe und frawde an jm haben."

[556] WA 10 I 2, 156, 7– 8: "denn was mit unlust, schweer und unwillen wirt gehalten, das ist fur gott gleych, als nicht gehalten."

salvation would become ultimately insecure. One's faith could therefore not withstand life's adversities or the devil's attacks. Even if there were no adversities or demons, the uncertainty would not end. How could anyone ever be sure that one had done enough in God's eyes (*satis Deo)?* Therefore, it is liberating to know that God has taken one's salvation outside one's own power of decision and kept it within his own (*salutem meam extra meum arbitrium tollens in suum receperit).* One may trust the words, "no one can snatch them out of my hand" (John 10:28), since the matter of salvation is completely in God's hands. As the basis of one's salvation is God's grace and forgiveness, it cannot be annulled by either the unreliability of one's own decision or the attacks of demons.[557]

However, Luther's solution does not assuage all insecurity, for the prominence of pleasure can cause ultimate despair. What if one does not feel joy ("the willingness, inclination and accord") in God at all? If feeling joy and pleasure is understood as a sign and consequence of faith, can anyone draw other conclusions than that lacking those emotions indicates a lack of faith? Here Luther uses another pair of words, *joy and consolation* (*freude und trost).* Whereas "*freude und lust*" deals with the basic motivation of Christian life, "*freude und trost*" is more of a pastoral concern. The expression "*freude und trost*" is an expression used especially when Christians encounter adversity and feel emotions contrary to joy, such as fear, sadness, or anguish. In a 1527 sermon on Christ's ascension, Luther comments on Eph 4:8 ("he led captivity captive") by observing that it is an unbelievable and impossible matter according to our own understanding. However, the prophets and apostles who were led by the Holy Spirit speak about it joyfully and certainly as if they had themselves seen it happen. They feel in their hearts and find joy and comfort (*trost und freude).* For others, on the contrary, it is difficult to perceive how sin and death are led captive. We

---

557 StA 3, 351, 13–30: "Ego sane de me confiteor, Si qua fieri posset, nollem mihi dari liberum arbitrium, aut quippiam in manu mea relinqui, quo ad salutem conari possem, non solum ideo, quod in tot adversitatibus et periculis, Deinde tot impugnantibus daemonibus subsistere et retinere illud non valerem, cum unus daemon potentior sit omnibus hominibus neque ullus hominum salvaretur, Sed, quod etiam si nulla pericula, nullae adversitates, nulli daemones essent, cogerer tamen perpetuo in incertum laborare et aerem pugnis verberare; neque enim conscientia mea, si in aeternum viverem et operarer, unquam certa et secura fieret, quantum facere deberet, quo satis Deo fieret. Quocunque enim opere perfecto reliquus esset scrupulus, an id Deo placeret, vel an aliquid ultra requireret, sicut probat experientia omnium stitiariorum et ego meo magno malo tot annis satis didici. At nunc cum Deus salutem meam extra meum arbitrium tollens in suum receperit, et non meo opere aut cursu, sed sua gratia et misericordia promiserit me servare, securus et certus sum, quod ille fidelis sit et mihi non mentietur, tum potens et magnus, ut nulli daemones, nullae adversitates eum frangere aut me illi rapere poterunt. Nemo (inquit) rapiet eos de manu mea, quia pater, qui dedit, maior omnibus est."

feel quite the opposite. We do not believe it, even less feel it, let alone find any joy or comfort in it.[558] It is obvious that, for Luther, faith is not just an opinion but also very essentially an experience. The problem at stake precisely concerns whether one experiences something that is contrary to joy and the certainty of faith. This is a matter of life and death, since one is devoured by death unless one believes that Christ has indeed taken death captive. The pastoral advice of Luther is that one should not judge oneself according to one's emotions. One may fear death and see before oneself hell wide open. Luther counsels his listeners to cling to the word that Christ "has ascended up on high, led captivity captive and given gifts to humans." There is no other way for a Christian to conquer sin and death, and this is not something that one learns instantly. It is a skill that needs to be practiced continuously. This occurs through hearing, reading, and singing the Word. When this trust is born in the heart, joy follows immediately.[559] This joy is a gift and work of the Holy Spirit in us. It is not an idle thought of the mind, but the Spirit's transforming activity, by which it makes us new. It is possible to derive three preconditions for Christian joy: 1) it is a gift of Holy Spirit; 2) it is given through the continuous exercise of the Word *im Schwang*; and 3) it is a

---

[558] WA 23, 717, 21–31:"Das sey von dem ersten stueck gesagt, Das Christus in die Hoehe gefaren ist und hat das Gefengnis gefangen, das ist, Er hat Suend, Tod, Teufel, Helle und alles unglueck uberwunden und uns, die wir gleuben, das es uns zu gut geschehen sey, den weg zum Himel eroeffnet. Das sind alles ungleubliche, ja unmuegliche wort, wenn wir unser vernunfft zu rat nemen, Aber die Propheten und Apostel, durch den heiligen Geist getrieben, reden so froelich und sicher davon, als sehen sie es fur augen, habens auch in irem hertzen gefuelet und trost und freude davon gehabt. Wir aber, weil wir nicht sehen noch tappen, wie die Suende und der Tob gefangen ist, sondern fuelen das widerpiel, gleubens nicht, viel weniger fuelets unser hertz, wil schweigen, das es trost und freude davon haben solte."

[559] WA 23, 718,19–719,19: "Das wird wol bleiben, das dich die Suende anfechten, der Tod erschrecken, Gottes gericht deinem gewissen angst und bang machen wird, so lang du lebest. Wie soltu aber hie thun? Da mustu bey leib dich nicht darnach richten, wie du fuelest, Du must nicht sagen: O weh, der Tod wil mich fressen, zetter, die Helle spert den rachen weit auff und wil mich verschlingen, sondern fasse einen mut und zuversicht auff Christum und trit solche gedancken mit fuessen und sprich: Es heisst nicht: O weh, der Tod wil mich fressen, sondern es heisst: Mein HErr Christus ist in die Hoehe gefaren und hat das gefengnis gefangen, Das in die Hoehe faren wird dirs, du leidiger Tod, wol verbieten, das du mich wol unverschlungen und ungefressen lassen must, Ich sol frey sein und bin auch frey umb des Mans willen, der in die Hoehe gefaren ist. Das ist die rechte einige weise, dadurch die Gleubigen die Suende, Tod &c.uberwinden, ... Aber diese kunst lesst sich so bald nicht fassen, wie viel dencken, wenn sie es nur ein mal hoeren, sie habens ausgelernet. Nein, Bruder, noch lang nicht, Du feilest weit, Es gehoert warlich ein fester starcker Glaube dazu, nicht ein loser wahn oder dunckel des hertzen, wie sichere Leut und Heuchler haben, sondern der mit gantzem erwegen und gewisser zuversicht darauff stehe und beruge, das Christus in die Hoehe gefaren sey &c.. Wo dieser Glaube ist, da kan der Mensch nicht verzweiveln, ja er wird von hertzen froelich drueber."

consequence of trust in God's Word. When these preconditions are fulfilled, it is possible to state that if one does not feel this joy, one lacks faith.[560]

5.2.2 Holy pleasure

What has made pleasure theologically suspect is that it is involved in the visible and tangible world, attached to our physical and temporary existence. Luther is associated with this tradition, but his thought contains traits that attest to a new appreciation of earthly pleasures. First, Luther's use of the word *voluptas* illuminates its distinctiveness as a form of joy, speaking of "pleasures of the throat and stomach" (*voluptatis ventris et gutturis*).[561] Luther also connects *voluptas* with *amor, libido, delectatio* and *laetitia*.[562] In the first *Antinomian Disputation*, Luther argues that it is not possible for a human being to sin without experiencing pleasure, since we do not sin against our will. Thus, *voluptas* and *voluntas* are strongly interconnected, as is evident in the above analysis of *The Bondage of the Will*.[563] Concerning the concept of pleasure, Luther adheres to Augustine, who considered pleasure to be a volitional matter so that to desire or delight in something involved only the will's consenting to the things enjoyed.[564] In the Aristotelian tradition, supreme pleasure was exclusively a matter of intellect; pleasure is a part of happiness, and the highest form of happiness, according to virtue, is the pursuit of wisdom.[565] As discussed in chapter 2, feeling pleasure has been perplexing for philosophers. The gratification of senses that pleasure implies has caused particular suspicion. In Greek philosophy, the reasonable joy was among *eupatheia*, the emo-

---

560 WA 23, 719, 22–33: "Solcher Glaube, wie gesagt, ist nicht ein schlefferiger muessiger gedancke im hertzen, sondern ein gabe und werck des heiligen Geists in uns, der uns wandelt und newe Menschen macht, solche unaussprechliche gnade Gottes, durch Christum erworben und geschenckt, mit ernst zu betrachten und im von hertzen dafur zu dancken ... Wo ein solche freude das hertz nicht fuelet, sondern ist eng und erschrocken, so ists ein gewis zeichen, das es on Glauben ist."

561 WA 4, 562, 33.

562 AWA 2, 420, 27.

563 WA 39 I, 378, 16–18: "Congenita est nobis illa concupiscentia et non est involuntaria, sed est voluptas et voluntas maxima peccandi et in peccato originali, nec possunt peccare involentes."

564 De civ. Dei XIV, 6 (PL 41, 409): "Interest autem qualis sit voluntas hominis: quia si perversa est, perversos habebit hos motus; si autem recta est, non solum inculpabiles, verum etiam laudabiles erunt. Voluntas est quippe in omnibus: imo omnes nihil aliud quam voluntates sunt. Nam quid est cupiditas et laetitia, nisi voluntas in eorum consensionem quae volumus?"

565 Aristotle: Nicomachean Ethics X, 7.

tions allowed in a wise man. Pleasure is also possible for animals, whereas joy (*gaudium*) presupposes the use of reason.[566]

Luther teaches that while humankind was still in the state of innocence, there was nothing problematic with pleasure. Pleasure was a part of the human condition in the beginning. Adam lived in a state of supreme bliss and confidence (*Adam autem in summa voluptate et securitate vixit*).[567] The reason for his uninterrupted bliss was that Adam was created as an image of God. Another source of endless pleasure was the dominion over nature and knowledge of it. We cannot perceive this pleasure, since it was lost in the Fall, and because every kind of human dominion over other creatures and other people has been contaminated by selfishness.[568]

Had humankind remained in its original state of creation, dominating the fish in the sea would have meant *voluptas sancta*, because greed did not yet contaminate human dominion. In addition to being used as a source of food, use of other creatures was admiring God.[569] After the Fall, our relationship to pleasure became distorted. Even though God has not ceased to be the source of supreme pleasure, humans have become more interested in the effects of pleasure than in the cause. Pleasures should not be pursued; they are a consequence of faith. "But seek first his kingdom and his righteousness, and all these things shall be yours as well" (Matt 6:33). Once there is faith, pleasure will inevitably follow.[570] Luther suggests the pleasure of faith in the *Lectures on Romans* when he writes that God must test and chastise us after giving us righteousness and other spiritual gifts, which are very lovable and which evoke enjoyment (*amabilia et fruitionem irritantia*). "The Lord disciplines the one he loves" (Heb 12:6) means that God teaches us to love him instead of his gifts. Through sufferings we learn to love our Father instead of the delightfulness of our inheritance (*dul-

---

[566] Sorabji 2000, 48; Knuuttila 2004, 245.

[567] WA 42, 47, 22–23.

[568] WA 42, 49, 29–3: "Hanc imaginis divinae particulam etiam amisimus, ita ut ne intelligamus quidem illam plenitudinem leticiae et voluptatis, quam ex totius creaturae animalis inspectione Adam habuit."

[569] WA 42, 54, 23–25: "Nec erat avaricia in eius posteritate futura, sed praeter victum, tantum ad admirationem Dei et voluptatem sanctam."

[570] WA 2, 98, 37–99, 5: "Dan das heyst selig sein, wan got in uns regirt und wir sein reich sein. Dye freud aber und lust und alles ander, das man begeren mag, durft man nit suchen noch bitten noch begeren, sundern es wirth sich als selbst finden und folgen dem reich gotis. Dan wie ein guter wein mag nit getruncken werden, er bringt von ym selb mit ungesucht seinen lust und freud, und mag nit vorhyndert werden, Also vil meer, wan die gnaden und tugenden (das reich gottis) volnkommen werden, so musz an unszer tzuthun, naturlich und unvorhyndert folgen freudt, fryd und selickeyt und aller lust."

cedo hereditatis). Our sinful human nature would rush to perdition if it had only the pleasure of God's gifts.[571]

The pleasure experienced in faith can be interpreted as a divine *condescendence*. The idea is parallel to the notion of the pedagogical use of music or to the rhetorical *delectatio*. Because humans are incapable of rising toward God through their own understanding and because the divine matters are unperceivable to humans, God in his affability chose to draw humans to himself through pleasure. This is a typical approach to the sensual language of Song of Songs. To quote but one author from the vast commentary literature:

> Since humanity has been closed from the delights of Paradise and has entered in the exile of the present life, its heart is blind to spiritual reality. If God's voice would say to this blind heart: "Follow God" or "Love God" – as it is said to it in the Law – it would not understand that because of its exile, frigidity and insensibility. Therefore the Word of God speaks with parables to this cold and insensible soul, and, speaking about things that the latter knows, secretly inspires in it the love it does not know.[572]

God needs to give us something that attracts us in order to make us hear his actual message. However, Luther uses the idea of condescention in a different sense.[573] In *Against Latomus*, Luther explains why scripture uses figurative language. Figurative speech has a powerful effect on humans, who are naturally inclined to hear it. Therefore the Bible is replete with the most beautiful and furnished imagery (*venustissimis et ornatissimis figuris*). Although here Luther is defending (against scholastic theology) the simple and historical meaning of scripture, he admits that the biblical use of images enriches understanding and gives pleasure to the soul. Luther offers an example of this divine condescendtion. In Deut 4:19, Moses does not simply say, "do not worship stars," but "do not worship things the Lord your God has designed for all the nations under heaven." Luther urges the reader to read these words *aloud* (in Hebrew) and promises that one will not hear anything as sweet, powerful, and perfect. Luther bases his explanation on the Hebrew verb *chalaq*, which can mean both "to distribute" and "to flatter."

---

571 WA 56, 305, 10–18: "Igitur optimus Deus, postquam Iustificauit et dona sua spiritualia dedit, Ne Impia illa natura in ea ruat fruitura illis, cum sint multum amabilia et fruitionem vehementer irritantia, mox tribulat, exercet, examinat, ne tali ignorantia homo pereat in-ęternum. Sic enim discit homo pure Deum amare et colere, dum non propter gratiam et dona, Sed propter ipsum solum Deum colit. Sic 'flagellat omnem filium, quem recipit'. Quod nisi faceret, filius dulcedine nouę hereditatis arreptus cito luxuriaret in fruitionem acceptę gratię et grauius post quam ante patrem offenderet."

572 Gregory the Great: Commentary in Song of Songs (SC 314, 68).

573 Sammeli Juntunen (2010a, 70–80) has discussed condescendence in Luther's christology. I approach this theme from the perspective of creation.

This dual meaning implies that the stars in the sky tell us that God has created them in order to flatter and persuade all the nations on the earth. This is simultaneously a pleasure (*voluptas*), a lesson of piety (*eruditio pietatis*), and an arousal of emotion (*concitatio affectuum*). However, it is not preliminary knowledge or a trick God must perform in order to get to the point. God reveals his innermost being precisely in the way he flatters us, as Luther writes:

> Just think, even as a mother fondles her child upon her knees, so the Lord God has given the stars of the heaven to all peoples as if to flatter and caress them, and in order to draw them to himself by his most sweet and tender goodness and to invite them to his love by these gentle benefits.[574]

This is the view of God that pleasure conveys, and it is not a preliminary view of God that should be corrected afterwards. The way God speaks to us in the Bible and even through stars in the sky is condescending, but it uncovers the heart of God precisely as being condescending. If one experiences God as a caressing mother due to the abundance of scriptural imagery and the endless number of stars, what is preliminary or theologically insufficient here? Stating that God uses our sense of pleasure as a starting point for something higher does not capture Luther's point, which is gaining pleasure from the categorical goodness of God. Pleasure does not come before understanding, but vice versa. To encounter God is to experience pleasure.

---

[574] StA 2, 464, 20 – 465, 17: "Proinde mihi Hebreistae illi no(n) placent, qui tot uni verbo significationes faciunt occasione Chaldaicoru(m) istoru(m) Onkeli (et) Ionathae, quorum hoc negociu(m) fuisse videtur, ut ea, quae scriptura venustissimis et ornatissimis figuris eloquitur, pro rudibus exuerent et crasso simplicite significato traderent. Hinc natae illae aequivocationes in ista lingua sine causa et quaedam Babylonica confusio verborum. Mire enim dispergitur er intelligentia et animus ista varietate, ubi si una simplici (quoties fieri potest) significatione proposita caeteras illius imagines et figuras iuxta posueris, placido et facili sinu omnem illam confusionem colliges, tum et memoriam et intelligentiam mirum in modum iuvabis, nec minus animum simul dulcissima voluptate capies. Nescio enim, quae sit figurarum energia, ut tam potenter intrent et afficiant, ita ut omnis homo natura et audire et loqui gestiat figurate. Nonne multo dulcius sonat: 'Coeli enarrant gloriam dei', quam istud: 'Apostoli praedicant verbum dei'? Et quando Moses Deutero. iiij. dicit de astris non adorandis: 'Ne forte adores ea, quae creavit dominus deus tuus in ministerium cunctis gentibus, quae sub coelo sunt', si hebraeum verbum sua simplicitate reddas, involuta metaphora, certe nihil dulcius, potentius, plenius audias. Sic enim sonat hebraice: 'Quae blandificavit dominus deus tuus cunctis populis sub coelo'. Obsecro, quanta eruditio pietatis, quanta concitatio affectuum, quanta voluptas in eo verbo est, quod dominus deus astra illa coeli omnibus populis dederit, velut adulatus et blanditus eis, quo eos suavissima et tenerrima bonitate sua ad sese alliceret et mollibus istis beneficiis ad sui amorem invitaret, non aliter quam sicut mater filio suo super genua sua blanditur?"

The *Heidelberg Disputation* determined human love to be directed to those things from which humans derive pleasure (*amor hominis fit a suo diligibili*). Therefore it appears to be contradictory to state that God is encountered in pleasure. Is the "theology of pleasure" merely another form of *theologia gloriae*, which Luther vehemently attacked in the Disputation? To answer that question, it is necessary to examine more closely the essentials of the theology of glory. The "theologians of glory" aspire to understand the invisible qualities of God (*invisibilia Dei*) through his works (*per ea quae facta sunt*). What is problematic regarding the theology of glory is not observing creation, but rather failing to see creation as it is. Theologians of glory are so determined to discern divine qualities such as wisdom, righteousness, and goodness that the realities of the world escape their attention. A "theologian of the cross," on the other hand, recognizes God in the "humanity, weakness, and madness" of the world.[575] In this respect, it becomes clear that finding pleasure in creation is the direct opposite of the "theology of glory." To be pleased with God's works is to acknowledge them as created, and as gifts of God. A theologian of glory would indeed detest the physicality and temporariness of earthly pleasures.[576] Luther's openness to earthly pleasures proves to be a trait that is not just a biographical detail, but reflects his understanding of God, faith, and love.

5.3.3 Sensuous pleasures in Luther's thinking.

A famous quote by Luther, though inauthentic, is: "Who loves not women, wine and song, he lives a fool his whole life long." While it has not been documented that Luther said this, it does not necessarily mean the sentence does not reflect Luther's ideas. One of the most significant testimonies to Luther's appreciation of

---

575 StA 1, 207,26–208,4: "Non ille digne Theologus dicitus, qui inuisibilia Dei, per ea, quae facta sunt, intellecta conscipit. Patet per eos, qui tales fuerunt, Et tamen ab Apostolo Roma. 1. stulti uocantur. Porro inuisibilia Dei sunt, uirtus, diuinitas sapientia, iusticia, bonitas (et)c (etera). haec omnia cogita non faciunt dignum, nec sapientem. [] Sed qui uisibilia (et) posteriora Dei, per passiones (et) crucem conspecta intelligit. Posteriora (et) uisibilia Dei sunt opposita inuisibilium, id est, humanitas, infirmitas, stulticia."

576 Kari Kopperi, who has thoroughly examined the Heidelberg Disputation, comments that the "theology of glory" seems to intend speculative theology, but, the whole disputation taken into account, it becomes obvious that for Luther human works are an essential part of the theology of glory (Kopperi 2010, 166). In his dissertation Kopperi entertains the possibility that the words per ea quae facta sunt can refer to the human works performed to attain righteousness. In any case, Luther does not deny that the creation can convey knowledge of God. Instead, humans tend to abuse it (Kopperi 1997, 127–138).

earthly pleasures is his letter to Hieronymus Weller written in June 1530. Weller suffered from sadness, so Luther wrote Weller to say that God is the God of joy and consolation, whereas sadness comes from the devil. In fact, Luther argues that to live is to rejoice in the Lord.[577] As a piece of pastoral advice against the spirit of sadness, Luther encourages Weller to seek company, play cards, or to have fun. He encourages Weller to undertake this with a good conscience, because sadness comes from the devil, not from God.[578] These earthly, perhaps even profane joys are also gifts of God. In accordance with what has previously been stated about music, one should not say, "they are gifts of God when properly used." The use or abuse of a gift of God does not constitute its being a gift of God, although it is important for the recipient of the gift. Eccl 3:12–13 states, "I know that there is nothing better for men than to be happy and do good while they live. That everyone may eat and drink, and find satisfaction in all his toil – this is the gift of God." For Luther, the ability to enjoy present things and to have a happy and joyful heart is also a gift of God.[579] The little pleasures of everyday life are therefore a twofold gift; a gift of things to enjoy, and a gift of joyous disposition that is willing to enjoy them. This side of faith, more typical of the old Luther than the young, is opposed to both monastic and puritan piety.[580] Luther's conception of Christian joy is not averse to earthly pleasures; on the contrary, the Christian attitude to temporary gifts is to receive them with gratitude and use them moderately. The biblical ground for the appreciation of wine, dance, and earthly festivities is the wedding in Cana (John 2), where the Lord created wine for people who were already drunk. Luther says that undoubtedly hypocrites disapproved of the Lord's conduct in the wedding, and, as he preaches on this text, Luther also feels obliged to emphasize restraint both in the consump-

---

577 WA Br 5, 374, 18–22: "Igitur ante omnia tibi statuendum est firmiter istas cogitationes malas et tristes a Deo non esse, sed a diabolo, quia Deus non est deus tristitiae, sed deus solatii et laetitiae, velut Christus ipse dicit 'Non est Deus mortuorum, sed vivorum'. Quid vero est vivere, nisi laetum esse in Domino."

578 WA Br 5, 374, 39–41: "Quare recte feceris, si potius luseris cum aliis aut alia iucunda tractes ac deinde de ludo nullam conscientiam feceris. Deo enim non placet tristitia illa vanissima."

579 WA 20, 64, 22–25: "Nihil est melius homini in tam calamitosis negociis quam frui praesentibus ac laeto et iucundo animo esse sine sollicitudine et cura futurorum. Verum istud posse facere donum Dei est."

580 Heiko A. Oberman (1989, 310) offers both recognition of and a complaint about the way German Lutheranism has fostered Luther's heritage, "The discovery of the world and earthly joys against the background of the adversary's threat to morality separates Luther from both monastic and puritan morality. German Lutheranism, with its cultural ideal of making music at home, has preserved a precious part of the Luther heritage. But when a cheerful round of cards is disdained as unrespectable or even disreputable, Luther has lost the game."

tion of wine and the activity of dancing. Nevertheless, the Lord did not disapprove of the earthly rejoicing at the wedding.[581] Luther's appreciation of earthly pleasures is a remarkable trait in his thinking, but not without tensions. The pleasures of music seem rather different from, for example, sexual pleasure, which is briefly discussed next.

The virtue of chastity is particularly difficult to maintain. Luther states in *A Treatise of Good Works* (1520) that even though only one of the Ten Commandments concerns chastity, "do not commit adultery" obligates us ceaselessly. This is because sexual lust is present in our body, in our thoughts, in our words, and in things we see and hear. Luther regarded sexual desire as something sinful, even in marriage. In this regard, there is no difference between Luther and Augustine, who has the reputation of being an anti-sexual thinker.[582] A difference is discernible in the thinking of these two in how Luther appreciates the sexual drive that existed in paradise. Originally, as part of creation, human procreation through sexual intercourse was a holy state of affairs. Luther never abandons this basic conviction. Without the Fall, human procreation would have remained pure and decent. As no man is ashamed to talk, eat, and drink with his wife, so would copulation be just as decent, or perhaps even more decent than that.[583] After the Fall, however, the relationship between the sexes became corrupted and the pure love between spouses deteriorated to a bestial level.[584]

---

581 WA 17 II 63,1–64,29.

582 Grimm 1999, 64: " Pour Luther – comme pour la tradition chrétienne – le procréation elle-même est toujours affecteé d'un mauvais désir. Bien qu'elle soit necessaire et utile pour la vie de l'Eglise et de la societé et qu'elle soit placée 'sous le commandement de Dieu', elle ne peut se réaliser sans pécher. Augustin n'argumentait pas autrement. Procréer – même selon l'ordre de Dieu – est devenu indécent! " What is noteworthy in the examples that Grimm has selected from Luther's works is that the most explicit statements concerning the sinfulness of sexual intercourse are from the mature work Commentary of Genesis, not from the texts written by the young monk.

583 WA 42, 177, 3–7: "Opus generationis est creatura Dei bona et sancta, est enim ex Deo benedicente. Ac si homo non esset lapsus, fuisset purissimum et honestissimum opus. Sicut enim nemo veretur cum uxore sua loqui, edere, bibere; honesta enim sunt haec omnia, Ita quoque generare honestissimum fuisset." In a sermon Luther gives a pastoral advice to the youth in the same vein: "Lieber knabe, scheme du dich nichts, das du eynß meydlin begerist, und das meydlin eynß knaben begeret, laß nur tzur ehe gelangen, nit tzur buberey, ßo ist dyrß keyn schande, ßo wenig alß essen unnd trinckenn schande ist" (WA 10 I 1, 708, 10–13).

584 Lähteenmäki 1955, 45: "Was ursprünglich ehrenhaft und gut gewesen sei, das sei nunmehr nach dem Sündenfall durch fleischliche Begierde und satanisches Gift besudelt. Die reine Liebe, purus amor, habe sich in abscheuliche Begierde, laeda libido, gewandelt. In die geschlechtliche Gemeinschaft sei sinnliche und blinde Gier eingegangen, die wie eine tödliche Krankheit anmute. Die erniedrige die Gemeinschaft zwischen Mann und Frau unter den Stand des Tieres."

Nonetheless, Luther is not completely straightforward in discussing this matter. He oscillates between the rehabilitation of marriage on the one hand and the inescapable sinfulness of conjugal life on the other.[585] The ultimate goodness of marriage is based on the fact that it is God's commandment. In *Vom Ehelichen Leben* (1522), Luther teaches that the words "be fruitful and increase in number" (Gen 1:28) are not merely a commandment but a work of God. Therefore it is not under human power to prevent it. Sexuality, as well as the organs related to it, is part of human nature.[586] For both Luther and Augustine, the power of sexuality is evidence against the freedom of human will. However, the emphasis of these two theologians is quite different. For Augustine, the inability to avoid sexual desire is a sign of the miserable condition of humankind.[587] In contrast, for Luther, the indispensability of sexuality attests to the fact that God institutes marriage, and therefore the monastic ideal to suppress sexual attraction is in fact sinful. The reality of original sin is not based on human procreation occurring through sexual intercourse, but that sin is ineradicable in humans. Although Luther may sound strikingly Augustinean in his concept of original sin, there is a small but significant difference. In commenting on the psalm verse, "I am conceived in sin," *Ego in peccatis conceptus sum* (Ps 51:5), Luther points out this cannot be interpreted as, "my mother sinned when conceiving me," *mater mea peccavit cum conciperet me*. Original sin does not mean that parents sin when they conceive children, but that sin is innate for humans.[588] In explaining Gen 6:2, "The sons of God saw that the daughters of men were beautiful, and they married any of them they chose," Luther highlights that it is not procreation that is prohibited, but the abuse. The argument continues with the statement that "the sons of God" were wrong in that they did not ask the will of God but instead married according to their lust. Furthermore, they also neglected natural law, which is

---

585 Grimm 1999, 80. Augustine considered the question of pleasure in paradise as being problematic. In De Genesi contra Manichaeos, he thought that Adam and Eve had spiritual bodies not designed for procreation. In The City of God, Augustine ascribes to them sexual bodies, but "if they had used their bodies then, they would not have felt neither lust nor pleasure." Sorabji 2000, 406–409.

586 WA 10 II, 276, 21–26: "Denn diß wort, da gott spricht: 'Wachsset und mehret euch', ist nicht eyn gepot ßondern mehr denn eyn gepott, nemlich eyn gottlich werck, das nicht bey uns stehet tzuverhyndern odder noch tzulaßen, ßondern ist eben alßo nott, alß das ich eyn manß bild sey, und noettiger denn essen und trincken, fegen und außwerffen, schlaffen und wachen. Es ist eyn eyngepflantzte natur und artt eben ßo wol als die glidmaß, die datzu gehoeren."

587 See e.g. De Civ.Dei XIV, 16.

588 WA 40 II, 380, 26–28: "Porro non loquitur de peccato coniugali seu parentum, quod parentes accuset peccati, de se dicit: 'Ego in peccatis conceptus sum', non dicit: mater mea peccavit, cum conciperet me."

understood in a positive sense as an institution of God. The spiritual moral of the incident is that the violation of the first table of the Ten Commandments leads immediately to the violation of the second table.[589]

Sexuality is part of humanity. Feeling sexual desire is not wrong as such, but if sexual desire is the main motive for human action, it becomes a sin. Therefore, Luther admonishes youths to ask God for a good spouse. In this way, marriage will take place in the right manner and not according to carnal desires. Whereas sexual delight is not an unreservedly positive thing in Luther's thinking, it is not altogether bad. To some extent, his attitude toward sexual pleasure reflects his positive assessment of earthly delights. All material things are pure and holy in faith and they are gifts of the creator. On the other hand, even the most spiritual and immaterial things may be harmful and sinful if they are used for one's own benefit and for gaining merits before God. Therefore, it is not sensuality or corporality that taints human sexuality, but the abuse of this gift of God. The holiness of sexuality is not based on abstinence or the marriage ceremony, but the Word of God, which says, "procreate" and "it is not good for a man to be alone."[590] Marriage is instituted in the Word of God and in natural law (*iuris naturalis et positivi*), which means admitting the power of sexuality. One of the most important and positive consequences of the Reformation was the rise of the status of marriage to the supreme form of Christian life. The purpose of marriage is not just to satisfy sexual desires, because marriage is not a play of passions but a holy estate meant to raise persons to serve the world and promote the knowledge of God.[591] Luther does not, however, overlook the emotional side of marriage. For example, in the *Large Catechism*, he stresses, "Wherever marital chastity is to be maintained, above all it is essential that husband and wife live together in love and harmony, cherishing each other wholeheartedly and with perfect fidelity. This is one of the chief ways to make chastity attractive and desirable."[592]

---

589 *WA 42, 268, 9–20: Sed mirum videri potest, quod Moses inter peccata videtur numerare procreationem Filiarum, quam tamen supra in Patribus laudavit, et est benedictio Dei etiam in impiis. Cur igitur inter peccata numerat? Respondeo: Non damnat simpliciter procreationem, sed abusum, qui est ex peccato originali. Nam regia maiestas, sapientia, divitiae, vires corporis sunt res bonae, quas habere etiam bonum est, nam divinitus conceduntur hominibus. Sed quod homines cum his donis proruunt extra primam tabulam et contra primam tabulam hisce donis instructi pugnant, deinde etiam secundam tabulam licentius violant: haec impietas est digna, quae damnetur. Ideo Moses quoque singularibus verbis utitur. 'Videbant, inquit, filias hominum filii Dei, quod essent pulchrae, et acceperunt Uxores ex omnibus, quas elegerunt', nullo scilicet habito respectu Dei, iuris naturalis et positivi.*
590 Lähteenmäki 1955, 67–68.
591 BC 414, 208.
592 BC 415, 219.

The pleasure that spouses can experience in each other's arms is not condemned. On the contrary, it is as a holy thing, a blessing of God. However, it is not of intrinsic value, but is a pleasure with a purpose. Its purpose is to procreate children or to fulfill natural need and restrain infidelity. Luther's thoughts on sexual pleasure present a new appreciation of pleasure – one can experience sensuous delight without sin –by God's commandment. Nevertheless, Luther's thoughts on sexual delight are still somewhat restricted and even contradictory.[593] Therefore it is remarkable that when Luther speaks about the delights of music, all reservations disappear.

5.3 The delight of music is sensuous and innocent

Luther declared his love for music by exclaiming, "I love music, because ... it creates innocent joy" (*quia innocens gaudium facit*). In *Frau Musica* he wrote about the joy of music, making clear to everyone that music cannot be sin. Instead, music pleases God more than all joys upon earth.[594] Furthermore, unlike anything else, music affords pleasure that is good before both humans and God.[595] This is a bold statement and the inherent perils are manifold. First, rejoicing in music is rejoicing in a human activity. We are so preoccupied with Luther's refusal of human efforts in theology that this idea seems to be incompatible with his other ideas. Furthermore, the pleasure of music is not intellectual but affective. As an affective delight, music is bound to the physical world and our time-embedded existence. The pleasure of music is also a momentary experience, music being one of the most transient of all artistic mediums. All these things considered, for Luther, music is the purest joy on earth. It is not a pleasure that serves a higher purpose, such as sexual pleasure in marriage. This pleasure

---

593 According to Juntunen (2010b, 200 – 204), Luther failed to incorporate his theology of love into sexuality, "Luther did not foresee the consequences that abandoning the ordo caritatis as the framework for his theology would have had for his sexual ethics. The Stoic understanding of concupiscence, which Luther inherited from Augustine, was so strong in this area of Luther's thinking that the irrational character of the sex act made it something dirty in itself, even within marriage" (p. 204).
594 WA 35, 483, 11–14: "Auch ist ein jeder des wol frey,/ Das solche freud kein suende sey,/ Sondern auch Gott viel bas gefelt / Denn alle freud der gantzen welt."
595 WA 35, 474, 2–7: "Das geystliche lieder singen gut und Gott angeneme sey, acht ich, sey keynem Christen verborgen, die weyl yderman nicht alleyn das Exempel der propheten und koenige ym allten testament (die mit singen und klingen, mit tichten und allerley seytten spiel Gott gelobt haben) sondern auch solcher brauch, sonderlich mit psalmen gemeyner Christenheyt von anfang kund ist."

is completely good and sufficient in itself. However, to use music as a medium for something else presents problems. The use of music may be understood from two angles – how God uses music and how humans use it. God uses music to proclaim the Gospel, gratify human souls, and drive away the devil. When people use music, they tend to use it wrongly.[596] Use becomes abuse when people make music a tool for their insane passions.[597] The right use of music is therefore to sing and enjoy it simply and with joy. To say that this kind of human activity, which affords sensuous pleasure, is something that deserves to be called "the best gift of God" is a remarkable statement. This presents Luther's theology in a new light, which may be called a "theology of pleasure."

In the course of the present study, theology of music has become theology of pleasure. Next, it is time to determine what kind of pleasure is discussed here. Kant used the term *disinterested pleasure* for aesthetic appreciation to refer to pleasure that is an end in itself. As the pleasure of music is, for Luther, an end in itself, it may be concluded that the pleasure of music pertains to the aesthetic realm. Except for applying Kantian definitions to Luther's theology, there is hardly anything controversial in this statement. Obviously, as a form of art, music is an aesthetic phenomenon. However, the role of aesthetic perception in Luther's thinking requires further examination in the present analysis.

6 Theology of beauty and the virtues of music

The pleasure of music has been demonstrated to be of the aesthetic kind. This necessitates the examination of Luther's aesthetics, a topic rarely discussed in previous studies. This chapter proceeds as follows: first, I will discuss Luther's idea of beauty (*Schönheit, pulchritudo*), which undergoes a certain development in the course of his career. Then I will investigate the aesthetic criteria by which Luther evaluates music. As was explained in the introduction, the key methodological problem in reading Luther's ideas about music is that much of the material is in *Table Talk*, which are second-hand reports on Luther's sayings. In the previous chapters, I have attempted not to use *Table Talk* as sources, except for the idiom *optimum Dei donum*. However, to discuss adequately Luther's aesthetics of music, *Table Talk* needs to be consulted, since it is for the most part the

---

596 AWA 2, 162, 15–17: "Usum musicae fuisse olim sacrum et divinis rebus accommodatum, successu temporum (ut omnia) in luxus et libidinis servitutem redactum."

597 WA 50, 373, 11–374, 5: "Et deprauatos animos, qui hac pulcherrima et natura et arte abutuntur, ceu impudici poetae, ad suos insanos amores... isti adulterini filii, rapina ex dono Dei facta, colunt eodem hostem Dei et aduersarium naturae et artis huius iucundissimae."

only source available on the subject. Methodological cautiousness is maintained by comparing the sayings of *Table Talk* with more reliable Luther texts. This kind of investigation will demonstrate the relevance of these sayings to Luther's theology as a whole.

This chapter also includes a comparison between the evaluation of the sweetness (*suavitas*) of music in Luther and Calvin. The purpose of this comparison is not to make a statement *ad maiorem Lutheri gloriam*, which unfortunately often occurs in studies written by Lutheran scholars. For the most part, Luther and Calvin converge in their musical theology, but the comparison nevertheless exemplifies the peculiarity of Luther's attitude. Finally, I will present some concluding remarks about Luther's musical aesthetics.

6.1 Luther as an aesthetic thinker

6.1.1 Luther and beauty

Luther does not occupy a place in the history of aesthetics. Even in the few accounts that exist on theological aesthetics, he is seldom mentioned. The reason is perhaps that Luther is associated with Protestantism, which is often labeled as a cold, intellectual, and anti-aesthetical religion. That view is based on some changes that took place in the worship renewals during and after the Reformation. Depicting the process negatively, the Mass, with its rich synesthesia (incense, chants, candles, images of saints) was changed into a preaching hour. As a result, all outward forms of piety vanished and religion became a matter of inner conviction, an intellectual belief. However, this interpretation of Protestantism is certainly not the entire picture. It should be remembered that the music of Bach, Schütz, and Telemann, as well as congregational song and chorales, all originated in the Reformation. Furthermore, translating the scriptures into the vernacular occasioned the cultivation of poetry and literature in German and other languages. Even the Pietists, concentrating as they were on the inner spiritual experience, cherished the musical heritage of Lutheranism. Another important point is in considering present Protestantism; there are many new worship renewals and movements that do not emphasize solely the inner faith but also the outer senses.[598]

---

598 Gestrich 2008, 143, 144. A good, thorough Protestant theological aesthetics – that takes also Luther into account – is Zeindler 1993. Wolterstorff 1980 and Begbie 1991 address modern aesthetic discussion with less attention to the history of theology.

The six-volume *Die Herrlichkeit* by Hans Urs von Balthasar is probably the most important account of theological aesthetics in the twentieth century. Its first volume contains a short review on Protestant theological aesthetics that illuminates the problem of Luther's aesthetics, namely its alleged non-existence. Luther's theology is portrayed as a strictly actualistic approach, where every contemplation, analogy, and ontology is excluded. Balthasar's Luther concentrates on the "flash-lightning" event of salvation, where a human is *simul iustus et peccator*. This means that faith cannot have a breadth or permanence in the world. The paradox of faith denounces all the ways of seeing the beauty of God in this world as *theologia gloriae*. Thus the contemplative element of faith – indispensable for an aesthetic approach – vanishes, and faith becomes the opposite of aesthetic. According to Balthasar, Søren Kierkegaard is a faithful Lutheran theologian when he asserts the "aesthetic" to be the lowest stage of human existence. Accordingly, Rudolf Bultmann's stance is fully developed, anti-contemplative Protestantism that espouses nothing else but the absolute inwardness of the decision of faith without any imagery or outward facts to rely on.[599] Despite Balthasar's acuteness in portraying the absence of aesthetics in Protestant theology, it is not difficult to conclude that his picture of Luther is antiquated. I hope that the previous chapters have provided sufficient evidence to attest to the importance that Luther ascribes to outward reality and sensuous delight. To be fair to Balthasar, it must be conceded that Protestant scholars have also neglected Luther's aesthetics. Indeed, the notion of beauty seldom appears in Luther studies. Therefore, by discussing the topic "Luther and beauty," we enter into a field where previous studies are of little avail.

One can distinguish between two approaches to beauty in Luther's works. The first is typical of the young Luther and considers beauty as being inward and paradoxical. This paradox never vanishes, but it is later accompanied by another approach that is sensitive to the outward beauty of the world.

---

599 Balthasar 1982, 45–70. Rodney A. Howsare, who has studied Hans Urs von Balthasar's relationship to Protestantism, states that Balthasar's interpretation of Luther's theology is discredited by the fact that he relies on two Luther studies that are less positively assessed even within Catholic scholarship, i.e. Paul Hacker's "Das Ich im Glauben bei Martin Luther" and Theobald Beer's "Der Fröhliche Wechsel und Streit: Grundzüge der Theologie Martin Luthers"; Howsare 1999, 37–91.

6.1.2 Young Luther and the beauty of the cross

The pre-Reformatory phase of Luther's thinking has sometimes been characterized as *humilitas*-theology. Its salient features are discernible in the young Luther's notion of beauty. Commenting on Ps 96:6, "Confession and beauty are before him," Luther defines beauty as the good will, the adornment of practical virtue, and the appetitive power by which the good will loves in itself what belongs to God and hates what is its own.[600] This means simultaneously to confess what we are in ourselves and what God is in us. In other words, confession and beauty belong together in such a manner that the soul is adorned with beauty at the same time as it confesses that it is nothing and it receives everything from God. Luther presents confession and beauty in the following semantic formula:

Table 2. The young Luther's semantic formula in "Dictata super psalterium"

Confession		beauty	
Praise	and	splendor	is the same thought
Glory		elegance	

The first set (confession, praise, and glory) is given to God from the soul, while the second (beauty, splendor, and elegance) is given back to the soul by God. Hence the following memorable maxims: "Be ugly to yourself, and you will be beautiful to God,"[601] "Those who consider themselves darkness and unworthy are righteous,"[602] and "Righteousness in the soul does not come about except out of a confession of unrighteousness."[603]

Commenting on Ps 50:2, "Out of Zion the loveliness of his beauty" (*Ex Zion species decoris eius*), Luther makes an analysis of the concept of beauty (*species*). The starting point is that the word *species* comes from the verb *specere*, "to look at." As a consequence, Luther concludes that beauty is that which can be seen and placed into the light (*qui videri potest et in claritate positus*). By making this emphasis on vision, Luther seems to take a Thomistic stance (*pulchra sunt quae visu placent*). On the other hand, Luther adopts the position of Albert the Great by stating that beauty exists even if there is no one to perceive it. Beauty re-

---

600 WA 4, 109, 26 – 28: "Sed 'pulchritudo' est bona voluntas, totus ornatus practice virtutis, vis appetitive: quo amat in se que dei sunt et odit que sua sunt."

601 WA 4, 110, 16 – 17: "Tibi esto fedus, et eris deo pulcher. Tibi esto infirmus, et eris deo fortis. Tibi esto peccator, et eris deo iustus."

602 WA 4, 111, 31 – 33: "Igitur qui sibi tenebre videntur et indigni, iam sunt iusti, quia dant sibi quod suum est, et deo quod suum est: ideo illis oritur."

603 WA 4, 113, 16 – 17: "Sed iustitia in anima non fit nisi ex confessione iniustitie."

quires vision, but it can also be concealed. In the old covenant, the beauty of Christ was indeed hidden in the letter, but now the letter has been discarded and the light brought in. Although the shadow of the letter did not permit this loveliness to be sensed, it could not prevent it from being beautiful.[604] This indicates that there is beauty that is not perceived. The word *species* refers to the beauty of Christ, which was hidden in the letter but then became manifest. The church is the loveliness of the beauty of Christ, because it was conformed to Christ and receives his fullness.[605] The beauty of the church is, however, concealed from the world, "to be sure, according to the body no beauty appears in the church, because she is downcast and despised."[606] The beauty of Christians is a paradox; who is most beautiful in the sight of God is the most ugly, and vice versa, whoever is the ugliest in his/her own sight is the most beautiful.[607] For Luther, the concept of beauty in *Dictata super Psalterium* refers to an inward, spiritual thing, which stays unperceivable for the world and conceals itself under humility and ugliness.

Perhaps the most important Psalm verse considering beauty in Luther's works is Ps 45:2, *speciosus forma prae filiis hominum*, "you are fairer than the sons of men." He refers to this verse in the above *Dictata* passage and often comments on it later. This psalm verse speaks about Christ, whose beauty is superior to the beauty of humans. In a sermon on the passion of Christ (1518), Luther explains the verse by saying that the Hebrew equivalent for *speciosus forma* means "beautiful beautiful," which means that beauty is at its most beautiful when it is in Christ, implying that even the ugliness of Christ is beautiful.[608] Furthermore, the beauty of Christ is paradoxical by nature. For example, as Isa 53:2 witnesses, Christ

---

604 WA 3, 281, 24–29: "Quia fuit quidem decorus, sed nondum species eius apparuit: ideo abiecta litera et adducta luce tandem apparuit veritas, quam umbra non sinebat esse speciem, licet decorem esse prohibere non posset. Et hoc in Monte Christus ostendit, quando decorem divinitatis et glorie sue foris protulit in speciem. Unde et species a specere venit, ut sit non nisi ille decor, qui videri potest et in claritatem positus."

605 WA 3, 281, 8–11: "Ecclesia est species decoris eius, scilicet Christi, quia ei assimilata et de eius plenitudine accipiens. Ipse decorus et omni decore pulcherrimus, a quo decore venit species, i.e. forma et imago eius in Ecclesia."

606 WA 4, 113, 32. Years later, commenting on Song 1:5, "I am dark but comely," Luther wants the readers to understand that the beauty of the Church comes from the Word, not from anything outer decoration. WA 31 II, 611, 27–30: "Sic Ecclesia quoque in speciem non desiderabilis, sed lacerata esse videtur et misere afflicta omniumque opprobriis exposita. Est autem ea consolatio nostra, quod nostra salus in verbo et in fide, non in externa specie est sita."

607 WA 3, 291, 23–25.

608 WA 1, 340, 17–21: "In hebraeo pro 'speciosus forma' dicitur 'pulcer pulcer' geminando, per quod exprimit excellentiam pulcritudinis, quasi dicat 'pulcra seu electa pulcritudo est in te. In aliis enim pulcritudo est, sed in te pulcerrima pulcritudo. Immo in aliis foeda pulcritudo est, in te autem pulcra pulcritudo, ita ut et foeditas in te sit pulcra."

had "no form nor comeliness" to attract us to him. This does not refer to the outer appearance of Jesus of Nazareth. This tells about his suffering and death, which are ugly and abominable. Moreover, in the cross of Christ supreme beauty is concealed under the basest ugliness. Beauty here is not something seen with one's eyes. It is the beauty of God's love, discernible for the eyes of faith alone.[609]

That God disguises his beauty in the ugliness of Christ's suffering is his way to reveal to us the essence of his love, which again turns out to be the most beautiful. The less beautiful and the more ugly the humiliation of Christ's passion is, the more precious his love proves to be. In brief, the beauty of God's love becomes apparent in proportion to the ugliness it suffers. According to this view, to attain supreme beauty it is necessary to endure the most appalling ugliness.[610] Moreover, the way God reveals the beauty of his love in the abomination of the cross instructs us also about our own ugliness – to know God and to know oneself concur. The lovely beauty (*species illa Formosa*) is God's and belongs essentially to him. By contrast, the ugliness and suffering of the cross (*foeditas et passio*) belongs to us and endows us with knowledge of ourselves. What happens here is the *commercium admirabile:* God takes our ugliness upon himself and gives his beauty to us.[611]

The paradoxical view of beauty is an abiding part of Luther's theology. This first idea of beauty, presented in *Dictata* and maintained throughout Luther's career, could be called *pulchitudo crucis.* This is beauty concealed in ugliness, glory hidden in lowliness, and God himself disguised amidst sin and death. It is also the beauty of God by which we are made beautiful – the aesthetical variation of

---

609 WA 1, 340, 26 – 33: "Quod ut intelligamus, notandum, quod Scriptura praedixit utrumque futurum, scilicet maximam speciem et maximam foeditatem, ita ut Iesaias 53.dicat: non erat ei species neque decor. Ideo diversimode oportet intelligere: iuxta enim oculos carnis eum aspiciendo fuit novissimus virorum et despectus, et sic loquuntur scripturae, quae eum futurum abiectum et sine specie praedicant, Secundum oculos autem spirituales nihil pulcrius quam ipse est. Hunc enim oculi carnis et animae, quae iuxta carnem sapiunt, non possunt videre: sic enim fuit vere speciosus forma prae filiis hominum."

610 WA 1, 342, 22 – 24: "Nam vere quanto minor est species et maior foeditas et indigna passio, tanto maior et mirabilior est caritatis eius dignatio pro nobis eam suscipientis."

611 WA 1, 342, 37 – 343, 5: "Secundo notandum pro intellectu etiam, ut, sicut in caritatis exhibitione Dei cognitionem hic discimus, ita et nostram quoque cognitionem discamus. Ista enim duo hic summe lucent. Nam species illa formosa, quae in ipso lucet, eius est et suam in illa manifestat nobis cognitionem. Sed foeditas et passio, quae in ipso est, nostra est et nostri nobis indicat notitiam. Nam tales nos indicat esse intus in anima, qualia ipse foris sustinet in corpore. Nam nostra suscepit, ut sua nobis daret. Vere enim ipse languores nostros tulit."

the justification. The *Heidelberg Disputation* declares, "The sinners are beautiful because they are loved; they are not loved because they are beautiful."[612]

The approach to beauty in the *Lectures on Hebrews* is slightly but significantly different from that of *Dictata*. Once again, Luther states that nothing looks outwardly more unlike the "throne of God" than the church. In fact, the church appears not glorious but disgraceful, a residence in a foreign land more than a kingdom. That is the experience of all belonging to that kingdom; "the ornaments of Christians are poverty, tribulations, and afflictions."[613] The decisive moment is not, however, the humiliation that precedes the glorification, but the entrance of faith that destroys everything that pertains to the human capacities so that the person is born anew. This means that human self-humiliation plays no part. The Holy Spirit is the only active agent in the birth of faith.[614] Later, commenting on Song 1:16, "Behold, you are beautiful, my beloved, truly lovely," Luther states that this verse is full of consolation. The Holy Spirit raises the certainty in our hearts that we are beautiful in the sight of God. That is the beauty of faith. We do not need to perceive God's beauty but to be certain about our own, because at the moment of tribulation it is not apparent in our sight that God is beautiful.[615]

In Luther's third psalm commentary of 1532, the Reformer discusses Christ's beauty and says that it is possible that Jesus was also outwardly attractive, with proportional limbs and a beautiful face. Christ's physical beauty notwithstanding, his essential beauty was in his actions. In other words, the beauty of Christ

---

612 StA 1, 212, 10 – 11: "Ideo enim peccatores sunt pulchri, quia diliguntur, non ideo diliguntur, quia sunt pulchri."

613 WA 57, 107, 16 108, 3: "Nihil enim dissimilius trono et Dei trono quam populus Christi, si consideretur secundum faciem, cum non videatur regnum esse, sed exilium, nec vivere, sed semper mori, nec in gloria, sed in ignominia, nec in diviciis, sed in extrema paupertate versari, prout et quilibet, qui huius regniparticeps fieri voluerit, cogitur experiri in semetipso. Ornamenta christianorum sunt paupertates, tribulaciones, morbi; [it]a ornari debet [thr]onus Dei, qui homo [es]t."

614 WA 57, 109, 15 – 23: "Evangelium vero dicit: 'Nisi quis renatus fuerit ex aqua et spiritu denuo, non potest intrare regnum celorum', ac sic nihil reservat veteris hominis, sed totum destruit et facit novum usque ad odium sui eradicans penitus amorem sui per fidem Christi. Frustra itaque est omnis iactancia erudicionis, sapiencie et sciencie, quia nemo illis efficitur melior, quantumlibet sint bona et laudabilia dona Dei. Imo ultra hoc, quod non faciunt bonum, fiunt operculum iniquitatis et velamen morbi nature, ut sint incurabiles, qui sibi in illis placentes sibi boni et salvi videntur."

615 WA 31 II, 25, 25 – 29: "Ecce tu quoque pulcher es, amice mi, et decorus.' Est abundantia consolationis. Spiritus sanctus dat testimonium in corde, ut certo sentiamus nos placere Deo et pulchros esse. Fit igitur vicissim, ut nos quoque confiteamur Deum esse pulchrum, id est: placere nobis etc. Haec autem pulchritudo non apparet in tempore tribulationis."

is spiritual, inner beauty. He alone is beautiful as other humans are disfigured by sin. Both the ugliness of sin and the beauty of righteousness is imperceptible to human eyes and therefore often neglected, since we are attracted to the outer appearance or, at best, to beauty as a metaphysical concept.[616]

In accordance with Luther's discovery of *iustitia Dei* as the righteousness with which God makes us righteous, the beauty of God is the beauty that makes us beautiful. This is the aesthetical variation of justification through faith alone. In his *Lecture on Romans* (1515/1516), Luther recounts how this takes place.

As a philosophical starting point, it is maintained that beauty as *forma* cannot be given to someone until he/she is devoid of it.[617] Only the formless can receive the form.[618] God's justice is more beautiful (*pulchrior*) than we are in three ways. The first is that God punishes wrongdoers. It is possible to claim that even the unjust can do that. But the second way by which God "is proved righteous" (Rom 3:4) is through comparison (*relative*). Compared to human injustice, the justice of God excels in beauty. The third point is the most perfect, that God is righteous (*iustificatur*) when he justifies us. This means that God reveals his perfect righteousness by making us righteous (*effective*). The aesthetic dimension of the doctrine of justification is displayed with an image of an artist; Luther says that an artist does not become established as a good artist merely by criticizing the work of others. Instead, when an artist is compared to others and seen to be more experienced, he/she can be called a good artist. Finally, a master artist is the one who can teach his skills to others and help them become good artists.[619] In brief, God acts like a master artist and shows his beauty by making us beautiful.

---

616 WA 40 II, 485, 17–25: "Forte fieri potuit, ut aliqui essent formosiores Christo, non enim legimus Iudaeos singulariter eius formam admiratos esse, sed nos de naturali et metaphysica forma non agimus, Sed de spirituali forma; ea est talis, ut simpliciter sit formosissimus prae filiis hominum, ut hic solus maneat formosus, pulcher, coeteri omnes deformati, defoedati, depravati mala voluntate, infirmitate resistendi peccatis et reliquis vitiis, quae naturaliter nobis inhaerent. Haec turpitudo hominum non apparet in oculis, non movet oculos, sicut nec spiritualis pulchritudo movet oculos, Quia enim sumus caro et sanguis, movemur tantum forma et pulchritudine metaphisica, quam oculi vident."

617 Forma in Luther and in medieval philosophy is the "actual reality" of a thing, opposed to its materia. Thus, when Luther calls the righteousness of faith formalis iustitia, it does not mean "formal" but "real" righteousness. Mannermaa 2005, 23–30.

618 WA 56, 218,21–219, 2: "Et Vt philosophi dicunt: Non inducitur forma, nisi vbi est priuatio forme precedentisque expulsio. Et: intellectus possibilis non recipit formam, nisi in principio sui esse sit nudatus ab omni forma et sicut tabula rasa."

619 WA 56, 220, 12–16: "Bonus artifex tripliciter commendatur. Primo, dum imperitos arguit et reprehendit, Vbi errant. Secundo, quando eis comparatus doctior apparet ipsis. Tertio, quando tradit suę artis perfectionem aliis, qui eam non habebant. Et hec est Vera commendatio. Quia

6.1.3 Old Luther and appreciation of outward beauty

The later works of Luther particularly retain appreciation of outward beauty as a gift of God. In *Genesis Lectures,* Luther provides a full account of Rachel's beauty (Gen 29:17), providing a medieval textbook example of *pulchritudo visu* – Rachel's face had the right proportions, her eyes, cheekbones, and body were attractive. Although Luther sees Jacob as being somewhat puerile, being at that point an octogenarian and still deeply committed to this kind of external beauty, Luther does not judge him since scripture does not. On the contrary, Luther notices that scripture praises the love between man and woman.[620]

Mature Luther's conception of the beauty and goodness of the world is contradictory, but not entailing the same paradox as in *pulchritudo crucis.* Luther's position is related to the Bonaventurean *vestigia* of God in nature, but his orientation toward the topic is somewhat different. The Platonic order was to proceed from the sensuous world to the eternal truths, *per corporalia ad incorporalia,* just as Augustine assumed with his treatises on liberal arts. However, Luther's apprehension of beauty stands in opposition to the Platonic orientation. For instance, Luther states in his Genesis lectures, "the better someone knows God, the more one appreciates the creatures."[621] That statement belongs to Luther's comments on why Abraham "went to mourn for Sarah and to weep over her" (Gen 23:2). Expressed succinctly, the tears of the patriarch do not witness his weakness, nor is expressing emotion wrong. The people of God harbor tender emotions and weep and mourn their parents, spouses, or friends when they are bereaved. This is not

---

non reprehendere alios Vel apparere artificem, hoc est artificem laudabilem esse, sed efficere artifices, hoc est artificem bonum esse." There is an interesting resemblance between Luther's and Albrecht Dürer's thought about the idea of a true artist. Dürer's literary output was aimed for helping other artists to benefit of what he had learnt during his career. Cf. Dürer, Schriften, 152: "Es ist not su gemeinem Nütz, dass wir lernen und das getreulich unseren Nachkummen mitteilen, ihn nichts verbergen. Aus solscs hab ich mir fürgenummen, etwas zu beschreiben, das den Jungen nit unbegierlich wird sein zu sehen."

620 WA 43, 631, 30 – 632, 1: "Rahel vero fuit pulchra. Et refertur ea significatio in Hebraea voce (*Thoar*) proprie ad quartam speciem in praedicamento qualitatis, ad figuram, quae continet formam et proportionem qualitatis. Oculi Rahelis habuerunt iustam figuram, frons item et genae ac totum corpus habuit suam dispositionem et convenientiam membrorum. Haec vera pulchritudo et venustas est, quando facies habet aptam et convenientem proportionem oculorum, frontis, genarum et aliarum partium. Atque hactenus descripsit Moses sponsum istum et amatorem Iacob satis iuveniliter, qui amore lepidae et formosae puellae tam longam et duram servitutem sustinet, unde colligi magnitudo amoris potest. Et observandum est, quod scriptura sancta non damnat, sed praedicat istum amorem in sponso."

621 WA 43, 276, 18 – 20: "Quo enim sanctior quis est, et quo propius Deum cognoscit, hoc magis intelligit et adficitur creaturis."

a sign of their human infirmity, but rather their feeling of tender passion for others is proof that they know God. Whoever knows God also knows and loves creatures, since vestiges of God exist in creation.[622] As was noted in the discussion of emotions, the peculiarity of a Christian's affectivity is a person's depth and warmth of emotions. The disagreement with Bonaventure's *vestigia* is that vestiges of God do not result in knowledge of God, but rather, knowing God leads us to acknowledge his vestiges in all of creation. Only then can Luther make use of the Thomistic distinction of the traces of the Trinity in creation. The substance of things is from the Father, the form (i.e. beauty) from the Son and the goodness from the Spirit. To the Spirit belongs, according to the scholastic formula, also *usus*. For Luther, the holy use of things that receive their being from the Father and their beauty from the Son are "for the glory of God and to the benefit of neighbors."[623] This means that one's aesthetic experience takes place *a posteriori* to one's faith. Furthermore, to praise God is to acknowledge the beauty in the world that he has created. Indeed, to see beauty, order, and goodness in the world is a confession of faith. In fact, it is possible to maintain that only a Christian can truly perceive the essential beauty of the world. However, recognizing the ultimate beauty of the world does not mean denying the horrible events that happen. In *The Beautiful Confitemini* (1530), the reason for gratefulness is that there is at least some goodness in the world and not merely war, bloodshed, and rebellion. A great beauty and blessing is concealed in the fact that ordinary life continues. This is a miracle that may be compared to the creation of the world out of nothing.[624]As for the church, one may detect heretics, parties, and sects there. Instead of being appalled by them, one is rather

---

622 WA 43, 276, 24–28: "Moti igitur sunt sancti patres humanae naturae casibus et calamitatibus, fleverunt cum flentibus, non fuerunt stipites et trunci, sed habuerunt motus et adfectus tenerrimos. Quia habuerunt agnitionem Dei. Qui autem cognoscit Deum, etiam creaturam novit, intelligit et amat. Quia divinitatis vestigia sunt in creatura."

623 WA 43, 276, 29–40: "Cum in principio crearet Deus coelum et terram, primum vestigium patris erat substantia rerum, postea accessit forma. Tertio bonitas. Istam differentiam in creaturis observant soli pii, impii non agnoscunt, neque enim Deum nec creaturas norunt: multo minus usum earum. Pertinet autem ad usum rei spiritus sanctus. Qui usum rei videt, spiritum sanctum videt, qui formam rei sive pulchritudinem cernit, filium videt. Qui substantiam et durationem rerum considerat, videt patrem. Haec tria non possunt separari, substantia, forma et bonitas. Avarus vero tantum videt in pecunia substantiam, figuram, pondus: non autem, quod sit vestigium filii, animadvertit, nec usum rei, hoc est, ad quid prosit, cogitat, nimirum ad gloriam Dei principaliter, deinde ad utilitatem proximi."

624 WA 31 I, 78,10–14: "Denn das nicht ymer on vnterlas eitel krieg, vnfride, theurüg, blut vergiessen, aüffrür, mord vnd iamer ist ynn landen, stedten, dorffern vnd allerley hand werck, handel vnd stende der narunge bleiben, das ist eben so ein grosses wunder vñd gewallt Gottes, als das er aus nichts die wellt gemacht hat vnd noch erhellt teglich."

obliged to think that it is a work of God that the Word, faith, and the Spirit are still in the church. This is an endless source of thanksgiving.[625] To express this succinctly, every moment is a unique gift of God. If God did not hold the world together, the devil and the powers of destruction would swallow it completely. Perceiving the outer beauty of the world is not a sign of a mind that is superficial or worldly, but a statement of faith. This means also that the greatest gifts are the most obvious and therefore we seldom bother to thank God for them. What would happen, for example, if the light of the sun would fail us for a moment? As a divine aesthetic, faith opens the human mind to see and receive the goodness of God in everything. This is one of the reasons why joy must be regarded as a sign of faith.

Occasionally Luther equates faith with aesthetic understanding. If it is true that Christ has taken away the sin of the whole world, then God must see nothing in the world but "purification and righteousness."[626] A Christian must observe the world similarly to God. To have a spiritual understanding of the world is to see nothing in it but the favors of God (*Spiritus videt in mundo nihil nisi dei beneficia*). Reason (*ratio*), on the other hand, sees everything that is wrong and horrible in the world and can only find the world displeasing. That is why reason cannot praise the goodness of the Lord, as that is only possible after observing the world through spiritual understanding. Faith makes it possible to sing, *Misericordia Domini plena est terra.*[627]

---

625 WA 31 I, 84, 9–13: "Was dasselbige fur eine gabe ist, kan diese gantze wellt nicht bedencken noch begreiffen. Denn das nicht eitel yrthum, rotten, secten, ketzerey, ynn aller wellt ist, Sondern das noch ettwa bleibt das wort, glaube, geist, tauffe, heilige schrifft, Sacrament, Christen &das ist, auch nicht menschlicher macht noch weisheit, Sondern lauter vnd blosse gnade vnd gabe Gottes."

626 WA 40 I 438, 16–17. "Deus nihil aliud videret amplius in toto mundo, praesertim si crederet, quam meram purgationem et justitiam."

627 WA 31 II 536, 20–28: "Racio non potest de beneficiis domini canere. Nam solius spiritus opus intelligere misericordias domini, ille sapiens incipit laudare, gracias agere. Racio per se hoc non potest, sed solum speculatur minas et terrores dei et mundi impietatem, tunc incipit murmurare, blasphemare. Quare? quia caro non potest numerare beneficia, saltem numerat mala et non bona, ideo non potest nisi murmurare. Racio mundum videt impiissimum, ideo murmurat. Spiritus videt in mundo nihil nisi dei beneficia, ideo incipit canere"; WA 25, 378, 10–16: "'Quis sapiens, inquit, et custodiet haec et misericordias Domini videbit.' Quando enim intuemur beneficia et misericordias Domini, quod dat solem, pluviam, proventum annuum frugum, divitias, vitam, salutem &c.., tunc totus mundus fit plenus gracia et misericordiis Dei sicut dicit Psal. 'Misericordia Domini plena est terra'. Ita fit, ut misericordiae Domini videantur. Inde sequitur Amor erga Deum et laus. Haec scire est sapere, dicit Psalmus."

6.2 In search of the aesthetical criteria of music

One of the most characteristic issues of *Table Talk* concerning music is dated December 17, 1538. Here Luther admires certain motets he has just heard, and wonders why God has poured out (*geschütt*) such great gifts in this lifetime, which is a mere *Scheishaus*. What shall it be like in heaven, where everything is perfect? After all, this is just *materia prima*.[628] That thought resembles the *Encomion musices* image of a divine roundelay, where different voices play around the tenor, exulting and adorning it, "so that those who are at least bit moved to know nothing more amazing in this world."[629] Above all other arts, music was the realm of beauty for Luther; the beauty of music anticipates the beauty of heaven. Moreover, the experience of beauty in music may be viewed as disinterested pleasure. To state the obvious, we do not listen to music because it is right, but because it is good; it gives us joy, pleasure, and relaxation. We likewise do not listen to music in order to become better persons, but to entertain ourselves. This characteristic of musical experience only appears to be superficial while in fact, it has been shown to express the right stance for a human before God, where one receives the goodness of God and enjoys it and praises the Giver with joy.

On the other hand, it has become apparent that not all music is good. Therefore a most pertinent question is: what kind of music is truly pleasing? What are the aesthetic characteristics of good music that produce the innocent delight that Luther talks about? We know something about what kind of music Luther liked, so one could analyze the motets of Josquin des Prez, Ludwig Senfl, and others of Luther's favorite composers, and thereby discover the stylistic and the harmonic criteria that Luther might consider to be normative for musical beauty. This approach is not adopted in the present study due to two reasons. First, there are methodological restrictions at hand; this study is not a musicological survey. Second, it is highly possible that analyzing early sixteenth-century music would produce evidence that is only historically relevant. Instead, if there are more general aesthetical criteria in Luther's thinking, it might have some bearing

---

628 WA Tr 4, 4192: "Musicae admiratio. 17. Decembris cantores quidam aderant canentes egregias mutetas. Quas cum Lutherus miraretur, dixit: So vnser Her Gott in diesem leben in das scheißhauß solche edle gaben gegeben hat, was wirdt in jhenem ewigen leben geschehen, ubi omnia erunt perfectissima et iucundissima? Hic autem tantum est materia prima." Cf. WA Tr 1,968,27–30: "Weil unser Herr Gott in dies Leben, das doch ein lauter Scheishaus ist, solche edle Gaben geschütt und uns gegeben hat, was wird in jenem ewigen Leben geschehen, da Alles wird aufs Allervollkommenste und Lustigste werden; hie aber ist nur materia prima, der Anfang." About materia prima, see note 357 above.
629 WA 50, 373, 1–4.

even today, despite the fact that the musical environment is completely different than that of Luther's time.

Defining theological aesthetic criteria is a complicated task, owing to the unreliable sources (e. g. *Table Talk*) and the ambiguity of several concepts. To begin with, how does one define "aesthetic perception"? In this regard, I tend to use the Kantian idiom "disinterested pleasure" without entering the philosophical discussion of its value. Furthermore, the unsettled conceptual vocabulary of theological aesthetics does not facilitate the task either. How does one evaluate these criteria from the point of view of Christian faith? Last but not least, one must consider the temporal distance between Luther and us. Our understanding of music is different from that of the early sixteenth century. Therefore, nothing more than a tentative account can be offered here. After attempting to analyze the four aesthetic characteristics that can be found in Luther's writings, it is possible to determine whether they are linked to Luther's theology or are merely matters of his personal preferences.

Oskar Söhngen discerned the two aesthetic criteria in Luther's musical thinking as simplicity (*simplicitas*) and sweetness (*suavitas*). Söhngen understands simplicity as the ability of music to express the message of the text. Sweetness, on the other hand, is related to affective expressiveness. Here Söhngen perceives there to be a connection to the aesthetics of Heinrich Glarean's *Dodecachordon* (1547).[630] These two terms, "simplicity" and "sweetness," are taken from a 1538 *Table Talk*, where Luther comments on a motet by Antoine de Févin,[631] "those four parts are a marvel of sweetness and simplicity. For simplicity in all the arts is delightful."[632] In addition, two features that have recurrently occurred during this study can be regarded as essential aesthetic characteristics of music – freedom (*libertas*) and joy (*exultatio*). One needs only to recall Luther's apotheosis of Josquin's music; according to Luther, the music of the Flemish master reflects the Gospel in its imminent sense of freedom. Joy, on the other

---

630 Söhngen 1967, 97: "Es ist wohl auch nicht zufällig, dass sich Luthers wichtigste ästhetische Kategorien: suavitas (Lieblichkeit) und simplicitas (Einfachheit) inhaltlich etwa mit den Forderungen decken, die Glarean, der Theoretiker der ‚Moderne,' 1547 in seinem Dodekachordon an den Affektgehalt und Ausdruckswert der musikalischen Werke stellt; dabei spielen delectatio (Vergnügen) und iucunditas (Lieblichkeit) eine wichtige Rolle." Wetzel (1954, 216) recognizes numeralness (numerus-gebundene Musik) as the sole aesthetic principle.

631 A French composer (1470–1511) whose style is portrayed as abandoning old-fashioned principles in favor of the new compositional procedures introduced by Josquin and other composers of the previous generation. (Mayer Brown&Keahey 2001).

632 WA Tr 4, 216, 1–2 (No. 4316): "Nam quatuor illae voces mirae sunt suavitatis et simplicitatis. Nam simplicia in omnibus artibus sunt iucundiora."

hand, is a reciprocal phenomenon in music. Joy is something that humans receive from music, and it is also something humans express in terms of music.

6.2.1 Simplicitas – communicativeness

Luther established simplicity as a primary aesthetic principle in *Table Talk* by stating, *simplicia in omnibus artibus sunt iucundiora*, "simplicity is beautiful in all arts." *Simplicitas* is a word Luther uses in different contexts. First, it is good to remember that, like beauty, simplicity is also an attribute of God. The highest simplicity is in God (*in Deo summa simplicitas*). As a theological notion, God's simplicity has traditionally meant that God does not consist of many parts. In this context, simple is the opposite of composite. Hence it is commonplace in doctrinal tradition when Luther remarks in a 1544 disputation that the doctrine of the Trinity does not make God less simple, since there is nothing added to Deity, but that God has been plural for eternity.[633] In the activity of the Trinity, Luther uses expressions like *simplicitas et bonitas Spiritus Sancti*.[634] In biblical exegesis, Luther considered the literal meaning to be the most important. This hermeneutical principle also reflects the preference for *simplicitas*, the literal meaning being "simple and true."[635] However, this does not necessarily make the Gospel any more accessible. In fact, the result is quite the contrary; the extreme simplicity of Christ's words sometimes prevented them from being understood, because listeners could not believe the words might hold a deeper meaning.[636] The simplicity of the Word of God also requires simplicity of the preacher. The preacher must address the simplest laypeople when preaching. In addition, the preacher must preach for both the good and bad people in a simple manner, which means that one speaks without hoping for glory or benefit to one's self.[637] Furthermore, Luther demands in *De servo arbitrio* for Erasmus both the simplicity of the subject matter (*simplicitas et puritas doctrinae*)[638] and the clarity in de-

---

633 WA 39 II,327, 17–19: "Ergo in Deo summa est simplicitas, neque dici potest esse pluralitatem additionis, sed est pluralitas aeternitatis, quae est simpicitas." The same idea is found in: WA 46, 436, 29.

634 WA 39 II, 96, 31.

635 WA 38, 662, 22.

636 WA 52, 199, 6–7: "Dise wort redet Christus so einfaltig, das niemand meindt, da sie so grosse ding inn sich haben."

637 WA 38, 509, 24–26: "Simplicitas est docere et vivere, utrisque scilicet bonis et malis indifferenter, sine spe gloriae et sine cupiditate vindictae." See also Stolt 2000, 63–64.

638 WA 18, 648, 6.

livering his address (*simplicitas et proprietas dialectica*).[639] Finally, *simplicitas* or *Einfaltigkeit* is an attribute of faith. This means that against the temptations of the devil, the believer must have a simple trust in faith.[640] There is also an affective power in simplicity. Another illustration of this is found in *Operationes in Psalmos*, where Luther is pleased by the way Psalm 13 begins, with the word *usquequo* ("How long") repeated four times (with the variation *quam diu* the third time), which evokes a strong sense of the emotions of a humiliated person.[641]

In other contexts, Luther connects simplicity with truth,[642] innocence,[643] and sincerity.[644] The following scripture verses are of importance here; "Be wise as serpents and innocent as doves"(Matt 10:16) and "Let us keep the feast, not with old leaven, nor with the leaven of malice and wickedness, but with the unleavened bread of sincerity and truth" (1 Cor 5:8).[645]

What could *simplicitas* mean in reference to music? Is good music simple? The praise of polyphony in *Symphoniae iucundae* does not easily lend itself to this interpretation, because when voices "play around the tenor" in a four-voice motet, it is far from simple musical texture. That Luther was an admirer of Josquin des Prez is another indication of the fact that *simplicitas* in music is not the same as "simple," because no musicologist would describe Josquin's music as being simple.

In fact, opinions that good Christian music is simple sound rather like a puritan view. Abolishing everything extravagant from church music was precisely the program pursued by Zwingli and Karlstadt in their liturgical renewals; simple is best. In other words, a song is best when it has fewer features that might dis-

---

639 WA 18, 662, 20.

640 WA 52, 175, 34–35: "…bleybe einfaltig bey dem wort in rechtem vertrawen unnd glauben." WA 52, 107, 111: "Ich … will einfaltig bey dem kindlein bleyben." WA 7, 476, 9–10: "simplicitas et robur in fide."

641 WA 5, 384, 30–32: "Simplicitas ista hebraea magis placet et non nihil ad affectum facit, qua repetit quater idem vocabulum 'usquequo', pro quo varietatis amans interpres in tercio loco 'quam diu' posuit, nec sine affectus iniuria."

642 WA 1, 263, 32; WA 3, 662, 22.

643 AWA 2, 418, 8–9: innocentia seu integritas seu simplicitas (haec enim hebreum sonat).

644 WA 8, 109, 4.

645 The words of Bridegroom in Sgs 2:14 "O my dove" gives Luther an occasion to comment on the simplicity of a dove, WA 31 II, 661, 24–31: "Columba in sacris literis semper laudatur. Primum ob simplicitatem et innocentiam. Deinde ob foecunditatem. Et notum est Christi dictum: 'Estote simplices ut Columbae et prudentes ut serpentes'. Ideo Ecclesiae figura est Columba, quae cum omnium iniuriis pateat, non tamen reddit iniuriam, sed patitur. Sic hortatur Paulus Corinthios, ut in synceritate et veritate ambulent, abiecta illa humani cordis nequitia, quae tum divina tum humana omnia vertit in suum commodum. Haec autem columbina simplicitas est quaerere, quae Dei sunt et proximi."

tract the mind from concentrating on the words. As a consequence, musical instruments were seen as vain and vocal polyphony needless. Moreover, to achieve simplicity in music, the melody should be without artistic subtlety. This kind of simplicity is doubtlessly incompatible with Luther's conception of music. In other respects Luther did indeed share a suspicion of extravagance. For example, in *To the German Nobility* (1520), Luther disapproves of the expensive taste of the Germans in their clothes and spices. Luther states that God has given us enough wool, feathers, and linen for reasonable clothing. As a consequence, there is no need to spend large sums of money for silk, velvet, golden cloths, or spices.[646]

While "simple" does not convey the musical idea of *simplicitas,* I suggest interpreting it with the modern word *communicativeness.* This means first that it displays *accessibility.* In short, that music is accessible means that it is not "art for art's sake." According to the principle of *simplicitas,* church music cannot be principally the artistic self-expression of a composer or a musician. There is always the concern of communicativeness involved, the need to be understood and approved by the recipients, which in this case are neither the critics, nor the audience, but the congregation. This concern does not challenge the artistic integrity of a musician at all. The musician is obliged to use all of his/her professional skills to accomplish the task. The accessibility of church music does not turn it into spiritual muzak or decrease its means of expression to the musical taste of a "common man." Examples of sixteenth-century polyphony (or those of Schütz or Bach) are always good to recall at this point. The second factor of musical communicativeness is *interactivity.* This concept of the Internet-era is an integral part of the Christian theology of music. Church music is basically not a performance but involves singing together. Even when professionals perform church music, there is a congregation present, not an audience.[647] Communicative music should at least incorporate the experience, or feeling, that "we are singing."

Assuming that we can trust the report of *Table Talk*, a closer look at the occasion where Luther advocates simplicity as a feature of all true art is illuminating. This is a *Table Talk* dated December 26, 1538. Luther's entourage sang Févin's motet *Sancta trinitas* in six parts. Two of the parts were not authentic, at which point Luther made the following observation:

---

646 WA 6, 465, 25 – 466, 12.

647 According to Herl (2004, 22), Luther regarded congregational singing as useful and desirable, but not at the expense of the choral liturgy. Luther's theology did not have a conflict between a choral liturgy and his desire for the people to sing. The German Mass of 1526, widely regarded as a congregational service, actually describes what was at the time of its publication mostly a choral mass. The choral mass in Latin remained the principal service in Wittenberg throughout Luther's lifetime.

> Someone wanted to improve on the original, forgoing simplicity as a result. For those four
> parts are a marvel of sweetness and simplicity. For simplicity in all the arts is delightful ...
> Therefore one should in each and every case leave the composition alone and not destroy
> [the composer's] voice.[648]

Simplicity is thus related to *authenticity*. One could conclude that it is not possible to rewrite another's composition without demolishing it. This means that the composer's genuine voice cannot be copied. The numerous attempts to finish Schubert's *Unfinished* symphony serve as witnesses.

Simplicity is also related to naturalness. In this regard, it is good to recall Dürer's aesthetics. Dürer was convinced that one "who wishes to do something properly ought not to take anything away from the nature nor add anything inappropriate to it."[649] That art imitates nature is an ancient idea. However, the naturalness of the Renaissance era was not exclusive faithfulness to the outward appearance of things but a genuine expression of the artist as well, with naturalness belonging to both the objective and subjective side of the artistic experience.

As a conclusion, it can be stated that there are at least three factors in *simplicitas* to discern: accessibility, authenticity, and naturalness. Moreover, naturalness implicates the sense of freedom, which is the next aesthetic characteristic of music.

6.2.2 Libertas – freedom

The quality that prompted Luther to utter his most courageous words about music was the sense of freedom in Josquin's music, *"sic praedicavit Deus evangelium etiam per musicam."* This celebrated *Table Talk* dated 1531 deserves to be quoted in its entirety, in both extant versions:

> What is Law is not done voluntarily, what is Gospel is done voluntarily. In this way God has
> preached the Gospel also through music, as may be seen in Josquin, from whom all com-

---

648 WA Tr 4, 4316: "Deinde canebant: Sancta trinitas, etiam sex vocum, sed duae errant adulterinae. Ubi dixit: Es hats ainer wollen besser machen et simplicitatem depravavit. Nam quatuor illae voces mirae sunt suavitatis et simplicitatis. Nam simplicia in omnibus artibus sunt iucundiora ... Darumb sol man einem ieden sein composition lassen vnd sol ym seine stim nit verderben." For closer musical detail see Leaver 2006, 54–57.

649 Tatarkiewicz 1974, 257: "... wer etwas Rechts will machen, dass er der Natur nichts abbrech ung leg ihr nichts Uunträglichs auf."

position flow gladly, willingly, mildly, not compelled and forced by rules, as *des fincken gesang.*[650]

What is Law does not come out successfully, nor does it go voluntarily from the hand, but resists and struggles, one does it reluctantly and without liking. But what is Gospel, that comes out successfully, delightfully and willingly. In this way, God has preached the Gospel also through music, as one sees in Josquin's music, that all his compositions gladly, willingly, mildly, and lovingly flows and goes forth, is not forced nor compelled and tightly and directly bound to the rules, as *des Fincken gesang.*[651]

This *Table Talk* has not merely puzzled the commentators for its theological content. Scholarly discussion has focused on its logical structure as well as the reference to *des fincken gesang.* The reason the words *des fincken gesang* are left untranslated is due to their ambiguous character. They have been understood to refer to "the song of a finch." The other possibility is to interpret them as referring to the composer *Heinrich Finck* (1444–1527). Another question is whether the word *sicut/wie* is connected to the freedom of Josquin's music or to music that is bound to rules. That is to say, does Luther mean that Josquin's music is free *as* the song of the finch or *unlike* the song of the finch?[652] Despite these difficulties it is not hard to determine what is special in Josquin's music for Luther. Freedom means to act voluntarily, not under coercion. The analysis of the concepts of joy and pleasure in the previous chapter has provided insight into the deep significance of freedom in Luther's theology. That is what he experiences when listening to Josquin. The music is played happily, willingly, mildly, and lovingly (*fröhlich, willig, milde und lieblich*).

---

650 WA Tr 2, 11, 24–12,1 (No.1258): "Was lex ist, gett nicht von stad; was euangelium ist, das gett von stadt. Sic Deus praedicavit euangelium etiam per musicam, ut videtur in Iosquin des alles composition frolich, willig, milde heraus fleust, ist nitt zwungen vnd gnedigt per regulas, sicut des fincken gesang."

651 WA Tr 2, 12, 3–9 (No. 1258): "Was Gesetz ist, das gehet nicht von Statt, noch freiwillig von der Hand, sondern sperret und wehret sich, man thuts ungern und mit Unlust; was aber Euangelium ist, das gehet von Statt mit Lust und allem Willen. Also hat Gott das Euangelium geprediget auch durch die Musicam; wie man ins Josquini Gesang siehet, daß alle Compositio fein fröhlich, willig, milde und lieblich heraus fleußt und gehet, ist nicht gezwungen, noch genöthiget und an die Regeln stracks und schnurgleich gebunden, wie des Finken Gesang."

652 Buszin (1946, 91) translated the end of the passage, "[Josquin's compositions] are neither forced nor coerced and bound by rigid and stringend rules, but, on the contrary, are like the song of the finch." Leaver (2006, 368, note 199) emphasizes that Luther makes the comparison as an antithesis. Josquin's compositions are free in contrast to the song of the finch, as the finch always obeys the rules. Østrem (2003, 51–80) interprets the reference to Heinrich Finck as being more credible and makes a profound musical comparison between the style of Josquin and Finck. My translation here follows that of Østrem.

From the point of view of music theory, it is less convincing that Luther depicts Josquin as a composer who does not obey musical rules. The claim is particularly indefensible if "the rules" refer to those of counterpoint. The rules of polyphonic counterpoint had been established by the beginning of the sixteenth century, and Josquin was a master of this art, not an *enfant terrible*. However, there is a contemporary professional assessment available on the compositional technique of Josquin. The author suggests that there was a unique kind of freedom in Josquin's music, to the point that Josquin sometimes neglected strict compositional rules. Glarean's textbook *Dodecachordon* (1547) was an epoch-making attempt in the theory of music. He added – as the title indicates – four more modes to the medieval eight and thereby promoted the modern Western understanding of tonality as having twelve tones. In the last part of the book, he praises Josquin unrestrictedly, yet regrets that Josquin did not have the knowledge of the twelve modes:

> If the knowledge of twelve modes and of a true musical system had fallen to the lot of this man, considering his natural genius and the acuteness of intellect through which he became esteemed, nature could have produced nothing more august, nothing more magnificent in this art. His talent was so versatile in every way, so equipped by a natural acumen and vigor, that there was nothing in this field which he could not do.[653]

Glarean's apotheosis of Josquin resembles the saying ascribed to Luther, "others do what they can, Josquin does what he wants." Moreover, in this passage Glarean recurrently refers to the "naturalness" of Josquin's music ("nature could have produced," "natural acumen"), which in the present discussion points to the simplicity of music. Josquin did not have the understanding of the twelve modes that Glarean had later arrived at. Therefore Glarean sees some technical defects in Josquin's composition:

> But in many instances he lacked a proper measure and a judgment based on knowledge and thus in some places in his songs he did not fully restrain as he ought to have, the impetuosity of a lively talent, although this ordinary fault may be condoned because of the otherwise incomparable gifts of the man.[654]

---

[653] Dodecachordon vol 3, XXIV: "Cui uiro, si de duodecim Modis ac uera ratione musica, noticia contigisset ad natiuam illam indolem, et ingenij, qua uiguit, acrimoniam, nihil natura augustius in hac arte, nihil magnificentius producere potuisset. Ita in omnia uersatile ingenium erat, ita naturae acumine ac ui armatum, ut nihil in hoc negocio ille non potuisset." Transl. Miller.

[654] Dodecach vol. 3, XXIV: "Sed defuit in plaerisque modus, et cum eruditione iudicium. Itaque lasciuientis ingenij impetus, aliquot suarum cantionum locis non sane, ut debuit, repressit, sed condonetur hoc uitium mediocre ob dotes alias uiri incomparabiles."

Some characteristics emerge that depict a romantic picture of a creative genius. From a purely technical point of view, Josquin has violated the rules of counterpoint. However, what would constitute a mistake for a mediocre composer (*vitium mediocre*) is excusable for a genius. Glarean continues by comparing Josquin with the poet Virgil, who was also a genius with respect to form and could adapt words to the subject matter, resulting sometimes in his neglecting formal rules. Despite any possible technical reproach, Glarean concludes his evaluation on Josquin:

> ... to say finally, has never brought forth anything which was not pleasant to the ears, and which the learned did not approve as superior in talent, which in short, even if it should seem less erudite, would not be acceptable to discerning listener.[655]

What has previously (in Chapter 2) been stated concerning the development of musical thinking in the Renaissance becomes apparent here; the final judgment of music is in the auditory experience. This means that a composition with formal defects may nevertheless be pleasing to hear and therefore beautiful.[656] That Luther heard freedom in Josquin's music is therefore based on musical grounds.

The freedom expressed in Josquin's music is theologically relevant. Luther assesses it to be a sounding image of the Gospel in contrast to the law. How then does music reflect Christian freedom? There are indeed some characteristics of music that can advance the notion of freedom. Freedom in music does not mean that one just starts to sing or play, disregarding the rules of music. That is, rather, an unmusical performance. As Josquin did not abolish the rules of musical composition, but was able to be released from them occasionally, he considered the constraints of tradition not as a straightjacket but as a platform, as something that made creativity possible. This state of affairs may be useful for understanding the basic dialectics of Lutheran theology between law and Gospel.

One of the most difficult struggles within the Wittenberg Reformation where the old Luther had to take a stance was concerning the role of law in Christian life and proclamation (the Antinomian struggle). The distinction between law and Gospel is the supreme art of a theologian. In *Commentary on Galatians* (1531), Luther says, "Whoever can rightly judge between the law and the Gospel, let him thank God, and know he is a true theologian. In the time of temptation, I

---

655 Dodecach. vol. 3, XXIV: "et ut in summa dicamus, nihil unquam edidit, quod non iucundum auribus esset, quod ut ingeniosum docti non probarent, quod denique, etiam si minus eruditum uideri poterat, non acceptum gratumque iudicio audientibus esset."

656 Interestingly, the musicologist Edward E. Lowinsky (1961) has explored even atonalistic traits in Josquin's music. Lowinsky suggests that in its own time, the way Josquin (and some other sixteenth-century composers) treated the medieval modes was equally revolutionary as Schönberg's dodecaphonic music in the beginning of twentieth century.

confess I do not know how to do it as I ought."[657] That task proved to be difficult indeed. At the beginning of the Reformation, it was important to disavow "the righteousness of works" and proclaim that the law belongs to the Town Hall and the Gospel to the pulpit. This attitude later confronted Luther through Johann Agricola and other Antinomians, who shared the opinion that proclamation of the law did not belong to Christianity. Luther was nevertheless insistent on refusing to dispense with the law. His standard was the statement, *qui tollit legem, et euangelium tollit,* "who abandons the law, abandons the Gospel, too."[658] Christians still need the law because they remain sinners and the purpose of law is to reveal sin. This means that Christian life is a continuous struggle against sin. Whereas the Holy Spirit gives us the power to love God and detest sin, the life of a Christian is repentance until death.[659] In this process we need the law to show our sinfulness and to drive us to Christ. A believer does not see the law as a burden, but also as a sweet yoke of Christ.[660]

Antti Raunio has studied the Golden rule (Matt 7:12) as the law of love in Luther's thinking and found a trait in Luther's teaching which overcomes the strict antithesis between the law and the Gospel. According to Raunio, the divine love that strives the best for others is both natural and spiritual love of the whole universe. Divine love therefore involves all creatures striving to benefit each other.[661] The sun shines and the trees bear fruits "selflessly." There is but one point (besides the devil) in the entire creation that does not function according the Golden rule – the human heart. Therefore this rule of universal love remains as a "foreign" law for a human until the Spirit makes human love the law of God and, finally, one gives oneself to one's neighbor. To employ Chalcedonian vocabulary,

---

657 WA 40 I, 207, 17–18.

658 WA Tr 3, 3650.

659 In the first Antinomian Disputation (1537) Luther says:" Deinde concipimus per fidem Spiritum sanctum, qui novos motus parit et voluntatem imbuit, ut vere incipiat Deum amare et peccatum detestari in carne reliquum. Quia vero illud semper redit et negotium facit nobis, ideo opus habemus poenitentiae, quae durat usque ad mortem." (WA 39 I, 395, 22–396, 1) It is worth noting that in the beginning of 95 Theses against Indulgences (1517) Luther had already said: "Dominus et magister noster Iesus Christus dicendo 'Penitentiam agite &c.' omnem vitam fidelium penitentiam esse voluit" (WA 1, 233, 10–11).

660 WA 39 I, 381, 9–10: "Ideo lex manet, sed onus seu iugum eius non premit cervices eorum, quibus Christi onus impositum est, quod suave et leve est."

661 Raunio 2001, 227–229: "Luther erkennt, dass die gesamte physische Natur dem Gesetz der Liebe dient. Die ganze Substanz der Schöpfung ist im Gesetz Gottes. Das Sein der gesamten Schöpfung ist in diesem Sinne Liebe, dass keine Kreatur sich selbst, sondern den anderen dient." ... "Die göttliche, sich-schenkende Liebe, in der die Kreaturen zugleich Gott die Ehre geben, ist also nach Luther in bestimmten sinne die Substanz der ganzen Schöpfung."

law and Gospel stay *inconfuse* but *inseparabiliter.* Love is something that liberates a person to obey God's commandments voluntarily. Ultimately, obedience is not something foreign to a person's self, but is the true character of the human being.[662]

Some qualities of music are particularly apt to display Christian freedom. Jeremy Begbie has investigated the theological significance of musical improvisation. In musical improvisation, the occasional constraints (of time, place, and habit) are not treated as something to be released from but as something upon which freedom is based. As musicians know, improvisation requires a good professional background. An improviser must master his/her instrument and the theory of music and the musical genre that is played. Only then will improvising sound like music instead of noise. A musical sense of freedom emerges from the constraints of instruments, traditions, time, place, and persons.[663] Roger Scruton has also reflected on freedom in music and says freedom means the consciousness of necessity.[664]

There is yet another *Table Talk* to consult on the topic of law, Gospel, and music. On the surface, this demands a thorough knowledge of sixteenth-century musical notation, but ultimately the idea is rather simple:

> The Gospel is the same as the b *fa* b *mi* as it is performed; the other pitches are the Law. And the same as the Law obeys the Gospel so must the written pitches submit to the b *fa* b *mi.* And in the same way that the Gospel is a lovely and gracious doctrine, so is the *mi* and

---

[662] Raunio 2001, 313–314: "Das Selbst, ausserhalb dessen der Mensch sein soll, bedeutet nicht seine Person als solche, sondern seine Verderbtheit. Wie Luther mit dem ‚eigenen Willen' die verkehrte Liebe des Menschen bezeichnet, so benutzt er auch den Begriff ‚Selbst' um die Verkehrtheit des Menschen auszudrücken. Dies folgt aus seiner Auffassung, nach der der Mensch vor Gott völlig von dem Wesen seiner Liebe bestimmt wird … Durch den Glauben, in dem der Mensch sich Christus übergibt, verwirklicht sich auch die Liebe, d.h. die Verkehrtheit des Menschen wird überwunden, und er wird gerecht, wahrhaft, frei und fromm, und erfüllt alle Gebote."

[663] Begbie (2000, 205) distinguishes between three kinds of occasional constraints: 1) physical space where the improvisation occurs (e.g. a concert hall) with its attendant sounds; 2) other improvising participants, the music they produce, and the audience; 3) the disposition of the improviser him/herself, mood, degree of nervousness, etc.

[664] Scruton 1999, 76–77: "In music we are given an unparalleled glimpse of the reality of freedom: and because, as Kant reminds us, reason deals only with necessities, we hear the free order of music as a necessary order: it is when each note *requires* its successor, that we hear freedom in music. Freedom is the consciousness of necessity. But it is a necessity imposed upon life. Kant observed that our understanding stops at the threshold of this paradox, and cannot resolve it. Yet the solution seems to be ineffably contained in those triumphs of musical organization (fugues of Bach, quartets of Beethoven) in which the 'must be' of reason orders and redeems the 'is' of life."

fa the most beautiful in all voices. But the other tone is a poor, weak sinner, which allows both b *fa* and b *mi* – mi and fa – to be sung.[665]

In this occasion, freedom means written musical notes are not constraining the performer. An experienced singer knows when to sing "b fa"(B-flat) or "b mi" (B natural).[666] If one sings strictly from the notes the result will be an unpleasant dissonance. Regardless of the details of musical theory involved, the essential point is that Gospel is *doctrina suavissima*, as the b *fa* and b *mi* are *omnium vocum suavissima*. In short, freedom is pleasant, because what is free is done willingly and with pleasure.

6.2.3 Suavitas – pleasantness

As a criterion for good music, pleasantness may seem superfluous. Is not the pleasantness in music (*suavitas*) tantamount to beauty (*pulchritudo*)? Therefore, is not claiming *suavitas* as an essential characteristic of good music the same as claiming that beautiful music has to be beautiful? To realize the difference between these terms, one has to recall the distinction that Augustine made in *De Ordine* between *pulchritudo*, which appeals to the principle of harmony in the mind, and *suavitas*, which causes pleasure directly in the senses. Following Augustine's distinction, it is possible to define *suavitas* as the ear-pleasing character of music.[667]

The significance of pleasure and beauty in Luther's thinking has been discussed above, and what he expresses about sweetness is hardly unpredictable. After all, *suavitas* is an aggregate of "beauty" and "pleasure." Yet it is worth saying that, for Luther, music cannot be too beautiful. His appreciation of the beauty of music differs remarkably from that of Augustine. Indeed, the scruples of Augustine in *Confessions* were utterly inconceivable for Luther. He did not see beau-

---

665 WA Tr 1, 816 (=WA Tr 3,2996): "Das Euangelium ist gleich wie das B fa b mi in der Musica, als die von ihm regiret wird; die andern Claves sinds Gesetz. Und gleich wie das Gesetz dem Euangelio gehorchet, also sind auch die andern Claves dem B fa b mi gehorsam. Und gleich wie das Euangelium eine liebliche, holdselige Lehre ist, also ist das Mi und Fa unter allen Stimmen die lieblichste. Aber der ander Tonus ist ein armer schwacher Sünder, der läßt im B fa b mi beide, Mi und Fa, singen.""In musica b fah miest euangelium, ceterae claves sunt lex, et ut lex obtemperat euangelio, ita b fah mi regit ceteras claves et ut euangelium est doctrina suavissima, ita mi fa mi est omnium vocum suavissima "

666 In sixteenth-century notation, the accidental marks (sharp, flat, natural) were not used in the printed scores. Given their theoretical training in hexachordal solmization, musicians were expected to know whether B flat or B natural was to be proded. Leaver 2007, 102.

667 See Section 2.4.2.

tiful music as distracting the mind from hearing words. According to *Table Talk*, Luther assumed that Augustine would have agreed with him if he had lived in Luther's time.[668] Luther does not deny that the sweetness of music can be misused, but so can all great gifts of God. However, the possibility of being seduced to sin through of music is not something that is characteristic of music itself, but rather a sign of the ubiquity of sin in human behavior. It is noteworthy that Luther never admonishes people to abstain from musical voluptuousness by restricting the sweetness of music. On the contrary, using music for selfish purposes may even help to distinguish the greatness of music as an art, since good music is seen more clearly as a contrast to its abuse.[669] Furthermore, Luther states that if one does not appreciate the beauty of music as a gift of God, then one is not worthy of it. Indeed, Luther's reproach to those who remain unaffected by music is more vehement than for those who abuse it:

> ... whoever is only mildly moved and heeds not the inexpressible marvel of the Lord, should not be considered human, and should not hear anything else than the bray of a donkey and the grunt of a sow.[670]

The more music pleases the ear, the better it fulfills its function as music. Some music is technically perfect, but lacks *suavitas*. Though music may look good on paper, the ear determines whether it is beautiful or not.[671] The significance of pleasantness is also discernible in Luther's Bible translation. For example, in the 1522 New Testament he renders "spiritual songs" in Col 3:16 *geistlichen, lieblichen Liedern.*[672] "Spiritual" on this occasion is equivalent to "lovely," which is consistent with Luther's theology of pleasure. In the same vein, Luther calls the songs

---

668 WA Tr 5, 4441: "Sed S. Augustinus illius conscientiae fuit, quod ex delectatione musices sibi peccatum finxisset. Es ist ein feiner man gewesen. Si hoc saeculo viveret, nobiscum sentiret."
669 WA Tr 2, 1515: "Die bosen vnd geitzigen fidler ienen dazu, ut sciamus, quam nobilis ars sit musica. Opposita iuxta se posita magis elucescunt."
670 WA 50, 373, 14–17: "Wer aber dazu kein lust noch liebe hat vnd durch solch lieblich Wunderwerck nicht beweget wird, das mus warlich ein grober Klotz sein, der nicht werd ist, das er solche liebliche Musica, sondern das wueste, wilde Eselgeschrey des Chorals, oder der Hunde oder Sewe Gesang vnd Musica hoere."
671 In a Table Talk Luther comments on a composition by Lucas Edemberger: "Artis sat habet, sed caret suavitate" (WA Tr 4, 4897).
672 WA DB 7, 235, 16: "Lasset das wort Christi vnter euch reichlich wonen, in aller weisheit. Leret vnd vermanet euch selbs, mit Psalmen vnd Lobsengen, vnd geistlichen lieblichen Liedern" [GLOSSA:b. (Lieblichen) Das ist, Troestlichen, holdselichen gnadenreichen etc.] I am grateful to Dr. Jochen Arnold for this notice.

of David *süsse, schöne Psalmen* and *liebliche, lustige Lieder*. The sweetness of song does not prevent, but rather advances, the spiritual understanding.[673]

6.2.3.1 Excursus: A comparison of the way Calvin and Luther value music

A comparison between Luther's *Encomion musices* and John Calvin's *Préface du Psautier Genevois* (1543) is illuminating in relation to the sweetness of music.[674] At the outset, one must notice that these two hymnal prefaces have much in common. Perhaps more than Luther, Calvin has been unjustly regarded as an anti-aesthetic thinker.[675] This notwithstanding, Calvin ascribes to music a hidden and almost unbelievable power (*vertu secrète et quasi incroyable*) and his preface includes a *laus musicae* almost as powerful as that of Luther. The difference lies in the subtle reservations that Calvin makes in the preface, due to the basic difference between Calvin and Luther regarding the relationship of affect and intellect and the role of *suavitas*.

At the beginning of the preface to the Genevan Psalter, Calvin states his basic conviction about the service of the church. For Calvin, it is necessary that everyone understand what is said and done in the church in order to benefit from teaching.[676] This emphasis was undoubtedly common to all Reformers. Luther also fought for vernacular services and toiled on a German Bible translation. Calvin continues by saying that God's intent was not to amuse the world but to instruct people. As the Apostle Paul states in 1 Cor 14:15, everything in an assembly must

---

673 WA 54, 33, 18 – 26: "Ja fur grosser freude fehet er an, tichtet schoene susse Psalmen, singet liebliche lustige Lieder, damit zu gleich Gotte froelich zu loben und zu dancken, Und auch die menschen nuetzlich zu reitzen und zu leren. Also rhuemet hie David auch, das er habe viel schoener, suesser, lieblicher Psalmen von dem verheissen Messia gemacht, die man zu lob Gott, in Jsrael singen solt, und auch gesungen hat, Darinnen zu gleich auch treffliche weissagung und hoher verstand dem volck Jsrael gepredigt und gegeben ist."

674 CR 34, 165 – 172. Garside (1951) gives a full commentary on this text. It is useful to know that the preface was first published in 1542 in a remarkably shorter version, and most of the part dealing with music is from the next version published in 1543. According to Garside's opinion, Calvin's thinking about music went through a slight change between these versions. The main difference is that in 1542 Calvin admits the great power of music but wants to restrict it, whereas in 1543, he speaks of music in a more positive manner and sees bad music as a misuse of God's great gift.

675 Zeindler (1993, 309 – 327) refers to hymn-like character of Calvin's descriptions of nature, which proves false the opinion that he was hostile to aesthetics. Cottin (2009) recognizes that the battle against idolatry and the emphasis on the second commandment have obscured the openness to aesthetics in Calvin's thinking.

676 CR 34, 165: " ... aussi est-il expédient et raisonnable que tous connaissent et entendent ce qui se dit et fait au temple, pour en recevoir fruit et édification. "

happen so that the church may be edified.[677] As common a reformatory notion as this may be, it is nevertheless indicative that entertainment (*amuser*) is opposed to edification, unlike the ideas put forth in Luther's liturgical treatises (e. g., *Concerning the Order of Public Worship*). Calvin envisions the Christian service as consisting of three parts: the preaching of the Word of God, public prayer, and the administration of the sacraments. In his preface, Calvin does not discuss preaching, and he mentions the Eucharist only briefly. Moreover, regarding the Lord's Supper, Calvin wants to emphasize the words "take and eat" instead of "this is my body." In other words, the meaning of the sacrament is not in the alleged change that occurs in the elements (wine and bread) but in one's faith.[678] Even though Luther also refused the doctrine of transubstantiation, his faith in the real presence of Christ in the Eucharist remained intact. It is also possible to see the aforementioned emphasis on *édification* underlying Calvin's thinking on the Eucharist.

Prayer is divided into spoken prayer and sung prayer. As a hymnal preface, Calvin's text concentrates on the meaning of song. Song has a great power and influence to move and to arouse the human heart to invoke and praise God with greater eagerness and ardor.[679] Luther would have agreed with this position. Calvin also makes his most unrestricted, positive evaluation of music when he claims that among the things that provide recreation (*volupté*) for humans, music is the first, or close to first, and should be considered a gift of God.[680] As for the moral use of music, Calvin refers to Plato, who said that one of the most powerful tools to move or change human manners is music. In this context, Calvin speaks about the hidden and almost incredible power of music. Like Luther, Calvin also comprehended the good and bad forces of music. In particular, Calvin cautions against *réjouissance folle et vicieuse*, "mad and vicious amusement." This warning is basically the same as the caution Luther expresses in *Encomion musices*. Calvin considers bad music a misuse of God's gifts. We should

---

677 CR 34, 165: " Car notre Seigneur n'a pas institué l'ordre que nous devons tenir quand nous nous réunissons en son nom seulement pour amuser le monde à voir et regarder, mais plutôt il a voulu qu'il en revînt profit à tout son people, comment saint Paul témoigne, commandant que tout ce qui se fait en l'Eglise soit rapporté à l'édification commune de tous. "

678 CR 34, 167–168: " Car il ne dit pas au pain qu'il soit fait son corps, mais il adresse la parole à la compagnie des fidèles, disant: 'Prenez, mangez, etc.' Si nous voulons donc bien célébrer le Sacrement, il nous faut avoir la doctrine par laquelle ce qui y est signifié nous soit declare. "

679 CR 34, 169–170: " Nous connaissons par experience que le chant a grande force et vigueur d'émouvoir et enflamber le Coeur des hommes, pour invoquer et louer Dieu d'un zèle plus vehement et ardent. "

680 CR 34, 169–170: " Or entre les autres choses qui sont propres pour récréer l'homme et lui donner volupté, la musique est ou la première, ou l'une des principales, et nous faut estimer que c'est un don de Dieu destine à cet usage. "

be careful not to use music for our condemnation, because originally it is a gift that God has dedicated to our salvation.[681] In short, Calvin's aesthetic standards for music are *poids et majesté*, "weight and worthiness," the opposite of which are light and frivolous (*léger et volage*) songs. Calvin distinguishes between music that is performed at home (*à table*) and music that occurs in church (*en l'Eglise*). Without further explications, it seems that there are clearly different criteria for music at home and in church.[682]

For Calvin, the importance in church music lies not in sweetness but in weight and worthiness. The difference between Luther and Calvin in regard to music becomes apparent on the last page of Calvin's preface. Here he discusses the "words of institution" of music (Eph 5:19). Calvin explains what it means to "sing with the heart." This primarily involves singing with understanding, *Or le Coeur requiert l'intelligence*. Unlike birds and other animals, the great gift of humans is to sing with understanding. The order is that the affect has to follow understanding. Calvin provides reasons for the predominance of intellect by saying that we have to memorize the song (*imprimé en notre memoire*) before we can sing it. This singing, therefore, continues ceaselessly.[683] Since the leading part in singing belongs to the understanding, Calvin is very consistent when he sees "weight and worthiness" (*poids et majesté*) as the aesthetic characteristics of church music instead of pleasantness (*volupté*). For Luther, the manner in which God uses music occurs through the affect, and therefore it is natural that *suavitas* is indispensable for music.

Calvin's preface introduces another discernible difference between the two Reformers. Calvin envisions the creative impact of humans in church music in a narrower sense than Luther. Calvin states, "No one is able to sing things worthy of God except that which he has received from him." This means that the Psalms of David are the best possible texts for a song. What Calvin attempts to do is to justify the use of psalms in a way that resembles the way Luther emphasizes the use of *Lord's Prayer*: "When we sing them, we are certain that God puts these in our mouths, as if he himself were singing in us to exalt his glory."[684] Calvin did

---

681 CR 34, 169–170: " Pourquoi d'autant plus devons-nous regarder de n'en point abuser, de peur de la souiller et contaminer, la convertissant en notre condamnation, où elle était dédiée à notre profit et salut. "

682 As Guicharrousse (1995, 238–239) mentions, it is noteworthy that Luther never makes this kind of distinction.

683 CR 34,171–172: " Après l'intelligence doit suivre lea coeur et l'affection, ce qui ne peut être que nous n'ayons le Cantique imprimé en notre mémoire, pour jamais ne cesser de chanter. "

684 CR 34, 170–171: " Or ce que dit saint Augustin est vrai, que nul ne peut chanter choses dignes de Dieu sinon qu'il ait recu d'icelui. Pour cette raison, quand nous aurons bien rode

not include in church music free hymn poetry, at least not in principle. If a song is made by the Holy Spirit it excludes human creativity. Luther's point of departure in this question is quite the contrary, as the Spirit makes us creative, which is precisely the next feature of good music.[685]

6.2.4 Exultatio – the creative joy

What has been said about the theological notability of joy (*gaudium, Freude*) need not be reiterated here. Joy is a noisy phenomenon. As an aesthetic criterion of music, joy refers to the musical expression of joy. For the sake of clarity, I reserve the word *exultatio* for this expressive side of joy. This solution is based in Birgit Stolt's analysis of Luther's use of the German word *fröhlichkeit*. Stolt notices that for Luther, *fröhlich* refers to a stronger feeling than is conveyed today by the same word. *Fröhlich* for Luther includes in addition to the mental attitude, bodily expressions such as jumping about and clapping hands. Its Latin equivalent is *exultare*, while the mental disposition of joy is better translated with *laetari*.[686] To clarify the point, *gaudium* is something one *perceives* or experiences in

---

partout pour chercher ca let la, nous ne trouverons meilleures chansons ni plus propres pour ce faire que les Psaumes de David, lesquels le Saint-Esprit lui à dictés et faits. Et c'est pourquoi, quand nous les chantons, noussommes certains que Dieu nous met en la bouche les paroles, comme si lui-même chantait en nous, pour exalter sa gloire. "

685 A Calvinist approach to music is traceable in a recent study of Calvin R. Stapert on musical thought in the early church (2007, 194–209). For Stapert, Tertullian's highly rejective stance towards pagan culture is a good example – although not the only model for Christians today. Stapert observes misleading ideas in the contemporary discussion concerning music of the church. The first is the attitude that "it is just a song." Then one also emphasizes that the church has to use the music of the ambient culture if it wants to grow. Yet another misunderstanding is the thought that "God has created music." Against this thought, Stapert states that God has created sound, but not music. "Sound, talent, and music [in the sense of musica mundana] are God's good gifts, but God did not make any 'pieces' of music."(198). To argue against Stapert's point is not to say that music could not also be pernicious according to the Lutheran view, but to refute the antithesis between human and divine creativity.

686 Stolt 2000, 105: "Als Luther daran ging, das Magnificat zu verdeutschen und auszulegen, hat er die Gefühlslage des Textes ausgelotet und die Freude Marias als den Grundton ihres Lobes hervorgehoben; dass Maria, ‚die zarte Mutter Christi' ‚mit frolichem springenden geyst hie sich rümet und got lobet, er hab ie angesehen' (WA 7, 548, 29ff). ‚Mit fröhlichem, springenden Geist': Hier tritt ein historischer Sprachwandel zutage, indem ‚fröhlich' bei Luther eine stärkere Freude bezeichnete als heute. Wenn heute das Deutsche Wörterbuch zu ‚fröhlich' angibt: ‚[...] der fröhliche ist gleichsam halbfroh, beginnt, sich zu freuen', will dies mit der Textstelle, die von ‚springender' Freude spricht, nicht übereinstimmen. Für die Zeit vor Luther und die Tradition der Psalterübersetzung gilt dagegen, dass ‚fröhlich' zu den Bezeichnungen für die Freude gehört,

music, whereas *exultatio* is something one *expresses* through music. They are often hard to distinguish, and one of the advantages of music is precisely that it confuses the subject-object relationship.[687] The benefit of this distinction will appear in the following analysis.

As the manifestation of Christian joy, *exultatio* justifies human creativity and musical playfulness. Christian joy is not a calm, intellectual opinion, but a warm, superabundant affect. Indeed, it is completely natural and desirable that Christian joy expresses itself in making music and writing poetry. The way in which Luther expounds "the words of institution" of music (Col 3:16) confirms that assertion. Luther defines "psalms, hymns, and spiritual songs" in that *Psalms* refer to the Book of Psalms; *Hymns* are other biblical songs (e. g., *Magnificat* and *Benedictus*); and *spiritual songs* are freely composed songs of the church. The latter are not officially canonized songs but are new songs that can appear every day.[688] What is important (likewise in comparison with Calvin above) is that there seems to be no order of superiority involved in this distinction. In fact, Luther notices that Paul gives the attribute "spiritual" solely to the last group of songs. Certainly this does not imply that "psalms and hymns" are non-spiritual. Rather, it means that he recognizes the first two groups of songs as spiritual *per definitionem*. In Col 3:16 three words are of importance for *exultatio* in music: *richly*, *wisdom*, and *grace*.

First, the apostle proclaims that the Word of Christ should dwell *richly (reychlich)* among Christians. This means that the Word has to be spoken, sung, and expressed in poems (*sage, singe und tichte*) everywhere. People should also sing praise and thanks from their heart to the Lord. As expected, to sing from the heart does not mean that one's mouth should remain silent. The song has to come *out* of one's heart (*herausgehen*). Spiritual songs that are created daily are a form of the Word of Christ to dwell among Christians.[689] Accordingly, in *For-*

---

die sich äusserlich zeigt, durch Aufspringen, Herumhüpfen, Händeklatschen, Jubeln etc. Es entspricht im Latein der Vulgata exultare, während ‚sich innerlich freuen' mit laetari bezeichnet wird."

687 This is the leading idea of Block's study (2002). The title of his book "Verstehen durch Musik" indicates that we do not understand music but become understood through it. Block quotes Christa Reich (1997, 19) who says, "Im Singen werde ich mit anderen in ein Geschehen hineingenommen, das um so intensiver ist, je engagierter jeder sich ganz und gar hineingibt. Es ist ein merkwürdiges Ineinander von Tun und Erfasst-Werden."

688 WA 17 II, 121, 8–9: "Durch geystliche liede aber die lieder, die man auffer der schrifft von Got singet, wolche man teglich machen kan."

689 WA 17 II, 122, 5–13: "Nicht meynet das S. Paulus, das der mund solle stille schweygen, sondern das des munds wort sollen aus hertzlicher meynung, ernst und brunst eraus gehen, das nicht heuchel werck sey und gehe zu, wie Isaias 28. spricht: 'dis volck lobet mich mit seynem

mula missae (1523), Luther planned to have "as many songs as possible" in the vernacular, which the people could sing during mass, and at that point only poets and composers were missing.[690] That situation was soon amended when the first songbooks of the Reformation were printed in 1524.

The Word of Christ should dwell among Christians *in all wisdom (ynn aller weysheytt)*. At this point Luther shares the concern of Calvin about the proper understanding of the Word. There can be an abundance of the Word without understanding. This is the way Luther sees the Word of God having been spoken and sung under the Papacy. Luther refers to the canonical hours and Gregorian singing that is not useful when not understood.[691] The situation requires human creativity. All Christians, not merely preachers, are invited to bring the Word of God *ym schwang*. Teaching and admonishing requires art and intelligence.

The third key word for the use of singing is *with grace (ynn der gnade)*. This has to do directly with *freude und lust*. For Luther, singing with grace means "the singing of spiritual songs is to be voluntary, uncompelled, spontaneous, rendered with cheerfulness and prompted by love; not extorted by authority and law, as is the singing in our churches today."[692] Ultimately, singing with grace contains all the aesthetical characteristics presented here. Singing with grace also implies freedom, that it is understandable (simple), is undoubtedly sweet, and expresses deep joy. On the contrary, singing without grace takes place under coercion or is undertaken for the sake of reward. When people sing as a meritorious work by which they attempt to attain God's favor, they neither sing *in all wisdom* nor want to know God better and therefore act against understanding. To sing with grace is to sing in all wisdom, which requires beauty and enjoyment.

> Hymns are to be rich, pleasing and sweet, which all hearers like to hear. That kind of singing is very properly called in Hebrew singing "with grace," as Paul has it. This is the char-

---

munde, aber yhr hertz ist ferne von myr'. So wil nů S. Paulus das wort Gottis so gemeyn und reychlich wonend haben unter den Christen, das man allenthalben davon sage, singe und tichte, und doch, das alles also, das es mit verstand und geystlicher frucht zu gehe und bey yderman lieb und werd sey und aus hertzen grund dem Herren also zu lobe und danck gesungen werde."

690 StA 1, 384, 19 – 20, 24 – 26: "Cantica velim etiam nobis esse vernacula quam plurima, quae populus sub missa cantaret, vel iuxta gradualia, item iuxta Sanctus et Agnus dei ... Sed poetae nobis desunt, aut nondum cogniti sunt, qui pias et spirituales cantilenas (ut Paulus vocat) nobis concinnent, quae dignae sint in Ecclesia dei frequentari."

691 WA 17 II, 120, 9 – 35.

692 WA 17 II, 121, 17 – 19: "Es sey gesagt von der gnade Gottis, das ist, das solche gesenge sollen geschehen on zwang und gesetz, aus freyer lust und liebe, nicht wie itzt der kirchen gesang mit gepotten und gesetzen erzwungen wird."

acter of the psalms and hymns of the Scriptures; they are good thoughts presented in pleasing words.[693]

In Luther's interpretation, grace becomes almost equivalent to pleasure. The richness of the Word of Christ is wisdom in grace – good thoughts in pleasing words and sweet music. These words function as guidelines to artistic creativity. Furthermore, hymns are to be created continuously according to the principles of wisdom and grace. To this end, speakers and singers need to strive toward intelligibility (wisdom) and pleasantness (grace).

As the creativity of joy aroused by grace, *exultatio* leads to two important phenomena that are typical of Lutheran hymns, free hymn poetry and the use of vocal (and instrumental) polyphony. Luther differs from other Reformers on this point. For example, Calvin understood the power of music and wanted to use it in the service of the Gospel. His concern in this regard was that music should be in agreement with the content of faith. As a result, the words sung should be as close as possible to the words of scripture and the melody should be as simple as possible, which meant that polyphony was excluded.

Luther's concept of joy is aimed at an opposite practical solution. The question is not how music should be in agreement with the content of faith but rather how one understands faith. The nature of faith is to produce joy and to cause an abundant *exultatio*. Faith expresses itself with an abundance of words and melodies. The problem is that no words or music in the world seem to be enough to express this joy. Luther's words in a Christmas Day sermon are instructive:

> But the spirit's joy bubbles over with cheery words, and still none are useless, yea, all is too little, and the soul can not pour forth itself as it gladly would desire, like Ps 45, 1 says: "My heart overfloweth with a goodly matter," as if he were to say, I would gladly tell it forth, but I cannot; it is greater than I can express, so that my speaking is hardly a hiccup. Hence the saying in Ps 51, 17 and other places: "My tongue shall sing aloud of thy righteousness," that is, proclaim, sing and speak it forth with rejoicing and jumping.[694]

---

693 WA 17 II 121, 31–122, 1: "Es sollen reyche, liebliche, susse lieder seyn, die yderman gerne hoeret. Das heysst eygentlich ynn der gnaden gesungen' auff Ebreisch, wie S. Paulus redet. Der art sind auch die psalmen und lobesenge ynn der schrifft, da guet ding ynnen und mit feynen wortten gesungen wird."

694 WA 10 I 1, 135, 21–136, 7: "Aber die freud des geystis geht alß ubir mit frolichen worten, und ist doch nichts ubrig, ia, noch alleß tzu wenig, unnd kunnen es nit ßo erauß schutten, wie sie gern wollten, wie ps. 44. sagt: Meyn hertz schluckt erauß eynn guttis wort, alß sollt er sagen: Ich wollts gern erauß sagen, ßo kan ich nit. Es ist grosser, denn ichs sagen kann, das meyn sagen kaumet eyn schlucken ist; daher kompt die rede ps. 50. und an mehr ortten: Meyn tzung wirt eraußhupffenn deyn gerechtickeyt, das ist, mit freuden und sprungen dauon reden, singen und sagen." Cf. To Magnificat-commentary 1521: "All words and thoughts fail us, and our whole

The nature of faith is joy, and in turn abundant joy is constantly expressing itself in new ways. This makes possible that a highly artistic musical setting with delicate words is a paradigm of church music. This is neither extravagant nor a question of *adiaphora*, but something that is born out of faith itself. Both Luther and Calvin state that music is performed *ad Dei gloriam*, for the glory of God. However, their approaches to human creativity in words and melodies differ. For Calvin, music is performed for the glory of God only when human creativity is minimized and the Word of God is clearly uttered. For Luther, full human creativity is required to celebrate the glory of the Lord. Luther's idea is also consistent in relationship with visual arts. In fact, Luther admonished artists to invent details that are not told in the Bible when painting pictures of the biblical stories. This especially pertains to pictures presenting the passion of Christ. Of course, the details of these pictures are not arbitrarily chosen but emerge from knowledge of the circumstances of the story and result from meditation on it.[695]

It is therefore no wonder that Luther's most ecstatic utterances on music are related to art music. One could even add *skill* (peritia) as a further aesthetic characteristic to the list presented here. There is a feature of musical craftsmanship, common to both Josquin and modern performers, which can be of use to understand the significance of skill. This is the ability to make the difficult sound easy. For example, the hearer to polyphonic motets of sixteenth-century masters may feel them to be extremely simple, but the performers know they are not; the simplicity of sound is very complex on a deep level. This is freedom based on the mastery of musical laws. When Luther admired the art and ease of birdsong, he called this ability *peritia*.

A full appreciation of musicianship is a consequence of *exultatio* as a feature of the theological significance of music. There were immediate practical results that occurred in the life of the churches of the German Reformation, of which the

---

life and soul must be set in motion, as though all that lived within us wanted to break forth into praise and singing (singen und sagen)" (WA 7, 554, 25–29).

695 Nicol 1983, 143–144; WA 28, 256, 16–23; the affective benefits of Christ's pictures is emphasized in *Against the Heavenly Prophets:* "So weys ich auch gewiss, das Gott wil haben, man solle seyne werck hoeren und lesen, sonderlich das leyden Christi. Soll ichs aber hoeren odder gedencken, so ist myrs unmueglich, das ich nicht ynn meym hertzen sollt bilde davon machen, denn ich wolle, odder wolle nicht, wenn ich Christum hore, so entwirfft sich ynn meym hertzen eyn mans bilde, das am creutze henget, gleich als sich meyn andlitz naturlich entwirfft yns wasser, wenn ich dreyn sehe, Ists nů nicht sunde sondern gut, das ich Christus bilde ym hertzen habe, Warumb sollts sunde seyn, wenn ichs ynn augen habe? syntemal das hertze mehr gillt denn die augen und weniger soll mit sunden befleckt seyn denn die augen, als das da ist der rechte sitz und wonunge Gottes." (WA 18, 83, 6–15).

organization of Lutheran *Kantorei* was perhaps one of the most important.[696] At any rate, it is useful to understand that the development that took place in Protestant church music up to the time of Schütz and Bach is not explicable merely in terms of the self-assertive professional integrity of musicians credited to the spirit of the Renaissance. At least as important is the theological explanation, the Lutheran emphasis on grace and joy.[697]

It can be concluded that the four virtues of music (*simplicitas, libertas, suavitas, exultatio*) demonstrate the convictions of Luther's reformatory theology. They do not only reflect Luther's personal musical taste but also pertain to his understanding of the Gospel. The Gospel and music share many features: they communicate directly to the human heart, make humans free, and allow them to recognize the beauty of the world and express their joy and gratitude to the creator.

6.3 Luther's musical aesthetics as an aesthetics of light

The examination of Luther's ideas about beauty in general and musical aesthetics in particular has established that aesthetic experience is neither a superficial phenomenon nor the lowest stage of human existence, but that it is genuinely possible only for one who has learned to know God.

Recalling the distinction between the "aesthetics of proportion" and the "aesthetics of light" in the background chapter, I will now proceed to assess the nature of Luther's musical aesthetics. At first sight, it seems to belong to the aesthetics of proportion, which is presumably the more musical approach of the two, as music consists of measured intervals of time and pitch.[698] Another word for proportion is harmony, which also evokes immediate musical connotations. Therefore it is quite natural to assume that even for Luther, the basis of the pre-eminence of music is due to its harmony. This argument is difficult to contest, because without harmony

---

696 There are political reasons, too. John the Steadfast disbanded the Hofkapelle of Ernestine Saxony after the death of his predecessor, Frederick the Wise, in 1525. Both Luther and Melanchthon reacted passionately against the disbanding but with no major result. However, this demolition of an institution of music of the state indirectly brought an institution of music of the church into existence – the Kantorei in Torgau. Sander 1998, 9. One of the rare occasions where the old Luther participated actively in Wittenberg university politics was the employment of a music teacher in 1541, which he saw as extremely important. WA Br. 9, Nr. 3583; Brecht 1987, 121.
697 Hermann Finck's *Practica musica* (printed 1556 in Wittenberg) demonstrates the aesthetic principles: the singers are admonished to judiciously add turns, neigboring tones, and other musical ornaments to the printed notes in order to beautify the music. Helmer 2009, 166–167.
698 For De Bruyne (1969, 27), that which charms us by virtue of its harmony is musical perception, and that which is pleasing to our sight, plastic.

music would definitely lack *suavitas*. On the other hand, I have somewhat harshly refuted the opinion that Luther's estimation of music would be based on *harmony of the spheres*.[699] I do not attempt to deny the fundamental importance of harmony to music, but rather suggest that the concept of harmony cannot sufficiently explain the theological import of music in Luther's thinking. The Augustinean *numerositas*, "numberliness," is not articulated in Luther's musical thought. It may be surprising that the "aesthetics of light" better encompasses Luther's theology of music. As was mentioned previously, the difference between the aesthetic of proportion and the aesthetics of light is that light affords us with immediate delight, whereas a sense of proportion requires a certain judgment based on (unconscious and instantaneous) calculations. In the aesthetics of light, aesthetic perception is a matter of joy and pleasure, rather than that of understanding and moral judgment. From the above examination of the concepts of joy, pleasure, and beauty that were proposed by Luther, one can draw the conclusion that Luther's idea of aesthetics is precisely that. Although "proportion" is a more musical concept on the surface and "light" pertains predominantly to the visual arts, Luther's aesthetics of music is, in fact, an aesthetics of light. In a manner that resembles the radiance of light, music overwhelms the listener immediately, generating and expressing joy and pleasure.

I have maintained that music reflects the essential tenets of Luther's theology. I will now conclude the survey by introducing the notion of aesthetics of light, which appears to be instructive for Luther's theology in general. The image of the sun perhaps best portrays the categorically giving God, who through his gifts of creation gives *himself*, regardless of recipients' belief or unbelief. Light has the quality of enlightening the object it touches. A powerful light also makes it impossible to discern the original ray of light from its reflection. The notion of light portrays the major theme of Finnish Luther scholarship on deification (*theosis*). In *Operationes in Psalmos*, Luther observes that faith is called "the light of the face of God" because in the illumination of faith, a ray of divinity is infused in our heart.[700] Besides musical imagery, Luther describes the Gospel in terms of light, "*Evangelium enim lux est et radius, in quo Christus*

---

699 See section 3.2.1.1.

700 AWA 2, 200, 3–201, 1: "Optime enim vocatur fides lumen vultus dei, quod sit illuminatio mentis nostrae divinitus inspirata et radius quidam divinitatis in cor credentis infuses." Peura (1990, 69) interpretes this as follows: "Das Licht und des Angesicht Gottes bezeichnen zunächst die Gotteserkenntnis. Das von Gottes Angesicht ausgehende Licht bewirkt im Christen aber nicht nur den Glauben als Erkennen, sondern es gibt ihm auch alle Güter Gottes, weil diese Güter in diesem Licht enthalten sind."

clarificatur."[701] The word "light" includes not only the cognitive aspect but also an ontological dimension. Light as *lumen vultus Dei* is not distinct from the deity of God as a mere cognition. Light is not knowledge of God but an entity that originates from the essence of God. The fact that illumination occurs through the real presence of God does not exclude the cognitive aspect. That faith "owns" God as present, means also to know God. Luther equates illumination with deification when he concludes that the God who enlightens (*deus illuminans*) and the heart that is enlightened (*cor illuminatum*) are one.[702]

The numerous instances of the word *lux* in the *Lectures on Galatians* (1531) also demonstrate Luther's theology as an "aesthetics of light." First, Luther refers to the law and the Gospel as two distinct lights, the first revealing sin and condemnation, the latter illuminating righteousness and the forgiveness of sins.[703] Ultimately, in the matter of justification, there should be no other light than Christ.[704] Christ is known through the Gospel, which as the very light of Christ is the teaching of grace, freedom, consolation, and life.[705] This light confers the knowledge of God, ourselves, and everything. It is not the light of God's terrifying majesty, but that of Christ's humanity that is full of joy and pleasantness.[706] The brilliance of this light generates new affects such as hope, fear, and faithfulness in the baptized through the work of the Holy Spirit. Luther employs auditory and visual images simultaneously when he argues that this light and these new spiritual movements are introduced by *verbum vocale*.[707] This

---

701 WA 13, 635, 9 – 10.

702 AWA 2, 201, 20 – 21: "Idem enim est et utrunque simul est: deus illuminans et cor illuminatum"; Peura 1990, 200 – 202.

703 WA 40 I 485, 28 – 486, 19: "Lex ergo etiam lux est quae lucet et ostendit, non gratiam Dei, non iustitiam et vitam, sed iram Dei Peccatum, mortem, condemnationem nostri apud Deum et inferos... Evangelium lux est quae illuminat et vivificat corda; ostendit enim, quae sit Gratia et misericordia Dei, quae sit remissio peccatorum, benedictio, iustitia, vita et salus aeterna et quo modo ista consequi debeamus."

704 WA 40 I 307, 17 – 19: "Oppone ergo mortem Christi simpliciter omnibus legibus et nihil scias cum Paulo quam Iesum Christum et eum crucifixum, ut prae eo nihil luceat." cf. the word "simpliciter" with "simplicitas" as an aesthetical virtue.

705 WA 40 II 2, 22 – 23: "Satan enim vehementer odit lucem Evangelii, hoc est, doctrinam gratiae, libertatis, consolationis et vitae."

706 WA 40 I 93, 24 – 28: "Tumque omitto speculationes Maiestatis divinae et haereo in Christi humanitate. Ibi tum nullus terror est, sed mera suavitas, laetitia etc. Simulque aperitur lux quae ostendit cognitionem Dei, mei ipsius, omnium creaturarum et omnis iniquitatis regni diaboli etc."

707 WA 40 I 540, 30 – 32: "Exsurgit enim in baptisatis nova lux et flamma, oriuntur novi et pii affectus, timor, fiducia Dei, spes etc., oritur nova voluntas." WA 40 I 572, 18 – 23: "Quando videlicet per verbum vocale concipimus ardorem et lucem, qua alii et novi efficimur, qua novum

process of purification, introduced by the light of the Holy Spirit, is not immediately discernible, because the flesh, the world, and the devil all fight against it. The light is not at once diffused in the whole body. Nevertheless, the little spark of light (*parvula lux fidei*) begins to enlighten us.[708] The renovating activity of the Spirit is like sunlight; it changes everything it touches. It is noteworthy that Luther claims that the Holy Spirit renews neither the intellect nor the affect alone, but renews the entire human sense of perception. This is because our ears and eyes perceive things differently in faith.[709] This does not imply any physical difference in the sensory organs of Christians, or even that they have a different psychological disposition. The metaphor of light releases us from anthropological speculations so that we perceive the light of God that also pervades us. The difference is caused by the overwhelming brightness of Christ – the light of Christ is so magnificent that it pervades our whole existence to the extent that we see no law, sin, or iniquity in the world.[710]

The metaphor of light in Luther's *Lectures on Galatians* is used in all respects that have been essential to this study: that the Triune God is categorically giving; that he awakens faith through physical, auditory word; that faith is an affective approach; and finally, that faith in God is a source of pleasure that makes us sing. Luther's theology can be viewed as an "aesthetics of light." In his sermons Luther sometimes views faith as aesthetic contemplation. When I see that Christ

---

iudicium, novi sensus et motus in nobis oriuntur. Ista mutatio et novum iudicium non est opus humanae rationis aut virtutis, sed donum et effectus Spiritussancti, qui cum verbo praedicato venit, qui fide purificat corda et spirituales motus in nobis parit."

708 WA 40 I 538, 19 – 23: "Quatenus igitur Christum fide apprehendo, eatenus abrogata est mihi lex. Sed caro mea, mundus et diabolus non permittunt fidem esse perfectam. Velim quidem, quod parvula lux fidei in corde diffusa esset per totum corpus et omnia membra. Non fit, non statim diffunditur, sed coepta est diffundi."

709 WA 40 II 178, 32 – 179, 18: "Nam ubi cor novam lucem, novum iudicium et novos motus per Euangelium concipit, fit, ut externi quoque sensus innoventur. Aures enim verbum Dei, non amplius traditiones et somnia humana gestiunt audire. Os et lingua non sua opera, iusticias et Regulam iactant, sed solam misericordiam Dei in Christo exhibitam cum gaudio praedicant etc. Hae sunt mutationes, ut sic dicam, non verbales, sed reales, quae afferunt novam mentem, voluntatem, novos sensus et actiones etiam carnis, Ut oculi, aures, os et lingua non solum aliter quam antea videant, audiant et loquantur, sed ut ipsa mens etiam aliud probet et sequatur. Antea enim caecutiens in erroribus et tenebris Papisticis somniavit Deum mercatorem esse, qui suam gratiam nobis venderet pro operibus et meritis nostris. Iam orta luce Euangelii statuit, sola fide in Christum sibi contingere iusticiam."

710 WA 40 I 304, 9 – 14: "Ego plane nihil videre volo prae illo Christo. Is tantus mihi thesaurus esse debet, ut reliqua omnia prae ipso mihi sordeant. Is denique tanta lux mihi esse debet, ut eo apprehenso fide nesciam, an sit lex, peccatum vel ulla iniustitia in mundo. Quid enim omnia quae in coelo et terra sunt, ad filium Dei?"

and his goodness are mine and that Christ is God that was concealed in my death, sin, and misery, I perceive the favor of God. *"Das freundlich ansehen und lieplich gesicht erhebt mich,"* it is a friendly contemplation and a lovely vision that elevates me.[711] The aesthetic, gratuitous perception is perhaps the best equivalent to faith as a happy acceptance of God's goodness. Moreover, the aesthetic perception sheds light on the article "by which the church stands or falls," the justification of sinners by grace alone. Instead of a legal procedure, justification can be understood as an illumination, in which sinners void of light are permeated by God's brightness in Christ so that they become radiant. This provides a new approach for the proclamation of the Gospel when the legal imagery of the Lutheran Confessions has lost its credibility or become offensive. However, the claim that theology of music offers a new perspective to Luther's theology as an aesthetics of light does not presuppose a certain interpretation of the doctrine of justification. Even if one understands justification in purely forensic terms, as an event where sinners are pronounced righteous, there is still an aesthetic vision at the heart of the doctrine. In other words, we become righteous because God regards us as righteous. Therefore one does not exaggerate by stating that both Christian theology in general, and Luther's theology in particular, are aesthetic by nature[712]

---

711 WA 10 I 2, 277, 18–37; see also the aesthetical contemplation of the birth of Christ in WA 9, 439, 14–442, 33.

712 In his profound analysis of justification, Eberhard Jüngel, while not quite agreeing with the interpretation of the doctrine of justification that is presented here, also refers to the grace of God as God's heartfelt devotion to sinners and His delight in them. Moreover, Jüngel employs the image of the flooding of God's love that resembles the image of sunlight that I employ, and mentions that grace makes ugly sinners beautiful: "... the sola gratia of the Reformers conveys the idea of sinners being constantly reliant on a gracious God and the unearned, and thus heartfelt, devotion of God to sinners. Grace is God's effectual delight in beloved human beings in defiance of the sin of vile sinners. And grace, when seen as God's delight in human beings, is effectual by making vile sinners fair. Grace is the flooding of God's love into the glut of human guilt." (Jüngel 2001, 196).

Conclusion

The aim of this study was to examine Luther's theology of music from the standpoint of pleasure. Although many scholars have written extensively about Luther and music, the role of pleasure has been neglected in previous studies. The emphasis has rather been on the relationship between the Word and music. However, even a superficial reading of Luther's texts on music is sufficient to convince one that a foremost advantage of music is its ability to delight human hearts. Three words are used in this study to signify contentment: joy, pleasure, and delight. For the most part they overlap but have different approaches; "Joy" describes the mental attitude, "pleasure" is more connected with the gratification of senses, and "delight" can also signify aesthetic perception.

The historical account of the theology of music presented in chapter 2 revealed that delight in music has been an object of both praise and suspicion. Although the prominence of music in pagan cults would cause suspicion, many church fathers praised the spiritual power of psalmody. Augustine, for example, wrote a highly speculative textbook on music and exhibited vulnerability to the beauty of music in the *Confessions*. Many medieval books of music belonged to the speculative pedigree that treated music as a mathematical discipline. Associated with the development of science, where the Pythagorean-Platonic abstract contemplation was superseded by the empirical methodology of Aristotle, the auditory experience gradually gained primacy in musical knowledge. Whereas many authors had treated music in psalmody as being subordinate to the words, Thomas Aquinas claimed that someone might be aroused to devotion without understanding the words when psalms are sung if one only understands why they are sung. In the fifteenth century, modern ideas of music began to flourish. Johannes Tinctoris represents the empirist and humanist understanding of music that denies the *harmony of the spheres* and emphasizes both the practical musicianship and the psychological power of music.

The theological treatment of music belongs to theological aesthetics. Although such an academic discipline has never existed, Christian theologians have discussed the notion of beauty. In medieval thinking, beauty was an attribute of God, one of the transcendentals with *one*, *true*, and *good* (or closely associated with them). According to Augustine, beauty was objective and was not dependent on the one who perceives it. Aquinas in turn defined, "things that cause pleasure when seeing them" (*quae visa placent*) as beautiful. Thus the aesthetic perception is a part of the definition of beauty. There are two approaches to beauty that were adopted in medieval thinking. First, the "aesthetics of proportion" means that beauty consists of harmonious relationships. Perception of beauty is a matter of mathematical proportions and "numberliness" (*numerositas*). Sec-

ond, the "aesthetics of light" is concerned with the immediate effect of beauty on our mind, and the aesthetic perception is a matter of delight. The delight in music is also related to the overall view of affectivity in Christian life. Terminologically this study preferred the words "affect/affectivity" for the emotional side of the soul. Emotions have been suspect both in Greek philosophy and in Christian theology in that they belong to corporeal existence and represent the lower parts of the soul. In the Stoic tradition, emotions were treated as something that should be extirpated altogether, whereas the Platonic-Aristotelian model considered them to belong to the essence of the human soul, needing only the guidance of reason. In medieval philosophy, there was some discussion whether emotions are volitional movements or not. Mostly it was maintained that an affective suggestion to sin is not a sin at all, and that one is guilty of sin only when one takes pleasure in that suggestion. Although emotions were mainly treated with suspicion as possible occasions to sin, they deserved a positive treatment when associated with the beatific enjoyment that awaits Christians in heaven. The mystical tradition also cherished the affectivity in Christianity by stating that knowing God is a matter of love, not of understanding.

To introduce Luther's theology of music, the principal chapter discussed the notion of music as a gift of God. The most recurrent statement about music in Luther's works is that it is a gift of God. Although not novel or surprising, this notion is nevertheless remarkable, because "gift" (*donum*, *Gabe*) appears to be a fundamental concept in Luther's theology. Luther defines God as the one who gives. The Father gives himself in the gifts of creation. The son gives himself on our behalf. The Holy Spirit is both the gift of God and God himself who comes into us wholly and completely. To receive the gifts of God means thus also to be united with him. This study adopts the idea of reciprocity involved in Luther's idea of gift that has been discovered lately. To be a gift presupposes a response in order that the gift is able to function as a gift. If a gift remains unnoticed and is not received, it is not a gift. "The economic gift-exchange" is a principle discovered by anthropologists that implies that all gifts include a counter-gift. Although on the surface this may seem extremely unsuitable to Luther, as he renounced all human efforts before God, it can nevertheless be reconciled with his theology. Our response to God's categorically giving goodness is thankfulness and praise. And praise, in turn, is an irrevocably musical phenomenon.

The first main chapter also includes the analysis of the primary source of Luther's musical thought, *Encomion musices* (1538). Here, Luther asserts that music, as a gift of God, comprises the phenomenon of sound, birdsong, other music of nature, human voice, and art music. Luther comments on the phenomenon of sound in Pythagorean language, arguing that nothing in the world is without sound or "sounding number" (*numerus sonans*). Luther thus exhibits traditional

insights concerning the cosmic dimensions of music. This trait of thought has sometimes been exaggerated, as Luther does not refer to the harmony of the spheres elsewhere in his discussion of music. Indeed, other features of music are important to him. Birdsong, and the song of the nightingale in particular, was for Luther an example of trust and joyfulness for all Christians. However, Luther considers the human voice to be the most wondrous musical instrument of all. According to Luther, to be able to utter one's joy and grief with one's voice is a miracle and a great gift. He further asserts that the highest stage of music is art music. A significant aspect for the theology of culture is Luther's discussion of polyphonic motets, that are works of art he calls the work of God (*opus Dei*). Music is therefore a part of creative cooperation between God and humans.

Praise is the musical response of the church to the good news of the Gospel. The liturgical service of the new covenant consists primarily of praise, it is both preaching and singing about God's great works. Singing spiritual songs is even counted among the *notae ecclesiae*. This bold statement, however, necessitates the discussion of the texts where Luther appears to contradict it. Luther occasionally speaks about musical phenomena in a very critical tone, but a closer examination reveals that the actual target of criticism is anything but music itself. Luther in fact criticizes the outward pomp and circumstance that have obscured the words of institution in the Eucharist since monks and priests sing reluctantly with no devotion. Singing is the best endeavor for a Christian, because when we encounter the goodness of God, all words fail us and music alone can express our feelings.

The most important feature of music for Luther is its ability to rule human emotions. Music is the governess of human emotions (*domina et gubernatrix affectuum humanorum*), and Luther's theology displays this affective character. The *Small Catechism* begins the explanations of the Ten Commandments with, "we must thus fear and love God." Faith is not a mere opinion, but *fiducia* that involves the heart and emotions. It is necessary to acknowledge that the *heart* in Luther's thought (and Christianity in general) does not just refer to emotions but to the very center of the human being, comprising intellect, will, and affects. The affectivity of Luther's theology does not mean that our love and longing grasps God without the intellect. Affect, in this regard, is not a privileged faculty of mind. Affectivity rather means, "to be affected." Intellect, will, and affect are equally blind and unable to attain God, unless God himself enlightens them. Luther does not portray the renewed emotional life of Christians as essentially properly controlled, but as exceedingly tender.

Music generates a variety of emotions such as love, hatred, fear, humility, calmness, and joy. As for the overall philosophical theory of emotions, music has a direct impact on affectivity. In general, emotions have cognitive content

– one is frightened by something that has happened or delighted in something one has attained. The peculiarity of musical emotions is that it is difficult to delineate the possible cognitive content of the emotions experienced in music. Although concentrating on the positive effects, Luther also acknowledges the unwanted influence that music can have on the mind. To Luther, bad and ungodly music is merely testimony to the omnipresence of sin and of the devil's cunning. More generally, however, music is and remains an excellent gift of God. The most significant effect of music is the delight it imparts to human hearts. This capacity enables Luther to argue that the Holy Spirit honors music as an instrument of its proper work (*sui proprii officii organum*). If one is to understand the theological weight of music in Luther's thinking, one must acknowledge that joy is not a frame of mind but a gift of the Holy Spirit. Accordingly, sadness is not just a feeling but also an attack of the devil. Therefore, the most important Bible verse regarding music in Luther's estimation was 1 Sam 16:23, "And so it was, whenever the spirit from God was upon Saul, that David would take a harp and play it with his hand. Then Saul would become refreshed and well, and the distressing spirit would depart from him."

Vocality contributes to the affectivity of the Word. It is commonplace that Luther regarded the Word of God principally as orally delivered word, *verbum praedicationis*. Speaking about the proclamation of the Gospel, Luther refers to it sometimes as "physical voice" (*leyplich stymme*). It can even be argued that the prominence of vocality challenges the aptness of the *Sola Scriptura* principle. *Solum Verbum* could be more faithful to Luther's ideas. Gospel is *gute geschrey*, "good clamor," and the Word of God is transmitted through the mouth and ears. The emphasis on the vocal and auditory character of the Word was a source of certainty for Luther in confrontation with spiritualists. The external word even has a sacramental dimension. In sacraments the Word is associated with the external element, and as in preaching, the Word is associated with the physical sound. Moreover, the audible word has affective power. This means that believing is not simply knowing what the Bible tells us but also applying this knowledge affectively. This requires the daily exercise of the Word – reading, hearing and singing the Word. That is the principle that Luther communicates in his liturgical renovations when he argues that the Word of God is *im Schwang*. The Word of God must therefore be read, preached and sung constantly and abundantly. In the daily exercise of the Word, the advantages of music become apparent; music has the ability to move human hearts without coercion, persuading them with its sweetness.

The perception of music allows us to define Luther's theology as a theology of joy and pleasure. The chapter dedicated to these two concepts, joy and pleasure, is based on Luther's main works. Joy is a consequence of Christian faith.

This means that if one does not rejoice, one has not properly understood faith. It also means that rejoicing is not actually possible without believing, because passing, profane joys are not real joys at all. However, the true difference between worldly and spiritual joy lies in their source. Spiritual joy is God's work, and it therefore means rejoicing in God. Luther defies the notion of spiritual joy being an inward and silent rejoicing when he states that it inevitably bursts out in song and laughter. Joy also indicates love. Loving God also entails being delighted with all his creation. According to the *ordo caritatis*, it was maintained that in order to reach God, one should be delighted only in God and abandon all lower things. Contrary to this, Luther states that God's love creates its object – God loves the sinful, sick, and insane and makes them righteous, healthy, and wise. And if God acts this way, then neither should we scorn lowly creatures but instead delight in them, regardless of their infirmity and transiency.

The notion of pleasure proves essential if we are to understand Luther's argumentation in *The Bondage of the Will*. Luther does not deny a human's ability to perform right actions. What remains impossible for a person, however, is to influence the delight of the heart, because one cannot force oneself to feel pleasure. Doing good with pleasure is nevertheless crucial, because before God, a work that is done reluctantly is not done at all. When the significance of joy and pleasure has been discovered, a danger arises that rejoicing becomes a merit people use to attain salvation or that it becomes a cause of despair for those incapable of it. Therefore Luther asserts that joy is a gift of the Holy Spirit, given through the exercise of the Word, whereby trust in God is increased.

As a word, "pleasure" has more sensuous connotations than "joy." The pleasures of life have been problematic in the history of theology. Luther teaches that in paradise there was nothing problematic about pleasure. Adam had *voluptas sancta* that would have remained the lot of humans had they not succumbed to sin. God has not ceased to be the cause of supreme pleasure, but humans search for pleasure in the wrong things. The words of Matt 6:33 also apply to pleasure: "But seek first his kingdom and his righteousness, and all these things shall be yours as well." Pleasure has also been treated as a divine condescendention, whereby God draws us near to him. God does this by attracting us with something that naturally pleases us in order to communicate his actual message. Luther, on the other hand, sees God's condescendention as God wanting to please and caress us with the goodness and beauty of the world, revealing what God is like. There is no deeper message than that.

Music also belongs to earthly pleasures alongside food, drink, and sex. Luther's position displays an appreciation of these temporary delights. This is a remarkable trait in comparison with both the monastic piety of Luther's predecessors and the puritan piety of his followers. Luther's appreciation of earthly pleas-

ures is not unreserved. His perception of sexual pleasure does not differ greatly from that of Augustine. Luther argues that sexual pleasure has a purpose, which is to procreate children or to fulfill natural needs and restrain unchastity. Compared to this, the pleasure of music appears to be the only pleasure that can be enjoyed without reservations. Indeed, music affords pleasure that is completely sensuous, time-embedded, and transitory. Nevertheless, it is the greatest and purest joy on earth.

The delight of music is, to use Kant's definition of aesthetical perception, disinterested pleasure. It is something that is delighted in for itself, not as a means to something else. It is hardly surprising that music belongs to the realm of aesthetics, but to interpret Luther as being an aesthetical thinker is less common. Luther has a dual opinion of beauty. The first approach is typical to the young Luther and can be called *pulchritudo cruces* – the one who is ugly in one's own eyes is beautiful in God's eyes. Furthermore, the beauty of God is concealed in the ugliness of sin and the cross. This view of beauty also communicates an aesthetic variation of the doctrine of justification that the beauty of God is that with which he makes us beautiful. The ugliness of sin belongs to us, the beauty of righteousness to God. In Christ, God takes our ugliness on himself and gives us his beauty, thus making us beautiful. The second approach, discernible in the writings of an older Luther, perceives the beauty of the world as God's gift, and even the ability to perceive beauty in the world is a gift from God. Mindful of the power of sin, death, and the devil, Luther even claims that to see beauty in this world is an act of faith. Because of Christ, God sees only purification and righteousness in the world, and Christians must observe the world as God does.

Although music is a realm of intrinsic beauty, not all music is beautiful. This study presented simplicity, freedom, pleasantness, and joy as the aesthetical criteria of music. The methodological problem encountered with these criteria is that most of the texts related to them are from *Table Talk*, and thus are relatively untrustworthy sources. First, to be exact, *simplicitas* in Luther's formulation of music is better rendered as communicativeness, containing the sense of accessibility, genuineness, and naturalness. Second, freedom is the criterion that occasioned Luther to attest that God also proclaims the Gospel through music, as in Josquin des Prez' compositions that flow "gladly, willingly, mildly, and lovingly." Incorporating freedom in music portrays well the concept of Christian freedom. In musical improvisation, the occasional constraints are not treated as threats to freedom, but as its basis. Freedom also belongs together with willingness. The third criterion was pleasantness. To say that music must be pleasant may sound superfluous, because presumably no one would claim that good music must be unpleasant. As an aesthetic criterion it is worth mentioning because, for Luther, music cannot be too beautiful.

At this point, this study offers a comparison between Luther and Calvin. Their discussions about music have much in common. Like Luther, Calvin also ascribes to music a hidden and almost unbelievable power to move human emotions and advance the proclamation of the Gospel. The difference between Luther and Calvin is that according to Calvin music should first and foremost promote understanding. Calvin understands the injunction that one must sing "from the heart" (Eph 5:19) to mean that one should sing more with understanding than with feeling. The fourth aesthetical criterion is *exultatio* – creative joy. The characteristics of Christian joy have been discussed in the previous chapter. For Luther, e*xultatio* or *Fröhlichkeit* comprises more than simply a happy mental attitude, but also includes physical expressions of joy. Christian joy expresses itself with all means available, also through artistic creativity. Accordingly, new songs are written in the church daily. The Word of God dwells richly among us (Col 3:16) when we use all our creativity to have the Word *im Schwang*. The problem is not in deciding what kind of music would be suitable to the Gospel, but in the realization that no music is sufficient.

It has become clear that the most important features of music are pleasure and joy. It therefore appears that Luther's musical aesthetics belongs more to "the aesthetics of light" than to "the aesthetics of proportion." Music overwhelms the listener immediately and generates and expresses joy and pleasure. Experiencing the pleasure of music does not require an understanding of the harmonious proportions of music. Harmony is undoubtedly implicated, but in Luther's theology, music works similarly to light. "Aesthetics of light" can also advance our understanding of Luther's theology as a whole. Justification should not be looked at as a legal procedure where righteousness is technically imputed to the sinner but as the brightness of God that permeates everything, even those who are completely dark in themselves. Although Luther employs traditional legal terminology, the light metaphor is concordant with his perception of the categorically giving God, as his wording in the great Galatians commentary suggests.

"Music can serve to enrich and advance theology, extending our wisdom about God, God's relation to us, and to the world at large." These words of Jeremy Begbie were quoted in the introductory chapter. Luther's theology, often enclosed in polemical writings and situated in the sixteenth-century discussions that are alien to us, is undoubtedly more accessible through his musical thinking. Without the notion of music, the positive approach to sensuous pleasure and the importance of aesthetic perception in Luther's theology would be considerably more difficult to observe.

Abbreviations

AWA	Archiv zur Weimarer Ausgabe der Werke Martin Luthers.
BC	The Book of Concord. The Confessions of the Evangelical Lutheran Church. Ed. by Robert Kolb and Timothy J. Wengert. Minneapolis. Fortress. 2000.
CCL	Corpus Christianorum.Series Latinorum.
CR	Corpus Reformatorum.
LQ	Lutheran Quarterly
LuJ	Lutherjahrbuch.
LW	Luther's Works. American edition. 55 volumes. St. Louis: Concordia and Philadelphia: Fortress. 1955–1986.
MGG	Musik in Geschichte und Gegenwart.
PG	Patrologia cursus completus. Series Graeca. Ed. J.P.Migne
PL	Patrologia cursus completes. Series Latina. Ed. J.P. Migne
SC	Sources Chrétiennes.
StA	Luthers Werke. Studienausgabe. Hrsg. H.-U. Delius.
TRE	Theologische Realenzyklopädie
WA	D. Martin Luthers Werke. Weimar 1883-
WA Br	Briefwechsel
WA DB	Deutsche Bibel
WA Tr	Tischreden

Sources

Martin Luther's works

1513 – 1516

    WA 3 – 4 Dictata super Psalterium

1514

    WA 1, 20 – 29 SERMO LUTHERI In Natali Christi A.

    WA 1, 94 – 99 Sermo de indulgentiis pridie Dedicationis. Sermone aus den Jahren 1514 – 1517.

1515 – 1516

    WA 56 Diui Pauli apostoli ad Romanos Epistola.

1517 – 1518

    WA 57 Vorlesung über den Hebräerbrief.

1518

    WA 1, 340 – 345 Sermo II de passione.

1519

    WA 2, 80 – 130 Auslegung deutsch des Vaterunsers für die einfältigen Laien.

    WA 2, 436 – 618 In epistolam Pauli ad Galatas M. Lutheri commentarius.

1519 – 1521

    WA 5 Operationes in Psalmos

    AWA 2, 1 – 648

1520

    StA 2, 96 – 171 An den Christlichen Adel Deutschen Nations.

    StA 2, 15 – 88 Von den guten Werken.

    StA 2, 263 – 309 Von der Freiheit eines Christenmenschen. (De Libertate christiana)

    StA 1, 289 – 311 Ein Sermon von dem Neuen Testament, das ist von der heiligen Messe.

1521

    StA 1, 314 – 364 Das Magnificat verdeutschet und ausgelegt.

    StA 2, 405 – 519 Rationis Latomianae pro incendiariis Louaniensis scholae sophistis redditae, Lutheriana confutatio.

1522

    WA 10 I 1 Weihnachtspostille.

    WA 10 II, 267 – 304 Vom ehelichen Leben

    WA DB 6, 3 – 12 Vorrede auf das Neue Testament. 1522/ 1546

    WA 10 III, 13 – 20 Ein ander Sermon D. M. Luthers Am Montag nach Invocavit.

1523

    WA 12, 31 – 17 Von Ordnung Gottesdiensts in der Gemeine.

    StA 1, 367 – 386 Formula missae et communionis.

1524

    WA 35, 274 – 275 Die Vorrede des Wittenberger Gesangbuches von 1524.

    WA 35, 483 – 484 Vorrhede auff alle gute Gesangbücher.D.M.L. Frau Musica.

    WA 15, 348 – 379 Der 127. Psalm ausgelegt an die Christen zu Riga in Liefland.

    WA 13,545 – 669 Praelectiones in prophetas minores.1524 – 26. In Zachariam prophetam.

1525

    StA 3, 177–356 De servo arbitrio.

    WA 10 I 2, 1–208 Adventspostille.

    WA 17 II, 109–123 Fastenpostille. Epistel S. Pauli zu den Colossern auff den funfften Sontag nach Epiphania.

    WA 23, 696–725 Eine gute Predigt von der Kraft der Himmelfahrt Christi. Predigten des Jahres 1525

1527

    WA 24, 1–710 In Genesin Mose librum sanctissimum Declamationes.

    WA 31 II, 1–585 Vorlesung über Jesaias 1527–30.

1528

    WA 35, 275–276 Die Vorrede von 1528.

    StA 4, 25–258 Vom Abendmahl Christi. Bekenntnis.

1529

    WA 30 I Grosser und Kleiner Katechismus.

1530

    WA 30 II, 396 Περι της μουσικης.

    WA Br 5, 639 Luther an Ludwig Senfl. Oktober 1530.

    WA Br 5, 320–321 Luther an Joh. Agricola in Augsburg. 15. Mai 1530.

    WA Br,5, 374–375 Luther an Hieronymus Weller. 19. Juni 1530

    WA 32 I, 299–554 Wochenpredigten über Matth 5–7. 1530/32.

    WA 31, 68–182 Das schöne Confitemini..

    WA Tr 1, 816 Veit Dietrichs und Nikolaus Medlers Sammlung

1531

    WA 40 I-II In epistolam S. Pauli ad Galatas Commentarius

    WA 38, 1–69 Allen fromen Christen. Summarien über die Psalmen und Ursachen des Dolmetschens 1531 bis 1533.

    WA Tr 2, 1258 Johannes Schlaginhaufens Nachschriften.

1532

    WA 20, 1–203 Annotationes in Ecclesiasten.

    WA 40 II, 185–610 Vorlesungen über die Psalmen 2. 51. 45.

    WA 32 I, 299–555 Wochenpredigten über Matth 5–7. 1530/32.

    WA Tr 2, 1515 Johannes Schlaginhaufens Nachschriften.

    WA Tr 2, 2387, 2545 Die Sammlung von Konrad Cordatus.

1533

    WA Tr 1, 555 Veit Dietrichs Nachschriften.

    WA Tr 2, 2996 Die Sammlung von Konrad Cordatus.

1535

    WA 38, 358–375 Eine einfältige Weise zu Beten für einen guten Freund.

1537

    WA 39 I, 359–417 Die erste Disputation gegen die Antinomer.

1538

    WA 50, 368–374 Praefatio zu den Symphoniae iucundae 1538.

    StA 5, 344–443 Die Schmalkaldischen Artikel 1536/1538.

    WA Tr 3, 3815, Anton Lauterbachs Tagebuch aufs Jahr 1538.

    WA Tr 4, 4145, 4192

1539

    Sta 5, 448–617 Von den Konziliis und Kirchen

    WA Tr 4, 4441 Anton Lauterbachs Tagebuch aufs Jahr 1539.

1540

    WA Tr 4, 4897 Nachschriften von Johannes Mathesius 1540.

1541

    WA 51, 469–572 Wider Hans Worst.

    WA Br 9, Nr. 3583 Luther an Kurfürst Johann Friedrich. 20. März 1541.

1542

    WA 35, 478–483 Die Vorrede zu der Sammlung der Begräbnislieder 1542.

1543

    WA 54, 22–100 Von den letzten Worten Davids.

1544

    WA 21, 195–551 Kaspar Crucigers Sommerpostille.

1545

    WA 35, 476–477 Die Vorrede zum Babstschen Gesangbuch 1545.

    WA 51, 60–67 Predigten des Jahres 1545. Predigt am 20. Sonntag nach Trinitatis.
                  (Eph.5)

1535–1545

    WA 42–44 Vorlesungen über 1. Mose.

From different years:

    AWA 4 Luthers geistliche Lieder und Kirchengesänge. Vollständige Neuedition in
        Ergänzung zu Band 35 der Weimarer Ausgabe. Bearb. von Markus Jenny.

Ancient and medieval authors

Ambrosius Mediolanensis

    PL 14, 123–274 Exameron libri sex.

Aristoteles

    EN Nicomachean Ethics by Aristotle. With an English translation by H. Racham. [The
        Loeb Classical library 73.] London. Heinemann 1934.

    Politics Politics by Aristotle. With an English translation by H. Rackham. The Loeb
        Classics Library 264. London. Heinemann 1959.

Augustinus

    PL 32, 583–658 Retractationes libri II

    PL 32,659–868 Confessionum libri XIII

    PL 32,869–902 Soliloquium libri II

    PL 32,977–1020 De Ordine libri II

    PL 32,1081–1192 De Musica libri VI

    PL 34,15–120 De Doctrina Christiana libri IV.

    PL 34, 121–172 De Vera Religione.

    PL 36–37 Enarrationes in Psalmos.

    PL 40, 101–146 De Diversis Queastionibus ad Simplicianum libri II.

    PL 42,819–1100 De Trinitate libri XV.

Bernardus Claraevallensis

    PL 182, 609 – 612   Epistola CCCXCVIII . Ad Guidonem abbatem et fratres Arremarenses.

    PL 182,1121 – 1132   Tractatus de cantu.

    PL 183,785 – 1198   Sermones in Cantica.

    De dil.deo   L'amour de Dieu; La grâce et le libre arbitre. Introductions, traductions notes et index par Françoise Callerot et al. [Sources Chretiennes 393] Paris. Les éditions du Cerf. 1993.

Biel, Gabriel

    Can. Miss. Exp.   Canonis misse expositio. Ed. Heiko A. Oberman&William J. Courtney. Wiesbaden. Franz Steiner. 1966

Boethius, Anicius Manlius Severinus

    Inst.Mus   De Institutione Musica. PL 63, 1167 – 1300. (Fundamentals of Music. Translated, with introduction and notes by Calvin M. Bower. Ed. Claude V. Palisca. New Haven. Yale University Press. 1989.)

    Arithmetica   De institutione arithmetica libri duo, ed. Godofredus Friedlein.Leipzig: B. G. Teubner, 1867

    Cons.Phil.   De Consolatione Philosophiae. Opuscula theologica. Ed. Claudio Moreschini. Monachii. Saur. 2005.

Bonaventura

    Itin   Itinerarium mentis in Deum. Works of Saint Bonaventure 2. Ed. by Philotheus Boehner and Frances Laughlin. With an introduction, translation and commentary by Ph. Boehner. New York. St Bonaventure University. 1956.

Calvin, John

    CR 34,165 – 172   Epistre au Lecteur. La Forme des Prieres et Chantz Ecclesiastiques. 1543.

Cassiodorus

    PL 70,1149 – 1218   De artibus et disciplinis liberalium litterarum.

Clemens Alexandrinus

    PG 8,48 – 246 Protrepticus Cohortatio ad Gentes.

    PG 8, 247 – 683 Paedagogus.

Cicero, M. Tullius

    Tusc. disp.   Tusculan Disputations ; with an English translation by J.E. King. [The Loeb Classical library 141.] London. Heinemann.1945.

Dionysios Areopagita

    PG 3, 586 – 760 De divinis nominibus.

Dürer, Albrecht

    Schriften Schriften und Briefe. Hrsg. Von Ernst Ullmann. Textredaktion von Elvira Pradol. Leipzig. Philipp Reclam jun. 1982.

Gerson, Jean

    TC   [Tractatus de Canticis] Isabelle Fabre: La Doctrine du Chant du Coeur de Jean Gerson. Edition critique, traduction et commentaire du "Tractatus de canticis" et du "Canticordum au pélerin." Genève. Librairie Droz S.A. 2005.

    OC   Oeuvres complètes. Introduction, texte et notes par Glorieux. Paris 1960 – 73.

Glarean, Heinrich

    Dodecach.   Dodecachordon. Basle: Henrichus Petri, 1547; reprint ed., New York: Broude Bros., 1967 (Glarean:Dodecachordon. Transl, trancription and commentary by Clement A. Miller. American Institute of Musicology 1965)

Gregorius Magnus
>CCL 143B   S. Gregorii Magni Moralia in Iob libri XXIII-XXXV. Cura et studio Marci
>>Adriaen. Turnhout. Brepols.1979.
>
>SC 314   Gregoire le Grand: Commentaire sur le Cantique des Cantiques. Introd.,
>>traduction, notes et index par Rodrigue Bélanger. Paris. Les editions du
>>Cerf. 1984.
>
>PL 76,1075–1312   Homilia in Evangelia

Gregorius Nyssensis
>PG 44, 431–615 Tractatus in Psalmorum.

Gualterus Chatton
>Rep. sup. Sent   Reportatio super Sententias. Liber I, distinctiones 1–9. Eds. Joseph C.
>>Wey and Girard J. Etzkorn. Toronto: Pontifical Institute of Medieval
>>Studiees. 1989

Guillelmus de Ockham
>Quodlib   Quodlibeta septem. Opera theologica, vol 9. Ed. Joseph C. Wey. St.
>>Bonaventure NY; St. Bonaventure University. 1967

Hieronymus, Eusebius
>PL 26, 443–554 Commentariorum epistolam ad Ephesos libri tres.

Ioannes Chrystostomus
>PG 55,155–166   Expositio in Psalmum XLI.

Ioannes Duns Scotus
>Lectura   Lectura in librum primum Sententiarum. prologus et distinctiones 1–7. Opera
>>omnia vol.16. Ed. C.Balic et al. Civitas Vativana. Typis Polyglottis
>>Vaticanis. 1960.
>
>Reportatio   Reportatio I-A. Eds. Allan B. Wolter and Oleg V. Bychkov. St. Bonaventure,
>>NY: The Franciscan Institute.

Isidorus Hispalensis
>PL 82,9–728   Etymologiarum libri XX.

Justinus Martyr
>PG 6,230–239   Oratio ad Graecos.

Mathesius, Johann
>Martin Luthers Leben Historien, Von dess Ehrwirdigen inn Gott seligen theuren Manns
>>Gottes, D. Martin Luthers ... Nürnberg. Berg, 1576; reprint Dr.
>>Martin Luthers Leben. St Louis. Concordia, 1883.

Melanchthon, Philip
>CR 5, 918–920   zu "Harmoniae Selectae" 1538.

Novatianus
>PL 4, 779–788   [Cyprianus Carthaginensis:] Liber de Spectaculis.

Petrus Aureoli
>Script.sup.Sent   Scriptum super primum Sententiarum. Vol.1. Prologue and distinction 1.
>>Ed. Eligius M. Buytaert. St Bonaventure, NY: The Franciscan
>>Institute. 1952

Platon
>Republic   Plato in twelve volumes.6. The republic; in two volumes. 1. Books I-V. with an
>>English translation by Paul Shorey. [The Loeb Classical Library 237.] London.
>>Heinemann.1969.

Timaeus Plato in twelve volumes,9. Timaeus, Critias, Cleitophon, Menexenus, Epistles.
  With an Engl. Transl. by R.G. Bury. [The Loeb Classical Library 234.] London.
  Heinemann. 1966
Richardus a Sancto Victore
  PL 196,1–63 De praeparatione animi ad contemplationem, liber dictus Benjamin Minor
Robertus Grosseteste
  Hexaemeron   Hexaemeron. Ed. by Richard C. Dales and Servus Gieben O.F.M. London.
    Oxford University Press. 1982.
  De Luce Die Philosophischen Werke des Robert Grosseteste, Bischofs von Lincoln.
    Münster. 1912.
Robertus Holcot
  In Sent. In quatuor libros Sententiarum quastiones argutissime. Lugduni 1518 (reprinted
    Frankfurt am Main; Minerva 1967)
Tertullianus, Quintus Septimus Florens
  PL 1, 627–662   De Spectaculis.
Thomas Aquinas
  S.Th.   Summa Theologiae. London. Blackfrlars.
  Super Eph. Super ad Ephesios. In Psalmos. S. Thomas Aquinatis Opera omnia 6.
  In Ps   Reportationes. curante Roberto Busa. Stuttgart. Fromman. 1980. 48–130, 445–
    465.
Tinctoris, Johannes
  Complexus effectuum musices. Liber de arte contrapuncti. -Johannis Tinctoris Opera
  theoretica, ed. Albert Seay, 3 vols. in 2, Corpus scriptorum de musica, vol. 22. Roma
  .American Institute of Musicology. 1975–78.
  De inventione et usu musicae. Johannes Tinctoris (1445–1511) und sein unbekannter
  Traktat "De inventione et usu musicae" Hrsg. Von Karl Weinmann.Regensburg: F. Pustet,
  1917, 27–46.

Literature

Abert, Hermann

    1929   *Luther und die Musik. Gesammelte Schriften und Vorträge.* Hrsg. von Friedrich Blume. Halle (Saale).

    1964   *Die Musikanschauung des Mittelalters und ihre Grundlagen.* Unveränderter Nachdruck mit einem Geleitwort von Heinrich Hüschen. Tutzing. Hans Schneider. [original 1905]

Aertsen, Jan A.

    1991   *Beauty in the Middle Ages; a Forgotten Transcendental?* – Medieval Philosophy and Theology. Vol. 1. 68–97

Anttila, Miikka E.

    2010   *Music – Engaging Luther. A (New) Theological Assessment.* Ed. Olli-Pekka Vainio. Eugene. Cascade Books. 210–222.

Asendorf, Ulrich

    1998   *Lectura in Biblia. Luthers Genesisvorlesung 1535–1545.* Göttingen. Vandenhoeck & Ruprecht.

Bader, Günter

    1996   *Psalterium affectuum palaestra. Prolegomena zu einer Theologie des Psalters.* (Hermeneutische Untersuchungen zur Theologie 33) Tübingen. Mohr-Siebeck.

Bainton, Roland

    2002   *Here I Stand. A Life of Martin Luther.* London. Penguin.

Balthasar, Hans Urs von

    1982   *The Glory of the Lord.* Vol. 1: *Seeing the Form.* Transl. by E. Leiva-Merikakis. Ed. by J. Riches. Edinburgh. T&T Clark.

Barth, Hans-Martin

    1967   *Der Teufel und Jesus Christus in der Theologie Martin Luthers.* Göttingen. Vandenhoeck & Ruprecht.

Barth, Markus

    1974   *Ephesians. Translation and Commentary on Chapters 4–5.* The Anchor Bible 34 A. New York. Doubleday

Barth, Markus & Blanke, Helmut

    1994   *Colossians. A New Translation with Introduction and Commentary.* Transl. Astrid B. Beck. The Anchor Bible 34B. New York. Doubleday.

Bayer, Oswald

    1990   *Schöpfung als Anrede zu einer Hermeneutik der Schöpfung.* Tübingen. Mohr-Siebeck.

    2008   *Martin Luther's Theology: A Contemporary Interpretation.* Transl. by Thomas H. Trapp. Grand Rapids. Eerdmans.

Beardsley, Monroe C.

    1966   *Aesthetics from Classical Greece to the Present. A Short History.* The University of Alabama Press.

Begbie, Jeremy S.

    1991   *Voicing Creation's Praise: Towards a Theology of the Arts.* Edinburgh. T&T Clark.

    2000   *Theology, Music and Time.* Cambridge. Cambridge University Press

2003 "Calvin: die Musik und Gottes Wort" *Berliner Theologische Zeitschrift* 20, 85 – 102.

2005 *Theology and Music – The Modern Theologians. An Introduction to Christian Theology since 1918*. Third Edition. Ed. David F. Ford with Rachel Muers. Blackwell.719 – 735

2007 *Resounding Truth: Christian Wisdom in the World of Music*. Grand Rapids. Baker Academic.

Beutel, Albrecht

1998 *Protestantische Konkretionen. Studien zur Kirchengeschichte*. Tübingen. Mohr-Siebeck.

Bizer, Ernst

1961 *Fides ex auditu. Eine Untersuchung über die Entdeckung der Gerechtigkeit Gottes durch Martin Luther*. Neukirchen. Neukirchner Verlag.

Blankenburg, Walter

1953 "Kann Singen Verkündigung sein" *Musik und Kirche* 23, 1 – 16

1957 "Luther und die Musik" *Luther*, 14 – 27

1960 "Luther, Martin" *Musik in Geschichte und Gegenwart* Bd. 8. 1334 – 1346.

1961a "Der mehrstimmige Gesang und die konzertierende Musik im evangelischen Gottesdienst". *Leiturgia. Handbuch des Evangelischen Gottesdienstes*. Hrsg. v. K.F. Müller u. W. Blankenburg Bd. 4. Kassel, 661 – 721.

1961b "Luther, Martin" *Encyclopédie de la Musique*. Tome III. Paris

1964 "Vom unaufgebbaren Platz der Musik in der Theologie" *Zeitwende, die neue Furche* 35, 21 – 29

1972 "Überlieferung und Textgeschichte von Martin Luthers 'Encomion musices'" *Lutherjahrbuch* 39, 80 – 104

1991 *Johann Walter. Leben und Werk*. Hrsg. Friedhelm Brusniak. Tutzing. Hans Schneider.

Block, Johannes

2002 *Verstehen durch Musik. Das gesungene Wort der Theologie: ein hermeneutischer Beitrag zur Hymnologie am Beispiel Martin Luthers*. Mainzer hymnologische Studien Bd. 6. Francke. Tübingen.

Blume, Friedrich

1975 *Protestant Church Music*. A History in Collaboration with Ludwig Finscher, Georg Feder, Adam Adrio, Walter Blankenburg, Torben Schousboe, Robert Stevenson, and Watkins Shaw. London. Viktor Gollancz.

Brecht, Martin

1986 *Martin Luther. Bd 2. Ordnung und Abgrenzung der Reformation. 1521 – 1532*. Stuttgart. Calwer Verlag.

1987 *Martin Luther. 3. Bd. Die Erhaltung der Kirche 1532 – 1546*. Stuttgart. Calwer Verlag

Brunner, Peter

1954 "Zur Lehre vom Gottesdienstes der im Namen Jesu versammelten Gemeinde" *Leiturgia. Handbuch des Evangelischen Gottesdienstes*. Hrsg. v. K.F. Müller u. W. Blankenburg. Bd. 1. Kassel, 84 – 361.

Bräuer, Siegfried

1974 "Thomas Müntzers Liedschaffen. Die theologischen Intentionen der Hymnenübertragungen im Allstedter Gottesdienst von 1523/24 und im Abendmahlslied Müntzers" *Lutherjahrbuch* 41, 45–102.

Burbach, Hermann Josef M.S.F.

1966 *Studien zur Musikanschauung des Thomas von Aquin.* Regensburg. Gustav Bosse Verlag.

Buszin, Walter E.

1946 "Luther on Music" *The Musical Quarterly*, vol. 32, no. 1, 80–97.

Chadwick, Henry

1981 *Boethius. The Consolations of Music, Logic, Theology and Philosophy.* Oxford. Oxford University Press.

Chamberlain, David S.

1984 "Philosophy of Music in the 'Consolatio'" of Boethius. *Boethius.* Hrsg. von Manfred Fuhrmann u. Joachim Gruber. Darmstadt. Wissenschaftliche Buchgesellschaft, 377–403.

Conzelmann, Hans

1990 *Die Briefe an die Galater, Epheser, Philipper, Kolosser, Thessalonicher und Philemon.* Übersetzt und erklärt von Jürgen Becker, Hans Conzelmann, Gerhard Friedrich. *Das Neue Testament Deutsch.* Bd. 8. Göttingen. Vandenhoeck & Ruprecht.

Cottin, Jérôme

2009 "'Le beau chef d'oeuvre du monde.' L'esthétique théologique de Calvin" *Revue d'histoire et de philosophie religieuses.* 89 n. 4, 489–510.

Dahlhaus, Carl

1983 *Analysis and Value Judgment.* New York. Pendragon Press.

De Bruyne, Edgar

1969 *The Esthetics of the Middle Ages.* Transl. by Eileen B. Hennessy. New York. Frederick Ungar.

Dyer, Joseph

2007 "The Place of Musica in Medieval Classifications of Knowledge" *The Journal of Musicology.* Vol. 24, 13–71.

Ebeling, Gerhard

1951 "Die Anfänge von Luthers Hermeneutik". *Zeitschrift für Theologie und Kirche.* 48, 172–230.

1971 *Einführung in theologischer Sprachlehre.* Tübingen. Mohr-Siebeck.

Eco, Umberto

1982 *Art and Beauty in the Middle Ages.* Transl.by Hugh Bredin. New Haven. Yale University Press

1988 *The Aesthetics of Thomas Aquinas.* Transl. by Hugh Bredin. Harvard University Press.

Elenius, Antti

2005 *Lutherin käsitys tunteista. Lisensiaattityö. Teologisen tiedekunnan kirjasto.* Helsingin yliopisto. [unprinted licentiate work]

Emrich, Britta
>   2010   "Lebendige Stimme. Zu Wesen und Bedeutung der menschlichen Stimme nach
>   Martin Luther" *Luther*. Zeitschrift der Luther-Gesellschaft. 81. Jhrg. Heft 2, 69–
>   89.

Forsberg, Juhani
>   1984   *Das Abrahambild in der Theologie Luthers. Pater fidei sanctissimus.* Stuttgart.
>   Franz Steiner Verlag.

Froehlich, Karl
>   1999   "Luther on Vocation" *LQ* 13 no. 2, 195–207.

Garside, Charles
>   1951   "Calvin's Preface to the Psalter: A Re-Appraisal" *The Musical Quarterly* vol. 37,
>   no. 4, 566–577.
>   1966   *Zwingli and the Arts.* Yale University Press.

Gestrich, Reinhold
>   2008   *Schönheit Gottes. Anstöße zu einer neuen Wahrnehmung.* Berlin. LIT Verlag.

Ghiselli, Anja
>   2005   *Sanan kantaja. Martti Lutherin kasitys Neitsyt Mariasta.* Suomalaisen Teologisen
>   Kirjallisuusseuran Julkaisuja 246. Helsinki. Diss.

Gnilka, Joachim
>   1971   *Der Epheserbrief.* Herders theologischer Kommentar zum Neuen Testament.
>   Bd. 10,2. Freiburg. Herder.

Grew, Eva Mary
>   1938   "Martin Luther and Music" *Music & Letters*, vol. 19 no. 1, 67–78.

Grimm, Robert
>   1999   *Luther et l'experience sexuelle. Sexe, célibat, mariage chez le Réformateur.*
>   Gèneve. Labor et Fides.

Guicharrousse, Hubert
>   1995   *Les Musiques de Luther.* Gèneve. Labor et Fides.

Gurlitt, Willibald
>   1933   "Johannes Walter und die Musik der Reformationszeit" *Lutherjahrbuch* 15, 1–102.

Harrison, Carol
>   1992   *Beauty and Revelation in the Thought of Saint Augustine.* Oxford. Oxford
>   University Press.

Helmer, Paul
>   2009   "The Catholic Luther and Worship Music" *The Global Luther: A Theologian for
>   Modern Times.* Ed. by Christine Helmer. Minneapolis. Fortress Press, 151–172.

Hengelbrock, J.
>   1971   "Affekt I." *Historisches Wörterbuch der Philosophie.* Bd 1. Hrsg. von Joachim
>   Ritter. Basel/Stuttgart. Schwabe & Co., 89–93.

Herl, Joseph
>   2004   *Worship Wars in Early Lutheranism. Choir, Congregation, and Three Centuries of
>   Conflict.* Oxford. Oxford University Press.

Hirvonen, Vesa
>   2004   *Passions in William Ockham's Philosophical Psychology.* Dordrecht. Kluwer.

Hoelty-Nickel, Theodore
>   1960   "Luther and Music" *Luther and Culture.* Martin Luther Lectures vol. 4. Luther
>   College Press. Decorah, Iowa.

Hoffman, Bengt
    1989   *Hjärtats teologi. Mystikens plats hos Martin Luther.* Bjärnum. Åsak.

Holm, Bo-Kristian
    2006   *Gabe und Geben bei Luther: das Verhältnis zwischen Reziprozität und reformatorischer Rechtfertigungslehre.* Berlin. New York. De Gruyter.

Honemeyer, Karl
    1941   *Luthers Musikanschauung. Studien zur Frage ihrer geschichtlichen Grundlagen.* Diss. Universität Münster.
    1974   *Thomas Müntzer und Martin Luther: Ihr Ringen um die Musik des Gottesdienstes.* Berlin. Merseburger.

Horn, Christoph
    1994   "Augustins Philosophie der Zahlen" *Revue des Études Augustiniennes* 40, 389 – 415.

Horne, Brian L.
    1985   "A Civitas of Sound: on Luther and Music" *Theology* 88, 21 – 28.

Howsare, Rodney A.
    1999   *Hans Urs von Balthasar and Protestantism: the Ecumenical Implications of his Theological Style.* Milwaukee. Marquette University. Diss.

Irwin, Joyce L.
    1981   "The Mystical Music of Jean Gerson" *Early Music History*, vol. 1, 187 – 201.
    1993   *Neither Voice nor Heart Alone. German Lutheran Theology of Music in the Age of Baroque.* New York; Berlin. Peter Lang.

Joest, Wilfried
    1967   *Ontologie der Person bei Luther.* Göttingen. Vandenhoeck & Ruprecht.

Joncas, Jan Michael
    2002   "Music as Worship" *The New SCM Dictionary of Liturgy and Worship.* London. 326 – 329.

Jenny Markus
    1966   *Zwinglis Stellung zur Musik.* Zürich.
    1983   *Luther, Zwingli, Calvin in ihren Liedern.* Theologischer Verlag. Zürich.

Junghans, Helmar
    1984   *Der Junge Luther und die Humanisten.* Weimar. Hermann Böhlau.

Juntunen, Sammeli
    1996   *Der Begriff des Nichts bei Luther in den Jahren von 1510 bis 1523.* Helsinki. Luther-Agricola Gesellschaft.
    2010a "Christ" *Engaging Luther. A (New) Theological Assessment.* Ed. Olli-Pekka Vainio. Eugene. Cascade Books, 59 – 80.
    2010b "Sex" *Engaging Luther. A (New) Theological Assessment.* Ed. Olli-Pekka Vainio. Eugene. Cascade Books, 186 – 209.

Järveläinen, Petri
    2000   *A Study on Religious Emotions.* (Schriften der Luther-Agricola-Gesellschaft 47) Helsinki.

Kant, Immanuel
    1790   *Kritik der Urtheilskraft.* Gesammelte Werke Bd. 5. Electronic Edition Berlin. Karsten Worm. 1998

Kitanov, Severin

2006   *Beatific Enjoyment in Scholastic Theology and Philosophy 1240–1335.* Helsinki
       University. Diss.

Kivy, Peter

1989   *Sound Sentiment: An Essay on the Musical Emotions Including the Complete Text
       of the Corded Shell.* Temple University Press.

1999   "Feeling the Musical Emotions" *British Journal of Aesthetics.* Vol. 39. No.1. 1–13.

Kleineidam, Erich

1992² *Universitas Studii Erffordensis. Überblick über die Geschichte der Universität
       Erfurt.* Teil 2: Spätscholastik, Humanismus und Reformation: 1461–1521. Leipzig.
       St.-Benno-Verlag.

Knuuttila, Simo

2004   *Emotions in Ancient and Medieval Philosophy.* Oxford. Clarendon Press.

Kolb, Robert

2005   *Bound Choice, Election and Wittenberg Theological Method. From Martin Luther
       to the Formula of Concord.* Grand Rapids. Eerdmans.

Kopperi, Kari

1997   *Paradoksien teologia. Lutherin disputaatio Heidelbergissä 1518.* (Suomalaisen
       teologisen kirjallisuusseuran julkaisuja 208) Helsinki.

2010   "Theology of the Cross" *Engaging Luther. A (New) Theological Assessment.* Ed.
       Olli-Pekka Vainio. Eugene. Cascade Books, 155–172.

Kraege, Jean-Denis

1983   "Luther théologien de la musique" *Etudes théologiques et religieuses.* 58, 449–
       63.

Krieg, Gustav A.

1990   *Die gottesdienstliche Musik als theologisches Problem. Dargestellt an der
       kirchenmusikalischen Erneuerung nach dem ersten Weltkrieg.* Göttingen.
       Vandenhoeck & Ruprecht.

Krokfors, Jockum

1993   *Musiken i församlingen. En studie kring betänkandet Musikfostran i
       församlingen.* Åbo. Åbo Akademis tryckeri.

Krummacher, Christoph

1994   *Musik als praxis pietatis. Zum Selbstverständnis evangelischer Kirchenmusik.*
       Göttingen. Vandenhoeck & Ruprecht.

Kurzschenkel, Winfried

1971   *Die theologische Bestimmung der Musik: neuere Beiträge zur Deutung und
       Wertung des Musizierens im christlichen Leben.* Trier. Paulinus.

Kärkkäinen, Pekka

2003   *Luthers trinitarische Theologie des Heiligen Geistes.* Helsinki. Diss.

Lanz, J.

1971   "Affekt II." *Historisches Wörterbuch der Philosophie.* Bd. 1. Hrsg. von Joachim
       Ritter. Basel/Stuttgart. Schwabe & Co., 93–100.

Leaver Robin A.

1994   "Review: Joyce Irwin: Neither Voice nor Heart Alone" *Sixteenth Century Journal.*
       Vol. 25, no. 2. 471–472.

1995   "Theological Consistency, Liturgical Integrity and Musical Hermeneutics in
       Luther's Liturgical Reforms" *LQ* 9, 117–138.

2001a "Luther and Bach, the 'Deutsche Messe' and the Music of Worship" *LQ* 15, 317 – 335.

2001b "Luther, Martin" *Grove Music Online*. Oxford Music Online. Accessed 24 Mar. 2009.

<http://www.oxfordmusiconline.com/subscriber/article/grove/music/17219>.

2004 "Luther as Musician" *LQ* 18, I no. 2. 125 – 181.

2006 "Luther on Music" *LQ* 20, 125 – 145.

2007 *Luther's Liturgical Music: principles and implications.*(Lutheran Quarterly Books). Eerdmans. Grand Rapids.

Leclercq, Jean

1987 "Introduction" *Bernard of Clairvaux: Selected Works*. Transl.G.R. Evans. New York. Paulist Press, 13 – 57.

Lippman, Edward A.

1992 *A History of Western Musical Aesthetics*. Lincoln, London. University of Nebraska Press.

Lohse Bernhard

1995 *Luthers Theologie in ihrer historischen Entwicklung und in ihrem systematischen Zusammenhang*. Göttingen. Vandenhoeck & Ruprecht.

Lowinsky, Edward E.

1961 *Tonality and Atonality in 16th Century Music*. With a Foreword by Igor Stravinsky. Berkeley. University of California Press.

Lähteenmäki, Olavi

1955 *Sexus und Ehe bei Luther* (Schriften der Luther-Agricola Gesellschaft 10). Turku.

Löfgren, David

1960 *Die Theologie der Schöpfung bei Luther*. Göttingen. Vandenhoeck & Ruprecht.

Mahrenholz, Christhard

1937 *Luther und die Kirchenmusik*. Kassel.

Mannermaa, Tuomo

1991 "Musiikin teologiasta" *Teologinen Aikakauskirja* 96 vsk. no. 1. 1 – 2.

1994 "Hat Luther eine trinitarische Ontologie?" *Luther und die trinitarische Tradition. Ökumenische und trinitarische Perspektiven*. Hrsg. Joachim Heubach (Veröffentlichungen der Luther-Akademie Ratzeburg 23) Erlangen. Martin-Luther-Verlag, 43 – 60.

2005 *Christ Present in Faith. Luther's View of Justification*. Ed. and introduced by Kirsi Stjerna. Minneapolis. Fortress Press.

2010 *Two Kinds of Love: Martin Luther's Religious World*. Transl., ed. and introduced by Kirsi L. Stjerna; with an Afterword by Juhani Forsberg. Minneapolis. Fortress Press.

Manns, Peter

1987 "Zum Gespräch zwischen M. Luther und der katholischen Theologie. Begegnung zwischen patristisch-monastischer und reformatorischer Theologie an der Scholastik vorbei" *Thesaurus Lutheri. Auf der Suche nach neuen Paradigmen der Luther-Forschung*. Hrsg von Tuomo Mannermaa, Anja Ghiselli und Simo Peura. Helsinki. Luther-Agricola-Gesellschaft, 63 – 154.

Marcuse, Herbert

1979 *The Aesthetic Dimension. Toward a Critique of Marxist Aesthetics*. London. Macmillan.

Mauss, Marcel
    1990   *The Gift. The Form and Reason for Exchange in Archaic Societies.* Trans. by W.D.
             Halls. Foreword by Mary Douglas. London. Routledge.

Mayer, Christian
    1993   "Gesangbuch, darin begriffen sind … Martin Bucer et la Chant liturgique" *Martin*
             Bucer and Sixteenth Century Europe. Ed. Christian Krieger, Marc Lienhard. Leiden.
             Brill, 215 – 226.

Mayer Brown, Howard & Keahey, T. Herman
    2001   "Févin, Antoine de" *Grove Music Online.* Oxford Music Online. 11. Nov. 2010
             <http://www.oxfordmusiconline.com/subscriber/article/grove/music/09569>.

McEvoy, James
    1982   *The Philosophy of Robert Grosseteste.* Oxford. Clarendon Press.

McKinnon, James W
    1987   *Music in Early Christian Literature.* Cambridge.
    1994   "Desert Monasticism and the Later Fourth-Century Psalmodic Movement" *Music &*
             Letters 75, no. 4. 505 – 521
    2001   "Ambrose" *Grove Music Online.* Oxford Music Online. 3. Nov. 2008
             <http://www.oxfordmusiconline.com/ subscriber/article/grove/music/00751>.

Metzger, Günther
    1964   *Gelebter Glaube. Die Formierung reformatorischen Denkens in Luthers erster*
             Psalmenvorlesung, dargestellt am Begriff des Affekts. Göttingen. Vandenhoeck &
             Ruprecht.

Mikoteit, Matthias
    2004   *Theologie und Gebet bei Luther. Untersuchungen zur Psalmenvorlesung 1532 –*
             1535. (Theologische Bibliothek Töpelmann. Bd. 124.) Berlin-New York. Walter de
             Gruyter.

Milbank, John
    1995   "Can a Gift Be Given. Prolegomena for a Future Trinitarian Metaphysic" *Modern*
             Theology vol. 11 no. 1. 119 – 161.

Mühlen, Karl-Heinz zur
    1972   *Nos extra nos. Luthers Theologie zwischen Mystik und Scholastik* (Beiträge zur
             historischen Theologie 46). Tübingen. Mohr-Siebeck.
    1977   "Affekt II. Theologiegeschichtliche Aspekte" *TRE* Bd. 1, 599 – 612.
    1980   *Reformatorische Vernunftkritik und neuzeitliches Denken. Dargestellt am Werk M.*
             Luthers und Fr. Gogartens. Tübingen. Mohr-Siebeck.
    1992   "Die Affektenlehre im Spätmittelalter und in der Reformationszeit" *Archiv für*
             Begriffsgeschichte Bd. 35. Bonn. Bouvier Verlag, 92 – 114.

Nicol, Martin
    1984   *Meditation bei Luther.* Göttingen. Vandenhoeck & Ruprecht.

Niemöller, Klaus Wolfgang
    2003   "Deutsche Musiktheorie im 16. Jahrhundert: Geistes- und
             institutionsgeschichtliche Grundlagen" *Geschichte der Musiktheorie* Bd. 8/1.
             Deutsche Musiktheorie des 15. bis 17. Jahrhunderts. Teil 1: Von Paumann bis
             Calvisius. Hrsg. Theodor Göllner et al. Darmstadt, 69 – 98.

Oberman, Heiko A.
    1989   *Luther. A Man between God and the Devil.* New Haven. Yale University Press.

Østrem, Eyolf

    2003   "Luther, Josquin and des fincken gesang" *The Arts and the Cultural Heritage of Martin Luther: Special Issue of Transfiguration – Nordic Journal for Christianity and the Arts.* 51 – 80.

Ozment Steven E

    1969   *Homo spiritualis: A comparative study of the anthropology of Johannes Tauler, Jean Gerson and Martin Luther (1509 – 16) in the Context of their Theological Thought.* Leiden. Brill.

Peura, Simo

    1990   *Mehr als ein Mensch? Die Vergöttlichung als Thema der Theologie Martin Luthers von 1513 bis 1519.* Helsinki. Diss.

    1998   "Christ as Favor and Gift: The Challenge of Luther's Understanding of Justification" *Union with Christ: the new Finnish interpretation of Luther.* Ed. by Carl E. Braaten and Robert W. Jenson. Grands Rapids. Eerdmans. 42 – 69.

Pinomaa, Lennart

    1940   *Der existentielle Charakter der Theologie Luthers: das Hervorbrechen der Theologie der Anfechtung und ihre Bedeutung für das Lutherverständnis.* Helsinki. Suomalainen tiedeakatemia.

Raunio, Antti

    1997   "Speculatio practica. Das Betrachten Gottes als Ursprung des aktiven Lebens bei Luther" *Caritas Dei. Beiträge zum Verständnis Luthers und der gegenwärtigen Ökumene. FS für Tuomo Mannermaa.* Helsinki. Luther-Agricola Gesellschaft.

    1998   "Natural Law and Faith: the Forgotten Foundations of Ethics in Luther's Theology" *Union with Christ: the New Finnish Interpretation of Luther.* Ed. by Carl E. Braaten and Robert W. Jenson. Grands Rapids.Eerdmans. 96 – 124.

    2001   "Rakkauden teologia" *Johdatus Lutherin teologiaan.* Toim. Pekka Kärkkäinen. Jyväskylä. Kirjapaja. 154 – 180.

    2001   *Summe des Christlichen Lebens. Die Goldene Regel als der Gesetz der Liebe in der Theologie Martin Luthers von 1510 bis 1527* (Veröffentlichungen des Instituts für Europäische Geschichte Mainz). Mainz. Von Zabern.

Reich, Christa

    1997   *Evangelium: klingendes Wort. Zur theologischen Bedeutung des Singens.* Stuttgart. Calwer.

Robinson, Jenefer

    1994   "The Expression and Arousal of Emotion in Music" *The Journal of Aesthetics and Art Criticism.* Vol. 52. no. 1, 13 – 22.

Ruokanen, Miikka

    1986   "Luther und Ekstase" *Luther in Finnland. Der Einfluss der Theologie Martin Luthers in Finnland und finnische Beiträge zur Lutherforschung.* Hrsg. von M. Ruokanen. 2. Aufl. Helsinki. Luther-Agricola Gesellschaft.

Saarinen, Risto

    1993   *Weakness of the Will in Medieval Thought: From Augustine to Buridan.* Helsinki. Diss.

    2005   *God and the Gift. An Ecumenical Theology of Giving.* Collegeville. Liturgical Press.

    2010   "Finnish Luther Studies: A Story and a Program" *Engaging Luther. A (New) Theological Assessment.* Ed. Olli-Pekka Vainio. Eugene. Cascade Books, 1 – 26.

Sander Katherine Joan
>   1998   *Johann Walter and Martin Luther: Theology and Music in the Early Lutheran Church.* Ottawa

Sariola Yrjö
>   1986   *Jumalan kunniaksi ja mielen rakennukseksi. Musiikin teologian peruskysymyksiä.* Jyväskylä. SLEY-kirjat.

Schilling, Johannes
>   2005   "Musik" *Luther-Handbuch.* Hrsg. Albrecht Beutel. Tübingen. Mohr-Siebeck, 236 – 244.

Schneider, Martin Gotthard
>   1997   "Martin Luther und die Musik" *Zugänge zu Martin Luther. Ringvorlesung an der Pädagogischen Hochschule Freiburg zum Lutherjahr 1996.* Hrsg. von Reinhard Wunderlich; Bernd Feiniger. Bern.

Schwanke Johannes
>   2004   *Creatio ex nihilo: Luthers Lehre von der Schöpfung aus dem Nichts in der großen Genesisvorlesung (1535 – 1545)* (Theologische Bibliothek Töpelmann 126). Berlin-New York. Walter de Gruyter.

Scruton, Roger
>   1999   *The Aesthetics of Music.* Oxford. Oxford University Press.

Sider, Ronald J.
>   1974   *Andreas Bodenstein von Karlstadt. The Development of His Thought, 1517 – 1525.* Leiden. Brill.

Seay, Albert
>   1965   *Music in the Medieval World.* New Jersey. Prentice Hall.

Siirala, Aarne
>   1956   *Gottes Gebot bei Martin Luther. Eine Untersuchung der Theologie Luthers unter besonderer Berücksichtigung des ersten Hauptstückes im Grossen Katechismus* (Schriften der Luther-Agricola-Gesellschaft 11). Helsinki.

Simon, Wolfgang
>   2003   *Die Messopfertheologie Martin Luthers. Voraussetzungen, Genese, Gestalt und Rezeption.* (Spätmittelalter und Reformation. Neue Reihe 22) Tübingen. Mohr-Siebeck.

Sorabji, Richard
>   2000   *Emotions and Peace of Mind. From Stoic Agitation to Christian Temptation.* Oxford. Oxford University Press.

Spelman, Leslie P
>   1951   "Luther and the Arts" *The Journal of Aesthetics and Art Criticism*, Vol. 10, no. 2, 166 – 175.

Stalmann, Joachim
>   2004   "Luther, Martin" *Musik in Geschichte und Gegenwart.* 2. neubearb. Ausgabe. Hrsg. von Ludwig Finscher. Personenteil. Bd. 11. Kassel. Bärenreiter, 636 – 654.

Stapert, Calvin R.
>   2007   *A New Song for an Old World. Musical Thought in the Early Church.* Grand Rapids. Eerdmans.

Stiegmann, Emero
>   2001   "Bernard of Clairvaux, William of St.Thierry, the Victorines" *The Medieval Theologians.* Ed. G.R. Evans. Oxford. Blackwell.

Stolt, Birgit

    2000   *Martin Luthers Rhetorik des Herzens.* Tübingen. Mohr-Siebeck.

    2009   "Luther's Faith of 'the Heart': Experience, Emotion, and Reason" *The Global Luther: A Theologian for Modern Times.* Ed. by Christine Helmer. Minneapolis. Fortress Press. 131–150

Sundkvist, Bernice

    2001   *Det sakramentala draget i Luthers förkunnelse.* Åbo. Åbo Akademis förlag. Diss.

Söhngen, Oskar

    1967   *Theologie der Musik.* Kassel.

    1979   "Zwinglis Stellung zur Musik im Gottesdienst" *Musica sacra zwischen gestern und morgen.* Göttingen. Vandenhoeck & Ruprecht, 31–46.

Tatarkiewicz, Wladyslaw

    1970   *History of Aesthetics.* Vol. 2: *Medieval Aesthetics.* Ed. by C. Barrett. Transl. by. R.M. Montgomery. The Hague. Mouton.

    1972   "The Great Theory of Beauty and its Decline" *The Journal of Aesthetics and Art Criticism.* Vol. 31. no. 2, 165–180.

    1974   *History of Aesthetics.* Vol. 3: *Modern Aesthetics.* Ed. by D. Petsch. Transl. by Chester A. Kisiel. The Hague. Mouton.

Thestrup, Petersen E

    1983   *Martin Luthers betydning for kirke og kultur.* Bonnerup.

Tobin, Henrik

    1996   *Den underbara harmonin. Aspekter på musikens teologi.* Göteborg. Verbum.

Vainio, Olli-Pekka

    2008   *Justification and Participation in Christ: the Development of the Lutheran Doctrine of Justification from Luther to the Formula of Concord (1580).* Leiden. Brill.

Vajta, Vilmos

    1952   *Die Theologie des Gottesdienstes bei Luther.* Stockholm: Svenska Kyrkans Diakonistyrels (Diss. Lund).

Veit, Patrice

    1986   *Das Kirchenlied in der Reformation Martin Luthers. Eine thematische und semantische Untersuchung.* Stuttgart. Steiner.

Viertel, Matthias Silesius

    1985   "Kirchenmusik zwischen Kerygma und Charisma. Anmerkungen zu einer protestantischen Theologie der Musik" *Jahrbuch für Liturgik und Hymnologie* 29, 111–123.

Waddell, Chrysogonus

    1992   "Chant cistercien et liturgie" *Bernard de Clairvaux. Histoire, Mentalités, Spiritualité* (Sources Chrétiennes 380). Paris. Editions du Cerf, 301–306.

Wagner Oettinger, Rebecca

    1999   *Music as Popular Propaganda in the German Reformation, 1517–1555.* Madison. University of Wisconsin. Diss.

Wetzel, Christoph

    1954   *Die theologische Bedeutung der Musik im Leben und Denken Martin Luthers.* Münster. Diss.

    1955   "Studie zur Musikanschauung Martin Luthers" *Musik und Kirche* 25, 238–243, 274–279.

1961   "Träger des liturgischen Amtes im evangelischen Gottesdienst bei dem Apostel Paulus und bei Marin Luther" *Leiturgia. Handbuch des evangelischen Gottesdienstes.* Hrsg. von K.F. Müller und Walter Blankenburg. Kassel, 270 – 340.

Wilson, Blake (et al.)

2001   "Rhetoric and music" *Grove Music Online.* Oxford Music Online, <http://www.oxfordmusiconline.com/subscriber/article/grove/music/43166> (accessed October 7, 2008).

Wingren, Gustaf

1948   *Luthers lära om kallelsen.* 2. upplagan. Lund. C.W.K Gleerups förlag.

Wiora, Walter

1988   *Die vier Weltalter der Musik. Ein universalhistorischer Entwurf.* Kassel. Bärenreiter.

Wolterstorff, Nicholas

1980   *Art in Action. Toward a Christian Aesthetic.* Grand Rapids. Eerdmans.

2004   "Art and the Aesthetic: the Religious Dimension" *The Blackwell Guide to Aesthetics.* Ed. Peter Kivy. Malden. Blackwell, 325 – 339

Zangwill, Nick

2008   "Aesthetic Judgment" *The Stanford Encyclopedia of Philosophy* (Fall 2008 Edition), ed. by Edward N. Zalta. <http://plato.stanford.edu/archives/fall2008/entries/aesthetic-judgment/>.

Zeindler, Matthias

1993   *Gott und das Schöne. Studien zur Theologie der Schönheit.* (Forschungen zur systematischen und ökumenischen Theologie 68) Göttingen. Vandenhoeck & Ruprecht.

Subject Index

Index of Names

Made in the USA
Monee, IL
06 November 2020